The Rorschach Technique

A Manual for a Projective Method of Personality Diagnosis

By BRUNO KLOPFER, Ph.D.

*Associate Professor of Psychology, City College of New York,
and Visiting Associate Professor of Psychology,
University of California, Los Angeles*

Clinical contributions by

DOUGLAS McGLASHAN KELLEY, M.D., Med.Sc.D.

*Associate Professor of Psychiatry,
The Bowman Gray School of Medicine of Wake Forest College*

With 1946 Supplement by Bruno Klopfer, Ph.D.,
and Helen H. Davidson, Ph.D.

Yonkers-on-Hudson, New York

World Book Company

WORLD BOOK COMPANY

THE HOUSE OF APPLIED KNOWLEDGE
Established MCMV by Caspar W. Hodgson

YONKERS-ON-HUDSON, NEW YORK
2126 PRAIRIE AVENUE, CHICAGO
BOSTON : ATLANTA : DALLAS : SAN FRANCISCO : PORTLAND

FOREWORD

THIS book grew out of seven years of "learning by teaching." My efforts to make the Rorschach method more comprehensible and thus more teachable were supported by almost every one of the more than eight hundred colleagues and students who participated in my seminars and classes. The first of these professional groups, consisting of Marion Cowin, Alma Paulsen, Dr. Zygmunt Piotrowski, Sadie Sender, and Gladys Tallman, started work on April 1, 1935. All members of this pioneer group have become well-known Rorschach workers; the founding of the Rorschach Research Exchange, outstanding publication in this field, is due to their efforts. They, as well as the others, contributed their alert questions and constructive criticisms, new ideas and sympathetic encouragement. Almost every conceivable question which might occur to those working with the Rorschach method came up at one time or another; I trust that the answers to most of them have found their way into this book.

Obviously, there is not room for a complete roll call of all the persons whose contributions I would like to acknowledge. I must limit the list of names to the dozen of my associates and colleagues who contributed so much time and effort to the tedious work of reading the manuscript in its various stages from its first rough draft to its final form. They include Dr. Max Hertzman, Dr. L. C. Hirning, Dr. Elaine Kinder, Helen Margulies, Dr. Ruth Munroe, Ruth Wolfson, and Dr. Austin Wood.

iii

Special acknowledgment is due to Pauline G. Vorhaus for her painstaking work with the manuscript and preparation of the Index; to Dr. Helen H. Davidson, who labored so diligently on the Bibliography; to Florence R. Miale for the sample case; and to Sadie Sender and Dr. L. J. Stone for critical reading of the proof. Even the members of my immediate family, Erna and Walter G. Klopfer, were drawn into the circle of co-workers and participated actively in the work on this book.

Many psychiatrists, by their vital interest and participation, showed a most generous attitude to the "invader" from a neighboring field. I appreciate especially that my friend Douglas Kelley could find the time to prepare the clinical part of this book during his two years as Rockefeller Fellow at the New York State Psychiatric Institute. This coöperative attitude is further evidenced in the Introduction by Dr. Nolan D. C. Lewis, Director of the Psychiatric Institute and a member of the Advisory Board of the Rorschach Institute.

This book appears at a time of emergency when we are all called upon to make the most effective possible use of our resources, whether these be men or materials. The Rorschach method is proving its worth in helping us to avoid waste of human resources in selection and training of personnel for many important emergency services, both in the armed forces and in civilian defense. If this book helps more people to become proficient in this method, I will be grateful for having had an opportunity thus to do my part.

Bruno Klopfer

New York City

CONTENTS

v

INTRODUCTION

THE Rorschach method is growing in popularity as a useful procedure in psychological work and in psychiatric diagnosis. When applied by those thoroughly trained in its use, it reveals the basic organization of the personality structure, including the fundamental affective and cognitive features of mental life. The method enables the investigator to recognize the spontaneous tendencies which form the basis of the subject's personality with a higher degree of reliability than has been demonstrated by any other experimental technique. Moreover, it is notably less time-consuming than any other clinical observation procedure which permits the formulation of conclusions of comparable validity.

The Rorschach method is remarkably effective in estimating the intellectual status of an individual; in revealing the richness or poverty of his psychic experience; in making known his present mood; and in showing the extent of his intuitive ability as well as in disclosing special talents and aptitudes. By virtue of its unique function in these areas, the value of the technique is becoming increasingly clear to psychologists in social service work, personnel administration, and vocational guidance.

In psychiatry, the validity of the method as a diagnostic instrument has been established. It points the way to new understanding of mental disorders, and it has gained a reputation for its service in identifying borderline cases and in differentiating among psychoses, neuroses, and organic brain disorders. Because the method differentiates reliably between normal groups with varying personality traits and subjects with mental disorders, it is finding a use in the United States, Canadian, British, and German armed forces for the detection of the unfit. Here as elsewhere it detects anxieties, phobias, and sex disturbances, as well as more severe disorders, and serves as a guide for appropriate treatment.

Furthermore, the results of therapy are more readily evaluated in the light of Rorschach findings. Residuals or "remnants" of delusions and other attenuated constellations of symptoms are often detected in patients who no longer display the ordinary clinical manifestations of their illness.

The limits of the research possibilities of the Rorschach method are not yet in sight, and it may be prophesied that many discoveries will be made through its use in competent hands. Although a great deal has been published on both the theoretical and practical features of the procedure, this is the first thorough treatise in book form that has appeared. Doctors Klopfer and Kelley have had extensive experience in Rorschach work and are recognized experts in the field. The text includes a complete, detailed account of the whole field from the historical beginnings on through the technique of administration and scoring, down to the special problems and interpretations. All professional workers and students in psychology, psychiatry, and personality problems should find a reliable guide in this comprehensive volume.

NOLAN D. C. LEWIS, M.D.

NEW YORK STATE PSYCHIATRIC INSTITUTE

PART ONE

PART ONE

CHAPTER

I

HISTORY OF
THE RORSCHACH METHOD

THE earliest recorded use of ink blots as psychological material is described in a book entitled *Kleksographien*, published in 1857 in Tuebingen, Germany. The time was approximately that of the dawn of modern psychology, the same period in which medicine was developing the beginnings of the specialty known today as psychiatry. The author of *Kleksographien*, Justinus Kerner, may in many ways be considered a pioneer in modern psychiatry. Kerner recounts that he accidentally discovered the possibilities inherent in the use of ink blots by noting how, as he observed them, they assumed various forms, which impressed him with their bizarre meanings. He then proceeded to the deliberate production of ink blots and thus opened a new field for investigation and experimentation which fired the public imagination, creating a "blotto" fad comparable to the one so widespread in American newspapers about twenty years ago.

Kerner's most interesting observation was that it seemed impossible to produce ink blots according to a preconceived plan; rather, the ink blots tended to impose their meaning and significance upon the producer. Thus he experienced the strong interplay between the objective features of the ink-blot material and the individual projections of the observer which is still the most impressive experience for everyone in a first encounter with Rorschach material. Kerner seems not to have realized fully that this interplay produces different results with different people; nor did he recognize the significance of these differences as affording a basis for a method of personality diagnosis.

It was a far cry from this early use of ink blots to their methodical application in psychological experimentation. The first person to sense their possibilities in this field was none other than Binet, the founder of modern intelligence testing. In 1895 [1] he suggested the use of ink blots for the study of various personality traits. Binet's attempts, and the investigations of a series of psychologists who followed in his footsteps, were reviewed in 1910 by Whipple,[2] who also published the first standard series of ink blots; Whipple's publication, in turn, was followed by a series of other studies. Although some of these early attempts to use ink blots as test material suggested the possibility of differentiating various individual characteristics or personality traits, the focus of attention remained on the content of the subject's responses to the ink blots. The ink blots were used primarily as stimulus material for free associations, indicating the nature of the subject's imaginative activity.

---

[1] Binet, A., and Henri, V. "La psychologie individuelle." *Ann. Psychol.,* 1895-96, Vol. 2, pages 411–465.

[2] Whipple, G. M. *Manual of Mental and Physical Tests.* Baltimore: Warwick & York, 1910. (Chapter XI, Tests of imagination and invention: test 45, ink-blots, pp. 430–435.)

Rorschach's *Psychodiagnostik* and the "Rorschach cards"
Herman Rorschach was born in Zurich, Switzerland, on November 8, 1884, the son of an art teacher. He studied medicine in various Swiss and German universities, receiving his medical degree in 1910. His preoccupation with ink blots started as early as 1911, and he pursued this interest throughout the next ten years, in the course of his work at various psychopathic hospitals. In 1921 he published the results of his studies in a monograph entitled *Psychodiagnostik*. This monograph is to be considered, as he puts it, a preliminary report on his findings, rather than a system of theoretical conclusions. In spite of their preliminary nature, however, Rorschach's working hypotheses penetrated into the theoretical foundations for his findings to an extent which is amazing to present-day followers of his method. He combined, to a marked degree, the sound empirical realism of a clinician with the speculative acumen of an intuitive thinker. Only a few months after the publication of *Psychodiagnostik* he developed peritonitis, following an attack of appendicitis, and died on April 2, 1922, at the age of 37.

The result of his ten years of experimentation was the selection, from among thousands of trial blots, of a standard series of ten ink-blot pictures to serve as the stimulus material in his diagnostic procedure. In five of the blots colored ink is used in addition to black ink. Reproductions of the ten blots (without the color) are shown on page 5 of the sample Record Blank inside the back cover of this book. In the standard series the blots are reproduced on cards 7 by 9½ inches, the cards being numbered from I to X. The cards were originally published as part of *Psychodiagnostik*.

The distinguishing feature of *Psychodiagnostik*, as compared with previous attempts at using ink blots as psychological material, is the complete shift of emphasis from the more or less imaginative content of the subject's response to certain formal characteristics in the concept formations. In other words, the interest is not so much in what the subject sees as in his method of handling the stimulus material. The interplay between the structural characteristics of the stimulus material and the personality structure of the subject is reflected in certain formal categories which describe characteristics of the concept formations, and which *Psychodiagnostik* established as the basis of an objective method for personality diagnosis.

Development of the Rorschach method

After Rorschach's death one of his closest medical coworkers, Emil Oberholzer, became the outstanding exponent of the Rorschach movement.   In 1923 he published a paper describing a number of amplifications and differentiations in the technique which Rorschach had developed in the short period between the publication of *Psychodiagnostik* and his untimely death.   After 1932 this paper was included in the German edition of *Psychodiagnostik*.

A translation (*283*)[3] of this posthumous paper was the first publication on the Rorschach method to appear in English in the United States.   It was published in 1924 under the title, *The Application of the Interpretation of Form to Psychoanalysis*.[4]   This paper contains a thor-

---

[3] Figures in parentheses refer to entries in the bibliography at the end of the book.

[4] A reprint of this paper under the title, *Manual for Rorschach Ink-Blot Testing*, is available through C. H. Stoelting Company, Chicago, Illinois.

ough analysis of a Rorschach record sent to Rorschach by Oberholzer, based exclusively on the objective evidence yielded by the record itself. The subject who produced this record was one of the patients being analyzed by Oberholzer. After Rorschach's death Oberholzer appended some explanatory footnotes and some supplementary passages on his clinical findings.

Apart from its historical interest, this document is of value in that it shows clearly the long and toilsome way a Rorschach worker must travel, starting with the careful treatment of the raw material in terms of the scoring and tabulation, and culminating in the interpretation. This interpretation is based on certain empirical assumptions, or working hypotheses, about the meanings of the various factors revealed in the scoring and tabulation. On the basis of these assumptions, clinical inferences may be drawn, yielding a consistent and amazingly elaborate personality picture.

The role of the various strata of interpretative information is clearly described in Rorschach's final summary. In general he distinguishes three such strata:

(1) The interpretation of the quantitative distribution of the various scoring categories.
(2) Certain qualitative characteristics of the responses.
(3) Psychoanalytic inferences, completing the picture.

The first two of these constitute what has since been developed as the Rorschach method; for the third, the use of psychoanalytic inferences, other procedures are at times substituted. The objective Rorschach findings may be combined with other available information, such as social case histories and clinical and psychometric findings.

Rorschach's posthumous article was, as a matter of fact, a paper read originally before the Swiss Psychoanalytic Society, which may account in part for the emphasis on supplementing ink-blot findings with psychoanalytic inferences. Be that as it may, the history of the Rorschach method for the last twenty years has demonstrated sufficiently that Rorschach findings can be valuable to interpreters not versed in, or not in agreement with, psychoanalytic thinking.

Several Swiss co-workers of Rorschach concentrated on the development of his theories and his procedures and their application to various fields other than clinical psychiatry. Among the more important published contributions are Furrer's paper (*88*) on the movement responses, published in 1925, and Binder's paper (*31*) on shading responses, published in 1932.

The first important extension of the Rorschach method to a new field of application was brought about through studies in child development reported by Behn-Eschenburg, Dubitscher, Loosli-Usteri, and Loepfe, starting in 1921. The contributions of psychiatrists and psychologists to the development of the Rorschach method in the field of psychopathology will be discussed in the chapters on clinical diagnosis.

Oberholzer was responsible not only for the first publication on the Rorschach method in the United States, but also for the training of the first Rorschach workers in this country. The Rorschach method was introduced in the United States by David Levy, who received his training under Oberholzer in 1923–1924. Under Levy's influence, Samuel J. Beck became the first American psychologist to work with the Rorschach method. He too received his training from Oberholzer, in 1928, and wrote the first American doctoral dissertation on the Rorschach method. Beck's earliest publication appeared in 1930 and was followed by one or more papers each year, culminating in his *Introduction to the Rorschach Method* in 1937 and his monograph, *Personality Structure in Schizophrenia*, in 1938. Another American psychiatrist, John D. Benjamin, received his Rorschach training in Switzerland and developed a center for the clinical application of the Rorschach method in Denver, Colorado.

A research center independent of the Rorschach-Oberholzer tradition was instituted in the Brush Foundation in Cleveland, Ohio. There, starting in 1934, Marguerite Hertz issued a series of papers concentrating on the study of adolescents and on validation procedures.

Approximately a score of other psychiatrists and psychologists in fourteen countries contributed to the expansion or growth of the method during the fifteen years between 1921 and 1936. Their work was reviewed in the first systematic surveys of the field by Vernon in 1933 and 1935 (*336, 339*), and by Hertz in 1935 (*136*).

During this first period of development the Rorschach pioneers encountered stubborn resistance, particularly in the United States. The psychiatrists, who would have welcomed a method which could give them a more complete and more objective understanding of their patients, were deterred by the cumbersome method of scoring and tabulation in the Rorschach technique; even more were they troubled by the fact that it was almost impossible to discover how a Rorschach interpreter arrived at his findings. The psychologists, on the other hand — academic psychologists as well as psychometricians — doubted the scientific value of a method which seemed to be applied in a rather subjective and experimentally uncontrolled manner.

This unfortunate situation was improved to a large extent by the appearance, in 1936, of the *Rorschach Research Exchange*, a quarterly publication devoted to the dissemination of research findings and theoretical discussions bearing on various aspects of the Rorschach method. The refined scoring system developed in the *Exchange* helped interested psychiatrists and psychologists to gain proficiency in the use of the method. After 1936 the method spread so rapidly, supported by the strong general interest in the study of personality, that in 1939 Rorschach workers in this country and abroad formed a professional organization, the Rorschach Institute, mainly as a clearing house for research and as a training center, in order to help satisfy the growing demand for skilled Rorschach workers in medical, psychological, and educational institutions. Today the skepticism which was quite prevalent as recently as five years ago has been replaced in many instances by an interested and even enthusiastic acceptance of the Rorschach method.

The Institute of Child Guidance in New York City, under the direction of David Levy, was probably the first institution in this country to use the Rorschach method as a routine procedure. The Bureau of Child Guidance of the Board of Education in New York City, under its chief psychologist, Morris Krugman, has used the Rorschach method extensively and systematically over a period of years. Starting in 1934, the use of the Rorschach method was gradually extended to psychiatric institutions throughout the country and within recent years has been incorporated by faculty members of a number of universities as a valuable part of their equipment. A conference arranged in the spring of 1941 by the Josiah Macy, Jr., Foundation between experimental psychologists interested in the study of personality and Rorschach workers represented the beginning of a research coöperation of mutual benefit.

The important stages in the development of the Rorschach method within the twenty years since Rorschach's *Psychodiagnostik* was published are summarized in two excellent papers. These papers were read by the first two presidents of the Rorschach Institute as their presidential addresses at the first and second annual meetings of the Institute and published in the *Rorschach Research Exchange (201, 128)*. To illustrate the variety of fields in which the Rorschach method has found useful application, it is necessary to list only a few of the more prominent areas in which research has been going on during the past few years: research on juvenile delinquents and adult criminals; studies of stutterers, epileptics, and alcoholics; investigations of twin differences; and anthropological field studies.

Large-scale application of the Rorschach method

The national emergency beginning in 1939 rendered more urgent than ever the problem of efficient utilization of human resources and served to emphasize the application of the Rorschach method as a device for the selection of personalities particularly suited for specific tasks. In the armed forces, the identification of satisfactory officer material and the location of personalities too unstable to withstand the rigors of army life are two functions which the method has been called on to perform. The Rorschach method seems able to reveal hidden weaknesses in the personality structure not disclosed either in overt behavior or by the routine physical and psychological tests.

Large-scale application of the Rorschach method for these purposes would have been utterly impractical without some modification of the traditional technique of administration and interpretation. Since its inception, the Rorschach method has been regarded by most experts in the field as essentially an individual procedure; the face-to-face contact between the examiner and the individual subject has generally been regarded as an indispensable administrative element, the loss of which would tend to vitiate the entire procedure. However, the urgency of the demand for widespread use of the method served to overcome or lessen these compunctions. During 1941, Harrower-Erickson (*106*) introduced a group method of administration which promises to make possible a far more extensive use of the method than has heretofore been the case. In the Harrower-Erickson technique, the Rorschach pictures are reproduced on slides and projected onto a screen; twenty to fifty subjects view the blots at the same time, each subject writing his own responses to the blots.

Results thus far reported indicate that little, if any, validity is sacrificed as a result of using the group rather than the individual method. Considerable experimentation remains to be done in this area, however; the more important differences between the two methods of administration and some of the problems to which these differences give rise will be discussed in Chapter III.

Another time-saving modification of the original Rorschach method has been the introduction of abbreviated evaluation procedures. These procedures do not attempt to construct individual personality pictures which shall be as complete as possible, but are aimed simply at selecting from the total Rorschach material the more conspicuous favorable or unfavorable patterns for particular selection purposes. More recently the term "inspection techniques" has been applied to such procedures by Ruth Munroe (*236*). Experimentation has revealed that these evaluation procedures can achieve a high degree of reliability and validity.

With the help of these two time-saving devices, it seems possible to reduce the time required for collecting and evaluating Rorschach records for 100 individuals, with a usual distribution of intellectual capacities and emotional difficulties, to a total of approximately twenty hours, or less than one quarter of an hour per subject.

It is interesting to note that during 1941 more than twenty proficient Rorschach workers, fellows or members of the Rorschach Institute, joined the military services of the United States and Great Britain as medical or psychological officers, and are now attempting to apply the Rorschach method along the lines indicated above.

Just as group tests of intelligence received their greatest impetus during the first World War, so the second World War seems likely to further the development of the group method of administering the Rorschach. It is to be hoped that the adaptation of group tests of intelligence to peacetime uses, particularly in the schools, which followed the first war, will be paralleled by a similar development in the case of the Rorschach method when the second war shall have drawn to a close.[1]

[1] See also 1946 Supplement, pages 431 ff.

CHAPTER

II

METHODOLOGICAL PROBLEMS

RORSCHACH'S aim in the development of his method was to help the psychiatrist to a better understanding of his patients on a more objective basis than routine clinical observation afforded. Rorschach's interest remained focused on the individual's personality structure; individual differences, as revealed by the ink-blot method, were only incidental to this primary concern. This point of view has been clearly expressed by Frank (*81*) in the following words:

"The Rorschach method offers a procedure through which the individual is induced to reveal his 'private world' by telling what he 'sees' in the several cards upon which he may project his meanings, significance, and feelings, just because they are not socially standardized objects or situations to which he must give culturally prescribed responses. The Rorschach method is essentially a procedure for revealing the personality of the individual as an individual, as contrasted with rating or assessing him in terms of his likeness or conformity to social norms of action and speech. It is just because a subject is not aware of what he is telling and has no cultural norms behind which to hide himself, that the Rorschach and other projective methods are so revealing."

In contrast to this approach to personality diagnosis, psychometry tries to establish rigidly controlled and standardized situations which force the individual to react in one specific manner, in order to be able to measure differences in the reactions of individuals as accurately as possible, and to insure that the resulting differences are genuine individual differences, not due to any uncontrolled factors outside the subject. A heavy price must be paid for this form of experimental control; the observer is deprived, to a large extent, of the possibility of understanding why and how the subject arrives at a particular result. Little or no insight is afforded into the interplay of various personality factors which produce one reaction rather than another.

The use of the questionnaire procedure in the study of personality is subject to a second disadvantage in addition to that just mentioned. The observer must rely on information which the subject is willing and able to furnish. The subject is as little able to say to what extent such information represents a true picture of his personality as is the examiner who scores and tabulates his answers.

Out of the need to bridge the gap between the merely subjective "understanding" of another personality gained through clinical observation, and the objective measuring of individual differences with little or no understanding of their origin or deeper meaning, there developed a new approach which may be described, as in the above quotation, by the term "projective methods of personality diagnosis."

The difference between the Rorschach method and other projective techniques using visual stimulus material and verbal reactions, lies chiefly in the degree of "structuralization" of the stimulus material, i.e., the degree to which the material has some objective meaning which it tends to impose upon the subject.   A projective technique using material which is more structured than the Rorschach material is Murray's "Thematic Apperception Test." The use of picture material in this test, instead of less meaningful ink blots, shifts the emphasis from the way of handling the situation to the imaginative content.   This picture content is naturally rather elusive with regard to objective comparison and more under the influence of conscious control.   In this respect the "Thematic Apperception Test" is more similar to Jung's free-association technique than to the Rorschach method.

A technique making use of less structured material than the Rorschach method is the "Cloud Picture" technique described by William Stern.[1]   The cloud-picture material does not offer supporting factors comparable to the symmetry and color of the Rorschach material.   The subject, therefore, is to a greater extent limited to the use of visual imagination.   This in turn limits the range of subjects who can react satisfactorily to the material; it limits, too, the opportunities for interplay of various personality factors such as is afforded by the reactions to the Rorschach material.

"Objectivity" of the Rorschach diagnosis

While all projective techniques have in common that they present what one might call a "total-action" picture of the personality, most of them offer little or no opportunity for an *objective* evaluation of their results.   The

[1] Stern, W. "Cloud Pictures: A New Method for Testing Imagination." *Character and Personality*, 1937, Vol. 6, pages 132–146.

term "objectivity" as applied to a psychological procedure usually implies two technical prerequisites:

(1) That the results obtained by such a procedure can be measured or counted.

(2) That most experimenters with the necessary skill and experience will arrive at the same or similar results in using the procedure.

It is often assumed that the fulfillment of these two technical requirements guarantees "objectivity" in the philosophical sense, implying that such a procedure is the best way of obtaining a complete and accurate or "true" picture of the object being observed. Actually, however, it is possible that a procedure satisfy these technical prerequisites and yet fall short of "objectivity" in this philosophical sense.

What is the position of the Rorschach method as regards objectivity? Does it fulfill the technical requirements and, if so, are the results it yields as true and complete as those obtained by other procedures, especially by the psychometric methods which are usually considered more objective in the technical sense?

A psychological procedure striving for such an "objective" basis must be much concerned about the scoring of the subject's reactions, since this is the starting point for any interpretative efforts. A *scoring system* which is expected to yield truly objective results must be composed of units, or categories, which satisfy the following conditions:

(1) The scoring categories must be so well defined that a given body of raw material will yield the same scoring in the hands of most skilled experimenters.

(2) The scoring categories must be selected in such a way that their interpretative significance is at least tentatively acceptable as a working hypothesis.

(3) Only those elements in the reactions of subjects which are produced by certain features of the stimulus material may be included in the scoring system. Thus the reactions of various subjects become comparable on a quantitative basis, since every subject is exposed to these same features and the differences in their reactions can be counted and measured in one form or another. This last point seems to be the most important from the point of view of "objectivity."

Such a scoring system, it would appear, can be reconciled with the essential qualities of the Rorschach method.

In the next interpretative step, *structural interpretation* of the scoring results, we find an important difference between the procedure necessary for the Rorschach method and most of the usual psychometric procedures. Whereas most tests achieve their results by adding up the scores of the different components such as vocabulary, repetition of digits, and so on, such a summative procedure is impossible in the Rorschach method. For instance, in evaluating the different components contributing to the picture of a subject's "intelligence," the Rorschach practitioner is concerned not with the sum of components but with a configuration or "Gestalt." He deals not merely with a sum of components, where each component contributes its maximal value to the total score, but with a configuration of factors where each factor must remain within an optimal range of values in order to contribute to, rather than subtract from, the total value. In scoring a Binet test, the maximal contributions of the vocabulary section, the repetition of digits, etc., are simply added to obtain the total score, while in the Rorschach a concentration of energy leading to a maximum in one component — e.g., form keenness — may under certain conditions have a detrimental effect on another — e.g., creativity.

This difference makes it impossible to arrive at a uniform score comparable to an IQ, but it does not seem in any way to be detrimental to the "objectivity" of the procedure. Experience has shown that in many cases this configurational or "Gestalt" picture of a person's intelligence gives a more complete and in that way a truer picture than a single quantitative score, since it shows not only what resources the subject has at his disposal, but also what other resources he might have, were it not for the blockings which interfere with the emergence of these potentialities. It completes and rounds out the picture still further by indicating the nature of these blockings. At the same time the usual prerequisites of "objectivity," that the objective evidence can be measured and counted and that various observers should arrive at the same result, are satisfied.

The situation with respect to objectivity becomes more complicated if our interpretative procedure carries us beyond a structural interpretation into an attempt to construct a full-bodied personality picture giving detailed descriptions of the behavior patterns in normal subjects, or of the clinical picture as summarized in a *clinical diagnosis* in the case of patients. In this phase of the Rorschach interpretation the interpreter must use not only the objective evidence yielded by the Rorschach record but must add to that a vast store of clinical knowledge; the combination will enable him to arrive by inference at a complete individual personality picture using all pieces of objective evidence as one would the pieces of a jigsaw puzzle.

There seem to be two possible ways of using the Rorschach method to arrive at a complete picture of the individual personality. The first is to limit the interpretation of Rorschach material to persons who have a vast store of clinical experience and demand as a routine procedure from these people a complete "blind interpretation," requiring as elaborate and full-bodied a personality picture as was given, for instance, in Rorschach's posthumous paper. The other possibility is to limit the use of Rorschach material for interpretative purposes to the structural interpretation, and to use all other sources of information, such as clinical observation, case histories, and psychometric results, as the necessary supplementary material to fill in the skeletal structure derived in an objective way from the Rorschach record. Used in this way, the Rorschach method can perform an important function in crystallizing all available information about the subject, making the subject's behavior, or a great part of it, understandable through a clarification of his underlying personality structure.

At the present stage of development the cultivation of both procedures appears most useful.

The role of statistical procedures

Another problem which merits discussion in this chapter is the role of statistical techniques in the Rorschach method. The quantitative approach is so deeply imbedded in current psychological theory and practice that it seems proper to inquire what contributions statistical methods may make to the Rorschach procedure and what the limitations of the statistical approach are in this field. In general there are three areas in which statistical techniques play an important role in the development of psycho-diagnostic procedures; namely, the investigation of validity, estimation of reliability, and the establishment of norms, or standardization, as this latter step is sometimes called. In each of these three areas, statistical methods have already made significant contributions to the Rorschach method and will, no doubt, continue to do so.

In the matter of validity, statistical procedures have been used to investigate the clinical significance of the various Rorschach categories from the very beginning. The Rorschach records of groups of subjects of known clinical differences are sometimes compared in order to determine whether any specific differences in the Rorschach reactions are associated with the clinically established differences. These preliminary validating efforts not infrequently give rise to working hypotheses as to the interpretative meaning of the scoring categories. In the verification of these hypotheses, statistical procedures may again be called into play.

As regards reliability, the problem of the consistency of results derived from repeated Rorschach tests, and the problem of agreement among various experimenters in their interpretation of given records, both necessitate a statistical approach.

There is finally what we may term the normative problem, — that is, the determination of the distribution of some of the scoring categories in a representative sample of records. This applies mainly to the selection of the most obvious blot areas (*usual details*) and to the frequency with which certain obvious concepts are chosen for the same blot or blot area (*popular form* and *popular responses*). This task, for the most part a simple compilation of data from several sources, offers no great difficulty from a statistical point of view.

A word of caution is in order about the possible abuses of statistical techniques in connection with the Rorschach method. It seems pointless to accumulate hundreds of thousands of records, noting how often a particular scoring category has been found in this or that group of subjects, if we have no clear idea about the meaning or significance of such a category. This would be particularly true in the case of a category so clumsily defined that it represents a whole series of divergent personality factors; e.g., the general category, "shading effects."

In an effort to compensate for the seeming "subjectivity" of the Rorschach method, as the method was conceived in the Oberholzer tradition, some Rorschach practitioners have over-emphasized the necessity for the accumulation of great numbers of records, as if the accumulation and summarization of these records would lend at least the appearance of objectivity to the method. It scarcely seems necessary at this time to suggest the futility of such a procedure.

It would naturally be absurd ever to expect to establish standardized tables based on statistical research which would enable one to determine whether a subject is schizophrenic, neurotic, or any other definite personality type — normal or abnormal. Anyone who has worked with the Rorschach method or, for that matter, who has had any experience with living human beings in clinical or consultation work, knows that such "standard" figures can never do more than direct attention to certain conspicuous traits which may have very different meanings for different personalities. It must be emphasized once more that a personality diagnosis can be made only by inference, using as one basis the information gained from the Rorschach material and as the other, either inferences as to how such a person behaves or the actual clinical information available.

From the foregoing considerations one may decide to what extent a "standardization" of the Rorschach method is feasible or necessary. There is no possibility of a rigid schematization, such as the establishment of standardized tables in which the scoring and interpretative value of every single Rorschach response would be listed, thus reducing the method to a seemingly foolproof mechanical procedure. Such a schematization would be incompatible with the basic principles of the Rorschach method and, in fact, with any true personality diagnosis, since it would induce the examiner to ignore the individual nuances and facets of any given record. On the other hand, if a refined scoring method induces the examiner to observe, more intimately and accurately than he otherwise could even with years of experience, just what the Rorschach record offers, then such a "standardization" could be considered a decided advantage.

Prerequisites for proficiency in the use of the method

The interpretation of a Rorschach record, especially the construction of a complete individual personality picture, presupposes such a wealth of general psychological experience that only a limited number can ever learn to realize the full potentialities of the method. However, many psychologists and psychiatrists will obtain satisfactory Rorschach records without such an extensive background. They may become efficient in collecting important research data under expert supervision, or contribute the Rorschach material within a clinical setup for use and interpretation by an expert. These Rorschach workers may be termed "Rorschach administrators" as distinguished from "Rorschach interpreters."

Proficiency as a Rorschach administrator can be gained within a few months. However, even those who are able and qualified to proceed to the next stage of proficiency as Rorschach interpreters usually will remain in a "learning stage" for two or three years. This period can be used to good advantage, especially by psychologists, to widen their background of experience in psychopathology. The Rorschach Institute demands as a general prerequisite for Rorschach administrators at least three years of graduate experience in medicine, psychology, education, social work, or allied fields.

It seems rather doubtful that proficiency even as a Rorschach administrator can be gained by a process of self-training without expert guidance. Heretofore this question has been simply decided by virtue of the lack of appropriate training material. Rorschach's *Psychodiagnostik*, even if it had been available in an English translation,[2] is definitely not a training manual; it is only after years of work with the method that one fully appreciates

---

[2] The publication of an English translation of *Psychodiagnostik* is announced for May, 1942, by Hans Huber, of Berne, Switzerland, publisher of the original edition.

what this book contains. Beck's *Introduction* stresses mainly the presentation of case material, assuming that the reader is "in broad outlines, at least, familiar with the objectives of the Rorschach method." This book attempts for the first time to present the accumulated experience of twenty years of application in terms of a technical description of the problems the beginner will encounter in his attempts to administer, score, and interpret a Rorschach record. While this book is hardly sufficient as a basis for self-training, it is hoped that it will be of considerable help when used in conjunction with other training facilities.

There is a final point to be considered, more delicate in its practical implications than any of the previous considerations. Provided a graduate student has been able to gain proficiency as "administrator" and "interpreter," how is he going to use his findings? As long as they serve merely as data in a research study, or as contributing evidence in a case evaluation, no serious problem is involved, but the situation changes radically if the subject, as an individual, is interested in the interpretation of his own Rorschach record. It should be considered an unalterable rule of professional conduct never to give a written Rorschach interpretation to the subject himself, since psychological terminology is so readily misinterpreted even by persons who should be familiar with it.

In case a psychotherapist or guidance expert working with a subject requests a Rorschach interpretation for his client, the report may be given to this expert in writing, provided he will understand and reinterpret to the subject in his own language what the Rorschach report says. Even in such cases it is much safer to come to an understanding in a personal discussion with the other expert, since Rorschach language is still so technical.

When the Rorschach expert deals directly with a subject, without any professional intermediary, a completely new problem arises. No one should be permitted by his own professional conscience to give to another person as penetrating information about his personality as the Rorschach provides, unless he has specific psychotherapeutic training. Any person who violates this rule of professional conduct uses the Rorschach method in an irresponsible way.

PART TWO

PART TWO

CHAPTER

III

THE TECHNIQUE OF ADMINISTRATION

THE function of Rorschach administration is obviously the acquisition of projective raw material for future evaluation. This function comprises two main objectives: (*a*) to get as much rich projective material as possible and (*b*) to avoid any distortion of this material by influencing the subject during the administration.

The atmosphere in which these two objectives may best be attained is one of relaxation. If the subject does not experience his contact with the cards as a "test," if it is more or less an interesting game with no concern for right or wrong responses or any "do's" or "don't's," the administration will have the best chance of resulting in a well-focused projection of his personality. Naturally, the extent to which such an atmosphere may be created depends a great deal on the subject; but to most Rorschach experts it is astonishing how much information the Rorschach yields even when the subject is embarrassed, self-conscious, or is actually trying not to reveal himself.

27

There is one inescapable limitation to the effort to create the most favorable atmosphere. The administrator must obtain an exact picture of the way the subject forms his concepts in response to the cards, if he is to get from the Rorschach material all that it can yield. This requirement can be fulfilled only if all the necessary questions are asked. Such questions, even when asked as tactfully as possible, are often very disturbing and tend to keep the subject from relaxing as much as he otherwise might. It is necessary, therefore, to ask the questions after the projective material has been produced. This situation gives rise to a division of the administrative procedure into three parts. In the first there is as little interference as possible with the subject's spontaneous reactions to the cards; this part is known as the *performance proper*. In the second all the questions are asked which are necessary to reveal how the subject arrived at his responses; this part is termed the *inquiry*. In many cases, however, even very judicious questions may not be sufficient to make thoroughly clear to what extent a subject is potentially able to react to the various features of the stimulus material. This leads to the third phase, the so-called *testing-the-limits* phase, in which the limits of the subject's responsiveness are tested at all those points about which the administrator is still in doubt. The three phases of the administrative procedure are discussed in greater detail in the following sections. This discussion applies only to the *individual* method of administration; a discussion of the *group* method follows at the end of this chapter.

THE PERFORMANCE PROPER

In the performance proper, as we have seen, the subject is given the opportunity of producing his responses to the cards as spontaneously as possible without any pressure or guidance from the examiner.

General preparation of the subject

The phase of administration preparatory to exposing the subject to the stimulus material is of greater importance in the Rorschach method than in most psychometric procedures because of the necessity of inducing an atmosphere of relaxation. The preparation of the subject for what is going to happen must naturally vary greatly with the age and cultural background of the subject and especially with regard to his previous experiences with test situations. It is almost always feasible, except with very small children, to explain how the cards were originally produced in order to assure the subject that there is no question of right or wrong responses. Such a preliminary explanation is very often of help later, if the subject is puzzled about the symmetry or some other features of the cards, since he may simply be reminded of this original explanation. Rorschach remarks in *Psychodiagnostik,* "Distrustful subjects will occasionally require a demonstration of how the pictures are made, but on the whole, the experiment is usually accepted even by distrustful and inhibited mental patients."

As a rule either the use of a trial blot, or the actual production of an ink blot before the subject, is to be avoided because it disturbs the very important succession of the ten cards. It is sufficient to say, "You know you can drop

ink on a sheet of paper, fold it, squeeze it, and when
you open it, find a picture." The examiner may accom-
pany this explanation with appropriate gestures. Most
subjects, children and adults, are able to link this explanation with childhood or play activities under different
names, such as "blotto," "ghostwriting," etc. This association is very likely to produce an easing of the "test
situation" and does not stress the imaginative factors as
strongly as would a comparison with looking at clouds,
for instance.

The introduction may then conclude easily with a statement that the figures on ten cards, lying upside down on
the table, have been made in the same way and that they
will be presented one by one to the subject.

Sometimes subjects are very anxious to know the purpose of the test, and if refused an explanation are likely to
develop an unfavorable attitude. In such cases it seems
advisable to explain that these ten cards were selected from
thousands of trial blots, because they give each individual
an opportunity to handle the task, to say what they might
be, in his own way, and that it is this personal way of
handling the task in which the examiner is interested.
Should subjects consider the method a test of imagination
or fantasy, it seems unnecessary to disillusion them.

Some experts have tried to avoid the preliminary tension
by exposing the subject to the stimulus material as immediately as possible. Schneider, for instance, in *Psychodiagnostisches Praktikum*, recommends the placing of
Card I before the subject without preliminary explanation,
with a statement such as: "I am going to put before you a
series of cards like this. Look at it." After giving the
subject a few moments to develop his own attitude to the

situation, Schneider adds the instruction, "Tell me what this might be." Usually, however, a more individual way of helping the subject to overcome the tension seems preferable.

Any attempt to standardize or routinize this preparatory phase seems to counteract the main function of such a preparation; namely, to create a relaxed atmosphere. Besides, a mechanical standardization as, for instance, the use of written instructions, is in reality a pseudo-standardization, since instead of controlling the experimental situation such a procedure actually has different and unmeasurable effects on different subjects.

Instructions to the subject

The question of how to tell the subject what he is supposed to do with the cards has been a puzzling one. The exact formulation of the task should eliminate as far as possible any misunderstandings, but there is quite a difference of opinion as to how fully the subject should be told what to do and what not to do, as, for example, with regard to the way he holds the cards.

A variety of formulations of the initial instructions have been used or tried out with English-speaking subjects. These formulations have one element in common; namely, each one offers some possibility of misunderstanding. A number of the most frequent "misunderstandings" are listed below. Of course, these "misunderstandings" are in one sense hardly ever accidental. They usually reveal a special bias on the part of the subject in the direction in which he "misunderstands" the instructions. Very often, changes in the instructions have no effect whatever on the actual behavior of the subject, even if he claims that

he would have done something else, had he understood
that the examiner meant one thing rather than another.
Nevertheless it is advisable to forestall as far as possible
any one-sided understanding of the task by repeating the
various forms of instructions, as soon as a particular bias
in the reaction of the subject becomes evident.

Consider the following formulation, which can serve as
a standard:

*"People see all sorts of things in these ink-blot pic-
tures; now tell me what you see, what it might be for you,
what it makes you think of."*

The first part of this instruction is occasionally misunderstood as calling for purely descriptive responses
listing all the various features of the cards, such as the
little dots outside the main blot in Card I, the symmetry
and the folding lines in the middle, the shading effects,
and so on.

Some subjects occasionally complain that they misunderstood the "it" in the second part of the instruction as
referring to each whole card and that they tried for this
reason to give only responses to the whole card. In most
cases the inner inconsistency of this claim is made evident
by the fact that almost invariably the subject actually has
given a few clear-cut detail responses. However, it is
very easy to test his capacity for giving detail responses
in the "testing the limits" period.

The formulation in the last part of the instruction, "Tell
me what it makes you think of," induces some subjects,
especially those with psychoanalytic experience, to give
free associations to the cards, to follow their train of
thought irrespective of the blot material, using the blot
mainly as a jumping-off place.

Although any one of these three formulations used by itself is susceptible of misinterpretation, the combined effect of all three when used together is to reduce such possible misunderstanding to a minimum. Furthermore, any one of these three may be repeated during the course of the performance when the responses of the subject reveal a tendency to be influenced too greatly in the direction suggested by either of the other two formulations. For example, in counteracting the descriptive or free-association trend, the examiner can rather bluntly tell the subject that he is not interested in either one of these procedures and ask him again what it might be for him.

In dealing with intelligent subjects, it can be emphasized that there are no further regulations in fulfilling the task and that this lack of regulation is essential for the test. Questions by the subject, such as, "Shall I say the first thing that comes to my mind or shall I say what it reminds me of, or what it looks like?" must be answered persistently with the words, "That is all up to you."

Some experts mention in their instructions the matter of turning the cards. Rorschach's only remark on this point is, "The subject may turn the cards as he likes." There has been much discussion as to the interpretation of this remark — whether to tell the subject that he may use the card in any position he likes or simply to permit, or encourage turning, when asked about it. Systematic experimentation with these methods suggests that it is preferable to say nothing about turning in the beginning, but to encourage it at any time the question arises. The fact that the subject continues or does not continue throughout to hold the card in the position in which it was given, or the particular point in the sequence of cards at which he thinks or asks about turning, are additional factors for interpretation.

The most important of the limitations in the instructions is that imposed by the necessity of avoiding any pressure during the performance proper. It is very important that the instructions simply set the task and leave the choice of procedure entirely to the subject. Therefore, a formulation such as "Look at each card as long as you like, only be sure to tell the examiner everything that you see on the card as you look at it," or even casual remarks, such as "What else?" after having received a response to a card, seem to emphasize the quantity of interpretations, which involves a restriction of the conditions.

It seems quite evident that any casual remark which has nothing to do with the task at hand, but serves the purpose of making the subject feel at ease, is not only permissible but desirable.

Technical arrangements for the presentation of the cards

Since it is important to create an atmosphere as informal as possible, any obtrusive technicalities should be avoided. There is only one indispensable arrangement: examiner and subject must be seated so that both are able to see the cards. It is preferable, but not necessary, that the examiner sit somewhat back of the subject in order not to disturb him. In cases where the subject prefers to sit beside the examiner, there is no objection to such an arrangement.

Before the performance, the cards must be placed face down on the table, in their proper sequence, so that Card I is on top and Card X is at the bottom. Each card is marked on the back with a number, indicating the succession and the position in which the card is to be presented to the subject.

As to the distance of the cards from the eyes of the subject, Rorschach recommends the length of the outstretched arm of the subject as the longest distance permitted. Such a regulation suggests that the subject shall hold the card in his hand(s). This also has the advantage of insuring a more personal handling of the cards than if they were to be put on a table or leaned against a wall and dealt with like pictures in a museum. Either daylight or artificial illumination may be used, with no apparent difference in results. The reactions even of color-blind subjects may be interpreted in the same way as those of subjects with normal vision. (*49*).

Recording technique

The ideal recording technique for the performance proper would undoubtedly be the use of a sound movie or at least a microphone-dictaphone combination which would not only record the actual responses but also the tone of voice and the remarks made by the examiner. However, these ideal techniques are neither feasible nor necessary in the great majority of cases.

What is necessary is that the examiner obtain as nearly literal a transcription as possible of everything the subject says. With some subjects who take a long time for each response and are not verbose in their formulations, this is rather easy. Other subjects produce an almost incessant stream of verbal expression, thereby greatly complicating the task of the examiner. This is particularly true in view of the fact that apparently only a small percentage of Rorschach administrators are skilled stenographers.

Experience has shown that the decision to allow the Rorschach administrator to toil along with an imperfect recording technique is a better alternative than the use of a stenographer to take down the responses. The presence of a third person interferes with the intimacy of the situation. This makes little difference in some cases, but in others it is very disturbing. Moreover, the skilled Rorschach examiner, even if he is unable to make a literal transcript, will at least know what is important and what is not, whereas even the most skilled stenographer will never be able to catch all the nuances of a Rorschach record, since the subject does not dictate but is supposed to give a free expression of his reactions, doing this often in a very informal way or in a very low voice.

Most Rorschach administrators divide the paper which they use for recording into two columns, using one column for the recording of the performance proper and the second column to fill in the information obtained later on during the inquiry, alongside the response to which this information refers.

Sometimes subjects become rather apprehensive about the fact that the examiner is writing down everything they say. It is fairly easy to reassure them with the explanation that it would be impossible to keep all their responses in mind and that since the examiner will want to consider these responses more carefully afterward, it seems better to eliminate the risk of forgetting, by writing them down at once. At the same time it seems clear that the subject must not see whatever descriptive remarks the examiner may put down about his behavior, and that the record of exclamations and asides must be made as inconspicuously as possible.

Time limits and time recording

Rorschach's statement, "It has not been found useful to fix a time limit to the responses," has been borne out by the experience of practically all experts. It cannot be denied that the use of a fixed exposure time for each card can produce interesting results (as it does in the group method of administration), but there seems to be general agreement that it involves a restriction of the full diagnostic possibilities of the method. In fact, when subjects seem to be very time-conscious, it has been found useful to emphasize that the time element is not important.

It sometimes happens that the subject cannot make up his mind to relinquish a card after having given some responses, or continues to force himself to give more and more responses as long as he is not stopped. In such a case it is good practice to state that the examiner cannot interfere with his handling of the card, because there are no limitations, but that it is entirely up to the subject to give up a card as soon as he thinks he is through with it and that the quantity of responses is of no particular moment. This procedure guarantees the spontaneity of the subject's attitude much more safely than does any arbitrary cutting off after a certain number of minutes or a certain number of answers.

The relinquishing of a card can be facilitated for a reluctant subject by telling him that his putting the card down on the table will be the signal to the examiner that he is ready for the next card. The subject can also be told to put the card away face down so that it will not distract him from the next card.

No particular degree of exactness can be specified for time recording. The measurements may be made to the

nearest five or even ten seconds. However, it is necessary
to record the following time elements: (*a*) the time between the presentation of each card and the first response
to it; (*b*) time for each entire card; (*c*) longer intervals
between successive responses to each card, produced by
shock or hesitation, which frequently (especially in Card
VIII) appear not before, but after the first response or
before a card is finally put away.

Recently, specific terms have come into general use for
the different time elements involved. The time between
the handing of the card to the subject and his first actual
response (not sounds or remarks) is usually called *reaction time,* while the total time during which a subject
holds any one of the ten cards is called *response time.*
The *total time* for the performance proper consists of the
sum of the response times for each one of the ten cards.
If the subject interrupts his responses to engage in purely
conversational remarks (as distinct from descriptive references to the cards), "time out" should be counted for these
interruptions. A simple measure of the *average response
time* may be derived by dividing this total time by the
number of responses produced in the performance proper.

Most Rorschach administrators find an ordinary watch
with a second hand adequate for timing purposes. A stop
watch may be more convenient, but ordinarily will tend to
produce too much of a laboratory atmosphere. Not even
a watch is necessary in all cases. Many examiners are
able to estimate time intervals well enough to make a dot
approximately every five seconds while the subject is not
speaking. The time elements which must be recorded
have this convenient feature in common, that the examiner
need not record anything else while he is noting the reac-

tion time, or the response time, or the time for longer silent intervals.

Recording position of cards and numbering the responses

The Individual Record Blank (reproduced on page 310) provides on its second page two columns, one for "Card Number and Number of Response," the other for "Time and Position" of the card. Loosli-Usteri (*210*) has proposed a very simple method for recording the position of the card: the symbols ∧∨<>, the apex always representing the top of the card. Even rarely chosen intermediate positions like ∧ can be accurately recorded in this way.

If the subjects turns the cards repeatedly before he says anything, it is not necessary to register every single position. If the cards are turned around completely once or several times, such a degree of turning can easily be symbolized by a spiral (☉) containing approximately as many inner circles as the number of complete rotations of the card. It is particularly important to record the final position in which a card is held when the subject gives a response.

For recording the response number it is necessary to know the distinction between responses and remarks, and between main responses and elaborations and explanations, as they are explained in the following chapter. Some Rorschach workers prefer to number the responses continuously through all ten cards in order to save themselves the trouble of totaling the numbers of responses to the ten cards. However, for purposes of location and other technical advantages it is preferable to begin the numbering of the responses to each card anew.

THE INQUIRY

In this second phase of the administration, the examiner ascertains how the subject arrived at his spontaneous responses and adds a further opportunity for the subject to enrich his spontaneous productions, should he feel more at ease after having seen all ten cards.

One of the inquiry's two main functions is to make the scoring and the interpretation of the spontaneous reactions possible; a satisfactory inquiry, therefore, is impossible without a thorough acquaintance with the scoring system and its interpretative values. The second function of the inquiry is to give the subject a chance to supplement and complete spontaneously the responses which he gave in the performance proper. This function is of particular importance where subjects of a high intellectual level are hampered by embarrassment or negative attitudes in expressing themselves adequately during the first encounter with the cards. In some cases only the combination of the responses given in the performance proper and the spontaneous additions in the inquiry produces an adequate picture of the personality.

Sometimes the blocking during the first encounter with the cards is so severe that the subject cannot produce more than two, three, or four responses. In the case of psychotic subjects it may be impossible to change the situation even after the performance proper is over. Many neurotics can overcome this blocking after the ten cards have lost their mystery and can produce a fairly adequate record in the second encounter. Occasionally the examiner is confronted by a situation in which the first encounter yields fewer than five responses and the second

encounter produces ten or more.   In such a case it seems
more practical to consider this second encounter a retest
rather than an inquiry to another performance, and to score
the responses of the retest by themselves.

Atmosphere of the inquiry

Where the performance proper has yielded fairly adequate results, the inquiry finds a relatively well-paved
road.   Nevertheless, the inquiry must be conducted with
all subjects, whether children or adults, whether feeble-
minded or of superior intelligence, in such a way that the
subject does not feel challenged in regard to his original
responses.   The examiner must formulate his questions in
such a way that the subject has no chance to feel that the
examiner thinks his answers are stupid and that he is trying to "show the subject up."   For this reason it is usually
quite dangerous to ask bluntly "Why do you think it
is . . . ?"   The subject may hide his resentment of such
a blunt challenge behind a polite façade, or may simply
give the rather negative response, "Because it looks
like . . ."
   In any case in which the subject becomes irritated or
bored or tired during the inquiry, the examiner does well
to assume that the inquiry has not been conducted in the
right spirit.
   The great majority of Rorschach examiners will have no
difficulty in developing a genuine interest in the reactions
of their subjects.   The more one develops a facility for
understanding the significance of the various reaction patterns, the more every single administration becomes a
rather thrilling game with tense expectations: "How will
the subject react to the next card?", "What will he do

about the colors?"; and so on. Regardless of whether the subject is feeble-minded or intelligent, well-adjusted, neurotic, or psychotic, the examiner will easily find a way of expressing this genuine interest, conveying to the subject the impression that he really wants to know more about his specific responses and that he wants to see them as clearly as the subject supposedly does. It is quite simple and natural to ask *where* all the interesting creatures and objects are and it is certainly quite natural to be interested in a question such as, "What was it in this particular card which made you think of this rather than something else?"

All questioning in the inquiry should thus be related to the cards and their particular features, instead of making the subject and his associations responsible for the choice of his concept. The techniques of questioning are further elaborated in the following sections; the main point, never to challenge the associations of the subject, but always to make the card and its qualities responsible for the concept formation, cannot be too firmly impressed upon the examiner. Another general suggestion, which is more self-explanatory, is the advice to be as naïve and as concrete as possible in one's questions. Every concept chosen by a subject offers some very obvious intrinsic and essential features, and it is a great sin of omission to fail to ask about these features before asking about specific or far-fetched elements. It seems best to consider what a small child would like to know about a concept when hearing about it for the first time, and then to relate the most concrete and essential features of the concept to the blot or blot areas used by the subject, before becoming interested in nuances and accessories. If, for instance, "two dogs kissing" is mentioned for Card II, the examiner must first know what portion of the card has been used, how much of the dog is seen (the whole dog or only his head and neck), and whether the ears and eyes are visible, before concerning himself with the use of shading for the surface appearance or with the particular implications of the kissing — such as, for example, whether it is more human or more animal-like.

If the examiner always starts with the most essential, concrete, and obvious features, he will soon find out in dealing with any given subject whether it is of any importance to go beyond these essential features in the inquiry, and in what responses, and how far to pursue the questioning.   Usually the inquiry about the cruder features leads automatically to finer nuances if and when the subject is responsive to them.   In this way the examiner can avoid many senseless and irritating questions which yield no results and interfere with a relaxed and coöperative atmosphere.

Starting point and main orientation for the inquiry

The most important principle for a satisfactory inquiry is to go over every single response with the subject, asking for all information necessary for the scoring, without asking any leading questions.   It is advisable to emphasize the coöperative character of this phase of the performance by putting the cards right side up on the table, handing them all together to the subject and telling him very simply — perhaps with some encouraging remarks about his performance — to show where and how he has seen the various things he has mentioned.

The main orientation of the inquiry is described by the

words "where" and "how." The term *location*, through
well-established usage, has come to designate the particular area of the Rorschach cards which forms the basis of
the concept formation; the full significance of the term
location is explained in Chapter V. The inquiry about
location seeks to answer the question, "Where on the card
has the concept been seen?" The term *determinant* is
used in describing the answer to the question "How was
the concept formed?" This term is applied to the various
qualities of the stimulus material such as form, color,
shading, and susceptibility to imaginative enlivening,
which determine the essential characteristics of the subject's concepts. Chapter VI explains the significance of
the various determinant categories. The other two major
scoring categories, namely the content of responses and the
popularity or originality of a response (i.e., the frequency
with which a given response occurs in the records of
specified groups), rarely necessitate any inquiry.

Inquiry about location

As a rule, the inquiry will first be directed to the location of the response on the card. A general question,
"Where is the . . . ?" or "Show me the . . . ," may in-
troduce this part of the inquiry. The examiner must proceed to a more careful determination: whether there was
an intention to use the whole, or virtually the whole, of the
card, or to select a specific part of it for the response.
Thus he will be able to distinguish clearly between the different types of whole and detail responses, as outlined in
Chapter V. Use of a wooden pointer, or any similar
method, is not necessary in the majority of cases, where
the most usual details are selected, and is insufficient in

the rare cases where the examiner has difficulty in recognizing figures seen by the subject somewhere in the shaded parts, or in very tiny spots, or by an unusual combination of adjacent parts.

1. *Use of the Location Chart.*[1] If the area used by the subject is reasonably clear, the examiner may, himself, mark it on the Location Chart, or picture sheet, drawing a line around the response area and marking this line with the corresponding number of the response, either by writing the number on the line or by connecting the number with this line if there is no room to write on it.

If, on the other hand, the examiner has difficulty in seeing exactly where the subject located his concept, there are several possible ways of handling the situation:

(1) He may ask the subject himself to outline the figure he has seen on the picture sheet.

(2) He may give the subject a piece of tracing paper and ask him to cover the selected part of the card with it and trace the figure as well as he can.

(3) A further possibility, now being studied,[2] consists of asking the subject to draw a freehand picture of his concept, first just drawing what he actually sees in the blot, then adding the part his imagination fills in, to make it a completed picture. This addition may be done with broken lines, or in any other way which would indicate that this part is not actually in the ink blot. Black and colored pencils should be at hand, so that the subject may use them or not, as he sees fit.

[1] Page 5 of the Individual Record Blank. (See inside back cover.)

[2] Doctoral dissertation by Kate Levine, now in progress at Columbia University.

It is important always first to ask the subject to point out his concept on the real card before the picture sheet is handed to him, since the smaller reproductions of the cards on the picture sheet look different in many ways from the cards themselves.

It is advisable to use pencils of a different color for distinguishing, on the picture sheet, main responses from additional responses.

2. *Record of spontaneous elaborations and explanations.* The general location is not sufficient for accurate scoring of the response. The examiner must also be informed about the elaboration and inner organization of each response. To use the example of the "bat" response to Card V, after it is known that the whole blot has been used, either with or without the light gray lateral extensions, a further description of the bat is requested. The subject may spontaneously point out the head, the body and the wings, as an answer to the request, "Describe the bat to me." If not, the examiner may proceed to ask for the head, the body, and the wings. Many subjects will volunteer further information about the particularly long ears of the bat, mentioning the vampire variety, the feet hanging down, or the position of the wings, which "should start lower down on the legs." Where these elaborations and explanations are not evident to the examiner, it is safer to mark the location of the more conspicuous elaborations on the Location Chart, appending the number of the response to which the markings refer. Naturally, all elaborations and explanations given should be noted on the record in the space left for the inquiry.

3. *Stimulation of explanations and elaborations.* If the subject does not volunteer the necessary explanations

and elaborations which enable the examiner clearly to see the concept, as it is projected onto the card, it becomes necessary to devise some forms of prodding which will stimulate the subject to produce the necessary information. There are two possible starting points for such a procedure:

(1) The concept with its main features may be used for this purpose; for example, if a human being or an animal has been seen, the examiner may ask for the head, body, legs, or arms.

(2) The examiner may, instead, start with the area which the subject has indicated as the location for his concept, by pointing to all the obvious subdivisions of this area and asking the subject which part of his concept they represent. The latter procedure is particularly important in the case of rather vague whole responses, including white spaces and various other complications.

Subjects giving the "clown" response to Card II usually skip the lower center red spot in their explanation; similarly, those who see two figures in action in Card III may not mention the three red spots. Most subjects will be guilty of minor omissions of this sort, and it has proved very useful to pin them down on just these points. Such conspicuous areas, besides the above-mentioned ones, are: the snake-like extensions at the upper sides of Card IV; the light gray lateral extensions of Card V; the "whiskers" and wing-like protrusions at the top of Card VI; the dark lower center spot in Card VII; and the blue section in Card VIII when the response is "animals climbing from rocks to a tree." In Cards IX and X one rarely finds

elaborate responses to the whole card which are characterized by such omissions.

Such questions may frequently stimulate additional responses which either add something to a response given
before or use the omitted parts for independent responses.
The examiner must ask whether or not the subject saw
these things in the performance proper, and, if he did, why
he failed to mention them in his spontaneous reactions.
Thus information is received about the different types of
mental behavior under pressure for explanation, but such
responses are not counted as *spontaneous* additions and
therefore are not scored.

Inquiry about determinants

Inquiry about determinants depends to a great extent on
a familiarity with scoring categories and their interpretative values. The qualities of greatest concern are form,
color, shading, and action. The principal danger so far
as the inquiry about determinants is concerned is that of
asking leading questions. For instance, the words *color*
or *action* or any questions using color or action concepts
should never be used by the examiner in his questions,
unless they are first mentioned by the subject.

Many examples illustrating the manner in which information about the determinants can be elicited without
the use of leading questions are interspersed in the following chapters on scoring. At this point only a few
general hints are given. In the majority of cases a general question such as, "What is it in the card which makes
you think of . . . ?" will suffice to bring forth the necessary information from the subject. Where this is not the
case, a series of special stimulating procedures must be

resorted to, of which the most important ones are listed below.

1. *Alternative concepts.* One method which is frequently used is that of offering the subject an alternative concept which differs from the concept actually chosen only in so far as it uses or does not use a specific determinant. For instance, if one of the colored blots is called a butterfly and the spontaneous explanations of the subject mention only the wings or the feelers or other form qualities, he may be asked whether it could be a moth as well as a butterfly. If the subject is actually not interested in the color it will make no difference to him. However, if he is interested in color, even only as a secondary determinant, he will make some remark about it under this provocation. Thus the inquiry is provocative without being leading.

2. *Analogy questions.* Very often the subjects themselves offer the necessary cues in some later responses. For instance, let us assume that no clear information has been elicited as to the use of color or action elements in some responses. In one of the other cards the subject mentions spontaneously something about color or action. This gives the examiner the opportunity to say, "In this case you said the color made you think of . . . ; how was it here?" These analogy questions should be left to the very end of the inquiry in order to avoid giving the subject the impression that any one determinant has a specific value. On the other hand, it seems legitimate to use such analogy questions provided they do not lead the subject to believe that one type of response is preferable to another.

3. *Specific stimulating procedures in various deter-*

minant areas. (Most of the specific procedures are contained in the examples interspersed all through the scoring chapters.)

For the color area, a procedure which has been frequently used, although not with decisive results, is the use of the question, "Suppose this were all gray or all black but the same shape it is now, would you think it is a . . . ?" This leads to conclusive evidence only if the subject answers "No." The answer "Yes" by no means excludes the use of color as a co-determinant.

Great difficulty is encountered by most examiners in the inquiry about movement. Questions like "What are they doing?" are definitely excluded. Usually answers to questions about the main parts of the human or animal figures seen, and their positions, give, as a by-product, indications as to the use of movement. Another indirect way of acquiring such information is through questions about adjacent parts and their relationships to the figure mentioned; for instance, questions about the black and gray lower center portions in Card III, as related to the two side figures (if the figures have been mentioned only as "Two figures"), usually produce an answer such as, "These are bags or hats they are holding."

Spontaneous additions during the inquiry

At the outset of the inquiry, after its purpose has been explained to the subject, it is desirable to state that if, in the process of going over the responses, something new comes to his mind which he would like to add, he should feel free to do so, merely telling the examiner whether he now sees it for the first time or had already seen it in the performance proper.

Such spontaneous additions may be completely new concepts which are simply scored in the three columns for additional scores (see sample Record), or they may be additional elaborations of concepts formulated in the performance proper. In the latter case the additional information may change the main score. For instance, assume that the subject has mentioned "two people" for Card III and explained during the inquiry how they are bending over, lifting something up. If the subject can explain convincingly that that is the way he saw it before, then the main score for this response is the symbol for human action (M), and not for form (F). If this action comes to the subject only as an afterthought, the main score is F for form and the spontaneous after-thought adds an additional score for human action $(F \rightarrow M)$. Spontaneous elaborations are also scored additionally where the elaboration does not actually change the main determinant, as it does in the example above, but only adds a new element; e.g., a stiff white collar to the two people. In this case it does not matter whether the white collar is an afterthought or has been seen before and just not mentioned.

These spontaneous additions contribute additional information about the subject, particularly if he gives any clue as to why he had not previously mentioned them.

TESTING THE LIMITS

In the testing-the-limits phase, as mentioned above, the examiner exerts pressure in a systematic and controlled way in order to provoke reactions in directions avoided or not clarified by the subject in his spontaneous reactions.

Importance and difficulties of testing the limits

The accumulated experience of the last few years has given more and more emphasis to this phase of the administration of the Rorschach method. Naturally the importance of this phase is in inverse proportion to the richness of the other two phases, the performance proper and the inquiry. The more results these phases yield, the less important "testing the limits" becomes. The more blocked and reticent a subject is in the performance proper and in the inquiry, the more important testing the limits becomes as an additional means of clarifying the subject's reaction pattern. As a rule, testing the limits will be particularly necessary where the performance proper and the inquiry produce few and meager responses.

However, it is almost impossible for the beginner to handle this phase of the administration adequately, since it presupposes that the examiner is fully aware of conspicuous omissions in the results of the performance proper and the inquiry. The more experienced the Rorschach administrator becomes, the more nuances he will get in testing the limits.

This phase of the administration deliberately departs from the otherwise strictly controlled experimental setup. The performance proper exposes each subject to the same series of stimuli and avoids any kind of pressure or direction. The inquiry adheres as closely as possible to the boundaries set by the spontaneous reactions of the subject. The only essential change in the experimental situation is that the subject is now familiar with all ten cards, a change which is identical for all subjects. The inquiry situation has this change in common with most

retest situations. Within this situation of greater familiarity the examiner takes the utmost care during the whole
inquiry not to lead the subject on in a direction he would
not have chosen spontaneously. The request for explanations is done at all times in the spirit of interest in what
the subject thought, and painstakingly avoids the impression that the examiner is putting new demands on the
subject or trying in any way whatsoever to make him do
things he would not want to do of his own accord.

This situation is entirely reversed in the testing-the-
limits phase. It is for this reason chiefly that the results
of the testing-the-limits, valuable and indispensable as they
often are, cannot be included in the scorable material.
The scoring affords a measurable comparison of the reactions of various subjects in a uniform situation; the
varying demands and pressures to which each subject has
to be exposed in testing his individual limits makes the
test situation one which is no longer evenly controlled.

As an external expression of the changed situation, and
for the general technical facilitation of the testing-the-
limits task, it is advisable to spread all ten cards face up
on a table before the subject when this phase of the administration begins.

The possible effect of the testing-the-limits procedure
on later retests has never been systematically investigated.
However, casual observation suggests that later retests are
not invalidated by whatever effects the testing-the-limits
procedure may have.

Reasons and aims of testing the limits

The need for testing the limits can arise from four
sources:

(1) One of the obvious features of the cards, like color, may be completely neglected in the subject's concept formation. The examiner must find out why he has failed to respond to it and to what degree he remains unresponsive under specific pressure.

(2) The subject may claim a "misunderstanding" of the instructions, stating, for instance, that he would have reacted differently if he had known earlier that he could turn the card, or use portions instead of the whole.

(3) In cases where the subject does not use the most obvious suggestions in the blot material to give the so-called popular responses, the examiner must find out whether these suggestions have been deliberately rejected because they were too "cheap" or too obvious, or because the subject did not conceive of the possibility of forming such concepts. In the latter case he must also find out whether the subject is able to accept them after they have been pointed out, and if not, why not.

(4) Certain features of the cards may be used in such an evasive, noncommittal, or crude fashion that the examiner is prompted to test the limits of the subject's capacity for a more refined or differentiated reaction.

Techniques for testing the limits

The various situations which create a need for testing the limits can be handled in a number of different ways. The examiner may, by indirect means, call the attention of the subject to the features in the blots in which he is interested; he can give specific tasks for the use of certain scoring categories; or he may offer definite concepts and ask for their acceptance and elaboration.

1. *Indirect prodding.* This first technique is most frequently advisable when the color in the cards has not been used for concept formation. A roundabout but often effective way of getting to this blind spot in the subject's reactions is to hand him all the cards, asking him to pick out the card he likes best and the one he likes least. It is of interest to note which, if either, of these cards is colored. If no colored card is used or color is not mentioned by the subject, the examiner may follow this by asking the subject to divide the ten cards into two equal sets of five cards each so that all cards in one set have something in common which the cards in the other group have not. If this procedure does not have the effect of calling the subject's attention to the color, the examiner may group the cards into the five achromatic and the five brightly colored cards and ask the subject about the dividing principle. If even that fails, he may point out the color and watch carefully to see whether the subject answers with scornful surprise at such an obvious point having been questioned at all, or what other reactions he may show.

2. *Special instructions.* As soon as the particular feature for which the examiner is prodding has been called to the subject's attention, the second technique can be employed.

Theoretically, any one of the various scoring categories may serve for the purpose of testing the subject's capacity to use the stimulus material. We will, however, limit our discussion of this technique to the most conspicuous blind spots or omissions, as outlined below:

(1) Where the subject always or virtually always uses a complete or incomplete whole card, a general introductory remark may be made to the effect that he has made things particularly hard for himself by his effort to get everything into a single concept, with an explanation that many people use separate unrelated details for their concepts. He may then be asked to pick out some such detail. If he seems to have difficulty in doing this, a number of obvious areas, like the side details in Card VIII or the center red spots in Cards II and III, may be pointed out, with an inquiry as to what these, for example, might be. If a particularly systematic check seems indicated at this point, the subject may be handed picture sheets on which all the usual details are indicated and asked to use as many of them as he possibly can to form independent concepts.

(2) Where color or shading has not been used or has neither been combined with definite form nor differentiated in any of the subject's spontaneous responses, he may be specifically asked to do that.

(3) Where no human figures have been seen in action, a general instruction may also be given to try to find such a concept in any one of the ten cards.

The remaining scoring categories do not require any specific testing of limits unless the examiner is interested in research problems related to them.

3. *The use of sample concepts.* If the specific instructions do not yield any results or if the subject seems unable to comprehend the meaning of such specific instructions,

the examiner must resort to sample concepts, thus combining a third technique with the previous ones. The beginner must be cautioned on a number of points in this matter of using sample concepts. First, it is very important to try to avoid giving the subject the impression that these new concepts which the examiner offers are necessarily better or richer than the ones which he has produced himself. The emphasis should be on the fact that different people have different ways of looking at the cards and that these are merely examples of ways which have been used by some other subjects, the examiner asking casually if the subject can see them.

Secondly, mere acceptance or rejection of the concept offered by the examiner is never sufficient evidence. If the subject rejects the concept, we must try to find out what element in the card makes the obvious concept suggested by the examiner difficult or impossible to accept. For instance, the reason for the rejection of the two people in action in Card III may be the shape of the head, which is to many subjects more animal than human-like, or it may be the separation of the details commonly used as legs from the part of the blot used as body. Sometimes the examiner must go into more and more detail in pointing out the concept in order to get specific reasons for rejection. If the general concept, "Two people doing something," is accepted, an elaboration must always be requested — what they might be doing, where their heads, arms, body, and legs are, and so on.

Finally, it is quite obvious that the examiner must always use one of the ten popular concepts (see Chapter VII, page 179) if he wishes to present a sample concept. After such a sample concept has been given, the subject may be asked to find similar concepts in any of the other ten cards, other creatures in human-like action like the figures in Card III, or other combinations of form and color like the caterpillars in Card X. If this demand produces no results, the examiner may point out a few more rather obvious concepts of the same category in order to find out whether they are accepted or rejected and whether the reasons given by the subject in either case show a reaction pattern similar to that found in the first sample concept. It is very important to use really obvious concepts for this purpose, and not to expect the subject to see the more unusual concept which happens to be a particular favorite of the examiner.

Group method of administration

The group method of administration, as described at the end of Chapter I, is marked by four fundamental deviations from the individual method of administration which has been described in this chapter.

1. The subjects are deprived of the opportunity of handling the pictures at will. The cards may, to be sure, be projected on the screen in various positions, but this kind of turning, since it is not done on the subject's initiative, is not satisfactory. Moreover, projection in several positions prolongs the administration time and does not seem to add to the validity of the results.

2. The subjects must formulate their responses in written language instead of in the quite informal way of oral expression which the individual method affords. As far as present evidence indicates, this requirement does not create disturbing inhibitions for most subjects.

3. All subjects must look at the pictures for the same

length of time. This requirement has the effect of inducing some subjects whose response time is comparatively short to increase the number of their responses in order to occupy all the time. Furthermore, the rather significant differences in reaction time cannot be observed.

4. The problem of inquiry is not yet solved. It would appear, however, that for most large-scale selection purposes a simple localization procedure suffices. Other forms of a modified "group inquiry" are still in an experimental stage. Probably a practical solution will be to add an individual inquiry to the group method of administration for doubtful cases.

CHAPTER
IV

GENERAL SCORING PROBLEMS

THE main function of the scoring is to extract from the raw material of a record the formal elements which constitute the basis of the objective interpretation. In Chapter II certain of the methodological considerations involved in this scoring task were described; as pointed out there, the "scoring" in the Rorschach method is similar in name only to the usual scoring procedures in other psychometric testing. The detailed scoring problems arising in the three main scoring areas — location, determinants, and content — are discussed in Chapters V, VI, and VII. This chapter considers some of the general scoring problems common to all three areas.

THE SYSTEM OF SCORING SYMBOLS

To construct a systematic, logical, and easily understandable system of scoring symbols, a few simple rules must be observed. These rules determine, so to speak, the vocabulary and grammar of the technical scoring language.

Choice of scoring symbols

For the choice of symbols the most obvious of rules is followed. As long as the letters used are as far as possible the first letter of the word representing a scoring category, such as *W* for *Whole,* there will be no difficulty in keeping the symbols in mind and associating them with the proper concept. The symbols used are of three kinds: capital letters, small letters, and combinations of letters.

1. *Difference between capital and small letters.* The use of capital and small letters in the scoring vocabulary possesses two advantages. First, it reduces the number of symbols necessary to describe the variety of approaches to the ink blots, and secondly, it enables the scorer to express, through the difference between capital and small letters, certain essential interpretative relationships among the scoring categories.

Four of the ten symbols used as capital letters are used also as small letters, one in the location area and three in the determinant area. In all four cases the scoring categories signified by the small letters are categories pointing in the same direction as the categories signified by the corresponding capital letters, but are of minor intensity or in some other way of reduced importance as compared with the capital letter category.

2. *Letter combinations.* We speak here only of letter combinations which form single unified scoring symbols, and not about combinations of symbols created through the scoring of main and additional elements. We shall distinguish the two kinds of combinations as *combination symbols* and *combinations of symbols.* The combinations of symbols must always be clearly separated, either by putting them into separate main and additional columns or

by inserting a comma between the main and the additional scores.

The combination symbols being discussed here are letter combinations which represent new and distinct scoring categories. In these combination symbols it was not possible to adhere as closely to the principle of self-evidence as in the choice of the basic letters. Into the choice of these combination symbols enter complicated theoretical considerations which are fully comprehensible only after one has read the following chapters.

Meaning of the symbols [1]

A brief explanation of the various scoring symbols follows. Fuller descriptions, both of their meanings and of their variations and combinations, will be found in the following chapters.

1. *Scoring symbols for location.* The location symbols consist mainly of three letters, *W, D,* and *S* used as capital and small letters in various combinations. The symbols and their meanings are as follows:

W	Whole blot area	*S*	Space
D	Large usual detail	*Dd*	Unusual detail
d	Small usual detail		

The last category, *Dd,* is further subdivided in order to describe the various sorts of unusual details:

dd	tiny detail	*di*	inside detail
de	edge detail	*dr*	rare detail

2. *Scoring symbols for determinants.* In the determinant area three capital letters are commonly used as symbols:

---

[1] A complete list of the scoring symbols appears in the reproduction of the Individual Record Blank inside the back cover.

M Movement (This symbol is restricted to human or human-like movement.)

F   Form [2]

C Color (C', called "C prime," indicates black, gray, or white used as surface color)

It was necessary to add a fourth letter which constitutes an exception to the rule about using the initial letter of the word which describes the scoring category. In scoring part of the fourth main area of determinants, shading, a fourth letter was introduced:

K "Chiaroscuro" or diffusion

K does not stand for the first letter of the determinant it represents, but rather the initial sound of the word "chiaroscuro," a term borrowed from the field of art which connotes the effect of light and dark.

The small letters used in the determinant area are:

m minor movement (abstract or inanimate movement)

k toned-down chiaroscuro

c texture or surface appearance (The small c is appropriate in that these responses point interpretatively in the direction of the qualities represented by bright color — C)

With the exception of the combination symbol FM, which is the symbol for animal action, all other combination symbols in the determinant area serve the same purpose: to describe the different roles form elements play when they are fused with movement, shading, or color effects.

The rules governing these combinations are simple: F

[2] The use of $F +$ and $F -$ is discussed on page 156.

before another letter (*Fm, Fk, FK, Fc, FC', FC*) indicates that the concept chosen by the subject is one with definite form. An *F* following one of the other letters (*mF, kF, KF, cF, C'F, CF*) indicates that the concept chosen is one which, by its very nature, has no definite outline; e.g., clouds or flames. If the six letters (*m, k, K, c, C', C*) are used without *F*, this indicates that considerations of form have not entered at all into the concept formation.

The outstanding exception to these rules is the category *M*. This category implies the definite use of form, but the traditional practice has been not to express this fact by adding an *F* to the scoring symbol.

In the symbol *FM*, the *F* has been added to indicate concepts which deal with animal-like rather than human-like action. There is no apparent logic in this discrimination between *M* and *FM;* it is merely a convention based on long usage and interpretative significance. There is, of course, as much definite form involved in concepts using human-like action as in those using animal-like action.

3. *Scoring symbols for content.* Special scoring symbols in this area have been limited to the most frequent content categories:

H	Human figures
Hd	Human details, parts of human figures
A	Animal figures
Ad	Animal details, parts of animal figures
Aobj	Objects made from animal parts, like skins, fur pieces, etc.
Obj	Other man-made objects
At	Anatomy
Pl	Plant

In other categories, which either have short names, or appear less frequently, the full name is used, like Art, Sex, Fire, etc.

Other terminological conventions

There are a few other terminological conventions which facilitate to some extent the use of descriptive language. It has probably become clear by now that the use of the term "location" is limited to a special sense. It does not describe the position on the card — top, bottom, or side — but rather describes whether the whole blot on a card, or any of its subdivisions, has been used for concept formation.

In referring to the position of a portion of a blot on a card the terms *center, left,* and *right* are used for the vertical subdivisions of the blot and the terms *middle, top* and *bottom* for the horizontal subdivisions. The terms *left* and *right, top* and *bottom,* are used in such a way that they vary with the position in which the card is held. For instance, the detail which is described as bottom center of Card IV with the card held in the original position is described as top center when the card is held upside down (∨).

WHAT IS A SCORABLE RESPONSE?

The first important task of the scorer is to divide the total of the subject's verbal expression into its natural units; in other words, to answer the question: What is a scorable response?

Independent concepts and elaborations

In many records the scoring units are obvious. Some subjects list with almost monosyllabic brevity the various items they see in the ten cards, adding few or no elaborations or introspective observations. In such cases the only difficulty is that of ascertaining whether the different items mentioned are entirely independent of one another or whether they form various elements of a single concept. A child, for instance, may say "a head, a foot, a tail," and only under special questioning will the examiner be informed that this head, foot, and tail are all parts of one animal which the child is describing. Sometimes it is difficult, or even impossible, to discover whether or not these different parts of a human or animal body belong together, especially in the records of children between four and five years of age, for whom the natural order of the different parts of the body is in a sort of prelogical state which does not conform to realistic adult requirements. Occasionally, children clarify their attitude by a formulation like "and this is its head, its foot . . ." Similar difficulties in establishing the unity of a concept may be found in the records of feebleminded adults, and occasionally in other pathological subjects. However, on the whole, cases in which difficulty arises in finding out how the parts of a body belong together are very rare.

Another difficulty on a higher level is presented by additional elaborations which do not form a natural part of a concept. For example, the two figures in Card III may be seen as holding in their hands all sorts of objects: "a kettle," "footballs," "muffs," and so on. To what extent are these accessories to be scored as independent concepts? The concept of *accessories* must be used as a guiding principle in arriving at a decision. For example, it is extremely unlikely that anybody would see the lower center portion of Card III as footballs without seeing two persons holding them. On the other hand, the butterfly in the center red spot of Card III may be seen either separately or flying between the two persons. In the latter case, the two concepts, the "butterfly" and the "people," are combined only loosely in order to establish a single concept, covering as much of the card as possible. In this instance it seems fair to consider the butterfly an independent concept which serves to make an incomplete whole more nearly complete. The same red spot seen as "the bleeding hearts of the two suitors who have been rejected by a fair lady, and are standing there with flower bouquets in their hands," is obviously not an independent concept but rather an accessory to the whole, and is to be scored only as an additional determinant.

Exclamations and remarks

An element frequently found in the records of more verbose subjects are exclamations and remarks which are clearly meant as asides rather than as fulfillment of the instructions to tell what the subject can see in the cards. These exclamations and remarks range all the way from sounds like "hmmmmm" or "oh" to phrases of considerable length like "Oh, this is pretty, now we have different colors."

In the case of such expressive remarks about colors there may be difficulties in determining whether to classify them merely as remarks or as responses. In the instance just mentioned there would be no doubt. However, if a subject says, "This is red and black," the examiner cannot be sure whether that is meant as a response or as a remark. Since color-naming responses are of outstanding interpretative importance, it is very essential to ascertain whether one is dealing, in such a case, with a response or a remark. The only way to find this out seems to be to use some clear-cut examples of mere exclamations or asides, or obvious responses during the inquiry and to ask the subject whether this particular phrase was meant in one way or the other.

The symmetry of the cards is another element which frequently evokes all sorts of observations, even where the subject has been told how the pictures were originally produced. *Symmetry responses*, as distinct from *symmetry remarks*, are rare and are usually given only as elaborations or amplifications of obvious responses. Such symmetry responses usually contain concepts like "balance" or "dividing force" or "central power."

Descriptive tendencies

One of the most perplexing difficulties in the task of ascertaining what are scorable responses is offered by descriptions of various elements in the cards. Subjects vary greatly in regard to the awareness of the fact that the ink blots have no objective meaning and that they may interpret them as they like. A certain number of subjects remain convinced that there is a real answer for these blots. Other groups try to evade the entire situation by taking literally the instructions to tell what they can see in the cards, and simply describe the blot as material without attaching any meaning to it. A repetition of the instruction that they are supposed to tell what it could be may or may not have an effect.

The interpretative and the descriptive attitude, moreover, may not be clearly separated and the examiner may therefore get descriptive responses intermingled with interpretative ones. For instance, a subject may see a bird in the upper side portion of Card I and then continue, "and here are little dots and there is a line and there are white spots . . . ," and conclude by pointing out the human figure in the center. The examiner may resort to the same procedure during the inquiry as just described in the section on remarks, but in many cases the subject will not be able to decide the question or will simply insist that these purely descriptive enumerations of certain features of the cards are responses. The reason for such an insistence may vary from quantity ambition or neurotic evasiveness to psychotic illogic. Whatever the reason, the problem of how to score such descriptions remains. Where they accumulate to a considerable extent so that five or more such descriptive elements are listed for a card, it seems appropriate to add to the other responses for that card one concept scored as a whole form description, or whole shading or color description.

In cases where these descriptive tendencies are fused with a more interpretative attitude, as, for instance, where colors are not simply described as "two colors" or "seven colors" but as "pastel shades" or "water colors" — that is, where the subject at least does something with the material besides naming it; or where the description of the middle line becomes an abstract uniting or dividing force, the examiner is obviously confronted with definite responses. Such responses must be scored, according to the determining element, as color descriptions (C_{des} or C'_{des}), or shading description (c_{des}) or k, or form (F), or abstract movement (m).

MAIN AND ADDITIONAL RESPONSES

After the examiner has learned to distinguish between responses containing a concept formation and side remarks or exclamations, his next task is to find out at what point in the stream of verbal expression a new concept is formed, and whether this concept is an independent one or only an elaboration of some other concept mentioned before, or some free-association-like story not directly related to the stimulus material. The basis for the distinction lies in the actual concept formation of the subject and the procedure by means of which he arrives at his concept.

The emphasis on the concept formation leads technically to the distinction between *main* and *additional* elements in the scoring. The *main score* serves to emphasize and delineate all the independent concepts formed by the subject during the performance proper. Concepts formed later as afterthoughts, or concepts withdrawn later by means of rejection, or elements also important for the concept formation but not independent concepts in themselves, are indicated by *additional scores*.

The use of this distinction between main and additional responses is quite recent, and there is consequently too little evidence for establishing a quantitative relationship between main and additional scores. In some cases it seems that the additional scores have almost the same weight, interpretatively, as the corresponding main scores. In other cases they may not have more than one half or one third of the interpretative importance of the main score. In all cases, these additional elements are not expressed in the same way as the elements scored as main responses but rather as *afterthoughts, accessories,* or *elaborations.*

This fact is sufficiently significant to make the differentiation between main and additional scores one of the most valuable means of getting a differentiated picture of the subject's reactions. For the time being we shall treat main and additional scores as two different kinds of scores, which in different ways are important as bases of interpretation. In general, the main scores seem to represent the ready-to-function elements in the subject's personality, while the additional scores represent a sort of potential.

Spontaneous additions and rejections

Spontaneous additions and rejections represent the most obvious basis for the distinction between main and additional scores. A concept which can be brought to the surface only during the inquiry, when the subject is more familiar with the cards and with the total Rorschach situation, is obviously less completely at the subject's disposal than is a concept formed during the performance proper. A similar situation is indicated when the subject rejects a concept which was originally formed — that is, when he does not feel, under further scrutiny, that he can adhere to it.

Within this area, two more refined distinctions are to be noted:

1. *Distinguishing between corrections and rejections.* One important method for distinguishing between corrections and rejections lies in noting the attitude of the subject to the original concept. Some remark such as "No, that's wrong, now I see what it is," indicates clearly that the original concept has been dropped and a new one substituted. Usually only the substituted concept should be

scored; the rejected concept should be scored additionally only if it contains some scoring element not implied in the new concept.

A different situation presents itself when the original concept is not totally rejected and the subject simply discovers a new variation of the old theme. For instance, suppose that Card V has been called a butterfly, and that the subject then says, "It could even be a bat; that fits the shape of the wings much better." The examiner can always make sure about the attitude of the subject toward the old concept by direct questioning. For instance, he may say, "I see that it looks very much like a bat; could it look like a butterfly, too, as you said at first?" Such a provocative question may evoke either a strong protest, implying a definite rejection, or a more equivocal attitude expressed in some such phrase as "Oh, yes, it could." In the latter case two independent main concepts are present, each to be scored separately, provided the correction occurs in the performance proper.

Turning of the cards frequently brings forth corrections. For instance, Card V turned upside down quite often elicits the observation, "This way it looks much more like a butterfly"; or in Card VIII, the animals in the side pink portions become much clearer and more definite when the card is turned sideways. If in these cases the concept is changed materially, as, for instance, by an interchange of feelers and legs in Card V, or by an interchange of tail and leg of the animal in Card VIII, the same situation exists as mentioned in the preceding paragraph. If the entire response is rejected, and if it did not contain any scorable elements omitted in the new concept, the scorer may simply forget about the first attempt at concept formation. If it is not definitely rejected and there are clearly two variations in the use of the same blot area, each one of the two concepts must be scored as a main response so long as both have been seen in the performance proper.

If a correction is made during the inquiry, it may be considered simply an elaboration of the original concept and scored as only one main response. Sometimes, however, the change in mind leads to a change in determinants. For instance, in Card V the subject may first see a moth, using the gray surface color as a determinant in addition to the form. Then the moth is rejected and replaced by a brightly colored butterfly, where the shading is imagined as photographic reproductions of color, scored as *Fc*. The gray color element must now be scored as an additional score, transferred from the main to the additional column by virtue of the rejection. This transfer is indicated in the scoring list by a little arrow pointing from the main to the additional column.

An essential question in all these borderline problems is whether or not a blot, or blot area, is used in various ways in order to arrive at several independent main responses. This elasticity of mind, permitting the subject to organize the material in different ways, is a very important factor. Compunctions on the part of the subject about using this elasticity of mind are among the main causes for rejections and corrections. The strength of such compunctions determines whether the independence of different concepts based on the same areas will stand up under examination during the inquiry or will be destroyed by insecurity and doubt. When the independence is destroyed to such an extent that one of the concepts is entirely disclaimed, there is, of course, a complete rejection. The following is an example of such a rejection: "Yes, I know I said a butterfly before, but I don't think it looks like it now. I have no idea what about the blot made me say it."

The score for such a rejected response must be moved to the additional column. Location and determinants can be scored only by guessing, since the subject does not give any further evidence.

2. *Distinguishing between spontaneous additions and elaborations.* Card II often furnishes a clear example of a spontaneous addition in the inquiry which serves only the function of an elaboration. In the performance proper only the "two clowns playing patty-cake" are mentioned. The subject, when asked in the inquiry to describe them, mentions the red hats and faces and says: "And now I see they are stepping on a firecracker," making it clear that this is a spontaneous addition which he had not seen during the performance proper. The old concept is here retained in its entirety, enriched and enlarged by the additions.

A more difficult situation frequently arises in Card X. Assume that the whole card has been called "a scene at the bottom of the ocean," without any further elaboration. In the inquiry the subject is asked to tell more about it and he points out the crabs, the corals, and the sea horses; in the course of this elaboration, moreover, he continues to interpret most of the other separate color spots, with or without reference to the original concept — seeing, for example, poodle dogs in the center yellows. It seems most appropriate to score all these details as spontaneous additions, giving each of them a location, determinant, and content score in the additional columns.

A new spontaneous addition not related to any of the previous concepts and using an entirely new blot area does not present any specific technical problem.

Additional location scores

For purely technical reasons location and determinants must be treated differently in scoring additional elements of a single concept which are not implied in the main score. Nearly every concept formed by an intellectually superior subject contains a long series of elaborations of details which refer to a great number of different places in the blot area used for the concept. For instance, the two gentlemen in Card III may have bald heads, goatees, sideburns, stiff high collars, flowers in their coat lapels, handkerchiefs in their vest pockets, the white strip of the vest showing between the "body" and the legs, the end of their cottails flapping in the wind, pointed shoes, and so on. In the first place the scoring procedure would become clumsy and unwieldy if one tried to score the location of all these elaborations additionally. Secondly, it is very doubtful that this enormous labor would lead to a better focusing of the personality picture. It may rather blur the difference between the subject who uses such different blot areas only for the purpose of elaborating his concepts and the subject who goes on and on, picking out larger and smaller areas for the formation of new concepts in the performance proper and the inquiry. At present it seems best not to express the degree of elaboration as a quantitative measure. For interpretation purposes, it is sufficient to classify the degree of elaboration as high, medium, or low. The remaining opportunities for additional location scores are described in Chapter V.

Additional determinant scores

The situation is very different in the determinant area. There is only a limited possibility of using a variety of different determinants for the same concept. Very rarely does one find a concept in the formation of which more than three determinants are involved. Thus it is both technically very much easier to score all the different determinants contributing to a concept formation, and, at the same time, interpretatively much more important. It is frequently of the utmost significance to note whether the subject makes use of a determinant only in the more reserved form implied in the additional determinant scores, or uses it as a main determinant. For instance, a subject may never use the bright color as a main determinant but he may, so to speak, "decorate" a number of his form or movement responses by giving, let us say, red hats to his "clowns" in Card II, or a colored backdrop for the stage setting in Card III, or, in Card X, by describing a "vista of the Eiffel Tower" with a road leading toward it, conceding that there may be red flower beds on both sides of the road.

The procedure described in the examples above is just as different from the procedure of a subject who never uses bright color at all as it is from the procedure of a subject who often makes color the main determinant.

1. *Determinants used for only part of a concept area.* The simplest situation for the scoring of additional determinants is presented where a particular determinant — for instance, shading or color — is used for only one portion of the total concept. In the side portion of Card V we may have the profile of a face, which is determined

mainly by the contour of the area. The light gray side protrusions are described as the gray whiskers belonging to that face (*D F, FC' Hd*). Another example is the "two clowns" in Card II seen as figures in action (disregarding the center red portion), with the hats and faces of the clowns described as red (*W M, FC H*). In all these cases the determinant forming the basis for the total concept is obviously the main determinant, and the determinants used in elaborating some of the details are scored as additional determinants in the additional column.

2. *Primary and secondary determinants.* The problem becomes much more complicated if the different determinants which serve in the formation of the concept all refer to the total concept area. For instance, the same clowns mentioned above in Card II are sometimes seen as colored all over, the red spots visible within the black areas seen as portions of a red undergarment visible through the furry overcoat and reappearing around the legs. Even if the use of color is not distributed over the blot as carefully as this, subjects frequently emphasize that they think of clowns because the picture is colorful.

For an unskilled observer it would be very difficult to decide which one of two or more determinants used in the formation of a concept is primary and which is secondary. Unfortunately, in this respect we cannot rely on information obtained directly from the subject. It is surprising to most Rorschach experts to what extent subjects are sometimes unaware of the determining factors of their responses. Especially when it comes to estimating the weight of these factors is the judgment of the subject frequently misled by his preconceived idea as to whether it is good or bad to have his responses determined by color, shading, and so on. Moreover, many subjects so take for granted determinants which they have been using that they are not able to isolate them in their thoughts.

The question may be raised, why in such cases of ambiguity must we establish a rank order among determinants; why can't we have two main determinants — for instance, a movement and color combination in the case of the above-mentioned clowns? The answer is that rigid adherence to the principle of giving one and only one main score for each independent concept in each of the three scoring areas (location, determinant, content) seems to lead to a clearer focusing of the structural personality picture. As a by-product we gain an important arithmetical check on our computations, since the total number of main scores in the location, determinant, and content areas will be equal and can serve as a check on computational errors.

In the experience of skilled Rorschach workers the number of cases where a careful inquiry does not produce an obvious distinction between primary and secondary determinant scores is very small, probably not more than one or two in one hundred responses. As a rule of thumb, in cases of doubt it has been proven to be safer to give M preference over any other score, and to give bright color scores preference over scores other than M. However, in most cases an indecision about the main determinant of a concept indicates mainly an incompleteness in the inquiry concerning this concept. The more descriptions and elaborations the subject produces, the easier it is to find out which is the most important determinant. Sometimes subjects see in half of Card IV held sideways a fantastic landscape with immense boulders and gnarled trees, and somewhere in the area a tiny detail represents a frightened human being. It is obvious that in such a case the rule of thumb does not apply, that the main determinant is the vista and the human action is an additional elaboration.

Another simple technical device is to consider a determinant which has been mentioned in the performance proper as more important than one mentioned only during the inquiry. There are, however, certain exceptions to this rule. Quite often a subject mentions the animals in Card VIII without saying any more about them. In the inquiry, quite spontaneously, he describes how they are stepping from one side to the other. In most cases it would be a mistake to assume that the form is a primary element in this concept formation and the animal action is secondary merely because it was not mentioned in the performance proper.

3. *Determinants used reluctantly.* Determinants which are used by the subject only very reluctantly offer another opportunity to use additional scores. This reluctance may be expressed in several ways.

For example, the subject may, during the performance proper, be in doubt as to the way he actually sees the concept. He sees a bird in Card I, without being sure whether the bird is flying or not. Or he sees animals in Card VIII, with the card held right side up, and wonders whether they are climbing up something or whether they are only part of a heraldic emblem, without any action of their own. Or he sees the center red spot in Card III as a bow tie and doesn't quite know what to do with the red color, since evening bow ties usually are black. At the same time he hesitates to disregard the color entirely, and finally, in the inquiry, solves this problem by calling it a "very modern bow tie."

In certain other instances these doubts may not be expressed by the subject until the inquiry makes it necessary for him to explain his concept in greater detail.

Still a third way in which this reluctant use of determinants may be indicated is by the subject's failure even to mention the determinants spontaneously during the performance or inquiry, but to reveal their use only indirectly during the inquiry. It is a very delicate question as to how far the examiner should push the inquiry in order to find out whether the determinant has been used even reluctantly. It would obviously be quite foolish to try to force a confession out of every subject in every instance in which he sees an animal, as to whether or not he sees this animal alive and in action. On the other hand, it is extremely conspicuous if a subject sees the animals in the side portions in Card VIII and does not see them alive and in action. The question therefore arises: What principle shall determine the amount of prodding desirable to elicit information in any individual case? The answer is in terms of frequency; if a subject fails to use a particular determinant in a response in which the majority of subjects do use this determinant spontaneously, it seems well to inquire further. Where it is not generally used, such prodding becomes unwarranted.

Typical examples of concepts where determinants other than form are ordinarily used are the human action for the figures in Card III, the texture of the animal skins in Card IV or VI, the animal action for the animals on the side of Card VIII, the color for the caterpillars or grasshoppers in Card X. Where any of these "popular" concepts is used and the subject gives no evidence of having employed the usual determinant, prodding is necessary.

However, these "popular" concepts are not the only ones which call for prodding. Sometimes a less popular concept is chosen by a subject, which implies by its very nature the use of a specific determinant, as, for instance, the response "coral" to the pink section in Card X. In case the subject remarks, during the inquiry, on the surface appearance, "which gives the impression of the roughness of coral," and does not mention color, we must do some prodding in order to find out whether he simply "forgot" to mention the color or was not aware that he used it.

The butterfly in the center of Card III may serve as an example of another form of reluctance. The subject, who has *not* mentioned the color spontaneously, concedes, under prodding in the inquiry, that the color may have something to do with the butterfly idea, because butterflies happen to be brightly colored, even if he has never seen one of this particular hue.

There are cases in which the use of a determinant which is obviously suggested by the concept is denied by the subject. For instance, he may deny that the shading effect in Card VI has anything to do with his "animal skin," which he thinks was determined only by the contour of the blot. In such a case we are not even entitled to score the shading as an additional, reluctantly used, determinant but can do no more than make a marginal note in the scoring list to the effect that this determinant was definitely rejected. The same thing happens more often with color, where, for instance, the subject denies indignantly that any butterfly could be as red as the center red spot in Cards II and III and states that the form alone was responsible for his concept.

CHAPTER
V

SCORING CATEGORIES FOR
LOCATION OF RESPONSES

IN THE scoring of location, as defined on pages 44 and 65, various possibilities present themselves. The subject may, in forming his concept, use the whole blot, or so significant a portion of it as to make it clear that the omitted portions are of no consequence for him and that he therefore intended to use the whole card.

The subject may, alternatively, use some portion of the card, definitely meaning to use a subdivision or "detail," and not the whole blot area. These details are further divided into *usual* and *unusual details*, which in turn have further subdivisions. The usual details consist of *large* and *small usual details*. The unusual details appear in four variations, to be described later.

Still a third possibility is that the subject may use the white space left within or around the blot area, as the location for his concept.

These three possibilities, and their variations, are fully discussed in the following pages.

THE WHOLE RESPONSE (W)

There are two main aspects of W's which must be investigated: their exact spatial delineation and their inner construction.

Delineation of the W response

Delineation of the W response is a relatively simple matter, since it implies that a subject uses all of a card for the formation of his concept. However, there are two major borderline problems — so-called "incomplete" wholes and "loosely combined" wholes.

1. *The incomplete whole* (W). Not every subject is very careful in using all of a card. Some subjects may intend to do so but there may be certain minor areas in the card for which they have no use in their particular concepts or which they simply overlook. The incompleteness of their whole response is frequently not revealed until the inquiry. It is safe to assume that the majority of W responses are incomplete in this particular way. Rorschach cited such an incomplete whole in his original delineation of location categories. It is the popular response to Card III, "two people" doing something, using all the black blot material but omitting the red spots. Other subjects are aware of discrepancies between their concepts and some minor portions of the card and indicate of their own accord that one would have to cut this off or eliminate that portion in order to see the blot as a butterfly or whatever the concept may be.

There are interesting qualitative differences between such "cut-off W's" (W) and inadvertently incomplete W's. However, they have this essential feature in common, that the intention of the subject is to include everything or, if that is impossible, to include as much as possible of a card in the formation of a concept.

This particular borderline problem occasionally creates a situation in which the area of the blot used for a concept does not in itself determine the location category, since the same area may be scored as a W or a D, depending on the intention of the subject. For instance, in Card VI, the popular concept of the bearskin rug may be formed simply by omitting or neglecting the top part of the card or a portion of the top part of the card. However, some subjects declare specifically that they cannot interpret the card as a whole, that the top part may be seen as a bird in flight and the bottom part as a bearskin rug. Where the formulation of the subject in the performance proper or in the inquiry does not reveal clearly the whole or detail intention, it seems quite easy after the end of the routine inquiry to select one clear-cut W and one clear-cut detail response and ask the subject directly whether his intention in the questionable case was more like his attitude in the W or in the D response.

2. *The loosely combined whole.* The second borderline problem in the W field is related to the question of whether a response of the subject represents one concept or a combination of several concepts. This borderline problem arises especially frequently in responses to Card X. Subjects who have a definite tendency to give to each card at least one response which covers the whole material of the card try very hard to find such a total solution for Card X. They may, for instance, discover the White Rabbit of *Alice in Wonderland* at the bottom center of the card, then search for other figures which could

come from the same background, and finally decide that
the whole could be a scene from *Alice in Wonderland*
with two Red Queens, the White Rabbit, and a number of
other figures. In such a case the result seems to be a successively and successfully built-up *W*, and the only problem is whether the stepping stones in the construction —
for instance, the rabbit — should be considered independent details or simply a part of an elaborated whole. The
decision turns on whether these particular details could
be seen by themselves without being part of the total scene.

Frequently the concept is much looser than the
example just mentioned. The subject may start out in
Card X with the idea of a scene on the bottom of the
ocean, pointing out crabs and corals, and then see dogs
and caterpillars and other creatures quite out of place in
such wet surroundings. Sometimes subjects do not become aware of this inconsistency; sometimes they simply
give up the original attempt to make every part of the
card fit into the whole concept. It seems best, in such a
situation, to score both a main *W* and, besides that, as
many main *D*'s as there are separate concepts.

In other cases, the entire combination is so loose that
the whole concept appears as a rather artificial adjunct to
a number of independent details. For instance, the subject may see several butterflies in the three center sections
of Card VIII and may refer to the thin connecting lines between these three sections as "ties which bind these
butterflies together and expose them to the two animals
on both sides." The artificiality of such a *W* justifies its
being scored as merely a *W* tendency. (See section 4.)

3. *Response to one symmetrical half of a card.* Another problem is presented by responses given to a com-

plete half of a card. Sometimes the subject tries to make the answer cover the whole card by saying, "The other half is a reflection in water or in a mirror of the half mentioned." Sometimes he is satisfied by simply saying, "Naturally the same is on the other side." As long as the subject uses each symmetrical half completely there seems to be no question that this concept is meant as a *W*. The situation is more perplexing if some areas around the dividing line in the center are not used in the concept formation. An inquiry, in the form described previously, as to the intention of the subject is necessary in order to clarify this point.

Another form of establishing a concept covering the whole card when only the main portion of one symmetrical half is actually used is to relate the two halves to each other by action. For instance, the two figures in Card VII may be talking, quarreling, or at least looking at each other; or the animals in the black portion of Card II may be balancing something on their noses, or rubbing noses, or kissing.

If none of these devices to construct a *W* is used and the subject still insists that he intended to use the whole card, taking for granted that the same thing is on the other side, we are dealing only with what is termed a "whole tendency," scored → *W*.

4. *Whole tendencies* (→ *W*). There is a definite limit beyond which it does not seem wise to allow a subject's whole intention actually to constitute a *W*. A typical example is a frequent response to Card VIII, where many subjects clearly see the animals in the pink side portions. In a perfunctory attempt to follow through with their efforts to form a *W* concept, they may say, "These animals

are stepping over something." It seems best to require
that the definitely interpreted part of a card must cover
at least half the total blot area before such a *W* tendency
may be scored as a *W*. For instance, in Card I, the
response, "Two Santa Clauses with Christmas trees under
their arms hanging up stockings on something," would
fulfill this minimum requirement, whereas the response
to Card VIII of "animals stepping over something" obviously falls short of it. The *W* tendency in such a case
can only be an additional *W*, scored $D \rightarrow W$.

It is very important to distinguish these normal *W* tendencies from the type of response which Rorschach called
confabulatory [1] *W* and to which he assigned the symbol
DW. The critical difference between the normal *W* tendency and this confabulatory *W* is the fact that the subject who produces *DW* has not enough logical control over
his thinking and is therefore carried away by his *W* tendency. He may discover a clear form in even a very
tiny portion of a card; for instance, in the tiny light gray
protrusion at the bottom of Card VI he may see the head
and beak of an eagle and, jumping at conclusions, declare
that the whole blot is an eagle. The only rational basis
for the concept which he can supply in the inquiry is the
small head and beak. If he gives any explanation at all
for the rest of the card, he will point vaguely to the sides
as wings and the center as body, and so on. The essence
of a confabulatory *W* is, therefore, that it is impossible,
even with a stretch of imagination, to reconcile the major

[1] The terms *confabulatory* and *confabulation* are rather an unhappy invention in this connection, inasmuch as their technical meaning, as described above, has little or no relation to the meaning of similar words in
the English language. However, they have become so familiar in
Rorschach literature that it seems inadvisable to replace them.

features of the remaining part of the card with the remaining parts of the concept. For this reason a confabulatory *W* always has a negative form accuracy value.

Sometimes a subject is carried away by his *W* tendencies to some extent but catches himself in time to arrive at a somewhat reasonable solution. Thus, the four thin whisker-like lines near the top of Card VI make many people think of cats' whiskers. An extremely meticulous subject will see only the whiskers. It is quite easy to use the whiskers with the topmost *d* as the "head of a cat." To include any more of the card in the cat concept requires quite a stretch of imagination. One solution which avoids the trend toward the confabulatory *W* is to call the whole card the skin of a cat. Such reconciled whole tendencies leading to a built-up *W* combination are scored as *W*. (See also page 85.)

Construction of the *W* response

Rorschach described in *Psychodiagnostik* some of the major *W* constructions found among normal subjects and some of the more conspicuous misconstructions of *W*'s which he discovered, mostly among psychotic patients. Using Rorschach's distinctions as a nucleus, we can build up the following system of *W* constructions.

1. *Arbitrary W responses.* Inaccuracy, in its most extreme form, is found in responses which do not in any respect take into consideration the particular features of the card to which the answer is ostensibly assigned. Such responses are obtained quite regularly from children below four years of age, but also occasionally from psychotic subjects. One special form of such arbitrary assignments of meanings to cards is a more or less complete persevera-

tion of a concept through all ten cards. For instance, if in the first card a concept such as "airplane" or "bird" has been formed, this idea is then used as a magic key for all or most of the following cards. In a similar way children often assign the most elaborate and varied meanings to their early drawings, describing the same "picture" consecutively as that of a parent, a train, a cow, etc., without any effort or apparent need to add to or change the structure of the drawing itself. In both instances there seems to be no effort to relate the structure of the stimulus material to the structure of the concept.

2. *Inaccurate, unorganized outline W's.* The first step away from the arbitrary assignment of meanings to the cards is made if the crudest features, at least, of the general outline of the cards are taken into consideration. On this level the concept "bird" or "butterfly" can be assigned to every one of the ten cards, always pointing to something in the middle as body and something at the sides as wings. More or less accidentally, this procedure leads to a higher achievement in some of the cards, such as Cards I and V, which lend themselves so readily to this kind of interpretation that the *W* constructions in these cases must be considered as fairly accurate.

The confabulatory *W* response described in paragraph 4, page 87, can be classified in this category, since it represents only a minimum of organization. Confabulation contributes nothing to the clarity of the concept but has a detrimental effect on the accuracy level.

One very frequent feature of *W* constructions on this primitive level is the use of position as a means of elaboration. Thus, for instance, almost any card may be called "a doggie" and some area at or near the top of the card is pointed out as a head, some area at or near the bottom as a tail, and some area in the center as a body. This poor organization and disregard of form qualities does not permit the placing of these responses in higher construction categories.

3. *Unelaborated, fairly accurate outline W's.* With this type of *W* construction we approach the area of popular responses, though still dealing with essentially unelaborated outline *W's.* The only elaboration elicited in the inquiry is a pointing out of the body and the wings of some kind of a winged creature as, for instance, in Cards I, II, IV, and V. The addition of feelers, ears or claws, legs or tails, indicates at least a tendency to rise beyond the minimum level of accuracy. The pointing out of any specific features such as the bat-like wings or rabbit-like ears establishes a higher level of elaboration.

4. *Crude determinant W's.* Crude determinant *W's* represent another type of *W* construction showing a minimum of mental effort within the area of popular achievements. The outline or other form characteristics of the cards are more or less completely neglected and the shading or color effect is the basis of the concept formation. Unelaborated animal skins for Cards IV or VI, or clouds for Card VII, or "bloody mess" or "fire and flames" for Card II, are typical of this category.

Responses of this sort frequently result from a neurotically evasive attitude on the part of the subject. For instance, any shaded card may be called an "X-ray picture of some part of the body" and any colored card an "anatomical chart" where the different colors indicate different parts of the body.

5. *Organized popular W's.* The most outstanding ex-

ample of this category, which represents a transition from
the inferior or mediocre to the superior forms of construction, is the popular response to the black portion of Card
III, "two people doing something"; another illustration
is the animals or heads of animals in some sort of contact, seen in the black portions of Card II. However, if
a subject adds any more unusual elaboration, such as the
sideburns, high stiff collars, and pointed shoes to the
people in Card III his response should be put in the next
category.

6. *Superior W constructions.* The superiority of *W*
constructions can be established along various lines.
These possibilities include unusual elaborations of *W* constructions, although the *W* itself is organized along the
most obvious lines, and refinements in the use of shading
and color even where the form remains quite indefinite.
All except the popular combinations of more or less definite form with other determinants such as shading, color,
or movement must be considered as superior constructions.
Another way of establishing superiority is by an adequate
and unusual organization of the major portions of a card
into integral parts of a whole concept.

The question raised by Rorschach, as to whether these
combinatory tendencies occur simultaneously or successively, seems to have only a limited interpretative significance and is very difficult to decide in many cases.

THE DETAIL RESPONSE (*D, d,* and *Dd*)

As soon as it is established that the blot area used for a
concept formation does not represent a complete or incomplete *W*, it is automatically clear that we are dealing
with a detail response. Within this area one of the im-

portant distinctions is that between *usual* and *unusual* detail responses.

Usual detail responses (*D* and *d*)

The concept of the *usual detail* includes two characteristics. First, the areas chosen by the subject must represent obvious subdivisions of the total blot area, in size and organization; second — probably because they are obvious — these areas must be used by any random group of subjects more frequently than other blot areas. The usual details are further differentiated into large usual details (*D*) and small usual details (*d*).

The most frequently chosen larger details are characterized by the fact that they emerge almost spontaneously at the moment when the subject tends to break up the whole blot into its natural divisions. These subdivisions, therefore, have the general properties of relatively independent "sub-wholes," in the sense in which this term is used by Gestalt psychologists. They are completely or almost completely "insular" in their positions, being either completely surrounded by the white space or bordering on another area which, either in color or in shading, is markedly and distinctly different from them.

Next to these most obvious subdivisions are found details of an intermediate nature. Their Gestalt properties can be described as "peninsular." They are not so large nor so significant with regard to the whole blot, nor so independent in their positions, but they are nevertheless obvious and easily recognizable parts. They occur usually in one of two ways; either they are very conspicuous protrusions, jutting out from the edges of the larger blots, or they occur through the breaking up of one of these larger detail areas into its natural subdivisions. These smaller details are still obvious enough to be chosen far more frequently than any one of the really unusual details. Among them are found some which show a degree of frequency actually in excess of the frequency of many of the larger usual details.

There is some evidence that Rorschach was not unaware of these *d* areas; he suggested that certain Gestalt factors may affect the frequency with which they are chosen; for instance, the position of these smaller areas near the symmetrical axis may cause them to be noticed more often.

Distinction between usual and unusual details

In distinguishing between usual and unusual details, Rorschach concentrated on the two extremes in the choice of detail areas where the quantitative and qualitative differences coincide. The most obvious large details are the ones most frequently mentioned, and most of the smallest details are rarely seen. Due to this concentration on the extremes, he did not fully recognize the significance of the *d* areas. *D* and *d* together comprise the usual details which are quantitatively different from *Dd*, the unusual details.

1. *Frequency distribution of usual and unusual details.* A simple frequency tabulation of all blot areas used by as great a number of various subjects as can be compiled will make possible the identification of "usual" details (those occurring with great or moderate frequency), and an endless number of areas which are used very rarely, some of them not more than once or twice among thousands and thousands of subjects.

Sufficient data to establish the statistically "normal"

large usual detail and small usual detail with a validity beyond that of particular groups, such as age or intelligence groups, have not as yet been compiled. To establish the usual details statistically with what might be called "universal" validity, it would be necessary to obtain a frequency distribution of details in records of a truly random sample of subjects, which no one has accomplished as yet.

However, in order that the beginner may have a tentative guide as to where to look for usual details, there is presented below a tentative list of *D* and *d* in the approximate order of their frequency of mention, arrived at through the use of figures published in the literature (*11, 133, 193*) and the additional compilation of several hundred records.

2. *Borderline problems.* The difficulties in a quantitative determination of usual and unusual details arise from the fact that very few subjects delineate their concept areas, particularly in the achromatic cards, so sharply that the examiner can always be sure of the area with which the subject is concerned. He must decide how much of the adjacent area the subject may be allowed to include without overstepping the limits of a usual detail, and how much of a usual detail area he is permitted to exclude or omit without establishing an unusual blot area. In the latter case the problem is similar to that of the distinction between incomplete *W*'s and *W* tendencies. Another complication is the subject's manner of treatment of these detail areas. There is a considerable qualitative difference between the indistinct use of the lower center part of Card IV as an animal head and the very elaborate construction of a scene with two people standing behind a tree trunk with only their

TABLE 1

LARGE (*D*) AND SMALL (*d*) USUAL DETAIL RESPONSES TO CARDS I-X, IN APPROXIMATE ORDER OF FREQUENCY

CARD I

Large usual detail (*D*)

Entire center ("woman's body") with or without lighter gray
  (transparent skirt) in lower portion
Entire side (witch, bear)
Lower center without lighter gray (thighs and legs)
Entire lower center (bell)
Upper side (dog's head with snout outside)
Upper third of center (crab)

Small usual detail (*d*)

Upper outer projections (wings)
Lower side (lady's head)
Upper, inner, claw-like extensions (hands)
Uppermost projections (bear's head)
Upper innermost details (heads)
Bottom projection (feet)
Small knob-like extension at lower side (sheaf of wheat)

CARD II

Large usual detail (*D*)

Lower red with or without black-red mixture (butterfly)
Upper red (Christmas stockings)
Entire side black (bear, dog)
Upper portion of black (one half to one third)

Small usual detail (*d*)

Upper center (castle)
Bottom outer projection (hen's head)
Bottom projection adjacent to preceding *d* (Indian head)
Upper side projection (stone head)

CARD III

Large usual detail (D)

Inner red (butterfly or bow)

Outer red with or without tail-like extension

Entire lower center (pelvis or mask)

Lower center black (Negro heads)

Lower side black (fish or hand)

Upper side black — head and upper part of body of the usual figure (bird on rock, card inverted)

Middle side black (airplane)

One of the two human figures

Lower center light gray (ribs)

Small usual detail (d)

Bottom side portion (high-heeled shoes) with or without lower part of "leg"

Top side black (head)

Side black lateral protrusion usually upside down as animal head (with tiny white space as eye)

CARD IV

Large usual detail (D)

Lower center (animal head)

Lower side black and gray sometimes including the upper side portion (boot)

Lower side light gray (dog)

Entire vertical dark center

Inner dark side detail (nuns, card inverted)

Small usual detail (d)

Upper side extensions (snake) sometimes with small adjacent portion (dancer with face in adjoining portion)

Uppermost portion (flower) sometimes including adjacent shaded portion (Japanese face)

Outermost lower side extension (head of dog)

Lowermost portion of lower center detail (crown)

CARD V

Large usual detail (D)

Entire side with or without light gray extensions (face or figure lying down)

Center vertical portion (rabbit)

Small usual detail (d)

Bottom (tweezers)

Side extension (leg) sometimes with adjacent thin extension (crocodile's head)

Top (rabbit's head), or top without uppermost protrusions, (policeman's head)

Contour of lower side detail (profile)

CARD VI

Large usual detail (D)

Entire lower portion (animal skin) or half of lower portion (boat or king's head)

Entire upper portion (dragonfly) sometimes including light gray uppermost portion of lower detail (lighthouse on rock with beacon)

Upper black portion only of center column (snake) sometimes without slightly shaded outer portion

Entire dark vertical center (spine)

Lighter part only of upper portion (wings)

Small usual detail (d)

Uppermost detail (snake's head) with or without "whiskers"

Lower lateral extensions (dog's head)

Two inner light gray ovals (mice)

Bottom inner projections (birds or eggs in nest)

CARD VII

Large usual detail (D)

Entire bottom portion (butterfly) sometimes each half separate (sheep)

Middle third (mask)

Upper third, with or without uppermost projection (women's heads)

Upper two thirds (dog)

Small usual detail (d)

Dark center bottom detail (canal)

Top projections (squirrel's tail)

Light gray projections on upper inner corner of top third (icicles)

CARD VIII

Large usual detail (D)

Side pink (animals)

Lower pink and orange (butterfly)

Top gray portion with or without center line (mountain and tree) sometimes including rib-like figure and/or blue portion

Middle blue portion (flags)

Rib-like figure in upper center (spine)

Bottom pink alone (bullfrog heads)

Bottom orange alone

Small usual detail (d)

Lateral extensions of bottom orange (lamb's head)

CARD IX

Large usual detail (D)

Green portion
Orange portion
Small inner portion at junction of green and orange (deer's head)
Lateral pink (man's head)
Entire pink portion plus center line (tree), card inverted
Entire pink or either half
Center portion between lateral greens (skull)
Center gray portion (candle), with or without preceding *D*
Inner pink portion (elephants' heads)

Small usual detail (d)

All or most of upper inner orange projections (lobster claws)
Eye-like portion in middle including green and white slits (eyes)
Arch-like light orange at top center

CARD X

Large usual detail (D)

Outer blue (crabs) sometimes with outer green
Inner green, dark portions only (caterpillars)
Entire gray portion at top
Gray "animals" at top, without inner gray column
Entire inner green
Outer gray-brown figures (mice)
Light portion between inner greens (rabbit's head)
Inner blue (birds)
Pink portion separately (mountain)
Inner yellow (lions or dogs)
Outer orange (collie dog)
Inner orange (wishbone)
Outer upper green (grasshopper)
Gray column at top without gray "animals" beside it
Outer yellow
Pink with entire top gray (flowers), card inverted
Pink with inner blue (man on a mountain or cliff)

heads showing and all sorts of animals and scenic effects seen as part of the picture. Such very elaborate organization of the material within a detail area frequently leads to the above-mentioned additions or omissions. For example, the subject may use the small lines connecting the center part with adjacent areas, and also part of the dark areas opposite the white spaces which separate the center from the sides, in the course of such an elaboration.

It seems impossible to lay down a mechanical rule for every possible case in which usual or unusual details are involved. However, since these important qualitative differences are not indicated in the location score, the examiner can be rather liberal in granting the subject a certain leeway in the delineation of his detail area, as long as he adheres in general to the obvious subdivisions of the card listed in Table 1. It may be taken for granted that he does this when the core of the whole concept remains located in the usual detail area and the additions or omissions can be characterized as on the periphery. As soon as an essential part of the concept is located in an adjacent area, the situation is changed. Thus, in our familiar example of responses to Card IV in inverted position, the two black figures seen as nuns, let us say, may be connected with the center area in some scene of action; in this case, the core of the concept has definitely spread from the usual D area into an unusual location.

To cite another example, the top center area of Card IV in its original position is a usual d if it is seen as a face. Very often some part of the adjacent area is included; e.g., Oriental eyes just underneath the top d and a beard reaching down almost to the center of the card. This concept may still be considered as a usual d with some extensions which do not shift the core of the concept. If, however, the whole top half of the card, excluding the side protrusions, is used as an animal skin, then the core of the concept has been definitely shifted into an area essentially different from the usual top *d*.

3. *Combinations of usual detail areas.* Another complication arises when the subject does not use some adjacent parts as accessories to a usual detail area, but rather combines several adjacent usual detail areas into a new concept area. Some of these combinations are so frequent that they must themselves be considered "usual" and are included in the list of *D* and *d* in Table 1. The combination of the pink and center gray areas, or the pink and center blue areas, or the pink and center gray and center blue areas, or the combination of the side blue and green areas in Card X, are all examples of these "usual" combination details. Again important qualitative differences in the kinds of combination are to be noted. Some subjects combine these areas solely for the purpose of creating a rather indistinct new outline area, such as a combination of the top gray and pink in Card X as "neck-bone and lungs." Others may work out a very elaborate scene with the Eiffel Tower in the background and a parkway with flower beds leading toward it.

Unusual detail responses

After every effort has been made to establish as clearly as possible all complete and incomplete *W* responses and all usual detail responses, it can be taken for granted that every concept formation which uses part of a blot not included in these categories must be considered an unusual detail response. However, the examiner need not rely

on such a purely negative definition. Fortunately the
number of ways in which a subject can arrive at an unusual location for his concept is limited. Since these
different ways all have their specific interpretative significance, it is worth while to distinguish them in the scoring.

1. *The tiny detail* (*dd*). One of the more frequent
forms of unusual detail selections is the use of little isolated spots like the dots at the bottom of Card I or tiny
protrusions such as those at the bottom of Card IV. There
does not seem to be any difficulty in delineating this kind
of unusual detail. Details of this sort are determined
mainly by their size and by the fact that they are completely or almost completely surrounded by the white
background of the cards, or by other blot areas which are
distinctly different in shading or color. The darker brown
spots in the center of the inner yellow portion of Card X
seen as "walnuts" are examples of such tiny details which
are inside another blot area but distinct enough to have the
character of independent tiny details rather than of *inside
details,* described below.

2. *The edge detail* (*de*). The *edge detail* is a less frequent selection and less easy to define. Where large edge
details, such as the whole inside edge of Card VII, are used
as the "course of a river" or "a flash of lightning," the
essential features of these edge details are quite obvious.
The contour of a blot area is used as sole basis for the
concept. This characteristic, however, is difficult to establish under two conditions. First, the part of a contour
used can be so small that it is difficult to distinguish the
edge detail from the tiny detail; secondly, it may be difficult to determine whether the contour only has been used

and not the contour with some adjacent parts of the blot area.

A frequent example of the latter is the "coast-line" response. Where the coast line is seen in a topographical sense or as an actual vista, using the shading to indicate the steep slopes or cliffs or sandy beaches, it is clear that we are not dealing with a pure edge detail. However, if a subject insists that his concept is based on nothing but the irregular contour, indicating fiords and other inlets and outlets, we may be dealing with a pure edge detail.

As illustrations of the former, one finds all sorts of profiles seen in practically every one of the ten cards in different parts of the contours. Most frequently the contours of Cards I and VI and of the pink portion of Card X serve this purpose. These profile responses retain their character as edge details (*de*) even if they include the area of some small protrusions for some part of the profile, provided that emphasis remains on the contour. If, however, the blot area is used in a silhouette-like fashion, or the shading is used, the response is a *dd* or *dr* (see below) response rather than *de*.

3. *The inside detail* (*di*). In discussing *dd*, mention was made of the difficulty often encountered in deciding whether a particular response is more truly a tiny detail (*dd*) or an *inside detail* (*di*). The essential point for establishment of *di*'s is that the subject "pierces" a blot area which seems to be an unbroken area to a preponderant majority of all subjects, in order to discover various objects or images, using the most minute shading differences for their delineation. A type of *dd* which may be mistaken for a *di* was discussed above. The most frequent examples of *di* are faces and figures seen in the

upper half of Card IV or within the lower side portions of Card I.   Any contact of such *di* areas with the outside contour would be purely accidental.   Lines like the light gray lower center line extending from the bottom of Card IV toward the middle of the blot area are *dd*'s rather than *di*'s.   The same is true of the folding lines visible in almost any one of the ten cards and sometimes used as "spinal cords."   Other kinds of *di* responses are the "eyes" which can be discovered in virtually any card, wherever there is a darker spot inside some blot area. More solid and independent darker spots, like the darker yellow brown spots within the inner yellow of Card X, or the gray brown portion of the outer yellow of Card X, or the lighter inner pink portion of the lower center red in Card II, have the independent nature of *dd*'s rather than the quality of artificial selection and severance of the *di*.

4. *The rare detail* (*dr*).   The *rare detail* is, in seeming contrast to its name, the most frequently found form of the unusual detail.   Its name derives from the manner in which subjects select this particular detail.   Instead of being limited and bound by the natural organization of the ink blots and their distribution on the cards, most intellectually superior subjects occasionally single out some areas according to the need of their concepts.   These rare details are usually characterized by careful elaboration and organization of the concept which determines its unusual blot area.   While it is true that any unusual detail area which has neither the characteristics of *dd*, *de*, nor *di* must be *dr*, it rarely happens that such a *dr* does not at the same time have the positive characteristics just described.   There is only one exception in which these positive characteristics may be converted into their oppo-

sites. Sometimes psychotics or very young children use some unusual blot area completely arbitrarily as the basis for their concept. Frequently it is very hard to decide whether these arbitrary *dr*'s which are not elaborated and not even clearly delineated are not exaggerated incomplete wholes rather than *dr*'s. The size of the blot area may be used as a yardstick: if the concept covers half or more of the blot area, it is considered a *W*.

THE WHITE SPACE RESPONSES (*S*)

The only portion of the cards left as a choice for concept areas after all usual and unusual parts of the blots have been considered is the white space. This is really an absence of blot, which appears in all the cards surrounding the blot area and, in some of the cards, in certain inside portions as well. Some of these white spaces offer themselves much more readily than others as an area for concept formation. However, the choice of the *S* area in itself is such a comparatively rare occurrence that it does not seem worth while to distinguish between usual and unusual *S* responses.

There are essentially three ways in which this white space can be used as the area for a concept formation.

Reversal of figure and ground

The most radical way of using the white space area is a complete reversal of the figure and ground relationship between the blot area and the white space. This procedure is particularly facilitated by the form of some of the spaces left inside the blot areas, especially in Cards I, II, and VII; e.g., the white space in Card II seen as a spinning top against the background of black. Any of the major white spaces in Card I may be seen as a figure on dark ground. The situation is somewhat more complicated in Card IX, where the greater part of the inner space between the green and orange portions is filled in with rather faint colors and shadings. If the total inside area, frequently interpreted as a violin or cello or vase, is used as a concept area, it may not be assumed that a complete reversal of figure and ground prevails; this is predominantly a *D* response which includes some additional white space areas.

This inclusion of some adjacent parts is possible in a number of other combinations. The white space in Card II seen as a "white porcelain lamp" is frequently combined with the lower red as some "fancy fringes" or as representing the "light shining out from under the shade." The white space inside the lower half of Card IV is sometimes seen as "a female figure" and the adjacent light gray portions as "the long golden hair flowing down her back."

In these cases an additional *D, d, dd,* or *dr* must be added in the score to take care of the other areas included in the concept.

Supplementary use of white space

An essentially different way of using the white space as a concept area is its use for supplementary purposes. In general, such supplementary use is of two kinds:

(*a*) Use of white space areas as "lakes," "roads," or "plazas" to fill in the general scenery; and (*b*) emphasis on the white spaces as cutouts for eyes and mouth in a pumpkin's face or as an entrance or exit of a cave or tunnel. The first of these two ways gives a certain solidity to the white space, but in the second only the absence of ink is used. A variation of the first procedure is the combination of white space with colored spots to form concepts of a brightly colored design or object, such as "the outside of a white tent with colored paintings on it" in Card X or the surface of a brightly colored vase or a dish of ice cream in Card VIII.

In all these cases, the use of white space is supplementary and the *S* therefore is scored only in the additional column, and *W, D,* or *dr* in the main column. There seems to be only one exception to this rule. If the total white space on a card is considered as the sky or ocean, with the existing blot as clouds or islands in it, we may consider the white space as the main determinant. However, this concept is extremely rare, and in most cloud or island responses the white space is not even mentioned or considered and need not be scored at all.

Fill-in *S*

The last and weakest way of dealing with spaces is the attempt to eliminate them under the pretext of filling in the inside or outside spaces, in order to get a better contour or surface for the concept formed. Many subjects handle the white space by simply pointing out that the "butterfly" or "animal skin" is torn or has a hole. Whatever the procedure in these cases, the white spaces obviously have only a very minor role and should either not be scored at all, or only as additional *S* when they are mentioned by the subject spontaneously during the performance proper, or in the inquiry without any special prodding or pointing out by the examiner.

CHAPTER
VI

SCORING CATEGORIES FOR DETERMINANTS

AFTER the various possibilities offered by the answer to the question, *where* does the subject see what he sees, have been exhausted, the important question arises, *how* does the subject see what he sees; in other words, what formal elements other than location determine the formation of the concept which the subject has chosen.

In his first ingenious choice of the various determinants, Rorschach selected three main categories: kinesthetic or movement elements, form elements, and color elements. A few months before his death he discovered the fourth main area of determinants; viz., the shading elements.

It is obvious that the delineation of these various categories was at first possible only in a rather crude fashion. The accumulated experience of the last twenty years has led to many new differentiations and realignments in the description of the various categories of determinants. In each case choice and delineation are guided by the same principles which dominate the entire scoring system: the greatest possible exactness of descriptive definitions, verifiable differences in interpretative significance, and relatedness to objective features of the stimulus material.

THE MOVEMENT ELEMENTS

Rorschach was interested in the tendency of many subjects to form concepts which projected some kind of action or life into the ink blots. He singled out one particular kind of such "kinesthetic" responses: human or human-like action. He insisted on differentiating this kind of projection from any other, even though he was not sure of its specific significance. The fact that he saw clearly that there are other such tendencies in addition to human or human-like action is shown in his posthumous paper in which he mentions as a special category a group of responses under the heading "form tending to movement." Here he includes some concepts containing animal action, inanimate forces, and abstract movement tendencies. Experience and evidence accumulated since then have led to a further differentiation, which will be described in the following sections.

Human or human-like action (*M*)

The great variety of responses mentioning human or human-like action have one characteristic in common; viz., the subject always has a picture of some kind of a creature doing something in such a way that its action becomes visible in the whole or part of a card. The following modifications and delineations of this general principle must be considered:

1. *Movement in whole figures or in parts of figures.* It is not always necessary that the center of the activity projected into the ink blot be entirely visible. A subject may see "kicking feet," "a pointing arm," "a head peering from behind a tree," etc. So long as the creature per-

forming one of these actions is thought to be present, such a response is a genuine *M*. Part of the figure may be hidden, even by some invisible obstacle represented by the white space.

A difficult point in this delineation arises in responses in which a subject sees a "symbolic" pointing finger; e.g., in the light gray bottom *d* in Card III, or "a threatening face" which is thought of, not as part of a living creature, but rather as an abstract symbol. Such peculiarly abstract responses are extremely rare. They will be discussed in the section on *m*. A question asking to whom the hand or face belongs will help to determine whether the response is to be scored *M* or *m*.

2. *Human action and live postures of living figures.* A second problem is whether external action or movement in space is necessary to constitute an *M*. Concepts such as dancing and jumping are obviously action responses. However, figures who sit perfectly still, sleep, or lie motionless on their backs may also contain the essential quality of an *M* response: a live creature in a live position. This still presupposes a kinesthetic projection, a feeling of muscular tension in the figure.

According to general scoring principles an extremely hesitant way of projecting life into the picture would be scored $F \rightarrow M$, and the score would be tabulated as a main *F* and an additional *M*. Frequent examples hovering around the border between *F* and *M* are found in responses given to the darker part of the lower center section of Card I. If the subject describes only the outline of a human figure up to the hips, calling it a nude feminine figure, it is a simple form response. A question during the inquiry as to whether the bottom *d* is part of the figure may elicit the answer: "This might be the feet. Maybe she is standing with her back to me." This would constitute an *M* tendency. If, however, the subject spontaneously describes the figures as standing with thighs and calves pressed together, it is a genuine *M*.

3. *Human-like and animal-like action.* Very often subjects see mythological animals like those in *Alice in Wonderland* who behave like human beings and not like animals. The score for these actions correspondingly must be an *M* or possibly *M → FM*, even though the content is a mythological animal (*A*).

On the other hand, a subject may see a mythological human creature or a winged monster flying through the air. Usually the very fact that these creatures are not considered animals indicates that the subject wants to differentiate their actions from simple animal-like action. However, there may be cases where the animal-like characteristics of the activity are so prominent that it seems a more adequate description to score the response as *FM* with a tendency toward human action (*FM → M*).

One of the most frequent borderline cases of animal-like and human-like action is the "kissing animals" response to the black portions of Card II. The subject must be asked what he means by kissing, in order to find out whether he means that they are touching noses, or smelling each other (*FM*), or whether he conceives of them as animated cartoon figures who behave like human beings (*M*).

4. *Human action and inanimate forces.* A new complication arises if human-like creatures are seen "carried on a cloud" or "hanging on to a parachute-like contraption" in the inner green *D* in Card X, inverted. In most of these cases the figures themselves are seen clearly

enough as alive, sitting, riding on a broomstick, or holding on to the parachute, to justify an *M* score. The inanimate forces acting upon these figures must be scored with an additional *m*. Occasionally it may be a more adequate description to reverse the position of *m* and *M*, as would be the case, for instance, if the figure in Card X is so undifferentiated that it might well be a lifeless object.

The additional *m* score is also in order whenever something happens in a scene which is not the outcome of the activity of a human or animal figure. If, for example, the two figures in Card III are seen as "bowing very politely to each other and a whirlwind is flapping their coattails in opposite directions," the whirlwind action must be scored with an additional *m;* whereas, if a dancer is seen whirling around and his clothing is swirling because of his action, there is no need for an additional *m* score.

5. *Modification of human action by emphasis on the medium of representation.* Many subjects incline toward *M*, but at the same time are uneasy about this free use of their imagination. They express their compunctions by emphasizing that these are not real figures but only "drawings," "caricatures," "clumsy pictures made by a child," or "silhouettes" of people doing something. Rorschach was inclined to think that such a modification excluded an *M* score. Our experience seems to indicate that the subject's reactions are more adequately described by an *M*. The counteracting compunctions are merely a modifying qualitative factor. Such responses are scored in the content area as *H*.

A limit along these lines is reached if the emphasis on the means of representation becomes so strong that it actually smothers the projected activity. For instance, in

Card VII the "two gossiping women with their hands pointing in opposite directions" still remains an M response if the subject calls them caricatures or even statues representing such women. However, if these figures are seen as statues with the middle side areas representing a part of their shoulders and busts, so that all that remains is the expression on their faces, the action has actually become so smothered as to preclude the use of the M score. It would be scored $F \rightarrow M$.

6. *Human action and expressive description of human details.* The last example leads us automatically to a new delineation. It is perfectly possible to see only the faces or even only a part of the face of a human being screaming for help, or looking terror-stricken at something, and still conceive the whole concept as so lifelike that the basic condition for a main M is clearly fulfilled. In a majority of cases where human faces or profiles are seen, there is basically a determination by form (a main F score) which is only amplified and enriched by a description of certain expressive qualities connected with this form. If such expressive qualities are couched in descriptive language, such as calling a face grotesque, or funny, or grinning, the scorer has no right to assume even a tendency toward an M. The utmost score for an enlivening tendency in such a case, if the descriptions are given quite spontaneously by the subject, is an additional m (see section on m). Only where it seems obvious that these expressive qualities are the residue of a repressed M, as in the example given at the end of section 5, is one justified in scoring an additional M, representing an M tendency (scored $F \rightarrow M$).

Animal or animal-like action *(FM)*

Most of the delineations for this category are implied in the previous section, either directly or by analogy. Thus, the borderline between *FM* and *m* is determined in exactly the same manner as the borderline between *M* and *m*.

1. *Animal action, live postures, and tendency to animal action.* The examiner should be less persistent in questioning about the live position of animals than of human beings, since the situation is slightly different in this case. A whole human figure is rarely seen in a completely static way. It is difficult to organize the material in such a way that it fits into the less variable concept of a human figure, as compared with the ease with which it can be made to fit the extreme variability of animal forms. In the great majority of cases where the subject is able to organize the material in such a way as to see a whole human figure, the concept is usually formed with the aid of kinesthetic elements. In other words, an entire human figure is not often seen unless it is seen in some live position. Since it is much easier to see animals, the likelihood that a subject will form such a concept without the aid of enlivening tendencies is greater.

It seems justifiable to score a response as a main *FM* if the action or live posture of the animal is pointed out by the subject spontaneously in the performance proper or without any special questioning in the inquiry, when the subject has an opportunity "to tell more about it," or if the subject can convincingly demonstrate during further questioning that he saw the animals in action from the very beginning and just didn't think of mentioning it earlier.

There are certain places in the ten cards where the objective features of the blots seem to suggest animals in action more strongly than in other places. The outstanding example is the side portions of Card VIII. Here, as with the "two people" in Card III, the situation demands investigation if the subject does not mention the action spontaneously. Sometimes action is conceded after special prodding with the help of questions such as: "Do you see these animals alive or dead?"; if they are seen alive: "What is it in the card that gives the impression that they are alive?", or by an inquiry concerning the position of the head or legs of the animal. In such cases it is more accurate to score only a tendency toward an *FM* or, to be more exact, a hesitant *FM*. The main score is *F* (or *FC* or *Fc* if color or texture is used) and *FM* is scored only in the additional column. This special prodding should be limited to those responses in which the majority of subjects see animals in action.

If a subject uses the formulation "with spread wings," they may be the spread wings of a butterfly pinned in a collection box (*F*) or they may indicate a graceful glide through the air (*FM*).

2. *Animal action in parts of animals and expressive descriptions.* An outstanding example of vivid action where only part of an animal is seen is the response to the light-gray side projections in Card V as the hindquarters of two animals "rushing toward each other" or "rushing into the bushes."

The situation is less well-defined where heads or faces of animals with open mouths are seen. It is necessary to find out what this "open mouth" means in order to determine the degree to which the *FM* tendency plays a role. If "the open mouth of a dog" means that the dog is barking, or "the open mouth of a crocodile," that it is "devouring its victim," it is scored *FM*, or, if special prodding is necessary, as a tendency to $FM(F \to FM)$. If, however, even a persistent inquiry produces no more than a description of the threatening expression of the animal, for example, the score is *F* with an additional *m*.

3. *Animals in action and under the influence of natural forces.* A borderline problem is presented by responses to the outer red spots in Card III, such as "a cat falling from a roof." An explanation that the cat could not be alive "because if it were alive it would not hold its feet this way" makes it sufficiently clear that we deal with the effects of natural forces rather than with an animal in action.

Minor movements (*m*)

This noncommittal heading, *minor movements,* covers a variety of dynamic projections in which no live creature is the center of the activity. This dynamic force may represent natural forces — e.g., gravity or air currents or explosions — or it may represent abstract powers of a magic or mysterious nature.

1. *Expressive descriptions.* There is a special group of minor movements which is scored by an additional *m*. These are the expressive descriptions of parts of living creatures, mentioned in the two preceding sections. They are the products of a peculiar type of projection. The *M* and *FM* actions are projected by the subject onto the cards in such a way that these actions become the actual properties of the imagined human being or animal. The expressive descriptions do not give these properties to the projected concept. These grotesque faces, or threatening images, or masks, are not imagined as if they, by themselves, could actually express any emotions or do any harm. They serve only as a screen, onto which the subject projects certain of his own feelings or emotions.

In the frightening "primitive mask" or "pumpkin face" seen in Card I, it is particularly clear that the subject is projecting fright onto a mask, which to other subjects might be amusing, or to still others merely of ethnological interest.

2. *Natural forces.* Usually the effect of natural forces constitutes only an additional determinant within a concept formation which is determined mainly by color, shading, or action. Wherever a blot is interpreted as flames, smoke, water, or lava, almost invariably the action of natural forces is included as one element. There are, however, occasional responses where these natural forces dominate the scene to such a degree that the other determinants become secondary. The subject's description of his concept is a more reliable basis for deciding which determinant is primary than is his subjective judgment.

Besides the rare cases in which natural forces dominate the determination by color, shading, or human or animal action, there are occasional responses which are clearly and exclusively determined by the visualization of natural forces. A good example is Card VII seen as "something falling apart," with the "something" left completely indefinite. While the concepts "pieces of rock" or "clumps of ice" would ordinarily call for a main texture or achromatic color score, with the "falling" only an additional *m*, the stress may be placed on the "falling" with some remark like "something is falling, I'm not sure what. It looks as though it might be pieces of rock or clumps of ice." This response is scored *mF*, possibly with an additional *cF*. Finally, if the moving objects have definite form, like "four masks tottering on a base," the scoring is *Fm*.

3. *Abstract forces.* A special variety of natural forces is represented by certain involuntary functions of human or animal bodies which seem to make living creatures the objects of natural forces and transfer the center of action from the individual to the biosphere. Among the most frequent symbolisms of this kind are the phallic or intercourse symbols without an accompanying body, seen in a variety of cards, especially in Cards II and VI. These responses are scored *Fm* rather than *M*.

Sexual concepts are more often formed without such an *m* quality, merely on the basis of the shape of a particular blot area, or by combination of shape and texture or color as, for instance, the "female organs" seen in the bottom center of Card II, or in the top *d* of Card IV, or in the bottom center *d* in Card VII. Only when the natural forces of the sex drive are actually visualized in the concept is the *Fm* score justified.

Some subjects use form elements — e.g., symmetry, the folding line in the middle, or tiny dots outside the blots — as a basis for descriptive responses. If, however, a subject uses the line in the middle of a card as a "force which divides," or the light-gray dots near the middle of Card VI as "a point from which all power emanates," the scoring is *mF*. Frequently, the symmetry of the blots serves as a basis for abstract interpretations of balance or conflict.

Abstract descriptive elements are used also to establish an artificial connection between independent details. Subjects who have a strong compulsion to build up concepts including everything on the card may, for example, use the tiny gray and blue lines between the various sections of Card VIII to serve as artificial bonds between independent concepts which may be "drawn together" or "pulled apart." In these cases it seems most appropriate to score each one of the entangled parts as a separate detail with its particular determinant, and bracket all these determinants together with an additional *m*.

4. *Ambiguous dynamic terms.* There are a number of terms which subjects use, such as "hanging," "stretched out," "spread out," "attached," which may or may not call for an *m* score. In order that such responses be scored *m*, the outline of the blot area used for the concept, or lines, or markings in the shading must show the effect of the mechanical force described in one of these expressions.

Often such terms are simply explanations of where such objects as "animal skins" would be found — for instance, "hanging up to dry," "spread out on the floor," "nailed to a board." It is not sufficient to ask the subject whether he really sees it stretched or hanging. If the subject answers "Yes," he must be asked, "What in the card gives this impression?" Only when the above prerequisite is fulfilled is an *m* score justified, as it is in the following example, in Card VI: "This is an animal skin which was nailed on a board. You can see that the nails have just been removed and it is beginning to contract, because of the unevenness of the edges and the lines in here."

SHADING EFFECTS

One of the discoveries made by Rorschach within the few months between the publication of *Psychodiagnostik* and his death dealt with the significance of shading effects for concept formations. The darker and lighter shading nuances appear in every one of the ten cards. In the brightly colored blots the shading effects are usually overshadowed by the color effects. They are more prominent or provocative in some of the achromatic cards, especially Cards IV and VI.

Rorschach initiated the use of the shading effects as a scoring category, giving to this category its first scoring symbol, and by so doing opened one of the most interesting chapters in the development of the scoring system. One of his Swiss colleagues, Hans Binder, contributed the most intensive study of the use of shading effects ten years after Rorschach's posthumous paper appeared (31).

The following description attempts to incorporate and integrate as far as possible all the significant differentiations in the use of shading effects.

Shading effects used as surface or depth impressions

It is fundamental to distinguish the use of shading for surface and depth impressions. It seems that these two procedures are opposite poles of an almost unbroken series of qualitative differences in the use of shading effects. Occasionally responses are found which use the shading effects in such a way that it is difficult to decide whether they are closer to one pole or to the other. A careful investigation will reduce such doubtful cases to an insignificant minimum. The two opposite poles represent the most significant differentiation as far as interpretative meaning is concerned.

With few exceptions, objects seen with shading effects are seen as three-dimensional. One of these exceptions is the use of shading as a photographic reproduction of bright colors, described later on page 141. Another exception is what may be described as "marble effect" — the use of shading as "mottling" of a smooth surface. Within the three-dimensional area, shading effects may convey one of two different impressions; they may appear as the clearly seen *surface* of a solid object (such surface impressions are obviously closely connected with the sense of touch — so closely that subjects not uncommonly use their fingers, stroking the card in order to feel the surface differences which they themselves have projected into the blots); or, they may produce an impression of *depth*, a sense of air-filled space between discrete objects, with implications of distance and perspective or of plain diffusion.

1. *Shading as surface impression* (*c*). The oustanding characteristic of the use of shading as surface impression is the fact that the subject sees the blot or blot portion which he uses as one solid object in which the shading effects, the mottling of the blot, indicate to him the way the surface of this object looks — smooth or rough, furry or rocky. The question naturally arises, Does the relationship between texture or surface appearance and three-dimensionality imply that every concept of a three-dimensional nature — human beings, animals, plants, and so on — is necessarily seen in such a way that shading is used as a determinant, whether main or additional?

The answer is that the fact that objects are seen as three-dimensional does not necessarily mean that the actual shading nuances in the blot or blot area were used in forming the concept. Skillful questioning should, however, disclose the intention of the subject. Thus, while it would seem as though calling an animal "fur-bearing" or a stone "rocky" implies the use of texture, it sometimes happens that, in asking the subject what in the card gives him the impression of fur or rock, the examiner learns to his surprise that it is not the shading but merely the rough outline which determined the concept. Even the response "animal skin" given to Card VI is occasionally related exclusively to the contour or shape of this blot (see end of Chapter IV). The scoring must express the actual attitude of the subject.

In every case where the concept formed by the subject suggests the probable use of shading for texture and the subject's response does not fulfill such an expectation in his spontaneous explanations, it is necessary to continue prodding in order to be sure how strong the rejection of the shading determinant is, since there is always the possibility that the subject simply forgot to mention the shading, taking it more or less for granted. In many cases it will be better to do this special prodding after the routine inquiry is finished, since in this way it may be seen whether the subject is persistent through all the ten cards in not mentioning shading effects. If the subject *does* mention shading as a determinant in some other response, then a very easy analogy technique is at the examiner's disposal: "You said in this case that the shading gave you the idea. How was it here?"

At this point it may be well to add that prodding for the use of shading as a determinant should be definitely limited to those blots which strongly suggest the use of shading (for instance, the "animal skin" in Card VI); in other words, to those cards or portions of cards in which the majority of subjects make use of shading. In most other cases the subject takes the three-dimensionality of the concept for granted, without being particularly interested in the specific surface appearance as related to the shading effects.

2. *Transitions between surface and depth impressions.* Where shading is used as a determinant, the question is whether it is surface texture or depth which is intended. In most responses this distinction is easily recognized. There are, however, some borderline cases in which one concept merges into the other, and it is difficult to decide which was uppermost in the mind of the subject.

The following three classifications, indicating points at which the emphasis shifts from surface appearance to depth, may help to clarify the differentiation.

(1) *Surface appearance and the play of light and shadow.* A classic example of shading seen as surface appearance is the frequent response to the upper center section of Card VI as a bed- or lamp-post or table leg, the small white lines at the center of the blot area often being seen in this connection as the highlights on a highly polished surface.

The play of light and shadows may not only highlight the surface effects but may create the effects of radiation, of rays of light emanating from an object, or of a dark shadow surrounding an object. As long as a definite object with its particular surface remains the center of the concept, it receives a main texture score, and the diffusion (K) and m elements are scored additionally. If the solid and concrete elements in the concept are submerged in the play of light and shadow, the texture score must be replaced by a depth or diffusion score.

(2) *Transparency.* One of the most difficult problems in this area of determinants is posed by concepts involving transparency. One type of transparency used quite frequently can best be described as "cellophane transparency." This description implies that the object seen through the transparent surface is really the main thing, and the transparent surface adds only a certain sheen or luster to it. The distance between the transparent surface and the inner object is a matter of no importance. The score, therefore, is *Fc.*

Only where distance gains importance, as, for instance, in a crystal ball through which distant scenes are discerned, or in an X-ray picture, where the different shadings indicate the relative positions of the different organs, do we deal with the use of shading for depth and diffusion rather than with the texture category.

(3) *Surface differences representing depth in plastic form.* The middle point between the two poles, surface and depth, is reached in concepts in which the shading differences are seen as concrete representations of actual depth differences. This happens occasionally with topographical map concepts, which are seen as actual relief maps formed in clay or other material. We also find occasional responses like "pelvis" to the bottom center section of Card III, where the lighter portions are seen as the bones in the back and the darker por-

tion as the bones in the front of the pelvic girdle. Here the score is $Fc \rightarrow FK$.

In such cases the degree of emphasis on surface elements will help to decide the scoring. For instance, Card IV is sometimes seen as a "wilted leaf," with the end of the leaf curled over so that the lighter portions of the card represent the turned-over portions of the leaf, and the darker portions the other surface, which is less exposed to light because of the curling. If the subject emphasizes that the back of the leaf seems to be more velvety than the front, or points to some other texture differences between back and front, the response receives a main texture score, with a tendency toward the use of shading as perspective indicated in an additional score $(Fc \rightarrow FK)$.

3. *Shading as depth impression or diffusion.* Two main ways of using shading effects as depth impression or diffusion may be distinguished: the unorganized diffusion and the organized perspective or vista (see page 128).

(1) *Diffusion responses* (K). Concepts like smoke or whirling water clearly related to shading effects are obvious examples of diffusion responses. A combination sometimes found is smoke with fire or diffused clouds with the color of the setting or rising sun. As a rule it will be quite safe to assume that the color is the main determinant and the smoke is only incidental to the fire or the diffusion of the clouds incidental to the colorful landscape.

Occasionally the center bottom *d* in Card VII is seen as a landscape visible through a break in the clouds. Here the problem arises, is the landscape seen through the break incidental to the clouds or vice versa? A very similar problem is posed if the same center bottom *d* is seen as a burning house and the rest of the card as the clouds of smoke enveloping it. One way of deciding the question is from the point of view of sequence. If the subject mentions clouds or smoke first, the landscape or burning house may well be merely an elaboration. This, however, cannot serve as a rigid rule. Something must be mentioned first, and the concept may well be seen simultaneously as an organized whole. In such a case the diffusion is related only to part of the concept and is scored additionally.

(2) *Diffusion and darkness.* A very similar use of the shading is made when the subject sees the darker shades as darkness — for instance, as the interior of a cave or a room, or as night surrounding some partly visible object. With some rare exceptions this use of shading is additional. A clear example of this additional use of shading is an answer to Card IV with the center portion seen as "the vague outlines of a skyscraper only dimly visible in the veiled light which shines through night and fog" (*FK, K*).

The use of shading as an impression of darkness becomes a problem of differential diagnosis when the subject uses the word "black" instead of "dark." So long as the term "black" applies exclusively to this impression of darkness or lack of light, and does not imply anything about the actual surface color of the object seen, the concept uses shading as diffusion or depth. However, this impression may change into the impression of a surface color. For instance, black clouds are sometimes described with their silvery edges and black center as if they were solid bodies with a surface color. It is actually very easy to see clouds in this way when the sun shines on them and makes them appear solid. In such a case the depth impression changes decidedly into a surface impression. The main determinant in such a case is the use of achromatic surface color, with texture or surface appearance as an additional determinant.

Only where darkness and light are seen as actual space-filling expanses can they be scored as *K*. Where the effect of light and shadow is seen only as a reflection on the surface of a solid object, shading is obviously used as surface effect.

When a subject calls Card I or V a "bat" and explains his concept formation with the words "the dark color reminded me of the night and, therefore, I called it a bat," it may seem as though shading is used in the direction of *K*, but in most cases this is deceiving. The subject would have to see the night around the bat, but since in virtually all cases the total blot is used for the bat concept and only the white paper is left as surroundings, it would be very strange to assume that this white paper represents the surrounding night. In reality the dark gray or black is used as the actual surface color of the bat and then a symbolism is attached to this dreary black color so that we deal with an achromatic color symbolism rather than with an actual *K*.

4. *Vista responses* (*FK*). The use of shading as depth is most frequently found and most clearly revealed in vista responses. The differences in shading nuances are interpreted by the subject as differences in distance from the observer's eye. It is unimportant whether the lighter shades are seen in front of the darker or vice versa. The main characteristic is always the recognition of discrete objects, usually parts of a landscape or an architectural setting, spread out in space. They are frequently connected by the white spaces which are seen as bodies of water or roads or simply as the empty space between the two walls of a gorge.

In most cases it is rather obvious that the shading nuances serve as a basis for the vista impression, but there are a number of borderline cases.

(1) *Perspective and architecture.* In a response like the one to the top center *d* in Card II, "A temple at the top of a hill, with a long stairway leading to it," shading is used obviously as the basis for the vista effect. However, there are architectural concepts in which the shape or outline seems to be the only determinant. If, for instance, Card I, upside down, is seen as the top of a pagoda, it is usually the contour with the white spaces which determines this impression. Sometimes the lighter shades of the center *D* are seen as parts of a building, of which both the front and the back are seen

simultaneously, with the back part visible through some openings. Such a response must be scored as a main *F* with an additional *FK*, additional because the vista is applied to only part of the total concept.

(2) *Linear perspective.* The limits of the use of *FK* are reached where the linear composition is really the only basis for the vista effect and shading plays no part at all in the concept formation. The pink *D* in Card X may be seen as a road with flowers on both sides which grows smaller and smaller in the distance. In this case the color-form combination seems to be the only determinant. However, when the top gray *D* is seen as "the Eiffel Tower" to which the road is leading, or the side pink portions are seen as "the steep walls of a gorge," then the shading nuances certainly are used, and scored as *FK*; the color-form combination may be primary or secondary.

This problem is presented most frequently by the concept "mountains." The top gray portion of Card VIII, or the upper edge of Card V, or even the whole upper edge of Card I, seen as "mountains" may be called "mountains" solely because of the peak or peaks indicated by the contour line. The subject must be asked how he sees the mountains in order to determine whether there is a vista element involved. The mountain seen "in the distance through a light mist" produces evidence for vista or *FK*. This effect is, of course, enhanced where such differentiations as, "wooded portions and bare spots above the timber line" are added. Where prodding for such elaborations is necessary there is only a tendency to vista, or an additional *FK*. Where even the prodding does not produce such evidence, *F* is the only determinant.

(3) *Vista and reflections.* The use of the two symmetrical halves of any one of the ten cards, in such a way that one half is seen as the reflection of the other, poses another problem. The shading differences may or may not serve as a basis for such a reflection response. Cards IV, VI, or IX held sideways, with the very rich shading around the dividing line, easily produce the impression of a body of water reflecting the landscape banking on it. It is easy to make sure about the actual use of shading by asking the subject whether he can see the water which reflects the other half or whether he just imagines there must be some reflecting agent. For instance, to Card VIII sideways, many subjects say, "There is an animal stepping along some body of water," a concept suggested by the blue detail, and add, "On the other half the entire scene is reflected." This cannot be based on visual impressions, because the body of water is much too small to reflect the whole scene if the water is associated with the blue detail only. In this case, as in many other cases, the reflection concept is pure inference based on the symmetry of the card and has nothing to do with vista impressions based on shading nuances.

(4) *Landscapes and maps.* One of the most frequent ways of using shading nuances for vista effects is

the discovery of coast lines along the rough edges of some of the cards. There are several different ways of seeing such coast lines, and it is important to find out which is being used. The subject may see a panoramic view, as from an airplane, a photograph, a topographical map, or merely an outline, the contour of which suggests a coast line. These various concepts may be determined primarily by form, or by shading used in various ways.

An example of a form (F) coast-line response is the use of the contour as "inlets, projections of land, and little islands off the coast." In such a case the subject is unable to say any more about the geographical features of the coast line, whether it is rocky or smooth, steep or shallow. The only determinant in such a case is F. On the other hand, if the subject sees these features, whether actually, as from an airplane, or as they would appear in a photograph, the determinant is FK.

If the coast line is seen as a topographical map, the vista is toned down too much to be scored as FK and is scored Fk instead.

(5) *Indefinite vista responses.* There are vista responses in which the shape of the parts of the landscape is almost completely indefinite. For instance, the black and white portions of Card II may be seen as an exit from a cave or tunnel. Many subjects do not clearly visualize the effects of light and shadow and call this area the entrance to a cave without realizing that the center space would appear dark and not light in such a case.

Not every subject is as careful not to violate the reality of the situation as the little girl who, having called the space "a hole in the ground," figured out that one has to be in the hole and look up through it in order to see it that way. It cannot be assumed that there is no shading effect involved if the subject calls this area the entrance to a cave. At first glance the symbol *FK* seems rather unjustified for responses with such an indefinite form element. One essential quality of vista is nevertheless retained even in such very simple vista responses; namely, the relationship between the outlines of the blot, indefinite as they may be, and the shading effects; therefore the *FK* score is still adequate.

A similar borderline problem is posed if subjects see Card VII upside down as a natural rock bridge. An appropriate question designed to find out whether there is really any vista involved has to do with the distance of the observer from the rock bridge. If he seems to stand directly in front of it, and the shading effects represent only the rough surface of the rocks which he can touch with his hands, the shading represents texture rather than vista. Only if the subject points out the depth impression usually related to the tiny lighter gray portions along the center edges of the blot is shading used as vista.

5. *Toned-down shading effects* (*k*). Many subjects react very strongly to the shading as a depth impression but are not able to form a definite picture, such as a land-

scape, or to form concepts of real diffusion. They use a simple device for toning down the shading effects into a two-dimensional concept. The two devices used almost exclusively are topographical maps and X-ray pictures.

(1) *Topographical maps.* Where a map is seen as a clay model or where somebody sees an actual landscape with specific mountain ranges in the form of an air view of that landscape, shading is used as texture or vista. However, if the general shading effect gives the idea of topographical maps without any details based on shading, the response is a toned-down or evasive shading response. This shading score is not affected by the subject's consideration or lack of consideration of the outline. If the outline of such a topographical map is that of some particular country, the response is scored *Fk*; if the outline is indefinite, it is scored *kF*.

(2) *X-ray pictures.* An even more evasive way of using the shading is to call a shaded blot an X-ray picture. It is rare to find a subject who makes this a specific X-ray picture, or indicates in a professional manner the different organs visible in the shading nuances. A response which did this might approach a real vista response. The usual X-ray concept serves simply as an excuse for an undifferentiated, non-committal reaction to the shading even when the subject pays some lip service to the contour of the blot. The scoring of such X-ray responses is *Fk* or *kF*, depending on whether or not the outline of the area is used to indicate the shape of an anatomical part.

Differentiated and undifferentiated use of shading effects

In the course of his elaborate contributions to Rorschach's original formulations, Binder discovered and described the distinction between the undifferentiated and the differentiated use of shading (*31*). By *undifferentiated* use of shading is understood a rather vague use of a whole shaded area, with little or no attention to the individual shading nuances. *Differentiated* use of shading, on the other hand, implies the utilization of these nuances for the elaboration of a surface or the creation of a vista. Very justifiably, Binder attached great interpretative significance to this distinction.

The other distinction which we have been discussing, that between surface and depth impression, cuts across Binder's distinction. It seems to be of a more incisive nature, both in regard to the description of the way the subject's mind works and in regard to interpretative significance. These two distinctions must be combined in order to crystallize the major types of shading responses.

1. *Form elements in texture responses (Fc, cF, and c).* In the majority of cases in which shading effects are used to describe texture or surface appearance, the subject sees a definite object with definite form. Typical responses showing the most complete fusion of form and shading elements are sculpture concepts: heads, faces, or profiles chiseled out of stone and seen in the shaded portion of some of the blots, predominantly in the upper center area of Card IV, the lower side areas of Card I, within the blue area of Card VIII, or at the edge of some blots, particularly the middle side edges of Cards II, IV, VI, and VII and the upper edges of Card V. Sometimes these stone figures are seen as mere outlines, but in most cases

they are based on elaborate descriptions of the sculptured details, using fine shading nuances to get the molding of cheek, eye, nose, mouth, and hair.

Occasionally one of the small areas with a somewhat darker shading than the surrounding area is used because of its shape. Examples of such responses are concepts like "an eye." Or, to give a more elaborate example, the darker spot in the upper half of the right side D in Card I may be called "a cup held by a hand like in New Year's greetings." In such answers the shading is used not to mold the surface but only to determine the outline and these answers are simply form responses.

A great number of texture responses are associated with one kind of concept: animal skins or rugs or pelts. Most frequently this concept is associated with all or approximately all of Card VI, almost as often with all or approximately all of Card IV, but it can also be found as a response to portions of Cards I and V, the black portions of Cards II or III, and is occasionally associated with the blue portion in Card VIII. Where subjects see only indefinite pieces of an animal's pelt the question of using definite form is clearly decided in the negative and the response is scored cF. However, where the subject sees the whole pelt of an animal, it is impossible to know how definitely the form is used without further investigation.

Most subjects point to the form qualities of the outstretched animal skin such as the head (or missing head), the tail (or missing tail), and the more or less disproportionate front and hind legs, without mentioning the shading effects of their own accord. In most cases they have simply taken the shading effects for granted. It is necessary to ask whether the inner or outer side of the skin is seen and what in the card makes it look that way, in order to elicit information about the shading. Where it is rather obvious that the shading effects have been taken for granted, the score *Fc* is appropriate. Where this is doubtful, it seems safer to score *F* with an additional *Fc*, thus registering the hesitancy in the use of shading.

In some cases the opposite attitude prevails. The furriness associated with the shading effects is mentioned immediately, and no attempt is made to elaborate the form qualities of the animal skin. Even the question, "What animal's skin might it be?" may elicit an answer referring to texture by pointing out that the hair is long or short or that the skin is striped or mottled. Such a differentiated use of shading in which the internal qualities of the shading nuances seem to be more important than the outline of the blot should be scored *Fc*, indicating a more differentiated use of shading, despite the lack of definite outline. *Fc* is more adequate here as a scoring symbol than the *cF* which implies a more crude and undifferentiated use of shading.

Such cases must be carefully distinguished from undifferentiated animal-skin responses — as, for instance, to Cards I or II where the white spaces are pointed out as holes torn in the skin. These responses, if neither the external contour lines nor the internal form qualities of the shading effects are used with any care, are *cF* responses.

A *c* implies complete disregard for any form qualities and should be scored where virtually every achromatic blot is called "fur" without considering differences in the shape of the blots or in shading effects.

2. *Form elements in depth and diffusion impressions*
(*FK, KF, and K*). It seems rather obvious that the inclusion of form elements makes a decisive difference between plain diffusion and vista responses. There is only
one type of response; namely, the indefinite vista response,
which is scored *FK* even though the shape of the blot may
play an unimportant role. The reason for this decision
is the fact that in such cases even the indefinite form qualities have a very specific relationship to the depth impression, which is not the case in plain diffusion responses.
Even in diffusion responses, to be sure, the form may
play some role. For instance, the subject may say he
considers Card VII "clouds" because of the shading and
the odd shapes (*KF*). If the subject does not register interest in the form of these clouds or smoke areas the score
for the response is *K*.

COLOR RESPONSES

Some of the general difficulties mentioned in Chapter
IV, notably those arising from the distinction between
remarks and responses, are particularly marked in the
scoring of color responses. The mentioning of color
within a response does not necessarily constitute a color
response, as many beginners mistakenly suppose. Color
is scored as a determinant only when the color actually
present in the blot plays a recognizable role in the concept
formation. It is not so scored if the existing color of the
blot is simply mentioned in pointing out the blot area for
the examiner. Subjects often say, referring to the side *D*
in Card VIII, "These red blots are animals," or they may
even say, "These pink animals on both sides look like
polar bears," or, for the center yellow *D* in Card X,

"There are two yellow dogs." In all these cases it is most unlikely that the color actually plays any role in the concept formation; at least, it cannot be assumed that it does without further information from the subject. A simple question, "What kind of dogs are these?" or "Are polar bears pink?" will instantly reveal whether the color was mentioned merely because it was there, or was actually used for the concept formation, as would have been the case if the polar bears had been seen "walking in a sunset."

On the other hand, sometimes subjects form a concept which is almost unthinkable without the use of the existing color as, for instance, "grasshopper" for the outer green *D*, or "caterpillar" for the inner green *D* in Card X, but do not mention in the inquiry that the color played a role. If further prodding results in a frank admission that such is the case and the subject simply did not think of mentioning it, the problem is solved. However, if the subject, even under direct questioning, refuses to admit that the color played a role, either by saying that caterpillars would be brown and not green, or by remarking that he "is not interested in the color at all," color cannot be scored; the score may be *F* or *FM*. (See also the discussion on page 81.) The color may have unconsciously influenced the subject, but the fact that he represses or rejects this influence precludes the scoring of such a response as a color response. Such an obvious color rejection may at the same time be a valuable qualitative contribution to the interpretative picture.

This rejection problem is more difficult where the concept used does not induce or imply the color concept to such a compelling degree as in the examples just mentioned. This is frequently the case when the red spots in Card II or III or any one of the symmetrical colored details around the center line in Card VIII, IX, or X are called "a butterfly." Often the question, "What was it in the card that made you think of a butterfly?" elicits the answer, "The shape of it." Even a more probing question, "Was it only the shape?" may not produce any further results. Usually the examiner must let the matter rest at this point till the end of the inquiry. If by that time the subject has clearly recognized the use of color for any of the concepts he formed, then an analogy question may be used: "You called this a sunset because of the color; did you use the color in these butterflies too?" This systematic pressure may result in a reluctant admission that butterflies are usually colored, and thus an additional form-color combination can be scored. Sometimes even this specific pressure produces only a further rejection like, "Butterflies would never be this particular color."

Achromatic color (*C'*)

Subjects use what we have termed the *achromatic color* — i.e., the black and gray nuances or the white color of the white spaces — as surface color instead of shading in their concepts to a much smaller extent than they use bright colors.

1. *Actual use or rejection of achromatic color.* The same problems described in the preceding section must again be considered with reference to the use of achromatic color. A formulation like "This white portion is a kitchen lamp" or a "spinning top" for the center *S* in Card II does not necessarily imply that the subject was thinking of a white porcelain lamp or a spinning top

painted white. Another example is the answer "mice" given to the outer gray *D* in Card X. The use of the achromatic color for the formation of this concept cannot be taken for granted, since actually there are three major possibilities: First, the subject may not have thought of mentioning it; second, he may actually have rejected it; third, he may say, "I called them mice because mice are usually this brown color." In the last case we deal with a form-color combination, but not with an achromatic one. Certain portions in Cards VIII, IX, and X, have such a faint or almost achromatic coloring that it depends entirely on the subject whether he conceives of these portions as gray or blue or green. The actual appearance of the card under daylight or artificial light seems to influence such a decision much less than the tendency of the subject to use achromatic or bright colors.

2. *Combination of achromatic and bright colors.* Sometimes the achromatic surface color is only part of a concept using bright color as well as achromatic color. Within this combination two possibilities may be distinguished: First, the white color may merely serve as a foil which enhances the brightness of the bright color. For instance, the white surface of a porcelain vase sometimes seen in Card VIII makes the bright color decoration on it more brilliant. In such a case, to score *C'* at all would be misleading. Secondly, the achromatic color may add a specific element to a colorful scene, in which case it gains some importance. Typical examples are the use of the inner white space in Card VIII as "snow" in a colorful mountain scene, or the top gray in Card X as a piece of steel-gray architecture in a colorful garden set-

ting. In such a case the achromatic element should be acknowledged with an additional C' score.

3. *Illumination effects.* The actual lighting conditions during the administration play a very insignificant role (page 35). However, illumination effects are sometimes visualized by the subjects, as in responses pointing out highlights or dark shadows on the smooth or rough surface of an object. These do not necessarily indicate the use of achromatic color. Only if the object — a piece of pottery, let us say — is imagined by the subject as made of white porcelain, may achromatic color be scored as the main determinant. The highlights and shadows add only the peculiar surface effects scored with a cF or Fc.

Other problems dealing with light and darkness, such as depth or diffusion impressions and the use of achromatic color, have been mentioned in the shading section.

4. *Photographic reproductions of bright colors.* A fairly frequent response to Card V offers another problem. A subject may call Card V "a tropical butterfly," pointing out the dark velvety surface. If he thinks of the butterfly as a black butterfly, then he certainly uses C' as a determinant. This is also the case when a subject calls the same figure "a dancer with a black velvet or chiffon costume." However, many subjects see multi-colored tropical butterflies reproduced in the blots as in a photograph. In these cases the achromatic color of the blot is not used as an achromatic color in the concept and cannot be scored as C'. A specific surface appearance is here used as a basis for imagining bright or brilliant colors in the concept and thus scored Fc as a main or additional determinant. This same scoring applies to the "marble effect" mentioned above (page 121).

Combination of form and color elements

The general principles governing combination symbols
in the determinant area have been discussed in Chapter IV
and need, therefore, simply be transferred to the color
area. The color area was the one in which Rorschach
discovered the idea of combination symbols. However,
the delineations between different combinations of form
and color, as he described them, have proved themselves
rather hazardous and indefinite. Rorschach thought he
could rely on the judgment of the subject as to which
determinant in the combination of elements he personally
considered as more important, scoring a concept *FC* or *CF*
correspondingly. There seem, however, to be very few
subjects whose judgment in these matters can be deemed
reliable. More objective criteria for differentiation between various form and color combinations are necessary.
They have been found in certain objective features of the
concepts formed by the subject. Some concepts seem to
be chosen by the subject for the very reason that they do
not demand any specific shape or form. They are indefinite by definition. Within the color area, the most frequent concepts of this type are "a drop of blood" (Card
III, outer red); "a splash of ink" (Card X, outer blue);
"a smear of lipstick" or "flames" (Card II, outer red);
"sunset" (Card II, center red); "colors on a painter's
palette" or "a tapestry or pottery design" (Card X). It
is not difficult in these cases to decide that color is important and form indefinite; accordingly, they are scored
CF. In other cases the object seen is so definite in form
that the only question in these cases is whether the color
is so intimately fused with the form that a real integrated

form-color combination results, or whether this is one of the loose or forced combinations to be described later.

There are some concepts which are open to question because one subject may see them with definite form and another may be indifferent as to their form. A frequent example of this kind of concept is the flower response either for the whole of Cards VIII, IX, or X, or for any one of their bright color details. Where the concept mentioned is a specific flower — e.g., "orchid" for Card VIII upside down, "rosebud" for any one of the pink sections in Card IX, "cornflower" for the outer blue details in Card X, or "snapdragon" for the outer yellow in Card X — the score is clearly *FC*.

Where the subject simply says "flower" and does not mention a specific flower even if asked, the scoring depends on the use of form in his elaborations. He must at least point out a stem and petals in order to suggest the use of definite form. An indefinite response such as "flowers" to all of Card X certainly seems to imply an indefinite form concept even where in the inquiry some details are pointed out as specific flowers; thus the indefinite use of form for the total picture is combined with the definite use of form in some of the details, and must be scored as main *CF* and additional *FC*. The same is frequently true about responses like "a scene at the bottom of the ocean" to Card X.

The complete disregard for form elements in the reaction to color can only be assumed if such indefinite concepts are given not only to one specified colored blot but if all red or pink portions, for instance, are called "fire" or "blood," and all blue portions "water" or "sky," regardless of where they are, what shape they have, and what other concepts are developed. If the concept "blood" is added wherever the subject finds a red or pink spot, but is used as an accessory to some "fight" going on or to some definite creature which is bleeding, this is scored as an additional *CF*, rather than a *C*, since the subject makes an attempt to relate his "bloody" impressions to some definite form concept.

These same principles can also be applied in the sphere of achromatic colors. However, the use of the achromatic color which the *FC'*, *C'F*, and *C'* all have in common is interpretatively so significant that it overshadows the importance of their differences, which therefore are not so noteworthy as are the differences between *FC*, *CF*, and *C*.

1. *FC responses.* An *FC* response is defined as a concept with definite form in which the actual color of the blot plays an integral part in the concept formation. This basic definition opens the way for a variety of different *FC* combinations.

(1) *Natural FC combinations.* Natural *FC* combinations are those in which the actual color of the blot approximates the natural or conventional color of the creature or object mentioned in the subject's concept. The outer bottom *D* of Card X is a natural *FC* combination whether seen as "brown woolly dogs" or as "a young lion cub" or as "carrots." The green *D* in Card IX seen as "an old bronze urn" in the shape of an animal and covered with green verdigris is another example.

Even man-made artificial colors can be considered in the same category when they represent a customary *FC* combination, as, for instance, the "red hair ribbon" frequently seen in the center red D of Card III. The same detail seen as an evening bow tie creates quite a problem for many subjects because the conventional tuxedo bow tie should be black. If a subject speaks of a "modern bow tie" or more specifically of "a tie someone might wear in a May Day parade," such a response must certainly be credited with an *FC* score.

(2) *Forced, arbitrary, or loose FC combinations.* While the majority of subjects do not bother about the pink color of the animals in Card VIII, some subjects feel compelled to include it in the concept, giving responses like "polar bears walking in the sunset," "chameleons who can change color," "baby rats, because they are pink." These rather forced form-color combinations are so adequate as to warrant a score of *FC*. The response "foxes, because they are red," is definitely less adequate, since in this case not only is the concept forced, to fit into the color mold, but the color itself is distorted, to fit into the "fox" concept. However, it still seems best to give the subject the benefit of the doubt and to score *FC*.

An even more forced combination, designated as a "loose" *FC* combination, is occasionally met in a response to the outer blue D in Card X; viz., "blue crabs." So long as a subject musters an unusual zoölogical knowledge and can tell that there really are crabs with a rather blue color, he may still be given a natural *FC* score. However, if the crabs only "look blue" because they are seen in blue water, the color-form combination is so forced as to require a different score ($F \Leftrightarrow C$). An original variation of such a forced combination is the sarcastic answer "blue-blooded crabs," which can best be described as $F \Leftrightarrow C_{sym}$. These scores are still tabulated in the main FC column.

Responses like "polar bears, which are made of pink sugar substance," or explanations that this creature or object seen is "simply painted that way," even though the choice of paint has neither a natural nor any conventional significance, are further examples of this loose form-color combination and are also scored $F \Leftrightarrow C$.

There is one further combination of form and color, scored F/C, in which the color, while used, is actually used in a colorless sense, in that it merely marks off or designates certain areas but has no color value. Such a "colorless" use of color would be found in those map responses in which color is used to mark off certain areas or sections, but where the choice of the particular color has absolutely no significance.

What has been said about F/C applies equally to C/F. The decision as to F/C or C/F depends on the adequacy of the explanations as to the outline and other form elaborations used by the subject. For instance, the response "anatomical chart" to Card VIII may produce the explanation that the different colors indicate different parts of the body. If the subject attempts to allocate the various portions of the card to the various parts of the body, starting with the rather obvious rib-like formation in the center, the score is F/C. If he merely vaguely calls it "an anatomical chart" and lets it go at that, the score is C/F.

(3) *FC— responses.* Without going too far into the problem of form accuracy to be discussed later (page 155) in this chapter, inaccurate form-color combinations must be mentioned for a specific reason. It seems very difficult for the beginner to distinguish between indefinite and inaccurate form concepts within a form-color combination. An inaccurate form-color combination implies a concept with a rather definite shape or form and a marked discrepancy between the form customarily associated with the concept and the form of the blot chosen as a response area. For instance, in the answer "butterfly" to the whole of Card II, where the center S is either filled in or actually seen as a body part, the discrepancy between the given shape and the shape of the concept "butterfly" is not marked enough to score this response as an $FC-$. It is naturally taken for granted that color has played a role as a determinant. If, however, the same response is given to the whole of Card VIII, the discrepancy is so marked as to cause the response to be scored $FC-$.

(4) *Additional FC scores.* The routine ways of producing additional FC scores, such as new spontaneous independent responses in the inquiry, reluctantly conceded use of color as a co-determinant, and use of a form-color combination for only part of a total concept, need not be discussed here. The only reason for bringing up this question here

is the occurrence of responses where the total blot area used is colored, but where the color of only a part of the total blot area is actually used for an *FC* combination. A typical example is the answer "rooster" to the outer red *D* in Card III. There are three distinct possibilities with regard to the use of color here. Some subjects disregard the color entirely even though they speak about "these red spots" looking like roosters. Other subjects conceive of the roosters as really red all over, since "there are such species of roosters." This may be a natural *FC* combination. Still other subjects, however, use the red color only for the comb of the rooster and not for the rest of the bird. In this case the *FC* combination can only be scored additionally.

If the entire Card X has been called "a submarine picture" or "a colored chart in a botanical or zoölogical textbook" and in the inquiry the subject points out "green sea horses" or "goldfish swimming in the water" or "cornflowers and daffodils," one or several *FC* combinations must be scored as additional elaborations to the main *CF* or *C/F* score.

2. *CF responses.* The distinguishing feature of a *CF* response is the fact that the color is the determining factor; in other words, the color is definite, the form is indefinite. Typical examples, such as "a smear of lipstick," have been discussed in the beginning of the section.

(1) *CF* and *C/F.* What has been said about the difference between natural, arbitrary, loose, or forced

FC can be applied to the *CF* combination as well. There is less difficulty with these differentiations, since the choice of a definite color with an indefinite form almost necessarily presupposes a natural or conventional color association as the main reason for the choice of the concept. The only type of really arbitrary, and at the same time evasive, *C/F* responses — e.g., "anatomical chart" — to any one of the colored cards has been discussed in the section on *F/C*. An explanation by the subject that the different colors simply indicate the different parts of the body solves the color problem in a very superficial way but makes it easy to recognize that the subject did not pay much attention to the individual color values. The same is true in answers like "political map" without any attempt to identify the shape of countries or to associate any customary or symbolic color values to various countries.

Occasionally modifications of such *CF* responses are given which bring them back to a more natural or conventional *CF* approach. For instance, in Card X seen as an anatomical chart, the pink and blue are used for blood vessels, yellow for the fat cells. A subject may change the concept from a *C/F* into a *CF*, but at the same time he approaches a new category, a *CF—* response.

(2) *CF — responses.* It may seem strange that a concept with form qualities which are by definition indefinite could still be so much at variance with the form of the blot as to warrant a *CF —* score. This score is appropriate only where the subject

uses a card area which strongly suggests some definite shape, but completely disregards the suggested form possibilities in order to form a concept with indefinite form. The most frequent example of this type is the answer "sunset" to all of Card VIII, without any attempt to differentiate such configurations as the animal-like shapes in the outer pink, which could be fitted into the concept by being seen as "bathed in the glow of the sunset." Answers like "a bloody mess," or "fire and smoke" to all of Card II seem to remain within the limits of an ordinary *CF* combination.

(3) *Additional CF.* Subjects who are deeply affected by the color but try to control this stimulation by first giving their attention to some other aspects of the card develop either *F*, *M*, or *FM* responses. Frequently they add color effects as a general background feature, using the red spots in Card III, for instance, as a colorful backdrop to the scene with the two people, or those in Card II as a sunset in a carefully described landscape which has first been built up mainly by using the shading effects, or those in Card II or III as some blood which has been shed during a fight or an accident. In all these cases we deal with additional *CF* scores. Only where the *F*, *M*, *FM*, or *FK* elements seem to be rather incidental elaborations within a very colorful picture does *CF* become the main score and the other elements secondary. This is usually the case in the colorful landscapes seen frequently in Card IX held sideways.

Pure bright color responses (C, C_n, C_{des}, and C_{sym})

The warning expressed repeatedly, not to confuse color remarks and color responses, applies particularly to pure color responses. Simple remarks about color, in the form of exclamations or descriptive statements, virtually always disregard form elements. Frequently the subjects express in their formulations the fact that they themselves are aware of the difference, by making side remarks, "How pretty these cards are," or "How disturbing the color effects are," or "Now they are black and red," and then going on to say, "I think it looks like . . . ," or "Now let us see what it could be. . . ." If these color remarks are the first verbal expression after the subject sees a colored card and if he afterward proceeds to give clearly formulated responses, then it is apparent, even where the subject does not make it clear in his formulations, that he only made a side remark.

The situation is not quite so clear where the subject limits himself to some statement about the color, putting the card away afterward, or where descriptive color statements are interspersed between other responses. Sometimes these color statements are actually a polite form of rejecting the card, "This is red and black and doesn't look like anything."

If the subject does not say anything except, "This is red and black," and puts the card away after this remark, it is difficult to decide what the subject's intentions were, whether rejection or color naming (see below). The same is true about descriptive statements referring to color interspersed between other responses. A statement like "There is a pink spot in the blue" (referring to Card VIII) may be meant as an aside and it may also be meant as one more response. In all these cases the only thing to do seems to be to wait until the end of the inquiry, to select then some clear-cut responses and some obvious exclamations and side remarks, and to ask the subject how the doubtful statements were intended, whether they were meant as responses or as remarks.

1. *Crude pure color responses* (C). The distinction between crude pure color responses and form-color combinations has been pointed out above. Only if a specific color is almost mechanically associated with a specific concept wherever it appears, and if there is no attempt to connect this concept with other interpretations, as, for instance, fire with something burning, blood with something bleeding, or a lake or sky with a landscape, do responses take the form of pure color responses. The decisive factor is not the frequency with which such a concept is used, but the way in which it is used. The difference between these crude color responses and $CF —$ and $FC —$ responses has already been suggested on pages 147 and 150.

2. *Color naming* (C_n). One of the most interesting variations of pure color responses is the naming or listing of colors intended by the subject as an answer to the question, "What can you see in these cards?" It is important to exclude in every case where there is a suspicion of color naming, not only the possibility that it was a side remark but also the possibility that the subject "misunderstood" the instructions as requiring merely description (see section on *Descriptive tendencies* in Chapter IV). If the subject after being reminded of his task still insists that this is a response, it must be scored C_n.

Color naming appears mainly in two forms: Either the subject lists the names of all the colors and color nuances which are present, sometimes naming even minute differences, such as "grayish-blue, greenish-blue," or he simply counts "here are three colors," "here are seven colors," etc., with or without adding the names of the colors to the figure.

Since a clear-cut case of color naming seems to be a highly significant pathological symptom, all other possibilities must be carefully excluded.

3. *Color description* (C_{des}). Descriptive statements which are not meant as responses may refer to the fact that colors are either separate or mixed, the variety of colors, or the degree of brightness. Color description responses usually add more specific statements about the artistic quality of the colors — e.g., whether they look more like pastel shades or water colors — or they may refer to other differences in the surface appearances of different colors. Such color descriptive statements may also be associated with some kind of material such as silk or velvet. An additional c to the main C_{des} score takes care of such shading effects. Where such responses are indefinite form concepts such as pottery or tapestry design, they must be scored *CF*.

Color descriptive responses seem to be between *CF* and *C*, from the point of view of the way in which the subject arrives at such responses. It is, therefore, important in scoring and tabulating pure color responses to keep these various categories clearly separated from one another.

C_n and C_{des} hardly ever appear as spontaneous additions in the inquiry. Occasionally, color descriptive elements are found in the elaborations of *FC* and *CF* combinations, but they need not be scored additionally.

4. *Color symbolism* (C_{sym}). Color symbolism is

never used in side remarks, and it is very easy to distinguish C_{sym} responses from other pure color responses. Answers like "This is the contrast of life and death" to Card III or "This is gaiety" or "spring" to Card X are classical examples. Frequently there are additional determining factors involved in color symbolisms, as, for instance, an m indicating the rhythm in the concept "gaiety" for Card X or a c in a response like "decay" to Card IX.

Still more often the symbolic value of the colors is attached to some actual FC or CF combination like a "red bow tie" expressing "gaiety", or "flickering flames" representing "the dangers of hell." It seems to be a more accurate description of what is going on in the subject's mind to add a "sym" index to the FC or CF score (FC_{sym}, CF_{sym}) and characterize these particular responses as such in the FC and CF tabulation, instead of adding an additional C_{sym} score.

FORM RESPONSES (F) [1]

Any response not determined in any one of the ways described in the previous sections of this chapter must necessarily be a form response. In making this statement it is assumed that these sections describe every possible way in which a subject can arrive at a concept formation except where the shape, the outline, or the contour of the blot is the sole determinant.

Form accuracy and form definiteness

The negative definition of F can be supplemented by a positive description of the various types of form responses. One of the most important differentiating factors within

[1] See also 1946 Supplement, "Form Level Rating," pages 435–452.

the area of form responses is the level of form accuracy. Another differentiating factor is the definiteness of form responses. It may seem rather surprising to speak about an "indefinite" form response; previously, the use of indefinite form concepts was found in responses in which another determinant like *m, k, K, c, C',* or *C* serves as main determinant. Besides these responses there are a great number of indefinite pure form responses like "islands," "maps," etc., where the outline and not the topographical features are important; or "bones" or "insides of a human body" without any specification as to their anatomical peculiarities. Close to these fully indefinite form responses are crude outline responses, like "leaves" or "torn leaves," which can be given to a great number of different cards or card details. Again it is taken for granted that the subject is not interested in such other factors as shading or color, but solely in the general form qualities of the blots in a more or less noncommittal way.

It is important to distinguish such responses, in which the subject deliberately avoids any test of accuracy by choosing such a vague or indefinite concept, from responses in which the subject wants to give a definite concept without being able to establish a sufficient degree of correspondence between his concept and the given form qualities of the blot, thus arriving at an inaccurate response. The noncommittal or evasive form responses lack the specifications necessary for characterizing them either as accurate or inaccurate. They are simply noncommittal.

The problems of form accuracy and its scoring have been central issues in the Rorschach literature almost from the very beginning. Rorschach made some very valuable suggestions as to determination and interpretation of form accuracy, which unfortunately were so vaguely expressed that they led to rather fundamental misunderstandings.

As a clinician, Rorschach was particularly interested in the pathological significance of intellectual disorders and deteriorations as expressed in inaccuracies found in the subject's concept formations. He was less interested in exact distinctions between inaccurate and noncommittal form responses, or between fairly accurate form responses and concepts of a superior form keenness. These differences could not be discovered and described in detail before a systematic inquiry provided the necessary evidence.

In Rorschach's original scoring, form responses were always scored either $F +$ or $F -$. The same is true of the indication of form accuracy of other determinants. For instance, he scored movement responses either $M +$ or $M -$. The only exceptions were C responses, which never had plus or minus signs, and CF responses which had minus signs only, where the indefinite form of a CF concept obviously varied from the given form. To this extent at least Rorschach recognized the principle of noncommital form.

The further development of the scoring system led to the decision to use the minus sign, the symbol for form inaccuracy, more stringently than did Rorschach. It is now reserved exclusively for the scoring of responses where the examiner finds evidence of marked discrepancies between the form qualities of the concept and the form qualities of the blot. Responses with indefinite form qualities, such as were described at the beginning of the section, and responses of a merely mediocre form accuracy, are indicated by the determinant symbol without any qualifying + or —. This procedure makes it possible to reserve the +, the symbol for form keenness, for use with a definite form which is markedly superior in accuracy to the mediocre. This is also true for the scoring of determinants implying definite form — *M*, *FM*, *Fm*, *FK*, *Fc*, *FC*, *FC'*. The + is indicated only where the implied form is on a superior accuracy level.

Form accuracy and frequency

Since the standard of form accuracy varies enormously among examiners, Rorschach recommended the use of the degree of accuracy exhibited in responses given by a great majority of all kinds of subjects as a more objective yardstick. Thus he established the relationship between the frequency with which the shape of a blot was used for a concept and its accuracy level. He never suggested any general correlation between frequency and accuracy. On the contrary, he clearly pointed out that these "popular" or frequent form interpretations may serve as a yardstick only by implying that both the more accurate and the less accurate responses are given less frequently than the popular ones. Form accuracies of responses probably are distributed normally. Concepts of a mediocre form accuracy are given most frequently; the more accurate or the more inaccurate a response is, the less frequently it is given.

Qualitative determination of form accuracy

How is form accuracy qualitatively determined? There are three elements to be investigated: (*a*) The form qualities of the concept as imagined by the subject, (*b*) the form qualities of the blot, and (*c*) the conventional form qualities of the same concept.

1. *Discrepancies between individual and conventional concepts.* Let us consider the relationship of (*a*) and (*c*) first. The importance of this relationship may be demonstrated by asking a group of people to describe or to draw the main features of a bat; one will be surprised by the number of variations in all major form characteristics.

As a rule, this fact causes little trouble. In spite of all variations, normal people can usually agree on some essential features characterizing the form qualities of a concept. The situation becomes more complicated in the case of feeble-minded, deteriorated, or psychotic subjects. How much leeway may be granted a subject in forming his individual concept? For instance, assume that a subject has the notion that snakes have feelers or whiskers. Correspondingly he interprets the center dark area of Card VI as a snake, pointing with special pride to the whisker-like thin lines near the top because they make his concept of a snake really complete. Does this zoölogical misconstruction constitute an inaccuracy in the logical thinking of the subject? Moreover, many normal subjects use their poetic license in making up snakes with wings and whiskers and any other conceivable caricaturistic combination they may fancy. Where is the borderline between this poetic license of a normal person and the arbitrariness of a schizophrenic for whom reality has so little weight that he can use any element in the card to create a new reality of his own? (See page 353 on "contamination.")

As long as a subject establishes a fairly good correspondence between the concept he develops and the blot he uses, and keeps his elaborations of this concept, unusual as they may be, within some logical order, his response may be called queer, abstruse, or bizarre, but it cannot be called inaccurate.   Usually the bizarre responses of psychotics are characterized by a lack of intrinsic logic in elaboration and in that way are quite easily distinguishable from the fantastic creations of an artistic or superior person who grants himself considerable poetic license.

2. *Discrepancies between form qualities of the concept and the blot.*   The discovery of discrepancies between (*a*) and (*b*) — between the form of a concept chosen by the subject, (conventional or not), and the form of the blot — is impossible without a careful inquiry.   A subject's form response may be noncommittal, or inaccurate to the degree of being nonsensical, or even so unique in its keenness that it is difficult for the average examiner to appreciate it without further explanations from the subject.

With regard to the interpretative significance of $F-$, it is important to define as clearly as possible under what conditions discrepancies between the concept chosen by the subject and the given form qualities of the blot are likely to be produced by some intellectual defect.   It is obviously an entirely unacceptable procedure for an examiner to score a response $F-$ because he himself is unable to understand how and why the subject called a blot what he called it.   The inquiry must clearly prove that the subject himself is unable to reconcile the particular features of his concept with those of the blot.

One way of making sure that the subject's rather than the examiner's intellectual functions are disturbed is to ask the subject to trace his concept on the picture sheet or, if it is very tiny, to trace it on a transparent paper placed on the card (see page 45). This helps to avoid misunderstandings which may be based on the difficulty of the subject in explaining verbally what he had in mind. It is quite easy to distinguish difficulties due to a lack of skill in drawing from difficulties due to a lack of clarity in concept formation.

Fortunately there seems to be only a limited number of mechanisms which produce form discrepancies between concept and blot. As far as we have been able to identify these mechanisms, they can be described as follows:

(1) *Completely arbitrary responses.* There is no particular need to explain the logical disfunctioning in responses having not the slightest connection whatsoever with the card. (See also page 88.)

(2) *Mechanical perseveration.* A concept may be formed in the first card, which, taken by itself, belongs in the category of fairly accurate but rather crude outline responses, such as "butterfly" or "bird." This concept is applied like a magic wand to all other cards with utter disregard for their individual characteristics.

(3) *Fixed idea perseveration.* Again a concept formed in one card is applied to all the others, but this time not in a mechanical way. For instance, "two Santa Clauses" are seen in the first card in a fairly well-organized form. This concept is carried through all ten cards with an attempt to take individual characteristics of each card into consideration. For instance, they may be "afire" in the second card and go through all sorts of transformations until they are "broken all to pieces" in Card X.

(4) *Partial perseveration.* Such perseverations can also occur as partial perseverations, or perseverating tendencies, but they rarely produce such extreme discrepancies between concept and blot as in the two complete forms of perseveration.

(5) *Confabulation* (*DW*). This mechanism for producing F — was described in Chapter IV, page 87. If the definition of confabulation is properly understood, it is clear that every *DW* response must be scored F —. The fact that in the literature an occasional *DW* $+$ score is found can only be explained as the result of a confusion of a different type of *W* construction with confabulation.

This occurs when a subject builds up a combinatorial *W* successively instead of seeing it simultaneously. He may start, for instance, with the bat-like wings, pointing only to the side *d* in Card I and continuing that "the whole thing could look like a bat with the center for the body and round ears." The same procedure is sometimes reflected in spontaneous statements by the subject like "It looks like a bat because of the wings" or "like a crab because of the claws." A demand in the inquiry for an explanation of the other parts of the concept or of the card will easily show whether the response is a successive combinatorial *W* or an actual confabulation.

(6) *Confabulatory combinations.* The nature of confabulatory combinations can best be described by a comparison with children's drawings showing pictures of a man in which various details are included but are more or less incorrectly placed, so

that arms and legs emanate from the face, ears are attached to the stomach, etc. The difference between this kind of response and real confabulation lies in the fact that in the former the subject has the spontaneous intention of identifying a number of details as parts of a whole concept, but is either not very concerned with or not capable of putting them into any logical order. The discrepancy in this case is not so much between the shape of the various blot details and the corresponding parts of the concept, but rather between the organization of these parts in the concept and the configuration of the blot material.

(7) *Inaccurate outline responses.* Another form of discrepancy is sometimes encountered, chiefly in the responses of feeble-minded subjects, who get a vague general idea of what the blot or blot area could be but are not cautious enough to leave their concept in the necessary noncommittal form. For instance, they may recognize that the side *D*'s of Card VIII resemble some kind of animal. However, instead of just saying "animal," they want to be more specific, so that they say "bird" or "fish," not on the basis of any rational consideration but because this was the kind of creature they happened to think of. On the other hand, somebody may call these same portions "fish," carefully cutting off the "legs" and using their stumps as "fins," elaborating head, mouth, and eyes, which response must certainly be regarded as accurate. The *F*— responses produced by guessing are invariably inaccurate outline responses.

(8) *Position responses.* A special application of vague guessing takes place when the position of a detail on the card serves as a determining factor. The whole card may be called a "doggie," but when asked to show the different parts of the "doggie," the subject may point to some area near the top as the head, some areas near the center as the body, and portions near the bottom as the legs or tail, with a clear disregard for the actual form qualities of these parts. A similar procedure is involved when a subject calls the center portion of some blot a "heart," for no reason other than the fact that it is the center and with no reference to any other concept.

Occasionally additional position elaborations occur. For instance, the whole black area of Card III may be called a "frog," elaborating the front legs and the big black eyes, and using the center white space as the main part of the body. The center red *D* may then be called heart or intestines, largely because it happens to be in this particular position. If color played a role, the additional score would be *FC*—. The inaccuracy in this combination is produced by the use of position as a determining factor.

(9) *Disregard for obvious form elements in the blots in indefinite concepts.* All the discrepancies described in the preceding paragraphs were found in concepts which demanded more or less definiteness of form. A discrepancy can also be created where the concept chosen by the subject does not demand any definite form, but where the portions of the

card used for the concept have such obvious form qualities that one must disregard the given form qualities to an outstanding degree in order to use this particular card or card portion for such a very indefinite form.   A typical example has been given in the section on color responses where the $CF-$ responses are mentioned.   Similar responses may be found when any of the other five determinants that can be associated with indefinite form ($mF, kF, KF, cF, C'F$) are used.

The mechanisms described in the preceding paragraphs cover the great majority of all possible $F-$ responses. The recognition of these mechanisms is necessary primarily for a descriptive delineation, which enables different administrators and even beginners to use the $F-$ score in the same way and for the same responses.   The ability to identify mechanisms which produce form discrepancies is also important from the interpretative point of view. Only a clear diagnosis of the mechanisms involved makes it possible to distinguish between various structural forms of mental disfunctioning like retardation, deterioration, and emotional disturbance.

It is obvious from the foregoing that the minus sign can be attached to any determinant except pure shading or pure color.

3. *Mediocre or popular form responses*.   In logical order the $F-$ responses are followed by responses which avoid all the mechanisms leading to striking discrepancies between the form qualities of concept and blot, but do not establish a concept on a particularly accurate or keen form basis.   These include:

(1) *Fairly accurate outline responses.* From the inaccurate outline responses it is a small step to responses which use only the most obvious and crude form characteristics of a blot but use these in such a way that they avoid striking discrepancies. For instance, if a subject limits his response "butterfly" to Cards I, II, IV, V, the top portion of Card VI, and the bottom portions of VII and VIII, but avoids calling the entire Cards III, VI, VII, or any of the last three cards "butterflies," he shows enough common sense to recognize where such a rather "cheap" outline response is tolerably acceptable and where he would encounter obstacles he could not surmount. Sometimes rather sophisticated butterfly responses are given even to the entire Card IX or X, using the blots mainly as designs and markings on the wings and establishing careful connecting lines between the given blot portions to indicate the general outlines of their concept. It is not difficult to distinguish such sophisticated, highly artistic, or imaginative responses from the "cheap" ones.

(2) *Evasive form responses.* A second type of response in the mediocre areas comes close to the indefinite form responses. Noncommittal form responses which avoid any obvious discrepancies between the concept and the blot material belong in the mediocre area. A subject may call Cards I, II (the black part), and V (without the protrusions) "mountains," without creating a discrepancy between his concept and the blot material. These "mountains" are based exclusively on the upper

contour lines of the blot as distinct from actual vista responses. Such mediocre evasive outline responses are always characterized by the fact that the subject is careful to use only such blot or blot portions as lend themselves to some degree to the concepts chosen.

(3) *Noncommittal determinant responses.* The combination of a concept which has indefinite form with one of the six possible other determinants (*m, k, K, c, C', C*) offers the widest variety of responses on a mediocre form level. Animal skins, clouds, something melting or dripping, patches of snow and ice or mud, blood spots, flames, indefinite flowers, and anatomical pictures or colored maps can be seen practically everywhere in the ten cards. Such responses are often given for the very purpose of avoiding any responses which necessitate form accuracy.

(4) *Popular form responses.* The frequency principle mentioned earlier in this section, on page 157, applies particularly to responses which belong to the mediocre area, for the very reason that here the subject uses form qualities of a blot which are so obvious and so suggestive that the great majority of all subjects cannot help using them in this particular way. For instance, even persons who show otherwise very little imaginative or organizing capacities may be able to see the black portions of Card III as "two figures bending over," or the side portions of Card VIII as "two climbing animals." The "butterfly" and "bat" responses to Cards I and V are examples in point.

If the subject is not able to be any more specific, for example, about these two people in Card III, than merely to point out their heads, bodies, legs, and maybe their arms holding onto something at the bottom center portion, the response surely is on a mediocre or popular form level. Any additional elaboration beyond these crude features, such as the "stiff collars" or the "coattails blowing in the wind," changes the rating of such a response from the mediocre to a more accurate or keen level.

4. *Form responses above average in accuracy.* A subject may go beyond the intellectual achievement level represented by mediocre or popular form responses into a concept formation which either shows a keener analytic mind in regard to choice of concept or degree of elaboration, or else shows higher synthetic capacities in more unusual organization of the given blot material.

(1) *Elaboration.* The term *elaboration* is here used to describe the tendency of the subject to use more and finer form qualities of a blot to specify his concept. For instance, the subject may call the side *D* in Card VIII "beavers," explaining, possibly in the inquiry, that he called them "beavers" and not "bears" because of the characteristic beaver-like tail, the head (clearly outlined in the shading with ears and eyes), and the particular form qualities of the heavy-set body. Another subject may use another of the popular concepts such as "bear cubs" for the black portions in Card II, but elaborate very carefully the shape of the

snout, the thick, woolly fur, and the appropriate curving-in of the head to form the neck.

(2) *Organization.* Concepts of more than mediocre form quality can also be created by organizing the given blot material in an unusual way. This can be done by transgressing the limits of the usual *D* and *d* in order to add some adjacent area which makes the concept more complete or more exact. For instance, in Card I upside down the dark top center portion may be seen as a "Buddha" with part of the dark area in the lower center added in order to outline the legs crossed in front of him.

Another way of organizing the given blot material is to relate various subdivisions of the card even if they are separated by other blots or by white space in order to see a scene with action or a carefully elaborated landscape interspersed with lakes or plazas. Here again the subject may be limiting himself mainly to form qualities of the blot or he may add any one of the other determinants to enrich his concept.

Consequently, the plus sign for form keenness is not limited to pure form responses. Any combination symbol describing a concept with definite form may also show signs of superior keenness. Thus there are $M+$, $FM+$, $Fm+$, $FK+$, $Fc+$, $FC'+$, $FC+$. An exception to this rule is the Fk combination. As a rule a superior keenness in the concept formation leads either to a real vista response (FK), or, if the use of shading remains toned down to the k level, the subject's procedure can be better described by scoring the response a

main $F+$ with an additional k. The vagueness
of the k as a determinant makes a thorough integration with keen form concepts impossible.

(3) *Degree and quality of elaboration.* Popular
form elaborations are characterized by the fact that
the peculiar shape or position of parts of the
body is not particularly specified. To call the
animals in Card VIII "climbing," or the human
beings in Card III "bending over," is obviously
still within the mediocre area. As soon as a subject describes the unusual politeness leading to
such a deep bow or the swinging gesture of hand
and hat with which they greet each other, or any
other such specific observation, the stage of keen
form responses is reached. An indispensable
prerequisite for form keenness is that these specifications and elaborations avoid all the mechanisms which create discrepancies between form and
blot and all illogical discrepancies between the individual and conventional concept.

A difficult problem is offered where a subject
supplements the given blot area with imaginary
lines drawn in the white space. As long as these
lines seem to be a natural continuation of the
given contours, as, for example, when a three-quar-
ter circle is imagined as a complete one, this may
actually be a superior procedure. If these imaginary additions to the blot areas have only a very
loose or an unintelligible relationship to the given
form elements, one of the mechanisms making for
inaccuracies is at work. For instance, a subject
may need a leg to complete the picture, and carve

it out of a white space which occurs where the leg should be, although nothing in the space resembles a leg.

(4) *Degree and quality of organization.* Any transgression of the usual detail areas exclusively for the sake of form keenness establishes the $F+$ quality no matter whether the transgressions are so insignificant that D and d can still serve as location scores, or a dr is chosen to establish a more accurate basis for the chosen concept. In passing, it may be said that sometimes the choice of dr is due to such mechanisms as fixed ideas, arbitrariness, or position responses.

Responses organized through the use of discrete portions of a card are usually based on a combination of form with some other determinant. So long as no mechanisms are involved creating real discrepancies, neither a minus nor a plus sign is added. The same is true if the organization results merely in a popular response. The organization of an unusual concept, however, establishes a superior F quality even if the correspondence between the form qualities of this concept and the form qualities of the blot area is no better than average. For instance, all of Card III is sometimes seen as a birthday cake in a basket with a red bow and handles decorated in red, using not only all the red and black portions with the intervening spaces but completing the picture with some imaginary lines which fit the given contours.

The $F+$ quality is doubly indicated where such an organization is amplified by careful elaboration.

CHAPTER
VII

SCORING CATEGORIES
FOR CONTENT

WITH a few exceptions suggested by Rorschach in *Psychodiagnostik*, the choice of content categories has varied rather widely in the Rorschach literature. In the great majority of all records a very elaborate system of content categories seems to be quite unnecessary. At least three fourths of the responses of most subjects deal with human beings and animals; the number of categories in which the other responses could be designated is small.

On the other hand, there are some specific contents like "fire," "blood," "clouds," "smoke," and "masks" which have such an outstanding significance that it would be very unsatisfactory from the interpretative point of view to include them under any other category.

The choice of the remaining content categories listed on the Individual Record Blank (see page 183) was determined by the frequency with which these categories occur. The Record Blank provides space for the addition of a number of content categories for responses which do not fit into the given categories, but it is important to list in the appropriate places all the contents which do fit into these definitions. The actual number of various content categories used is also significant.

DELINEATION OF CONTENT CATEGORIES

In this section only such content categories as offer
some problems of delineation will be discussed. They
include human, animal, nature, science, art and abstract
concepts.

Human figures

Responses which indicate concepts based on the figures
of one or more human beings are very frequent, and we
shall consider these first.

1. *Human figures and human anatomy (H, Hd, and
At).* Human figures and parts of human figures as a
content category must first be distinguished from anatomical concepts. No difficulty arises where human figures are seen as alive, even if only parts of these figures
are visible. A problem is presented in cases where subjects are exclusively interested in the shape of some part
of the human body; for instance, "the calf of a woman's
leg" in the side *d* of Card V. As long as this leg is seen
in a silk stocking, it is clearly not an anatomical concept.
Even where the leg is seen unclad without the rest of
the body and without the foot it would still be scored
as *Hd,* as long as the subject does not himself associate
it with anatomical dissection.

In general the best distinction between *Hd* and *At* is
produced by a question as to whether the hand, foot, leg,
and so on is seen as one would see it on a living body,
or whether it shows any marks of dissection or decay.
The problem becomes rather complicated if subjects see
parts of the human body ordinarily not visible in everyday contact with our fellow human beings, as, for instance,
the tonsils or a whole tooth. A question as to where or

how one would see this reveals easily whether the subject was thinking about an anatomical textbook or an everyday situation in a doctor's or dentist's office.

2. *Symbolic use of parts of human figure* (*Hd, Abs*). Sometimes parts of the human organism are seen which are entirely invisible in a living body, but are imagined without any association with anatomy; for instance, the heart. A "bleeding heart" is rarely associated with the sphere of anatomy but is used more in an abstract or symbolic manner. Likewise in a symbolic way "warning fingers" may be seen. A similar shift of emphasis from the human body to some other sphere is encountered in the response "seven league boots" to Card IV, which frequently take on the aspect of parts of the human body walking steadily along. "Artificial teeth" is another response which is so closely associated with the human body that it would be misleading to tabulate it simply as a man-made object (*Obj*); it should be scored as *H obj*.

3. *Caricatures and mythological figures.* Other variations frequently encountered within the sphere of human figures are caricaturistic pictures of human beings, fantastic or mythological figures which show a peculiar combination of human and animal-like features; e.g., creatures out of *Alice in Wonderland,* or ghosts, or genii, or monsters. It seems to be advisable to distinguish these human-like concepts from ordinary human beings by enclosing the *H* in a parenthesis. A mixture of human and animal-like features may still be scored (*H*) instead of (*A*) if the human features seem to dominate the behavior of the creature.

4. *Sexual concepts.* In view of the fact that the great majority of subjects are rather hesitant in calling sexual

concepts by their real names, it seems wise to use the content designating sex wherever there is reason to assume that a sexual connotation was in the mind of the subject. Responses like "the lower part of a human body" are obviously of this kind. It makes no difference whether these parts of the human body are seen as one would see them on a living body or in an anatomy book, or as a diagram in a textbook; the most important element involved in such responses always seems to be sex.

Animal concepts

1. *Parts of living animals and animal objects (Ad, Aobj).* The distinction between parts of living animals and animal anatomy follows the same lines as the distinction between *Hd* and *At.* A new variation is introduced by objects derived from or connected with the body of an animal such as a "fur rug," or a "bleached skull nailed to the gable of a house," or a "horseshoe." If it is clear to the examiner that there is little or no association in the mind of the subject between these man-made objects and the animals from which they were derived, the response may be either an animal object or a manmade object, but not an animal detail.

The distinction between animal objects and objects depends on the extent to which the subject is aware of the derivation of the object. No one would call a lady's bag an animal detail or an animal object because it is derived from alligator skin. However, the bleached skull mentioned above carries the earmarks of its derivation clearly enough to call it an animal object.

The differentiation between animal anatomy and such animal objects is quite simple because the animal objects always serve some decorative or practical function, or are in a stage of preparation for such function, as, for instance, "the skin of an animal hung up to dry."

2. *Animal anatomy and food.* Usually the formulation of the subject will enable the examiner to discriminate between responses representing food concepts and those based on animal anatomy. Thus the subject will generally make clear whether a fish is visualized as having been cut in half for the purpose of some zoölogical study or in order to be put into the frying pan. Wherever the subject does not mention this connotation by himself the question, "Where would one see such a thing?" reveals what the subject was thinking about.

Nature and geography, plants and botany

A distinction of some interpretative significance in this area is the distinction between real landscapes, flowers, or trees and more schematic abstract geographical or botanical concepts.

1. *Landscapes and maps.* The dividing line between landscapes and maps is sometimes very fine. A landscape may be seen from an airplane so far removed that it takes on the appearance of a topographical map rather than that of a natural landscape. Still, as long as the subject feels inclined to say, "One could see this particular bit of country in such a way from an airplane," he seems to be interested in the natural appearance more than in a schematic scientific representation. Lakes, mountains, rivers, and other parts of a natural scenery are likely to belong to the category *N* rather than to the category *Geo* as long as they are not seen as part of a map.

2. *Flowers and botanical charts.* The same distinction

plays a role in the botanical field. A subject may see in Card X only parts of flowers, as, for example, individual petals, but still they may be seen as "floating in the air." Another subject, however, may call Card X "a page out of a botanical textbook."

Art and abstract concepts

It must be emphasized that only those responses should be listed in this category which do not fall into human, animal, or nature responses. The fact that a response is labeled "a picture of something" does not, in itself, create an art response, since in most of the cases the formulation "picture of . . .," "drawing of . . .," "statue of . . ." indicates merely an emphasis on the form of representation, but the core of the concept lies in what is sketched, sculptured, or painted. Only responses such as "how the palette of a painter looks" or "a childish play with water colors" can be put under the art category. In other words, only if no specific content is mentioned, or if the content mentioned seems to be incidental to the artistic technicalities, is the content to be tabulated under "art."

Exactly the same is true about abstract concepts. Main abstract responses are responses like "a power" or "a dividing line" which have no other concrete connotations; the *abs* score is more frequently an additional score.

POPULAR AND ORIGINAL RESPONSES

The terms *popular* and *original* refer to the frequency with which certain contents are associated with certain cards or card details. A response is classified as a *popular* response if it is one which is frequently elicited by a given blot area; if it is only rarely associated with the given area, it is termed *original*. These definitions are elaborated below.

Popular responses

The term *popular* refers to one extreme of a theoretical frequency distribution of all possible responses. These are the responses given most frequently by any number of subjects to a particular blot area. In this definition of *popular* all Rorschach experts agree. There is no agreement, however, on a clear-cut line of demarcation between very frequent and less frequent responses. Rorschach originally suggested that responses be classified as "popular" if they occurred with a frequency equal to or greater than once in three records. Other experts suggested a frequency of once in six records. No Rorschach expert has yet been able to assemble and tabulate a sufficient number of records to claim universal validity for his frequency counts.

1. *Universal and group frequency.* The term *group frequency* suggests the obvious fact that certain responses are more popular among three- or five-year-old children, for instance, than among adults, or that certain concepts will be found quite frequently among the Hopi Indians or among the Behrens River Indians which are not so "popular" among the population of New York City. In this sense, a specific frequency distribution might be established for any group, whether the group is determined by age, cultural environment, educational background, or sex. The value of establishing such a group frequency for any concept is undeniable. However, it does not detract from the importance of the concept of *universal frequency*. To

every Rorschach expert who has seen records from many different groups it is rather surprising how many concepts even the most divergent groups have in common. Thus it seems worth while at least to aim at the establishment of a universally representative frequency distribution of concepts.

It seems reasonable to use the total number of subjects rather than the total number of responses as a basis for determining the frequency with which a concept has been selected, since the same subject, once he has used a concept, may continue to use it with variations, thus increasing the numerical score for that concept without increasing its significance.

2. *Selected popular concepts as substitutes for statistically verified ones.* Since a frequency tabulation of universal validity is not available, we are substituting a selected sample of popular responses which meet the following qualifications:

(1) These responses must be frequent in any published collection of records even if this collection is limited to a certain age or cultural group.

(2) They must embody the various determinants frequently used by any number of subjects, such as the most popular *M, FM,* and *FC.*

(3) They must represent concepts which every clinically "normal" subject should be able to accept. If they have not been spontaneously formed in the performance proper or during the inquiry, their acceptability should at least be conceded in the testing-the-limits period.

(4) They must be responses to a complete or incom-

plete whole or to a usual detail, since usual details are themselves determined by frequency.

In the light of these qualifications, the following ten popular responses were selected:

1. To Card I as W or W :   Any creature with the body in the center D and wings at the sides.

2. To the black area of Card II (either as an organized incomplete W, with or without the top center d, or as D):   Any animal or part of an animal of the dog, bear, rabbit, bull, or rhinoceros variety.   Common characteristics include a rather large head (which frequently suggests puppies or bear cubs), a thick neck, invisibility or foreshortening of rest of body, and, frequently, emphasis on the surface of the skin.

3. To the entire black area of Card III: Two human figures in a bending position (bowing, lifting, carrying, or dancing).   It seems to matter little what object these figures are holding in their hands; the important thing is that the legs are seen in the side bottom D and that the figures are really seen in action.   Dressed-up animals instead of people may still represent the popular concept. When the legs are seen where the arms usually are seen (for instance, as genii) or where the animals are seen as real animals with two pairs of legs instead of arms and not as dressed-up animals, there is at the most a tendency toward P which is scored with an additional P.

4. To the center red D in Card III: "Bow tie," "hair ribbon," or "butterfly."   The shape alone and the

combination of shape and color are used with about equal frequency.

5. To Card V as W or W : Again any winged creature with the body in the center D and wings at the sides. The same concept can be applied with the card held upside down.

6. To Card VI with or without the top D: The skin of an animal. The use of shading for the impression of furriness or for the markings on the inside of the skin is essential. This response may be given as a W or W or as a D.

7. To the side D in Card VIII: Any kind of four-legged animal in any kind of motion. If the animals are inaccurately called birds or fish, only a tendency toward P can be scored. The same is true of animals not seen in action. Usually the color is not used; when it is, it must be scored with an additional original score.

8. To the outer blue D in Card X: Any many-legged animal such as a spider, a crab, or an octopus. Usually the color is not used; when it is, it must be scored with an additional original score.

9. To the center green D in Card X (without the light green D between the darker green areas): Any elongated greenish animal such as a caterpillar, a garden snake, or a tobacco worm. In this case the popular concept includes the use of color. The exclusion of the color by a subject limits the scoring to an additional P.

10. To the light green D in the center green area of Card X: The head of an animal with long ears or horns such as a rabbit, a donkey, or a goat. Any

addition, such as the darker green *D*'s seen as "something coming out of the eyes of the animal," or the white space as "the body of a white rabbit," adds an original element to be scored as an additional original.

Original responses

Rorschach workers are unanimous with regard to the statistical definition of original responses. The commonly accepted statistical requirement is that a response can be scored as original if it does not appear more than once in a hundred records. However, even if an examiner has completed his first set of one hundred records he cannot be sure about his original responses. As long as one hundred records are collected from a homogeneous group, it seems safe to assume that any response found not more than once among these hundred records is likely to be original — at least, for a group of the same general character as the group tested; on the other hand, if the group from which the hundred records were obtained is fairly heterogeneous, there would still be the possibility that a response "original" within such a heterogeneous group might be comparatively common within a group similar to the one subject who produced this response.

Any attempt to list representative samples of *O* responses would be a hopeless enterprise, since the number of original responses is by definition unlimited. Virtually every superior adult is expected to produce at least a few new original concepts. The only practical expedient for the beginner is to consult the existing lists of sample responses *(3)*. An examiner may safely assume that he is dealing with an original response so long as he neither encounters this response more than once in any hundred records he has collected nor finds it reported in the literature.

The originality in the choice of a concept is not limited to the choice of unique concepts. Many subjects use either popular concepts or other concepts which are definitely used by more than one per cent of all subjects, but give them an original twist, or add some rather unique elaboration. Such original additions to a basically unoriginal concept are scored with an O in the additional column.

Due to the very nature of original responses, they usually are characterized by rather extreme features with regard to their form accuracy level. They may reveal a particularly keen sense of observation and a sensitiveness to possible elaborations which escape less discerning subjects. On the other hand, such responses may be the product of a rather suspect way of changing and distorting concepts in some bizarre manner. Original responses of these two types are scored, respectively, $O+$ or $O-$.

Original additions to non-original concepts are scored with an additional $O-$ if these additions contain marked form inaccuracy.

CHAPTER
VIII

THE TECHNIQUE OF TABULATION
AND THE USE OF THE RECORD BLANK

TO FACILITATE the summarization and interpretation of the material obtained from each subject during the administration of the Rorschach test, an Individual Record Blank has been prepared. This Blank is a 6-page folder, 8½ by 11 inches. Page 1 includes spaces for the subject's name, age, sex, and other identifying information, directions for using the Record Blank, and spaces for a brief summary of the personality description. Page 2 is the so-called *Scoring List*, the function of which will be described later. Page 3 is the *Tabulation Sheet*, likewise to be described below. Page 4 provides for summarization of the relationships among the various scoring categories and includes provision for a graph of the determinant categories. Page 5 is the so-called *Picture Sheet*, on which there appear reproductions of all ten blots, to be used in indicating the areas chosen by the subject for his responses. Page 6 contains a list of the scoring symbols and their meanings. A copy of the Individual Record Blank, slightly reduced, has been inserted inside the back cover of this book.

THE SCORING LIST

Many beginners prefer to write scoring symbols for each response alongside the text of the response. In most cases this leads, naturally, to an extension of the list of scoring symbols usually over several separate sheets of paper.

To be effective, however, the use of the list of scoring symbols as part of the interpretative process requires a more compact picture; the interpreter must be able to obtain a concise and simultaneous picture of what has been going on in the mind of the subject. No really thorough interpretation is possible without a complete simultaneous picture of the subject's reactions, containing as many nuances of his reactions as possible. A list of the total scoring for every response, concentrated on one page, is an invaluable aid in longer records, and is absolutely indispensable in the formation of the personality picture.

For this reason it is necessary that the Rorschach administrator transfer his complete scoring list to the space provided for this purpose on page 2 of the Record Blank, if he has been scoring his responses on his original record. The separation of responses into main and additional columns is a further valuable aid for the tabulation of the scoring.

THE TABULATION SHEET

While the Scoring List permits a careful step-by-step analysis of the sequence in which the subject formed his concepts, the Tabulation Sheet makes it possible to observe at a glance the distribution of the various scoring categories among the ten cards. As the following chapter on interpretation will show, it is very important not only to know how often the subject used the entire card, for instance, but which of the ten cards were used for these *W*'s. If there were many *W*'s, it is important to know whether they were evenly distributed over the ten cards or were concentrated on the first five, six, or seven cards, or whether there was a completely irregular distribution. Similar considerations are important for almost every other scoring category.

The technique of tabulation

The Tabulation Sheet provides for two kinds of total scores:

(1) The number of responses scored in a specific category — e.g., *W* or *M* — for the ten cards can be added along the horizontal lines; these sums represent obviously the total number of *W*'s or *M*'s used in all ten cards.

(2) The various location, content, or determinant categories used within each card can be added vertically to yield the total number of main responses given to that card, since every response receives only one main score in each one of the three sections (location, determinant, and content).

Thus the Tabulation Sheet affords a duplicate check on the tabulation procedure. The totals of the main scores for the various categories within each section (location, determinant, content) must equal the total number of responses given by the subject. If there are any discrepancies among the totals for the three sections, the source of such discrepancies can easily be discovered by adding up the main scores separately for each card within each section. In other words, the arithmetical trouble can be localized within the card in which it occurs, without need for checking all horizontal and vertical totals.

It is evident that the totals for the additional scores are not necessarily equal within the three sections, since they stem from so many different sources.

It is advisable to use tally marks of different colors (or pencil and ink) for tabulating main and additional responses; otherwise main and additional scores may be confused in adding the responses for a given category along the horizontal lines.

The tabulating of the number of main and additional *P* and *O* does not require any specific comment.

IMPORTANT RELATIONSHIPS AMONG SCORING CATEGORIES

The full significance of the entries on page 4 of the Record Blank will be clear only after studying the chapters on interpretation. At this point only the technical problems which one may meet in establishing these figures will be discussed. In computing the percentages called for, only the number of *main* scores in each category is used as a basis. In dealing with absolute figures instead of percentages, the number of additional scores in the same category may be added with a plus sign. Another method for distinguishing between main and additional scores in the determinant area is described in the next section.

The graph showing the distribution of determinants

The most important of the quantitative relationships among categories is the total distribution of determinants. The device used to portray this distribution is an ordinary bar graph. The number of main scores in each category is represented by a fully outlined bar; the number of additional scores in the same category is shown by an upward extension of this same bar, the extension being drawn with broken or dotted lines instead of solid lines. The size of the bars and the scale of the graph depend on the greatest number of responses in any category. The outline for the graph provided at the top of page 4 of the Record Blank has nineteen units on the vertical axis. If the sum of main and additional scores in any category does not exceed this number, the height of each space may represent one score. If the highest sum of main and additional scores in any scoring category is between nineteen and thirty-eight, the height of each space may be used to represent two responses. If the highest sum exceeds thirty-eight, one space may represent as many responses as the quotient of the highest sum divided by nineteen.

Provision is made on the base, or horizontal axis, of the graph for only the major categories of determinants; therefore the sub-categories, as, for instance, the various types of C, must be combined into one bar. However, it is very easy to distinguish the different types of C scores within that one C bar by dividing the bar into as many horizontal sections as there are sub-categories and simply writing the symbol of each sub-category in the appropriate section. Thus the bar might, if the record called for it, be divided into four horizontal sections — the first designated C_{des}; the second, C_n; the third, C_{sym}; and the fourth, pure C. The height of each section, naturally, should be proportional to the number of responses in the sub-category.

Another device for making the bar graph even more

telling is to characterize with diagonal lines all portions of the various bars where the determinants show form inaccuracies which are scored with a minus sign.

Proportion of location categories

A table which helps in evaluating the proportion of responses in each location category is provided in the lower right-hand corner of page 4. Parentheses and underlinings are used to indicate underemphasis or overemphasis, respectively, in the use of any one of the five major location categories. First, the total number of any one of the major location categories, and the percentage which this number is of the total number of responses, must be determined. It is advisable to note these percentage figures in the spaces above the box-like table. It can then be determined, by reference to the table, whether the percentage actually found in the subject's record represents an underemphasis or overemphasis in the use of a particular category and in what categories either of these conditions occurs.

A completely "even" distribution of these five categories is indicated in the third line of the table. This kind of distribution is found among subjects who show no preference whatsoever for any one of the major categories. In most cases the actual percentage figures are lower or higher. Thus there are three possibilities:

(1) Conformity with the expected distribution, indicated by allowing the location symbol above the column to stand unchanged.

(2) Underemphasis on a category, indicated by enclosing the symbol in single or multiple parentheses.

(3) Overemphasis on a category, indicated by single or multiple underlining of the symbol.

It is suggested that a check mark be placed in each column of the table opposite the range of percentages which describes the subject's performance. Thus, if a subject had 40 per cent of responses in the *W* category, a check mark would be placed opposite "30–45 *W*." These check marks make it possible to identify the areas of over- and underemphasis, if any, at a glance.

Succession

The term *succession* refers to the order in which the subject uses the major location categories in his responses to each card.

A *systematic order* is one in which the sequence *W, D, d, Dd,* and *S,* or its exact reverse, is strictly adhered to. Not all five categories need be used, but if they are used, they must be used in this order.

An *unsystematic order* is one in which there is any violation of this sequence; for instance, the use of *Dd* or *S* between *W* and *D,* or the insertion of *W*'s somewhere in the middle of the stream of responses. Sometimes the subject may start a series of responses with a new *W* after turning a card; this is not to be regarded as a violation of systematic sequence.

No succession exists where only one response is given to a card or where only one location category is used.

In scoring the succession and determining the appropriate point to be checked on the succession scale in the Record Blank, the following rules are applied:

(1) If not more than one card shows either a systematic or an unsystematic order, succession cannot be scored.

(2) If there are any cards in which there is no succession, the number of such cards is added to the number of systematic or unsystematic cards, whichever is greater.

　　If the number of systematic and unsystematic cards is equal (2, 3, 4, or 5), the succession is termed *loose*.

(3) After adding the number of cards with no succession, if any, to the number of systematic or unsystematic cards as directed in (2), the type of succession may be read from the following table:

No. of Systematic Cards	10	9	8	7	6	5	4	3	2	1	0
No. of Unsystematic Cards	0	1	2	3	4	5	6	7	8	9	10
Kind of Succession	Rigid	Orderly			Loose				Confused		

Other relationships among factors

The quantitative results and proportions listed in the lower left-hand quarter of page 4 of the Blank offer no particular technical problems. It is advisable to use absolute numbers instead of percentages in all places where the percentage sign does not appear on the Blank, because in all these cases the absolute numbers are more significant than percentages. This also makes it possible to include the additional scores, separating them from the main scores by a plus sign as described at the beginning of this section.

A few words should perhaps be said about the computation of sum *C*. This tabulation feature goes back to a

suggestion by Rorschach in *Psychodiagnostik*. It serves
the purpose of combining into a single measure the various
types of color responses, with the proper weight assigned
to each type. Rorschach suggested that in combining the
various color responses a weight of one-half should be
assigned to *FC* responses, unit weight to *CF* responses,
and a weight of one-and-one-half to *C* responses. The
formula for computing sum *C* shown on the Record
Blank $\left(\text{sum } C = \dfrac{FC + 2CF + 3C}{2} \right)$ is simply a convenient
device for assigning the proper weights to the three com-
ponents of the sum *C* score; the indicated division by 2
takes care of this weighting.

The "estimate of the intellectual level" is based on a
qualitative analysis which will be discussed in later
chapters.

PART THREE

CHAPTER
IX

GENERAL INTERPRETATION PROBLEMS

THE theory of the Rorschach method is still in the process of development; it is a field, therefore, for advanced research rather than for beginners. For this reason it has no place in this technical manual except for such references and explanations as are basic to an understanding of the technical procedure. The various points essential for a general orientation have been surveyed in Chapter II. Since a recognition of the difference between *structural* and *clinical* diagnosis, briefly mentioned in Chapter II, is basic to an understanding of the technical procedure of interpretation, a fuller explanation of this difference is included at this point.

The *structural interpretation* is the result of the direct use of the total evidence which a Rorschach record provides, without the assistance of other checking material or clinical inferences. The qualitative and quantitative material contained in a complete Rorschach record leads to a configurational picture which reveals the interplay between various major intellectual and emotional factors in the personality of the subject. From this picture the following structural aspects may be deduced:

(1) The degree and mode of control with which the subject tries to regulate his experiences and actions.

(2) The responsiveness of his emotional energies to stimulations from outside and promptings from within.

(3) His mental approach to given problems and situations.

(4) His creative or imaginative capacities, and the use he makes of them.

(5) A general estimate of his intellectual level and the major qualitative features of his thinking.

(6) A general estimate of the degree of security or anxiety, of balance in general, and specific unbalances.

(7) The relative degree of maturity in the total personality development.

This list does not represent a complete account of the personality aspects revealed by the Rorschach method. It simply enumerates the major structural elements in the configurational picture which the Rorschach material reflects.

Since overt behavior results from an interplay of the environmental situation and the personality structure, so that relatively similar personality structures may display markedly different behavior patterns, it becomes important, in estimating the expected behavior of a subject in various life situations, or in evaluating his specific clinical picture as a patient, to use some method of studying this environmental situation in addition to the structural personality diagnosis. The *clinical diagnosis*, compounded of clinical observation, case histories, and psychometric data, is such a method.

There are two final steps in the Rorschach technique of personality diagnosis, both of which present accurate pictures of the personality, although they represent very different approaches. Both, in their application, are beyond the scope of a technical manual of this sort, and we mention them only briefly here. The first is the so-called "blind diagnosis" of the expert, a term which implies that the diagnosis is made entirely on the basis of the Rorschach record, without any personal contact with, or any information about, the subject except sex and age. Such an interpretation, if it attempts to give a full behavior picture, reaches beyond the sphere of scientific techniques into the realm of intuitive art. The second is based on a complete integration of all available information. On the basis of the experience of the last twenty years, it may be predicted that the Rorschach method will, at some future time, develop into a crystallization point for combining all available sources of personality diagnosis — clinical, psychometric, and projective. However, the time is not yet ripe for writing a technical manual for such an integration technique.

THE VARIOUS STRATA OF INTERPRETATIVE INFORMATION

The information obtained during the successive phases of acquiring the raw material in the performance proper — the inquiry, testing the limits, scoring, and tabulation — organizes itself into various "layers" or strata. These layers may be described as follows:

(1) *The quantitative results of the tabulation,* representing the crude totals for the major scoring categories.

(2) *The configurational results of the tabulation,* showing some important interrelationships, both among the figures for the various scoring categories within a given record and in comparison with standard figures.

(3) *The distribution of the quantitative scoring results for all ten cards,* as seen on the Tabulation Sheet, representing the general responsiveness to the specific features of each one of the ten cards.

(4) *The sequence analysis of the Scoring List,* showing the succession of various location and determinant scores within each card and tendencies permeating several or all cards such as perseverating tendencies or color dynamics.

(5) *The qualitative analysis of all individual responses* as to organization, form accuracy, and integration of various determinants.

(6) *Analysis of the general symbolic characteristics of the content,* especially in movement, color, and original responses showing such specific emotional qualities as aggression or submission, or such general moods as depression or elation.

(7) *The use of conspicuous behavior* exhibited during the Rorschach administration, *characteristic features in the verbal formulations, asides, remarks,* and other unscorable elements, for a differential diagnosis in unusual or unfocused structural personality pictures.

In the course of the interpretative process, these layers may be used either successively, starting from one end or the other, or simultaneously, crossing back and forth from layer to layer.

SIGNIFICANCE OF THE MAJOR SCORING CATEGORIES

It would greatly facilitate the use of the Rorschach method of personality diagnosis if the interpretative significance of each of the various scoring categories was fixed and unchanging for all individuals. Unfortunately, this is not the case. Due to the very nature of the human personality, features or traits which may be considered similar or identical units can play such a markedly different role in various personality composites as to change their significance entirely.

Consider, for example, the trait of alert responsiveness to outside stimulation, to actions and reactions in the environment, usually called "sensitiveness." There is fairly general agreement, even among exponents of different theories of personality, that this is a trait which can be analyzed and isolated to a certain degree, that people can be distinguished as possessing a high, medium, or low degree of this "sensitiveness." If we were to observe the role which this trait plays in different personality structures, we would surely be impressed by the different significance which this same trait may have for various individuals. One subject may use or rather exploit this "sensitiveness" in the almost paranoid fashion of a persecution complex, relating everything going on in his surroundings to a very over-sensitized ego, interpreting chance situations as personal affronts or signs of neglect. Another subject, mature and well balanced, may use the same degree of "sensitiveness" to sense the reaction of various people in his surroundings to any given or impending situation, to forestall friction and pour oil on the turbulent waters of emotion. A low degree of "sensitiveness" may appear in one person as a component of a "happy-go-lucky" behavior and may make of another person the typical "bull in the china shop."

From these considerations one must draw the general conclusion that an attempt to give definite or dogmatic interpretative meanings to any individual Rorschach category would actually be misleading. At the same time it may be assumed that the various Rorschach categories reflect specific structural elements or components in the personality, as, for example, the number of Fc responses reflects the degree of sensitiveness as described above, but they change their meaning and significance with each total setting just as the role of the "sensitiveness" shows a marked changeability from one personality structure to another.

Another complicating factor which reflects the same interwovenness of the meaning of one scoring category and the total structural setting is the *quality of the scoring categories*. The W category may serve as an example: One subject may use the whole card in each response because of a complete inability to organize the given material into meaningful subdivisions. The result of such an incapacity for organization is, naturally, either completely noncommittal W's like the perseveration of the response "insides of a human body" through all ten cards, or, at best, fairly accurate crude outline responses like "butterflies," "birds," or "leaves." Another subject may produce a series of ten W responses because he greatly enjoys using his immense and almost unlimited organizational abilities to form a concept in each one of the ten cards which incorporates and uses every single one of the clearly perceived and organized natural subdivisions of the blot.

To a certain extent the scoring system can take care of such qualitative changes as long as they are based on measurable differences, as, for instance, through the addition of plus and minus signs, or the combination of F with other scoring symbols to express the definiteness of a concept in regard to its form qualities. However, these qualitative differences, even though they are based on measurable differences, can be quantified and thus made scorable only to a limited extent.

Another item of limited quantifiability is the relationship between *main* and *additional* scores. As mentioned in Chapter IV, the Rorschach reactions which are scored with additional scores represent a sort of potential — elements in the subject's personality which are less ready to function than those represented by the main scores. Therefore, these additional scores should never be entirely neglected; on the other hand, neither should they be given equal weight with the main scores. They may serve as modifying factors where the number of main scores indicates the lack of a certain capacity, or as a tendency to overflowing where the number of main scores indicates strength in a given capacity.

It may be worth while to become acquainted, in a preliminary way, with the interpretative meaning of the major scoring categories, through a general description of the interpretative significance of the various scoring areas, accompanied by suggestions as to the directions in which future Rorschach workers are likely to find satisfactory theoretical explanations for these meanings.

Interpretative meaning of main scoring categories

The location categories lend themselves to summary treatment in this general survey, as components of one interpretative area—"the mental approach." The significance of the four major determinant categories, however, calls for a more specialized treatment.

1. *The location categories.* The choice of the areas upon which the subject projects his concepts seems to reflect his typical mental approach to the problems and situations with which he is confronted. In a majority of cases this choice even reveals specific qualities of the subject's mental activities, such as a preference for sweeping generalities, the tendency to get lost in unrelated details, the compulsive habits of a perfectionist, or the arbitrary digressions of an undisciplined mind.

It is obvious that a complete interpretation of the scoring categories must use all the layers of interpretative information listed in the previous section; it is not sufficient to know only the absolute number and the proportion of the various scoring categories and their relationship to standard figures. It is also necessary to study the distribution of the *W*'s and *D*'s over the ten cards in order to see, for instance, whether the *W*'s are present only when the cards themselves invite their use, or are spread out over all ten cards, or even predominate in cards which do not seem to call for them. Naturally, the order in which the subject uses a whole card and its larger and smaller subdivisions is very important, as is also the degree of organization used within each area. The content and the formulation of the responses show whether the subject has tried to do his best or merely to "get it over with quickly."

Later we shall consider a number of other interpretative approaches for which the location scoring categories can serve as a starting point. For instance, the proportion of usual details may indicate the awareness of the obvious and the immediate problems of everyday living; preference for the use of the white space left by the blots may indicate some oppositional tendencies.

2. *Form responses.* The number and quality of responses which use the shape of blots as a determinant, either exclusively or predominantly, is, interpretatively, a keystone between intellectual and emotional aspects of the personality structure. On the one hand, it is the most important supplement to the location categories in reflecting the mental approach of a subject, his way of dealing intellectually with his life situations. On the other hand, it shows the role which intellectual or conscious control plays in the total emotional balance of the personality.

The concentration of a subject's interest on the purely "formal" qualities of the blot material seems to indicate the degree to which the subject is inclined to repress or control less "formal," more personal, or spontaneous reactions to the stimulus material.

It is evident that here again — as, indeed, at every point of the interpretative process — all the various layers of information must be used. There is reason to assume that a healthy balance between control and spontaneity is lost when more than half of all the subject's responses are of such a "formal" nature. It is interesting to know, for example, whether the first responses to each card are always *F,* only followed later on by more spontaneous reactions, and so on.

3. *Movement responses.* Movement responses represent one way of deviating from a "formal," impersonal relationship to the stimulus material. The projection of action onto the objectively static ink blots presupposes the use of the subject's imagination. This use of the imagination may be facilitated or stimulated by some cards more than by others. Such a stimulation seems to be so strong in some of the cards — e.g., Card III for human action and Card VIII for animal action — that either a pathological lack of imaginative capacity or an extreme repression of the use of imagination has been found where the subjects do not react with action responses to these cards.

The forces which give rise to such imaginative projections vary. They may range from the lucid quality of original ideas and thoughts, or the colorful products of a brilliant fantasy, to the rather foggy stirrings of instinctive impulses or inner conflicts. In all cases these "promptings from within" take advantage of the Rorschach situation to make themselves felt, to project themselves into the subject's reaction to the stimulus material.

Among the various strata of interpretative information the symbolic meaning of the content usually plays a more important part in the action responses than in any other scoring area, a fact which is understandable in terms of the nature of these responses.

4. *Color responses.* Responses using the actual color of the blots as a determinant for the concept formation seem to deviate from form responses in a direction which can almost be considered as opposite to the direction of the

action responses. Both represent a higher degree of spontaneity than form responses; but while the spontaneity of the action responses points toward "promptings from within," the spontaneity expressed in the color responses seems to reflect the reaction to "stimuli from without." Both forms of spontaneity are based on the emotional structure of the personality. The formulation "responsiveness to stimuli from without" contains an implication which is not immediately evident. It represents not only the general readiness of the subject to establish a relationship with the world around him, but it seems to involve more specifically the *emotional* qualities of this relationship, both the intensity and quality of his emotional relationship to other people.

Many subjects experience the color in the stimulus material very clearly and distinctly as an intruding element, frequently even as a disturbing factor. Whether the color is exhilarating or shocking, it always seems to be a force which tends to get the subject away from a purely formal, impersonal, matter-of-fact handling of the Rorschach situation.

The sequence analysis of the Scoring List is particularly important for the color responses. The color is very carefully distributed within the ten cards in such a way that the sequence of the cards tends to enhance the color effects. When color appears for the first time in Card II, it appears in the form of rather striking red blotches quite thoroughly fused with the achromatic part of the card. When color for the first time almost covers the whole blot material, in Card VIII, it is preceded by an unbroken series of four achromatic cards and happens in such a way as to create the strongest discrepancy between color and form qualities. These objective "color dynamics" will be dealt with in detail in Chapter XII.

5. *Shading effects.* The interpretative significance of this scoring area was the last to be discovered. It is technically the most complicated one and at the same time it seems to yield the finest nuances in the structural personality diagnosis.

The use of shading effects for the creation of a depth impression seems to reflect inner stirrings, either in the form of anxieties or in the form of introspective tendencies resorted to in an effort to dispel such anxieties. The scoring categories describing the use of shading effects as depth impression or diffusion are located in the distribution graph between the action responses (reflecting the "inner life") and the form responses, in order to demonstrate the close relationship of these shading reactions to the inner life of the subject.

The use of shading as surface impression seems to deal with an approach to the outer world which is more cautious or less outspoken than is the use of color in color responses. For this reason the scoring categories for texture responses are located in the distribution graph between the form responses and the color responses.

The undifferentiated use of shading effects seems to reflect very vague and general emotional reactions which can also best be described as undifferentiated emotional reactions. These may include the vague and general anxieties reflected in diffusion responses, or vague and undifferentiated desires for contact as reflected in the touch-feeling element of undifferentiated texture responses.

The differentiated use of shading effects changes the depth impression into vista and the touch-feeling expression into clearly conceived objects with their specific surface appearance. Both forms of differentiated use of shading effects have in common an element of caution and refined control. The *FK* or vista responses seem to reflect an adjustment tendency in the direction of the relationship to oneself. The *Fc* responses seem to reflect the adjustment process where the outer world is in the focus of attention.

Due to their very nature, the shading effects play a role in all major aspects of the structural personality diagnosis, both in the intellectual and in the emotional field, and particularly in the area which may be called *basic personality configuration.*

The number of responses using shading effects is comparatively small, so that any one of the shading categories becomes significant as soon as a record contains three or more responses of this kind.

INTERPRETATIVE SIGNIFICANCE OF OTHER SCORING ELEMENTS LISTED IN THE RECORD BLANK

In this section only those three groups of items listed on page 4 of the Record Blank which are not dealt with in one of the following chapters will be discussed. The other items will be treated in Chapter X, "The General Personality Structure," and Chapter XI, "Intellectual Aspects of Personality."

Number of responses (*R*) and rejection of cards

1. *Significance of the total number of responses.* Little specific significance can be attached to the total number of responses, *R*. It is of some interest to know that the range of responses found most frequently in all large-scale

investigations of adults seems to be between twenty and forty. This result was found in a large group of records taken from a non-literate American Indian tribe in Northern Canada, as well as in European or North American groups of subjects of different intellectual levels. Children below ten years of age, subjects with severe lesions of the central nervous system, severely blocked subjects, and subjects with a subnormal intelligence seem to have an average of less than twenty responses.

It would be incorrect to assume that a higher intellectual level is always a concomitant of a larger number of responses. Many highly intelligent individuals prefer to give just one response or an average of two or three responses to each card. On the other hand, records containing fifty or even more responses are sometimes given by subjects who are either somewhat superficial or else neurotically disturbed. Such persons indiscriminately discover feet or tails in any protrusion, eyes in any dark inside spot, spines in any center line, or an unlimited number of faces around the edges of the blots.

Thus, R is interesting only in conjunction with the quality of the responses. In itself it may be indicative in very extreme cases, in records of fewer than nine or more than seventy-five responses. Fewer than nine responses are rarely found in the records of adult subjects who could be called normal in a clinical sense — that is, who do not show clinically manifest psycho-pathological disturbances. More than seventy-five main responses are hardly to be expected except among really brilliant, productive subjects. Occasionally there are subjects with an artistic ability which seems to make it impossible for them to stop, even after having given twenty or more responses to a card. These persons could go on and on without any effort.

2. *Significance of rejections.* Records having fewer than ten responses are necessarily produced by subjects who reject one, or several, of the ten cards. Card IX with its complicated color and shading effects seems to be the only card frequently rejected by normal subjects. Cards II and VI vie for second place, depending on whether the subject is more shocked by the first appearance of color in Card II or by the sexual implications which Card VI seems to contain for the majority of subjects. Strong shading shock occasionally finds expression in the rejection of Card IV.

The rejection of these four cards — Cards II, IV, VI, and IX — seems to be less significant than the rejection of any of the other cards. This is also expressed in the fact that such rejections occur quite often even in records with a greater number of responses, while rejections of more than four cards, or cards other than the four mentioned, are virtually limited to records with less than ten main responses. Subjects with such strong blocking rarely give more than one or occasionally two responses to the cards they do not reject.

It is extremely rare to get no response at all to any of the ten cards. This is true even when the examiner strictly avoids exerting any pressure during the performance. Only one such case has been observed in more than five thousand records seen by the authors. It was a schizophrenic girl who managed to avoid responding by not looking in the direction in which the card was held or by looking at the extreme corner of the card away from the blot when specifically asked to look at the cards. Her pseudo-responses when she was pressed were, "It looks like my grandmother," "It looks like your uncle," and so on, to the various cards. It is taken for granted in this discussion that the subject has at least superficially consented to coöperate in the experiment. In working with very young children, however, it frequently happens that they simply do not want to look at the cards, and not even this superficial type of coöperation can be elicited.

It is almost as rare to find subjects who confine themselves to a single response. One such record in the writer's experience was produced by a twenty-one-year-old boy with an incipient schizophrenia who was afraid of being sent to an institution. After calling Card I "a butterfly," he rejected all the other cards obviously because he was afraid his responses might reveal his insanity. Another subject producing only one response was a thirty-five-year-old woman with Pick's disease, who, despite the greatest effort, could discover nothing but the animals in Card VIII. She was too conscientious and controlled to permit herself to resort to one of the evasive perseverations like "insides of the human body" which other patients with similar severe diseases of the central nervous system quite frequently produce. In our collection of over two hundred records of subjects at the preschool level, no records were found with fewer than two responses, and only sixteen were found in which two or more cards had been rejected.

It seems quite obvious that the general significance of the rejection of cards is a blocking or resistance against the situation. This may spring from a variety of causes, ranging from intellectual or emotional incapacity to cope with the situation to an aggressive negativism directed, in some instances, more against the examiner than against the task.

There are two elements which can throw further light on the significance of rejections: (*a*) persistence in rejection during the inquiry and in the testing-the-limits period; (*b*) the choice of the cards rejected.

A characteristic difference between neurotic and psychotic subjects is that neurotic subjects in the majority of cases are able to overcome their blocking either spontaneously during the inquiry or by a special request during the testing-the-limits, while psychotic subjects persist in their rejections. The ease with which rejections can be overcome may serve as an indicator of the severity of the emotional block. Naturally, where the rejection is based on an intellectual incapacity to fulfill the task, added pressure in the testing-the-limits period can at most produce inaccurate or nonsensical responses.

The choice of cards for rejection sheds light on the same question as does persistence in rejection. Neurotic subjects will usually reject the cards referred to as presenting difficulty even for many more or less normal people; namely, Cards II, IV, VI, and IX. In some cases one or two other cards may be added or substituted, especially Cards VIII and X, where a neurotic is unable to cope with the color situation, or Card VII because of the shading. Sometimes Card I is rejected because of an initial resistance, but in that situation a response to this card is usually offered spontaneously during the inquiry. Cards III and V are less likely to be rejected except occasionally when a subject has very strong resistance to the movement stimulus in Card III or to the blackness of Card V.

In most cases the subject either reveals the reason for

the rejection spontaneously or is able to give some reason on request. The rejection of more than four cards points with some emphasis in the direction of psychotic disorder, particularly when some of the more normally difficult cards mentioned before are not rejected and some of the usually accepted cards are rejected for no obvious reason, or for reasons, given under prodding in the testing-the-limits period, which appear to the examiner as arbitrary or utterly illogical.

Further discussion of the significance of rejections is given in Part Four (pages 386ff).

Time factors

(For definitions of the various time factors the reader is referred to the section on time recording in Chapter III.)

1. *Average time per response* (*response time*). There are no large-scale investigations giving a universally valid statistical picture of the average time for a response. The figures mentioned here are merely a preliminary estimate based on experience with more than five thousand records.

It seems that the average as well as the median lies somewhere between half a minute and a minute, probably considerably closer to the half-minute than to the minute mark. In other words, an average time per response of less than half a minute is a quick response time and an average time per response of more than a minute is definitely a slow response time.

The lowest time ever found in our records is a total response time for all ten cards of between one and two minutes, producing approximately ten responses. This record time was achieved on a few occasions in a group of children between eleven and twelve years of age, subjects of a longitudinal study, who had developed an unusual skill in the handling of test situations.

At the other extreme, an average time per response of more than a minute and a half is very rare and is usually found only among subjects with some rather severe pathology or extreme inhibitions. Occasionally a more or less normal subject may do so much talking "off the record" between his responses that he prolongs his response time beyond the half-minute limit. Conversational discussions between cards, after one card has been put away and the next one not yet looked at, may be counted as "time out," so long as the total time is considered as the sum of the times the subject was exposed to the ten cards.

2. *Average time before first response to each card (reaction time).* The Blank divides the computation of the average reaction time into two parts: The average reaction time to the achromatic cards and the average reaction time to the cards containing bright color elements. It is important to note the actual reaction times for each one of the ten cards in order to get a clear idea as to whether or not some cards show a marked prolongation of the reaction time (possibly due to blocking) as compared with the usual reaction time of the particular subject for the rest of the cards.

It must be borne in mind that extreme prolongation in one card may distort the picture completely. For instance, a subject may have a rather quick reaction time to Cards II, III, VIII, and X, but be "stumped" by Card IX to such an extent that his first response comes only after a struggle of more than a minute's duration. This fact may raise the average reaction time for colored cards above the average reaction time for the achromatic cards, in spite of the fact that four of the colored cards have a shorter reaction time than any of the achromatic ones.

Making allowances for such possible distortions, the comparison of the average reaction time to the achromatic cards and to the colored cards gives a clue, in most cases even at first glance, as to whether there is an indication of color or shading shock. Roughly, the difference between the two average reaction times should be at least ten seconds before any interpretative significance is attached to it. In order to avoid as far as possible the distortions just mentioned, it seems best not to count the time spent with a card before it is finally rejected as reaction time, but to use the average of the times for cards not rejected.

The range of average reaction times is the same as the range of average response times, from less than ten seconds to more than a minute, with the same qualifications as mentioned there.

Relationships among content categories

1. *Percentage of animal responses* (*A%*). The percentage of animal responses (*A%*), regardless of whether they refer to whole animals or parts of animals, is one of the old stand-bys in Rorschach interpretation. The importance of *A%* is based on the fact that the animal kingdom, with its endless variety of forms and shapes, offers itself more readily as a concept than any other content area. Moreover, the animal kingdom is within the field of experience of virtually every subject. For this reason it has become customary to expect that a considerable percentage of the total number of responses of every subject will fall into the two categories of *A* and *Ad*. The extent to which this is the case thus gains a new interpre-

tative significance. The more a subject is able to choose his concepts outside this most obvious area, the less likely he is to be confined to the obvious, the stereotyped, or a narrow range of interests. Involved in this interpretation, naturally, is the assumption that the animal kingdom is not replaced by another area — as, for instance, geography or anatomy — to which the subject may confine himself even more exclusively than do other subjects to the animal kingdom, unless the interests or occupation of the subject make such responses meaningful. A physician, for example, could well make a large number of anatomy responses, without thereby indicating stereotypy, but these responses would be marked by an unusual keenness of form or by the selection of unusual areas for the responses. As a matter of fact, it happens surprisingly rarely that the professional background determines the choice of content to any extent, and when it does happen it usually indicates that the subject is clinging to his professional interests as a support for his personal insecurity.

Other factors, such as the number of content categories outside human and animal responses, and the percentage of responses in these other categories, are used as indicators of the diversity of interests (cf. Chapter XI on "Intellectual Aspects"). Certain other modifications must be mentioned in connection with the interpretation of the $A\%$ as an indication of a stereotyped mind. Some subjects have a strong inclination to use cartoon animal figures or mythological creatures instead of actual animals. This may occasionally indicate another limitation, a tendency to escape into a fairy-tale world, but it would not be comparable to the ordinary concept of stereotypy. Another modification has to do with subjects with an unusual interest in and knowledge of zoölogy. The same principle would apply here as in the case of the physician with a large number of anatomy responses. We would, under these circumstances, again find a large percentage of original animal responses or animal responses with original additions, which would definitely modify the meaning of the $A\%$ as an indication of a stereotyped mind.

2. *Popular and original responses.* As described in Chapter VII, it seems more meaningful to use the absolute number of popular and original responses than a percentage, since the chance of producing popular responses is quite limited as long as it is restricted to the ten selected possibilities, while the total number of possible responses is more or less unlimited. There is not yet enough statistically valid evidence to make definite statements about the significance of the number of popular responses. This factor seems to reflect one of the more peripheral elements in the personality structure, and one which is more subject to change in retest experiments than many other factors. However, it seems certain that the use of less than four popular concepts indicates a lack of conformity on the part of the subject. Not to use the most obvious concepts used by the great majority of other subjects may mean that the subject is not able to think along the lines of other people or that he is not willing to do so.

The use of five or more popular concepts seems to assure that the subject possesses capacity and interest in thinking along the same lines as other people in sufficient degree. The tendency to popular responses or the additional use of popular concepts in the inquiry can constitute a partial substitute for the lack of P.

In order to facilitate the comparison of P and O, it is

again desirable to use the absolute number of O rather than a percentage. As a rule, in the record of a definitely superior subject the number of O reaches or exceeds the number of P, provided that there is a minimum of five in either case and that the quality of the original responses is sufficiently high.

If the number of O is equal to or greater than twice the number of P (again provided that there is a minimum of ten O), some criterion is necessary to gauge the significance of such a high number of O. In such a case the percentage of O within the total number of responses is an important factor. A subject producing one hundred or more responses may well have between twenty and fifty O responses among them, even if his number of P by virtue of our P limitations remains close to the figure of ten. Such an excess O production, if it is characterized by a high quality of form accuracy, organization, and combination of elements, can only be an indication of a really brilliant and creative mind. If any of these various modifying factors are missing — if the number of P is below five, if the O's are of doubtful quality — and if, moreover, the somewhat questionable O's form more than half of the subject's total responses, this excess O production demands a more reserved or critical or even negative interpretation. The subject may be a not overly intelligent "show-off," or a careless hypomanic, or possibly psychotic.

3. *Whole figures and parts of figures* $(H + A):(Hd + Ad)$. The majority of subjects tend, wherever possible, to see a more or less complete human or animal figure rather than only a part of such a figure. For this reason a subject must have a special, although possibly unconscious, motive if he prefers to see only profiles, heads, legs, and

hands or any other parts of a human or animal body. In virtually every case this motive is a tendency to be more critical toward the given form qualities of the blots than the average subject. It seems (as a rough estimate, not based on valid statistical research) that the threshold for such a critical attitude is reached if the number of $Hd +$ Ad exceeds half the number of $H + A$.

The significance of this tendency to be critical in the individual personality structure depends on its relation to all the other factors.

GENERAL INFORMATION ABOUT THE SUBJECT NECESSARY FOR A STRUCTURAL PERSONALITY DIAGNOSIS

A structural personality diagnosis is usually made without benefit of information about the subject gained from sources other than the Rorschach situation. However, there are certain facts which seem in many cases to be indispensable even for the purely structural interpretation. For instance, one would have to examine the records of some four-year-old children very minutely to distinguish them from the records of some psychotics if the age of the subject were not known. It would also be very difficult to estimate the intellectual level of a subject if his chronological age were not known.

Another piece of information which seems to facilitate the structural interpretation considerably is the sex of the subject. There are not yet any large-scale investigations which have shown sex differences in Rorschach records beyond some rather vague guesses and assumptions. On the other hand, the symbolic meaning of content, for instance, gains much more significance when it is known whether the subject is male or female.

A third bit of general information which sometimes becomes important is an account of the behavior and attitude of the subject during the administration. For instance, in a record containing a minimum of verbal expressions the paucity of words may be due to a distaste for verbosity, a pathological incapacity for verbal expression, or a resistance to the test situation.

1. *The age of the subject.* Recent experience, not greatly systematized as yet, indicates that there are typical Rorschach reactions for various age levels, so that a response may gain or lose in significance in relation to age. On the preschool level these reactions are markedly different from year to year. At the adult level the exact age of the subject does not seem so important; as a rule, knowledge of the subject's age within a range of about ten years will suffice. However, Rorschach experience seems to confirm the assumption that the biological development of the personality is not completed with physical maturity; that there are definite biological crises — the menopause, to mention only one — which are highly important for deep-reaching personality changes.

Rorschach, speaking of the changes during the course of the individual's life, mentions that a general introversial trend occurs around the thirtieth year. This seems to be a similar reaction, on a new level, to that which has been observed during the climax of the puberty crisis. This second maturation period seems to be limited to subjects with a high degree of intellectual and emotional differentiation. To mention another instance, it seems that women about forty display particular concern with the problems of reproduction, frequently seeing a pelvis in their very first response to Card I or repeatedly in some other cards.

2. *The sex of the subject.* As mentioned before, there is as yet little reliable or valid information available about sex differences. It seems that girls as a group show earlier reaction to color in the lower marginal age group for Rorschach reactions (2–4 years). Also they attempt to reconcile form and color, in some reasonable way, at an earlier age than do boys. Some other differences have been pointed out — and contradicted — between adolescent boys and girls. The literature contains only unsubstantiated hints about sex differences in records of adults.

3. *Behavior of subjects during the administration.* One rarely sees a Rorschach record giving a detailed description of the subject's behavior during the performance. Naturally, the information about the reaction time and the turning of the cards, which is expected in every satisfactory record, gives some clue in this direction, which, indeed, suffices in most cases. Some behavior description is always helpful, as in any test situation; however, the richer the record, the less important is any additional behavior description.

CHAPTER
X

THE GENERAL PERSONALITY
STRUCTURE

IT IS unnecessary for our purposes here to become entangled in the warring camps fighting for their particular theories of personality structure. The general psychological assumptions made in Rorschach interpretation are so few and simple that nobody will have any compunction about accepting them. Thus, it is assumed that the actions and reactions of human beings are stimulated or prompted both from without and from within. The stimulation from without has never been doubted. It seems equally clear that most psychologists agree in assuming that promptings from within form a working part of actual life.

One object of Rorschach interpretation is to discover the role which the different areas of stimulation play in the life of a subject, their strength, and their importance in his general life situation. In this sense, and in this sense only, does the Rorschach terminology distinguish between people who are predominantly prompted from within (introverts) and people who are predominantly stimulated from without (extraverts).

A second assumption (to be checked by further research) may be made that this susceptibility to be stimulated from within, or to be stimulated from without, is distributed in mankind according to a normal curve. This suggests that the majority of all people are about equally responsive to stimulation from without and to promptings from within, while relatively fewer are predominantly determined by one kind of stimulation only. It is true, of course, that cultural factors play an enormous role with regard to this kind of distribution of life energy. There seems, for instance, little doubt that pre-depression America set a high premium on an extraversial life. This interplay between cultural values and pressures on the one hand and the individual's personal tendencies on the other creates a whole host of emotional problems for the individual. One could find an appalling number of subjects in the United States who were trying desperately to run away from their basically strong tendency to be prompted from within, because being an "introvert" seemed to be identical with being a neurotic (nor was this only the lay opinion). These distortions of one's own tendencies create more neurotic tensions than the other solution; namely, being what one is naturally inclined to be, and then dealing from the firm basis of a healthy and fully developed personality with the environment and its values as best one can.

It is amusing to discover that many people known for the ease and smoothness of their contacts with other people and considered in terms of this as typical "extraverts" are in reality so firmly rooted within themselves and so definitely directed by promptings from within that their outside relations never have the slightest chance of becoming a source of disturbance.

The introversion-extraversion problem, in the sense in which we have been using these terms, forms the core of Rorschach's own personality theory and appears over and over again in *Psychodiagnostik* under the untranslatable heading *erlebnistyp.*

The above discussion illustrates what is meant by the term "structural personality concept." Most personality concepts in modern psychology are based either on content elements like aggression — submission, or optimism — pessimism, or on topological elements like density of wall, vector, gradients, etc. The content-determined concepts do not lend themselves easily to objective research methods; on the other hand, topological concepts are so "impersonal" that the individual personality all but escapes their grasp. The structural concepts used in Rorschach interpretation seem to hold a middle position between these two extremes. There has been a definite trend toward such structural concepts in the recent development of personality tests. The structural aspects of personality as discussed in this chapter may be summarized as follows:

(1) *Control.* Under this heading are included both the degree and mode of control which the subject exercises over his various spontaneous impulses. The term "control" as used here includes the various meanings of inhibiting, repressing, directing, and stabilizing.

(2) *Adjustment and maturity.* Here the interest centers on the extent to which the subject seems to follow his natural inclinations, to possess tenden-

cies to run away from himself, to fear his imagination, to shy away from his own ideas, to fear contact with the outside world, or to display other signs of insecurity or anxiety.

The general level of maturity on which these tendencies or conflicts are handled is also evaluated here — whether these tendencies lead to infantile reactions or to more mature solutions.

(3) *Erlebnistyp.* This aspect of personality structure, as we have seen, refers to the extent to which a subject is responsive to promptings from within or from without.

The "normal" personality

Some readers may ask how the discussion of the general personality structure in this chapter is related to what might be called the "normal" personality. In considering the problem of the normal personality in relation to Rorschach interpretation, three concepts of normality must be distinguished.

(1) *The statistical concept of normality.* Normality in the statistical sense of mediocrity or usualness is of limited significance in the Rorschach method. It is of importance, for example, in the establishment of popular responses and of usual details. However, the fact that an individual is "normal" with respect to all the scoring categories in this statistical sense by no means guarantees that the personality structure as a whole is a normal one. A mere compilation of average ratings in all the scoring categories may as little depict a normal personality structure as superimposed photographs of a thou-

sand New Yorkers would represent the typical New Yorker.

(2) *The clinical concept of normality.* The clinical concept of normality is somewhat more relevant to the problems to be discussed in this chapter. Clinically, the normal personality is defined as the human being who has no clinically manifest signs of neurosis, psychosis, or organic lesions of the central nervous system; in other words, a clinically healthy person.

It is safe to assume that the Rorschach picture of a person who has manifest clinical disturbances will always be distinguishable from the picture which is normal in the statistical sense. However, the Rorschach reactions of a person without any clinical signs of disturbance, and within the limits of statistical normality, may still indicate a personality which has not reached the optimum of social and personal adjustment. This points to the third sense in which the term "normal" is used.

(3) *The "ideal personality structure."* In discussions about the normal personality, the concept of an ideal personality structure, implying an optimum personal and social development and adjustment, is often confused with the two meanings of normal personality which we have just described. It seems quite obvious that no single uniform pattern of Rorschach reactions can reflect the myriad solutions which various individuals with differing endowments, confronted with different life situations, work out in attempting to arrive at the optimum state of adjustment.

The section in this chapter which deals with adjustment
and maturity may appear to be a meager substitute for
what many beginners no doubt expect to find in this book,
namely, the Rorschach picture of the "normal personality";
but, in our judgment, the material in this section represents
the best guide for beginners as to the manifold solutions
which individuals can work out for their personal and
social problems, all well within the realm of normality.

MODES AND DEGREES OF CONTROL

There are within the personality structure several forms
of control which one can exercise over his spontaneous impulses, just as there are various mechanisms in a speed-
ing automobile by means of which its movements may be
controlled. The major control functions, as they are revealed in Rorschach findings, are described as follows:

1. *The outer control.* One way of controlling one's
impulses in emotional contacts with the outer world is an
attempt to "channelize" them into "proper" forms of expression. In other words, without attempting to repress
the attraction or repulsion or any other emotion which one
may feel for anything outside, one seeks to express it
in a form which does not violate the rational implications
of a given life situation.

In the Rorschach situation this attitude seems to be expressed in a tendency on the part of the subject to use the
color elements which he finds in the cards, but to incorporate them into a concept which at the same time takes
into consideration the given form elements. The *FC* response is, therefore, the principal representative of such
an *outer control*. A number of variations will be discussed later (page 229).

2. *The inner control.* In most cases, efforts for an outer control of emotional impulses demand some degree of *inner control,* both as a prerequisite and as a support. Only when the attitude toward one's instinctual drives, toward the whole of what may be called the "inner life," is stabilized to some extent, is one able to exercise the outer control just described. The essential property of this inner control seems to be the acceptance of promptings from within as something positive and constructive, and not as an uncontrollable force which is constantly interfering with the security of one's existence.

This positive attitude toward promptings from within is expressed in Rorschach reactions by a readiness to use such promptings in a concept formation which projects action into the cards. For reasons which will be discussed later the M is the manifestation of such an attitude.

3. *The repressive or constrictive control.* Where the two forms of control described thus far are not sufficient to guarantee rational behavior, where a human being is afraid that he may not be able to control his emotional impulses, he resorts to an attempt to repress the spontaneity of his reactions and to put in its place an impersonal, matter-of-fact, cold way of dealing with situations.

When this form of control plays a dominant role in the personality structure, we describe the behavior of such a person as *constricted.* Thus, constriction in this sense means lack of personal spontaneity.

This form of control appears in the Rorschach situation as a preoccupation with the form qualities of the blot material. The percentage of responses which are determined exclusively or primarily by form, $F\%$, is a Rorschach expression of this form of control.

Outer control

Besides the simple form of control expressed in *FC*, there are other ways of striving for the same result expressed in the Rorschach material, as outlined below.

1. *Various forms of "sublimation."* Where the affective implications of color are too strong to permit the subject to incorporate them directly into a concept with a definite form, he may at the outset be carried away by the color element. Thus he may see beautiful landscapes with sunsets and other color effects, without paying much attention to the form of the various components of the picture. The controlling or modifying element is introduced through elaboration of vista effects within the scenery.

Another constructive way of handling affective elements implied in the color effects is to make them part of a concept dominated by promptings from within. A frequent example of this modification is a stage scene with two actors seen in Card III. The red spots are called "decorations on the backdrop" or some other artistic means of expressing the gaiety of the scene. Another example, in the same card, is the response, "The two figures are rebuked suitors and the center red a symbol of their bleeding hearts."

Where color symbolism or color description is the main determinant, the crudeness of the affective stimulation is also modified by a striving for sublimation. This, however, does not attain such a degree of effectiveness as would constitute an actual outer control.

2. *Genuineness of outer control.* The Rorschach expression for the difference between artificial and genuine control is described in Chapter VI, in an explanation of the differentiation between natural, arbitrary, loose, or

forced *FC* combinations. If colors are used in a completely "colorless" way — in other words, if the actual
values have neither a natural nor a conventional significance for the concept the subject chooses — one certainly
would not expect the emotional control expressed in such
responses to be deep and genuine. The most frequent examples of such artificial control responses are the various
anatomical charts or colored maps seen in any one of the
colored cards, and scored *F/C*. The position of the actual
color responses between the natural and the arbitrary pole
may reflect the position of the subject between natural
control and artificial or merely conventional "good man-
ners" of a kind which lacks real poise.

The *FC*— response, as described in Chapter VI, is an
expression of an attitude which intends or pretends to
combine emotional stimulation with rational considerations
but in which the "rationality" of the subject shows
marked discrepancy from the "rationality" of the world in
which he lives. This kind of *pseudo-control* is frequent
among psychotics who are convinced that their behavior is
perfectly rational but whose actions do not impress the
observer in the same way. Occasionally such reactions
also occur in more or less normal subjects.

3. *Degree of outer control.* There are several ways of
measuring the degree of outer control with the aid of the
quantitative Rorschach results. The significant values for
this purpose are as follows:

(1) The ratio of *FC* to $(CF + C)$.

(2) The ratio of all bright color responses $(FC + CF + C)$ to all achromatic responses $(Fc + c + C')$.

(3) The relationship of sum *C* to *M* and to *F%*. (See end of Chapter VIII.)

The full implications of these three quantitative criteria will be discussed in Chapter XII, "Emotional Aspects of Personality." At this point some rough indications will suffice.

(1) As a prerequisite for sufficient outer control, FC must as a rule equal or exceed the sum $CF + C$. This demand may be modified by the various indications of sublimation attempts, mentioned before, and by very favorable proportions in the other relationships.

(2) If the total number of all achromatic responses exceeds the total number of all bright color responses, an excess of outer control is to be expected. This reaches the point of a real "contact shyness" or overcautiousness in emotional contacts if the total number of achromatic responses is at least twice the total number of bright color responses.

(3) It is very difficult to give any definite figures for the relationship of sum C to M and $F\%$, because the amount of sum C needed for a favorable outer control depends very much on the natural disposition of the subject. If M exceeds twice sum C, and if F exceeds 50 per cent of the total R, there are indications of too little affective energy in the emotional contact with the outside world, due either to withdrawal or to repression. Where sum C exceeds twice the number of M, especially where there are only three M or less and F is below 30 per cent, color responses must be very well balanced within themselves to guarantee the necessary amount of outer control.

Inner control

1. *The control function of M.* The problems of inner control are thoroughly bound up with the general emotional structure. The reasons why *M* alone, and neither *FM* nor *m*, seems to indicate the emotional qualities necessary for the function of the inner control will be discussed in Chapter XII. At present only this need be said: The subject who feels enough at home with himself to take his own outlook and ideas seriously and to enjoy the workings of his imagination has a temporary retreat when emotional contacts with the outer world become too complicated. This offers him an opportunity to "mull it over," to digest an emotional impact, before being forced by his impulses or by circumstances to do something about it

2. *The degree of inner control.* The number of *M* necessary to guarantee a sufficient degree of inner control depends on the intellectual level of the subject and on his natural inclination to follow promptings from within. A well-adjusted subject of more than average intellectual capacity should produce a minimum of three *M* responses, even if his natural inclination goes more in the extroversial direction. If an introversial direction is indicated by the total record, the number of *M* responses should be five or more. Otherwise the inner life of such a subject is not rich enough to give him the necessary poise and security for his dealings with the outer world.

Another indication of the degree of inner control which *M* represents is the readiness with which the *M* responses are produced: whether they are the first responses to the cards in which they occur or are preceded by several *F* responses, or whether there are signs of reluctance on the part of the subject, such as hesitancy in admitting action or a tendency to withdraw it in the inquiry.

Constrictive control

While the estimate of outer and inner control demands a rather careful study of the total record in its quantitative and qualitative aspects, the repressive or constrictive control is one of the first impressions one can glean from a glance at page 4 of the Record Blank.

1. *The significance of F and the center area of the "graph."* As soon as the graph showing the distribution of the main determinants is constructed, a tentative impression of the relationship between spontaneity and control can easily be formed. The center area of the graph, containing the F column in the middle with the FK column to the left and the Fc column to the right, is the first object of attention. The percentage of responses in all three columns $\left(\dfrac{FK + F + Fc}{R}\right)$ and in the F column alone $(F\%)$ is investigated. These two sets of figures serve to differentiate further between crude control and refined control.

2. *Extreme constriction.* A subject who gives virtually nothing but popular or crude form responses may be thus "impersonal" because his personality is too colorless, his inner life too meager, his emotional responsiveness too poor, to enable him to do anything but that. This represents a picture of *crude control,* the word "crude" being used to mean simple or primitive, implying that there is little to control. Sometimes pathological conditions, for example brain diseases, bring about such an impoverishment of personality. A record of such pathological

subjects can easily be distinguished from those of unintelligent healthy subjects by the following two factors: First, in pathological subjects crude whole responses usually predominate, while unintelligent healthy subjects prefer D; and second, a complete perseveration of the content is frequent in pathological subjects (as, for instance, the response "insides of human beings" for each one of the ten cards, with feeble attempts to allocate the different parts of the card to different parts of the body) while unintelligent healthy subjects show only a high degree of stereotypy ($A\%$ is more than 50) as distinct from perseveration.

A different kind of subject may give a great number of responses, including many original ones, unusually accurate and keenly perceived details, most minute elaborations and delineations of all concepts, but almost exclusively based on form as the determining element. Why must this subject spend so much effort on the accuracy and correctness of his responses? He was asked only to say "what it might be." He is aware that he deals with random ink blots which really represent nothing. Why doesn't he use his imagination more freely? Why is he not more affected by the shading and the color of the blots? The answer is simply that he cannot afford to be spontaneous. The possible causes of such a rigid control could not be discussed without inserting into this section an entire book on neuroses. It must suffice to indicate a few general psychological aspects of rigid control, or constriction.

Constriction, as revealed in Rorschach reactions, can be defined quantitatively: The control of any subject of more than average intelligence, whose record contains more than 50 per cent F,[1] can be called *constrictive*.

Obviously, the more closely $F\%$ approaches 100, the higher is the degree of rigidity. F percentages above 80 are, as a rule, only to be found in pathological cases, not in merely neurotic ones. Among presumably normal adult subjects any $F\%$ between 50 and 80 invariably corresponds to signs of inflexibility, or, in clinical terms, constriction with compulsive elements.

The same conclusions seem to be valid for children of school age. On the preschool level there is rarely an opportunity to get a clear enough picture of the determinants to rely on such percentages. As a rule, one can expect either a very crude reaction approaching the picture of simple crude control, perhaps even resembling the pathological form, or else a high degree of spontaneity.

To determine more accurately the nature of such a rigid control, the two columns on either side of F must be investigated. Are they affected by the rigid control? Is even the use of texture which could refine objects mainly determined by their form excluded? Is form never used in combination with the diffused aspect of shading to create vista or perspective? If this is the case, the picture is that of a very rigid constriction. Frequently in such cases only a very few responses are exempted from such an extreme regimentation: possibly the popular M in Card III, the "climbing animals" in

[1] To avoid confusion, the difference between the $F\%$ used here and the traditional $F+\%$ must be emphasized. Rorschach's $F+\%$ indicated the percentage of accurately seen F in the total F. $F\%$ as used here $\left(\frac{F}{R}\right)$ is not at all applicable to the traditional system as Rorschach left it, a system which counts every response between F and M and between F and C' as F.

Card VIII, and, perchance, a sole response combining form and color, such as the "green caterpillars" in Card X. Such a picture produced by a subject without other pathological signs invariably indicates a high degree of compulsion neurosis or a severe form of depression. In both cases there is an almost complete elimination of spontaneity.

3. *Modified constriction.* The picture changes somewhat when the F column is only slightly under or over 50 per cent and is accompanied by well-developed FK and Fc columns — all three columns adding up to 75 per cent or more of R. Naturally, this leaves little leeway for responses outside the center area, but it indicates that the subject has at least developed sufficient insight (FK) and tact (Fc) not to trouble other people too much with the ill effects of his rigidity (so long as he does not live too closely with them).

4. *Refined control.* For a person to be adjudged free from constriction, his record must fulfill two conditions: First, the number of all responses in the center area ($F + FK + Fc$) shall not reach 75 per cent; second, the number of F shall not exceed 50 per cent.

On the other hand, how many F does a subject need in order to indicate a normally functioning control? The answer here is not so simple because the amount of control a person needs depends to a large degree on the vividness of his imagination, the strength of his emotional impulses in dealing with outer reality, the degree of security or anxiety, and the amount of sensuality he has to control. The details of this problem must be postponed until the manner in which such emotional qualities express themselves has been investigated. Only then can it be determined whether or not individuals show signs of efficient control. The whole center area usually contains at least 20 per cent of the total R in records of subjects who show efficient control in their personality picture.

5. *Qualitative indicators of balance of control* ($F-$, FK, Fc). An investigation of the determinant graph will clarify the main qualifications for a balanced control. As far as the center area is concerned, a few special indications must be considered.

(1) *The significance of $F-$.* It seems quite obvious that any amount of $F-$ indicates a damage to the effectiveness of control. A few less extreme $F-$, within a generally very spontaneous record, are naturally much less damaging than any $F-$ in a more rigid control system.

(2) *The significance of FK.* If a subject uses the differences in shading to create a three-dimensional expanse, he uses the form and shading of the different darker and lighter portions of a blot to create foreground and background in an air-filled space. Interpretatively, this procedure seems to have something in common with other responses enlivening the dead ink blots. Though not representing the same free use of the imagination as is found in movement responses, the enlivening process involved in FK responses seems to point in the same direction — the direction of the subject's inner life. This careful fusion between form and shading elements indicates, as far as our experience suggests, the attitude of introspection. More than

three *FK* responses seem to indicate that the tendency to introspection may be accompanied by self-consciousness. Lack of *FK* in a record, however, does not necessarily indicate lack of introspective capacities. Such responses seem to be used only by those subjects who need this introspective function as an outpost or shock absorber in their relationship to their own inner life. Balanced subjects without *FK* are those who have so satisfactory a relationship to themselves that they have no need constantly to cling to introspection for reassurance.

For the same reason the *FK* responses cannot be counted among the indicators of introversial tendencies; they have the function of supplementing the adjustment to the outer reality by smoothing out the relationship to one's own self. This is also the reason why Rorschach and Binder in their evaluation af shading responses did not differentiate between *FK* and *Fc* as signs of adjustment.

(3) *The significance of Fc.* The use of the shading nuances for pointing up the surface appearance of a given object obviously is related to contact sensations. It happens frequently that subjects, even adult and intelligent ones, react so strongly to a contact sensation of this sort that they stroke the cards with their fingers, as if they expected actually to feel the softness or smoothness, the hairiness or the roughness, of the object they see in the blot. When consideration for form is completely submerged or pushed aside by the sensation experience, and the finer nuances of the shading effects

are not used for differentiating the surface appearance, then such a reaction merely expresses sensuality or a general desire for contact, scored *cF*, and has no balancing function.

For this balancing function, two types of texture responses are important; namely, one in which considerations for the form qualities of the blot have a controlling function and the texture stimulus is fused with the form to emphasize the surface appearance of a clearly seen object; and another, in which a very delicate elaboration of the texture nuances serves the same purpose as a form-texture fusion. For instance, one subject, seeing the "animal skin" in Card VI, may elaborate the form details of the outline, pointing out the front legs and the hind legs, the fur around the neck, and the part where the tail is missing; another subject may be less concerned with these form details, but point out the dark stripe in the fur along the back of the animal, spots where the fur seems to be worn off, and other elaborations of the texture nuances.

Such a combination of *F*, indicating control, and texture, indicating sensation, reveals an awareness of things going on in the surroundings and represents, if it is part of a well-functioning control system, what is commonly called "tact." This "tact," as a form of behavior, can be distinguished from its structural basis, which we may call "discernment." A person may be painfully aware of what is going on around him, but because of his own insecurity may fail to demonstrate tact in the social sense.

Occasionally the *Fc* category contains more responses than any other determinant, even more than *F;* this may indicate a state of over-refinement or a lack of necessary aggression in the subject's relationship to the outer world.

(4) *Ratio of F to sum of Fc and FK.* For a favorable balance, the sum of *Fc* and *FK* should be within the range of $\frac{1}{4}$ to $\frac{3}{4}$ of the number of *F*.

Other expressions of over-control or constriction

Occasionally subjects with definite compulsive or constrictive patterns in their clinical picture do not show any of the quantitative patterns indicating repressive over-control. A qualitative analysis of the Rorschach record of such subjects will easily yield conspicuous signs of some form of perfectionism, as described in the section on compulsiveness. For instance, the subjects may make painstaking efforts never to omit any portion of any one of the ten cards in their responses, or may adhere to a rigid systematic order in the sequence of the choice of areas, starting with *W*, following with one or several *D*'s, occasionally adding one or several *d*'s. As a rule such compulsive traits are also expressed in the *F%* or in the $(FK + F + Fc)\%$, but an intelligent subject may have enough mental elasticity to use other determinants and thus keep these percentages within reasonable limits.

Another Rorschach pattern behind which such constricted personality structures may hide is found in records with very evasive and noncommittal responses, such as "designs" and "maps," color descriptions, and abstract movement responses. (See also the section on evasiveness, page 244.)

ADJUSTMENT AND MATURITY

These two aspects of personality structure are so closely interwoven in their Rorschach expression that they must be treated together. Up to adolescence the degree of maturation is mainly determined by the ratio between developmental age level and the chronological age of the subject. From adolescence on, lack of maturity necessarily implies certain signs and forms of maladjustment.

Some specific aspects of maladjustment appear in the chapter on Emotional Aspects of Personality. At this point only adjustment problems of a more general structural nature will be described. They include Rorschach signs of insecurity and anxiety, as opposed to signs of a balanced personality structure. Other signs of neurotic disturbances, and general signs of a pathological personality disorder are discussed in Part Four, dealing with clinical application.

Rorschach signs of insecurity and anxiety

The structural difference between *systematized* and *unsystematized* anxiety may serve as a starting point in the discussion of anxiety as revealed in Rorschach reactions. Anxiety recognizable in behavior can be reflected in Rorschach reactions in various ways. If the anxiety is *systematized*, i.e., has produced a neurotic defense system expressed in marked changes of the personality structure of a hysterical or compulsive character, open and conspicuous expressions in the Rorschach record of the subject are less likely to occur. Reactive depression, or a state of anxiety, or any other form of "free-floating" *unsystematized* anxiety, affects the Rorschach record much more immediately.

1. *General expressions of insecurity.* Often the language used by the subject, the formulation with which a response is introduced, reveals to some extent open insecurity or anxiety. Frequent expressions like "It might be, I'm not sure," expressions of curiosity as to what other people might see, constant attempts to improve or change the concept, doubts or evasiveness, a tendency to escape into a more descriptive attitude, noncommittal contents, especially of an anatomical or geographical nature, are all indications of insecurity.

2. *Diffusion responses.* Plain diffusion responses (K) and toned-down shading effects (k) invariably indicate insecurity and anxiety of the free-floating type. The physical qualities of these shading effects seem to reflect the corresponding qualities of the inner life of the subject: haziness and fogginess, created by free-floating anxiety. K and k seem to indicate a flight from the more sensuous shading effects, whenever these effects arouse so much anxiety and guilt that the subject is not able to accept them. For this reason the diffusion responses often have a dysphoric tinge.

It is understandable that K reactions have a tendency to associate themselves with m in such responses as "clouds driven by a storm" or "smoke rising from a fire." The inhibition conflicts indicated by m are likely to create anxiety of the sort expressed in K, and the anxiety is likely to create misgivings about any promptings from within.

The k indicates an intellectual attempt to "de-personalize" or objectify the haziness expressed in K. The subject speaks of topographical maps or X-ray pictures, projecting his haziness into a concept which is legitimately vague.   Many subjects combine a secondary motive with such an attempt.   Such general anxieties are frequently accompanied by feelings of intellectual inadequacy.   The choice of "scientific" concepts, like X-ray pictures or topographical maps, offers an opportunity to demonstrate an educational background or an interest in scientific matters, thus covering up actual insecurity along these lines.   It matters little whether the form of the blots is entirely neglected, or some feeble attempt is made to identify a specific country in the outlines of a topographical map, or a specific part of the body in an X-ray picture. In all these cases the attempt to intellectualize anxiety is merely more obvious.

The significance of such responses changes as soon as they achieve a genuinely professional character, as, for instance, when a geographical expert points out a country with fairly accurate outlines, indicating the main mountain ranges and valleys in the shading.

The response "clouds" to Card VII may be insignificant if given as the only K in a record.   Subjects who do not suffer from any degree of anxiety either do not emphasize the diffusion effect in this response, or else modify it in the direction of surface effects.

Every single k response and every K response other than the one just mentioned may be considered as an expression of some anxiety.   On the other hand, the role of such anxieties within the total personality picture is not pronounced, unless at least three K or k are present in one record.

3. *Achromatic responses as an indication of depression.* The term "achromatic responses," as distinguished from "achromatic color responses" (C'), includes texture as well

as achromatic color responses. Achromatic responses in general (*Fc, c,* and *C'*) are indicative of depressive tendencies only if they outnumber bright color responses (*FC, CF,* and *C*) at least two to one.

C' responses are found mainly in two situations. First, they occur in records of subjects with a very rich and variegated reaction to all sorts of stimuli from without. This combination clearly represents an artistic impressionability. Second, they may represent a "burnt child" reaction, the reaction of people who are basically responsive to emotional stimulation from outside but have experienced a series of traumatic experiences. Such subjects tend to withdraw from the "hot" bright-colored area into the safer realm of the less affective gray, black, and white hues.

The white, gray, and black surface colors used in an artistic record are often part of a bright color combination, like the white porcelain of a gayly decorated vase. In such cases it is unlikely that the use of achromatic color has any significance as an indication of depression. Such achromatic colors, forming a significant part within a concept, like snow in a colored landscape, may indicate some cold or frigid element in an otherwise warm-blooded personality.

Whenever a concept is chosen wholly because of its achromatic color, it would appear that the subject is interested in the less colorful aspects of life. Where the subject has a pronounced tendency to look for black, gray, or white objects rather than for bright ones, even when he is especially asked in testing the limits to use the color, a depressive tendency reveals itself beyond any doubt.

4. *Evasiveness.* Insecurity and anxiety can also take

the form of evasiveness. A noncommittal attitude expresses itself either in responses limited to the most obvious popular form or in an inclination toward the use of vague general outline responses. Favorite concepts for general outline responses are butterflies and birds, or leaves and trees, responses where the symmetry of the card is utilized with the least risk of becoming involved with too specific form characteristics of the cards.

Naturally it is taken for granted here that the subject would be able to give a more elaborate or specific response from the point of view of his intellectual capacities. Whether this is the case or not can usually be ascertained by a careful inquiry or, if necessary, in the testing-the-limits period. For instance, if the subject has been so evasive that his total responses consist of only one such noncommittal response for each card, it may be very useful to ask him in the testing-the-limits period to give at least three responses to each card in order to see how well he can do under pressure.

Where the evasiveness expresses itself in a very general concept category, such as "animal" or "some figure with wings," he can always be asked for a more detailed description: "What kind of an animal?"

The most evasive attitude within the form area is expressed in responses such as "a line in the middle" or "little dots on the outside" — an attempt to avoid any risk by simply describing given form elements in a completely noncommittal way instead of interpreting them.

Another way of avoiding the risk of being wrong is the complete avoidance of definiteness of form. Only on a very primitive level can this be done without the use of other determinants. "Islands" in the geographical field and "bones" in the anatomical field are virtually the only completely indefinite pure form responses. Other geographic concepts — e.g., "bays," "inlets," "peninsulas" or "emblems" — are evasive responses on a slightly higher level. As a rule such very evasive subjects are particularly disturbed and attracted by the shading effects, as mentioned before. "X-ray pictures" and "topographical maps" are the new editions of the "bones" and "islands" on this level.

In the area of action responses such an attitude easily leads to vague abstract forces like "balance" or a "dividing force" or "power emanating from a central point." Where such evasive subjects are sufficiently responsive to bright color, they may give responses like "a bloody mess" for Card II or "spattered paint" for Cards VIII, IX, or X.

Generally evasive subjects display an inclination toward a descriptive rather than an interpretative attitude.

5. *Compulsiveness.* Compulsiveness as an expression of anxiety indicates that the anxiety has taken on a more systematized form. We find compulsive traits to a certain degree in people with no clinically manifest neurosis. For this reason the discussion of compulsiveness has been placed in this chapter dealing with structural personality diagnosis. Signs of compulsiveness occur mainly in three forms: whole compulsion, accuracy compulsion, and completeness compulsion.

   (1) *W compulsion.* One of the most frequent forms of compulsiveness is a strong tendency to use all the blot material in one card within the framework of one concept whenever possible or as far as pos-

sible. Occasionally subjects give a W response to each card with such ease and pleasure, so obviously enjoying the organizational activity involved, that these W responses do not appear to be the product of a compulsion but rather the product of a superior organizational ability keenly relished by the subject. In such a case the subject has no difficulty using the subdivisions of the blot in elaborating and organizing his concepts; a special request to give detail responses in testing the limits will be fulfilled without any particular difficulty. However, these cases are definitely rare; a W compulsion may usually be assumed in records in which the W responses (including the incomplete W and W tendencies) represent more than two thirds of all responses.

Very often such a whole compulsion is projected by the subject into the instructions. The subject may claim that he simply misunderstood the instructions to mean that he should always use the whole card. Such an excuse can easily be exposed in testing the limits by specific instructions to find responses to details. Almost invariably the subject himself is stunned by his difficulty or incapacity to do so. Even if the subject is handed a picture sheet where all the possible usual detail areas are clearly marked, he will still have considerable difficulty in utilizing them, succumbing occasionally to his whole tendencies and performing the task with a distinct feeling of dissatisfaction.

(2) *Accuracy compulsion.* The compulsion to be overly accurate with regard to the form qualities

of the concepts can express itself in constant corrections and rejections of given responses, or in a sort of helpless dissatisfaction with any response given, without the ability to improve it.

On a higher intellectual level the accuracy compulsion invariably leads to a tendency to select smaller and smaller portions of the card in order to avoid even the most minute discrepancies between the form qualities of the concept and the form qualities of the selected card area. This trend away from W and D toward d and Dd usually is accompanied by a predominance of Hd and Ad over H and A.

(3) *Completeness compulsion.* A more organized form of compulsion with less one-sided results than either the W or accuracy compulsion is the tendency of the subject to utilize systematically all the given possibilities and aspects of a card. The blots may be used in all their natural organization as W's, D's, and so on. However, in a real completeness compulsion the same procedure must be systematically followed in every card, the subject always starting with a W, continuing with the most obvious D's, and finally selecting some of the more obvious small areas.

Another sign of this completeness compulsion is the fact that such subjects cannot omit any portions of the card in their systematic procedure. If by chance they come across some blot area which does not resemble anything for them, they must at least state apologetically that this particular area does not look like anything.

As a rule, such subjects do not think of turning the cards. If they do get the idea of changing the position of the card, this again is done in the same systematic way, with an attempt to give responses in every one of the four main positions.

Color and shading "shock"

In addition to the specific signs of insecurity and anxiety mentioned in the preceding section, certain general reactions of anxious or insecure subjects to the color and shading effects have been traditionally considered as the Rorschach signs of emotional disturbance.

The most complete description of the various effects produced by color shock is contained in an article by Brosin and Fromm (*49*). The ten criteria of color shock listed there can be applied to shading shock as well. They may be summarized as follows:

(1) Significant increase in the reaction time to colored or shaded cards.

(2) Emotional exclamations referring to color or shading effects.

(3) Other significant comments indicating anxiety, irritability, or passive resistance.

(4) Significant differences in the productivity for colored or strongly shaded cards as compared with others.

(5) Decline in the form quality of responses.

(6) Impoverished content, based on a decline in richness of invention, and in the variety of interest.

(7) Rejection of a card either by inability to give responses or by obvious reluctance to touch it, getting rid of it quickly, or even tossing and bending it.

(8) More irregular succession in colored or shaded cards than in others.

(9) A decreased ability to see popular responses though they have been easily seen in other cards.

(10) Avoidance of the use of texture or color as a determinant. In the case of color this can be limited to color shyness — avoidance of the red and pink portions.

A further discussion of these signs and of the different meaning of color and shading shock will be found in Chapter XVIII.

Rorschach signs of a balanced personality structure

As mentioned at the beginning of this chapter, the following discussion of Rorschach indications of a balanced personality structure is, in a sense, an approach to the problem of the "normal" personality.

1. *Characteristics of a well-balanced distribution of determinants.* While it is important to be able to discern symptoms of maladjustment and inadequate control in the determinant graph, it is equally important to be able to recognize signs of a well-adjusted and balanced personality. The most significant of these signs may be described as follows:

(1) *The center area.* A well-balanced, mature, and adjusted personality structure can be recognized by certain characteristics of the center area of the determinant graph. Naturally the intellectual capacities of the subject must be taken into account. The F column cannot be accompanied by modifying shock-absorbing FK and Fc columns unless

the subject has the intellectual capacity to differentiate, elaborate, and combine the elements in the cards in the way necessary for vista responses or for responses with an elaboration of the surface appearance. Where the intellectual capacity of the subject would permit such a differentiation, a lack of FK and Fc definitely becomes a sign of maladjustment. This applies more in the case of Fc than in that of FK, as explained in the section on FK. The sum of FK and Fc should approximate half the number of F.

The whole center area should be present in the graph, without having too dominant a position — i.e., without exceeding two thirds of the total responses.

(2) *Movement responses.* In the area of movement responses the maturity problem is particularly closely associated with chronological age. M is very scarce up to an eight-year level, averaging less than one; a predominance of FM over M is the natural state up to puberty; and m should not play any conspicuous role at any age level.

A mature, well-adjusted person, of not more than average intelligence, usually does not produce more than three M, unless he has very strong introversial inclinations. An adult with superior capacities should show at least five M, regardless of whether he is more on the introversial or the extraversial side, unless he limits himself to one response per card. The usually desirable relationship between M and FM in a mature, intelligent adult is one in which M exceeds FM. If there are 5 or more *M*, however, a slight predominance of *FM* over *M* does not distort the picture. Where, for example, both *M* and *FM* occur in unusually large numbers — for instance, 12 *M* and 15 *FM* in one record — and where these *FM* show marked ease and vividness in the description of animal action, such a slight excess of *FM* over *M* indicates a well-rounded, buoyant personality rather than an immature one. On the other hand, *FM* should not be completely lacking or repressed. Three or more *m* would certainly cast some doubt on the inner adjustment of any subject.

(3) *Texture and color responses.* A well-adjusted subject, even if strongly introversially inclined, should produce some color responses. These color responses remain within the limits of "adjustment" whether they exceed the achromatic responses or are exceeded by them, so long as, in the latter case, they are not outnumbered by more than two to one.

The distribution of responses within the bright color area again depends on the chronological age. Up to eight years it is natural that the *CF* should outnumber the *FC*. A young child who has more *FC* than *CF* is either precocious or overadjusted, a willing victim of an overdose of discipline. After puberty, however, the *FC* column should be the largest column in the bright color area. The sum of *CF* and *C* responses should not outnumber the *FC*. *C* responses should never be of the crude quality, but rather color descriptions or color symbolisms.

2. *Maturation signs in the intellectual sphere.* Referring back to the preceding section on insecurity and anxiety, it can be stated that the intellectual approach of a subject may be one-sided (showing a preference for W or small details) as long as this one-sidedness is the result of a natural gift or inclination and not of neurotic limitation. Normally an even distribution of all categories of mental approach according to expectation is a sign of balance. Where an overemphasis on one category of mental approach has a constructive basis, this category contains the keenest, most elaborate, and most original responses of the subject.

THE ERLEBNISTYP

The meaning of the term "Erlebnistyp," one of the traditional terms of Rorschach theory, was briefly explained at the beginning of this chapter. It is not intended as a means of pigeonholing subjects, not even in the more legitimate form of pigeonholing; namely, in the experimental investigation of individual differences. The importance of the Erlebnistyp as one of the structural elements lies in the fact that the Erlebnistyp may be a source of conflict or maladjustment.

Because of its importance it was necessary to supplement the indication for Erlebnistyp established by Rorschach; namely, the ratio of M to sum C, by other signs intended to reveal whether or not the subject follows his natural inclinations, and, if not, whether a conflict has arisen from this source. The two signs which seem to fulfill this purpose are the quotient $(FM + m)$: $(Fc + c + C')$ and the percentage which responses to the last three cards are of the total R.

The ratio of M to sum C

This ratio compares the number of M responses with the general weight which bright color has in the concept formation of a subject. Rorschach has devoted much space in the theoretical part of *Psychodiagnostik* to the justification of the selection of these indicators. However, these indicators reflect the balance between promptings from within and stimuli from without only in so far as the subject can utilize these motivating forces. An inclination to respond to outside stimulation which is either not accepted or is repressed does not lead to the use of color in the concept formation of the subject, affecting instead the achromatic responses or the mere number of responses to the colored cards.

The same is true for introversive tendencies which are not accepted or are repressed. The actual strength of an introversial inclination can only be measured if M tendencies, additional M, and the total configuration in the area of movement responses are considered together.

The ratio of $(FM + m)$ *to* $(Fc + c + C')$

The ratio $(FM + m) : (Fc + c + C')$ represents introversial and extraversial tendencies not fully accepted or utilized by the subject. When the weight in this ratio is on the same side as in the ratio M to sum C, this quotient serves to strengthen and confirm the impression conveyed by the quotient of M and sum C. If, however, the preponderance of the introversial and the extraversial tendencies in this quotient has changed sides as compared with the quotient of M and sum C, the subject seems to be in a state of transition as far as his Erlebnistyp is concerned. The quotient $(FM + m) : (Fc + c + C')$ points to the direction in which the subject is heading at that particular phase of his life — either toward a more extraversive expansion or toward a more introversive concentration.

Percentage of responses to last three cards

The percentage of responses to Cards VIII, IX and X seems to indicate a responsiveness to stimuli from without which is even less under the conscious control of the subject than the use of action and color elements.

1. *Underproduction in the last three cards.* Underproduction of responses to the last three cards is clearly established if they produce less than 30 per cent of the total *R*. A tendency to underproduction can be assumed where the last three cards produce less than one third of all responses. The cause of such an underproduction can be associated with color effects in two ways: Either the color merely has no particularly stimulating effect, or the color actually has a disturbing effect on the subject.

The first of the two alternatives seems to obtain if the subject shows a preponderance of introversial inclinations in both other ratios, M : sum C and $(FM + m)$: $(Fc + c + C')$. A neurotic unresponsiveness to color is indicated if either one of the two ratios shows a preponderance on the extraversial side.

2. *Overproduction in the last three cards.* It is more difficult to determine the threshold for overproduction in the last three cards. All three of them, but especially Card X, facilitate the breaking up of the whole card into details to such an extent that approximately half of all possible *D* areas are located in the last three cards. Since half of all responses are expected to be *D*, this leads automatically to an expectation of 40 per cent of re-

sponses in the last three cards, even without assuming any particular color stimulation.[2] It is clear that the color affects the number of responses if more than half of all responses are given to the last three cards, and this color effect may be suspected where the last three cards yield more than 40 per cent of all responses.

This overproduction is less significant if more than half of all responses to the last three cards are given to Card X, because in such a case it seems obvious that the overproduction is based on the particular facilitation of *D* in Card X rather than on the color which cards VIII, IX, and X have in common.

More important than the exact percentage in the case of overproduction is the relationship of this overproduction to the other two ratios; i.e., *M* : sum *C* and $(FM + m) : (Fc + c + C')$. Where the last three cards yield proportionately more responses, while at the same time very little or no use is made of the color for the concept formation, a conflict between natural inclination and conscious attitudes within the subject is indicated. It has been observed in some experiments, comparing Rorschach reactions in the normal state with Rorschach reactions under the influence of alcohol, that the percentage of responses in the last three cards increases with the tendency to repress color and decreases with the tendency

---

[2] This may be shown readily as follows:

The responses to the last three cards include *D* responses and non-*D* responses. If *R* = total number of responses, then $D = \dfrac{R}{2}$ = non-*D* (since half of responses are expected to be *D*). *D* in last three cards comprise half of all *D*, or $\dfrac{R}{4}$. Non-*D* in last three cards comprise $\dfrac{3}{10}$ of all non-*D*, or $\dfrac{.3R}{2}$. Thus, *D* + non-*D* in last three cards = $\dfrac{R}{4} + \dfrac{.3R}{2} = .4R$.

to give color effects a free play in the concept formation. These experimental findings suggest that overproduction in the last three cards without use of color is a sign of repression of responsiveness to outside stimulation.

Illustrative use of the quotients

A simple example may help to illustrate the use of these three quotients. Assume that a subject has 3 M, 4 FC, 4 CF, and 2 C_{sym}. According to the weighting system for sum C discussed at the end of Chapter VIII, sum C is 9. Therefore M : sum $C = 3 : 9$.

The subject seems to be definitely extraverted on the basis of this quotient. On the other hand, suppose there are 6 FM and 10 m and only 6 responses in the whole area covered by Fc, c, and C'. Therefore $(FM + m) : (Fc + c + C') = 16 : 6$ — a complete reversal in the introversial-extraversial relationship.

Assume finally that the total number of responses (R) is 70 and the number of responses to Cards VIII, IX, and X is only 20—i.e., 28.6% of R.

The subject has obviously forced himself into emotional relations with his surroundings, but has neglected the development of his inner life. The high number of m indicates the strong inner conflict he has to suffer for the violation of his own nature. The low number of M, coupled with the prevalence of FM over M, proves that these conflicts have left him on a less mature emotional level that he could otherwise have achieved.

His intellectual control is somewhat rigid, since he has an $F\%$ of almost 50 (with few Fc and no FK) and a high number of W's (20 W's to 3 M). This indicates an unfavorable balance between capacity and productivity.[1]

[1] See page 277 (*Relation of W and M*).

CHAPTER
XI

INTELLECTUAL ASPECTS
OF PERSONALITY

THE intellectual aspects of personality, as revealed in the Rorschach reactions, can be summarized quantitatively in an estimate of the general intellectual level of the subject, and qualitatively by describing the way he chooses his blot areas as a reflection of the way in which he typically approaches everyday problems.

MANNER OF APPROACH

The mode of approach to problems varies greatly from one individual to another. One person prefers a meticulous observation of details and hesitates to draw general conclusions; another may start with a general survey of the situation before turning his attention to details; a third may be inclined to jump at conclusions. Rorschach used the term "Erfassungstyp" to describe these various procedures; this term may be approximately translated as "manner of approach." The element in the Rorschach reactions which reflects the manner of approach is the choice of location.

The following tabulation, taken from the Individual Record Blank, gives the distribution of each of the location categories with the possible deviations. *W, D, d, Dd,* and *S,* without any underlining or parentheses (as we find it in the third line of the table), represents a distribution of these categories in which the subject follows the Gestalt qualities of the cards without any predilections for one type of area or another.

W	D	d	Dd $^{\text{and}}_{\text{or}}$ S
< 10% ((W)) 10–20 (W)	< 30% ((D)) 30–45 (D)	< 5% (d)	
20–30 W	45–55 D	5–15 d	< 10% Dd S
30–45 $\underline{\text{W}}$ 45–60 $\overline{\underline{\text{W}}}$ > 60 $\underline{\underline{\text{W}}}$	55–65 $\underline{\text{D}}$ 65–80 $\overline{\underline{\text{D}}}$ > 80 $\underline{\underline{\text{D}}}$	15–25 $\underline{\text{d}}$ 25–35 $\overline{\underline{\text{d}}}$ 35–45 $\underline{\underline{\text{d}}}$ > 45 $\underline{\underline{\underline{\text{d}}}}$	10–15 $\underline{\text{Dd S}}$ 15–20 $\overline{\underline{\text{Dd S}}}$ 20–25 $\underline{\underline{\text{Dd S}}}$ > 25 $\underline{\underline{\underline{\text{Dd S}}}}$

As this tabulation implies, a subject following completely these Gestalt qualities of the cards is expected to use a whole card in about one quarter of the total responses, the usual detail areas in about one half to two thirds of his responses, and only the remainder of his responses, usually not more than 10 per cent, will be located in unusual detail areas or in the white space.

That this distribution is not necessarily an optimal distribution for every subject either intellectually or emotionally has been discussed in the paragraph on maturation signs in the intellectual sphere, on page 252, it is only the most natural from the Gestalt point of view.

Significance of *W*

A relatively high number of *W*, according to the tradition of the Rorschach literature, represents an emphasis on the abstract forms of thinking and the higher forms of mental activity — as, for instance, the logical or constructive activities, philosophical or religious speculation, esthetic or ethical understanding, etc.

This tradition cannot be accepted unqualifiedly; not every *W* can be evaluated in this manner. Certain *W*'s are achieved by a mental inability to organize the whole card into subdivisions, an inability frequently found in certain severe forms of brain diseases. Furthermore, vague or noncommittal *W* interpretations, made in a high-handed manner, as butterflies, maps, islands, X-ray pictures, undefined anatomical cross sections, etc., show a minimum of effort to organize the stimulus material, to build up an all-inclusive concept; they merely utilize the crudest features of the general outline or employ a vague shading effect.

A high number of such simple or popular *W*'s represents either a pathological condition (easily revealed by other features) or, at best, a somewhat fruitless effort to attain a higher level of mental activity without possessing the necessary qualifications. Such a trait may be called "quality ambition" (as distinct from "quantity ambition" which tries to impress with a large number of answers). To be sure, even the most brilliant subjects use some simple *W*'s, but never in excess of half the *W*'s produced.

The percentage of *W*'s needs to be further qualified in the light of the form accuracy level. The fact that a record contains a high number of *W*'s which are neither simple nor evasive does not guarantee that they represent substantial achievements in the realm of higher mental activity, as witness the various types of definitely pathological *W*'s which are rich with the richness of nonsense.

The absence of a proportionately high number of good *W*'s does not necessarily prove that the subject lacks capacity for higher mental activities. It may merely mean that he does not use this capacity in a way expressed by *W*'s of high quality. For example, a very intelligent compulsion-neurotic may express an enormous drive for form accuracy and will not give a single *W* because he will discover in each card something which does not fit into a whole concept. However, his intellectual capacities will be revealed in other ways.

Significance of *D* and *d*

Traditionally it was assumed that about two thirds of all responses of an intelligent adult should be usual details. This is correct if *D* and *d* are considered together. Both *D* and *d* represent the subdivisions which offer themselves most readily as separate areas for responses. Therefore their use in approximately two thirds of a subject's responses simply means that he has enough common sense to use the most obvious material before he starts seeking the unusual. This obvious material corresponds in the actual life situation to the routine problems of daily life, which cannot be overlooked without endangering the smooth flow of life.

In more theoretical spheres of mental activity this attitude represents an interest in crude facts, rather than a drive for daring combinations or a search for unusual aspects.

The differentiation of *D* and *d* clarifies further nuances in the mental make-up of a subject; the intelligent subject will not only locate half of his responses in the obvious areas of the cards but, besides, will place 5 to 15 per cent of his responses in other portions which are not so obvious as *D* but are conspicuous enough to attract his attention.

A higher proportion of *d* does not necessarily mean a lack of ability to see the obvious, as long as *D* and *d* together reach 60 and do not exceed 70 per cent of *R*. Subjects who have a somewhat critical attitude combined with sufficient common sense to keep them from being far-fetched in their criticism frequently shift their emphasis from *D* to *d*. This state of mind is the typical reaction of many normal children in the pre-puberty phase when they start to find fault with their parents and other adults.

There is no evidence that underemphasis on or even a complete lack of *d* necessarily indicates a lack of critical capacities. Many subjects use the portions of the blots designated as *d* very freely for the elaboration of responses to larger areas, instead of using them as independent concepts.

The same may be said in more exceptional cases about the total absence of or underemphasis on *D*. For example, in some brilliant 10-response records the majority of the 60 available *D*'s is used for the elaboration of the 10 *W*'s. It is not important whether these elaborations are given in the performance proper or in the inquiry, so long as they are spontaneously produced. With this exception, however, a lack of *D*'s, especially in cases where they comprise less than one third of *R*, indicates a definite lack of recognition of the problems of everyday life. An overemphasis on *D*, as a rule, indicates that a person employs common sense as a main basis for his mental activity. Whether this is due to the absence of other capacities or to neurotic limitations in the use of such capacities may be determined by other factors.

Significance of *Dd* and *S*

The other portions of the cards which are selected besides *D* and *d* have one feature in common: they are unusual and not selected by the majority of subjects. For this reason the percentages of these two categories (*Dd* and *S*) are considered together. The average subject may or may not occasionally select some tiny detail or some of the more obvious white spaces between or around the ink blots — for instance, the center white space in Cards II, VII, or IX — but he does not select unusual details or white spaces as locations for more than 10 per cent of his responses.

A total lack of any *Dd* or *S* responses is in no way remarkable, if any such portions have been used for elaboration; e.g., the eyes and tusks of the animal head in the lower center portion of Card IV, or the white spaces in Card I as the eyes and mouth of a pumpkin face. This additional use of *Dd* and *S* indicates that the subject's mind has enough elasticity to observe less obvious but rather interesting details in a body of facts and occasionally to look at his problems from an unusual angle. If there are neither such elaborations nor any main *Dd* or *S* in a record, a lack of intellectual differentiation would be indicated.

1. *Even distribution among different types of unusual details.* The higher the percentage of unusual details in

a record, the more important it is to investigate whether it is *Dd* or *S* which creates the surplus of unusual responses and also the prevalent type of unusual details. If no particular type of unusual detail has a dominant position compared with the other unusual details — if tiny details, edge details, inside details, rare details, and white space responses are evenly distributed — such a record shows either rich artistic responsiveness or intuitive sense for the unusual. Naturally the percentage of some other category — *W, D,* or *d* — must be more or less underemphasized to make room for these unusual detail responses. If all three of these categories are replaced to a slight degree and indications of a rich and original achievement level are present, this manner of approach, although unusual, is still a balanced one.

The situation is different if only one of the three categories is displaced by the expansion of the *Dd* and *S* responses beyond 10 per cent. If *D* and *d* maintain their normal proportion, *W* alone being reduced, it may mean that the subject is somewhat too hesitant in drawing general conclusions from his rather fine and detailed observations, preferring to stick to the facts and shun theories in whatever field he may be working.

If the percentage of *W* is normal, of *Dd* and *S* above normal, and only *D* is reduced, the mental approach is less balanced; in this case the subject is too much concerned with mental activity and too little with everyday problems.

The constellation becomes increasingly one-sided when a general trend away from *W* and *D* to *Dd* and *S* appears. If a record contains less than 10 per cent *W*, less than 10 per cent *D*, about 20 per cent *d*, and more than one half of all the responses are distributed over *Dd* and *S*, then a trend toward mental escape from reality is indicated. If this is combined with lack of popular responses, far-fetched originals, and a lack of intellectual control, there are reasons to suspect psychotic disintegration.

2. *Emphasis on a particular type of unusual detail.* A particular type of unusual detail may be said to be emphasized when it accounts for more than two thirds of all unusual detail responses in a given record. Psychological implications of the different types of unusual details have not, as yet, been sufficiently explored. The following observations are suggested as a guide:

A predominance of tiny details (*dd*) has been found in a few cases with strong obsessional traits.

A predominance of human profiles, based on parts of contours of all blots (*de*), has been found in cases of anxiety neuroses, combined with a strongly introversial personality constellation. This clinging to the edge details seems to indicate a fear to go deeply into anything.

A predominance of inside details (*di*) is very rare. It has been found in records of schizoid subjects who are fighting against the disintegrating forces of their unconscious. In selecting these unusual areas, they are piercing a blot area which is usually perceived as an unbroken one. This seems to serve these subjects as a magic procedure which deprives these blot areas of their threatening shading qualities.

A predominance of rare details (*dr*) is found, for the most part, in subjects with strong artistic sensibilities, usually accompanied by a quick and elastic mind. If it occurs in combination with a lack of *D* and *W*, it suggests an arbitrariness in the mental approach.

3. *Emphasis on S.* S responses have been the subject of considerable theoretical discussion. It has been assumed that they are significant even if there are not more than three main S's in one record. Rorschach suggested that they indicate some kind of oppositional tendencies. The subject reverses the relationship of figure and ground, and thus expresses a tendency to use an unusual approach.

This general assumption can be clarified along three main lines:

(1) Oppositional tendencies may be directed against the environment or individuals in it; they may be directed against the self in the form of self-critical or self-destructive tendencies, such as feelings of inadequacy; or they may lead to a form of "stalling," to ambivalence and indecision.

(2) Oppositional tendencies may be expressed in observable negativistic behavior, or they may be part of the personality structure without being expressed in forms of overt opposition.

(3) Oppositional tendencies may be purely emotional, or they may find intellectual expression.

These considerations suffice to explain the presence or absence of S responses and their specific significance under various conditions. Rorschach discovered the fundamental relationship between S responses and the basic personality configuration. If they are present in an introversial setting, they indicate opposition against the self; in an extraversial setting, they indicate overt opposition against the outside. In a situation in which there is no emphasis on either the introversial or extraversial side, they indicate ambivalence and doubt.

Overt oppositional behavior may take intellectual forms, such as argumentativeness; it will then be expressed in *S* responses. Purely emotional aggression is more likely to be represented by a predominance of *CF* over *FC* and of *FM* over *M* responses. The same is true of inadequacy feelings: when they are vague and diffuse, they are more likely to be represented by *K* and *k* responses. Only where they invade the thinking of a person are they likely to be expressed in a combination of *S* and *FK* responses.

THE ESTIMATE OF THE INTELLECTUAL LEVEL

The first question to be raised is whether or not the intellectual level of the subject can be adequately estimated on the basis of the Rorschach information. More validation experiments have been made for this purpose than for any other aspect of personality diagnosis. Roughly speaking, the Rorschach results have been found to correlate as highly with intelligence test results as the results of different intelligence tests correlate with one another. However, this does not seem a decisive point. If the Rorschach method could do nothing else but estimate the intellectual level of the subject as well as the usual intelligence tests, these tests would be preferable since they are simpler to apply. The importance of the Rorschach method for the intellectual aspect of personality diagnosis lies in something which no intelligence test attempts, the differentiation between potential capacity and actual efficiency.

In general, the estimate of the intellectual level based on the Rorschach reactions utilizes two aspects of the Rorschach material:

(1) The form accuracy level of the responses which indicates the logical or analytic capacities of a subject.

(2) The degree of organization and combination of areas and determinants which indicate the synthetic intellectual capacities.

These two main aspects are the essential features of the scoring elements traditionally used for the estimate of the intellectual level, namely the following:

> Number and quality of W
> Number and quality of M
> Form accuracy level
> Number and quality of original responses
> Variety of content
> Succession of responses

Number and quality of W

The significance of the number of W's was discussed in the section on the manner of approach. The quality of W's demands some further elaboration. The sections on the construction of the W's in Chapter V may serve as a starting point.

Only W's with a superior construction are indicative of superior intellectual capacities. As few as two or three such superior W's may be a reliable indication that a subject has higher or superior intelligence. Among subjects with an IQ of 100 or less, one rarely finds any W's of a higher quality than organized popular W's. These considerations seem to be valid at all age levels, with the exception of the preschool level, where only crude organization can be expected from all but decidedly superior children.

Number and quality of *M*

The general significance of *M* will be fully discussed in the chapter on "Emotional Aspects of Personality." However, certain intellectual aspects of *M* must be mentioned here.

The differentiation between average, higher, and superior levels can be based on the degree of strength or obviousness of the stimulus necessary for seeing *M* in any card. Card III, naturally, furnishes the most obvious of such stimuli. Card II (the "clowns"), Card VII (the "gossiping women" or, upside down, the "dancing girls"), and Card IX (the "clowns" in the orange portion) seem to vie for second place. Card I (the two side figures, and the figure in the middle with the upraised arms), Card IV (the "giant" walking or sitting on a stool or, upside down, the "two dwarfs" or "witches" in the dark portion) rank next. Card V (the "person in the bat costume"), Card VI (upside down, the "two figures back to back"), and Card X (the "two pink figures with the gray heads") follow.

It is not usual to find any *M* other than the two figures in Card III in records of subjects with merely average intelligence. The greater the number of *M* responses, the farther they go beyond the most obvious *M* stimuli, and the richer the original variations from the usual responses, the more the *M*'s are indicative of a brilliant mind, provided emotional factors do not interfere with the production of *M*. Beck's assumption that no *M* responses, or one *M*, represents a low level of intelligence; two to four, a medium; and five or more, a high level, agrees with our experience, if by a "medium level" is meant what is usually called the higher average intelligence. Rorschach suggested in *Psychodiagnostik* a further differentiation of the medium area, assuming that one or two *M*'s represent a non-creative, predominantly reproductive intelligence and that three to five *M*'s represent more specifically a medium intelligence around an IQ level of 110.

The quality of *M* responses is an important factor; rich *M* responses, including careful form elaborations, naturally indicate the optimum of coöperation between rich imagination and keen thinking. Definitely inaccurate forms in *M* usually indicate some hypomanic state, where the imagination overwhelms rational thinking, or they may indicate a psychotic lack of control over the imagination.

Form accuracy level

The evaluation of the form accuracy level has been discussed in Chapter VI. In evaluating the form accuracy level, not only the level of the pure *F* but also the use of the *F* elements implied in *M, FM, Fm, FK, Fc, FC'* and *FC* must be considered. It is of particular interest to note whether the form accuracy level remains the same when other determinants participate in the production of a response or whether any of these other determinants — movements, shading, or color — has a beneficial or a detrimental influence on the form accuracy level. Here is one of the points in which not only the basic intellectual capacity but also the factors enhancing or interfering with its efficiency may be studied — as, for instance, a sweeping fantasy, a strong anxiety, an all-permeating sensuousness, or an over-strong emotionality.

1. *Popular F and F+*. Records which contain only popular *F* usually represent merely average intelligence. When subjects of superior intelligence produce only such

F, there are always modifying factors as, for instance, when the F are kept on a popular and noncommittal level for emotional reasons. That would indicate a cutting down of the efficiency of the higher intellectual capacity. The more F there are above the popular F level, the more certain is the impression of superior intellectual capacity.

2. *Significance of $F-$.* The $F-$'s have a very different significance when they appear in a record containing only popular F from that which they have when they appear in a record together with superior F's. (The traditional way of figuring the $F+$ per cent: $\dfrac{\text{total } F \text{ minus } F -}{\text{total } F}$, cannot express this difference because it does not distinguish between plain popular F and $F+$).

In those extreme cases in which several excellent $F+$ and several definite $F-$ occur in one and the same record, it is well to look for other signs of a psychotic disorder. In milder forms a few less extreme violations of the objective form qualities in the response may occur together with a great number of very original $F+$ responses. These must be records of artistically gifted, but not very logically controlled, subjects. A somewhat stable general F level without any brilliant aspects interspersed with some definite $F-$ responses represents the picture of a partial mental deterioration, as it is occasionally produced by some organic impairment of the central nervous system.

In records containing $F-$, without any mitigating $F+$ concepts, the intellectual level of the subject must be below the average IQ level. It is not possible to suggest any numerical relation between the percentage of $F-$ and a corresponding IQ level because too many modifying factors are involved. However, some rough suggestions may be made.

Barring other indications suggesting higher capacities, 10 per cent to 20 per cent $F-$, with the rest of the F on the popular level, seems to indicate the borderline area between deficiency and dull normality — an IQ level around the range of 70 to 80. If more than one half of all form responses are less accurate than the popular ones, a more decidedly feeble-minded level is suggested.

Number and quality of original responses

The selection of this particular factor for the estimation of the intellectual level is based on the expectation that every person of more than average intelligence should find at least a few solutions in the ten cards not found more than once among one hundred subjects. Lack of sufficiently broad statistical compilations of response frequencies precludes more exact numerical suggestions. However, our experience agrees well with Rorschach's suggestion that the higher average intelligence with predominantly practical interests produces up to 10 per cent original responses; really superior intelligence, up to 30 per cent; and only intelligent people with a rich imagination or definite artistic gifts, more than 30 per cent original responses on an accurate form level.

Original responses with marked form inaccuracies must arouse a suspicion of some kind of mental disorder. Some other suggestions about the interpretative meaning of original responses and their relation to popular responses have been made in Chapter IX (pages 216–217).

Variety of content

The variety of content indicates the intelligence level in two ways: in the percentage of the predominant categories and in the number of content categories used.

1. *Percentage of predominant categories.* Rorschach experts agree that subjects with higher intellectual capacities should not produce more than 50 per cent animal responses (including whole animal figures and animal details, but not including objects made from dead animals, like skins, skulls, etc., which are scored as *A obj.*). According to our experience, we must be more lenient with children under about eight years of age because up to that point life experience plays a more important role in the choice of content than does the basic intellectual capacity.

2. *Number of content categories.* As a rule, animals, human beings, anatomical and geographical concepts, and perhaps a few plants and objects are the stand-bys in a great majority of all records. Subjects with a limited range of interests usually have more than three quarters of their responses in the *H, Hd, A,* and *Ad* categories. A minimum of 25 per cent of *R* outside of these four categories distributed over at least three other categories seems to be the prerequisite of the wider range of interests accompanying higher intelligence. It is important to consider also correlated factors — as, for instance, the rigidity of control (usually *F%* and *A%* are in about the same range) and the form level of the responses. A broader selection of categories indicates higher intellectual capacities in a roundabout way, since a more alert subject will pick up more concepts and will have them more at his disposal than a duller person.

The manner in which concepts from the general area of science and arts are used must be carefully studied, for often a subject tries to impress the examiner by displaying his far-reaching education, and responses in these categories may be quite shallow and evasive.

Succession

Succession has been defined as the sequential use of W's, D's, d's, Dd's, and S's within the responses to one card. Subjects with simpler mental capacities rarely present a problem in the matter of succession, usually giving only one response to each card or, at most, a few which are mainly D. Only where there is a richer manner of approach can a study be made of the way different categories follow one another.

1. *Rigid and orderly succession.* Whereas a rigid order presupposes a certain intellectual capacity, it does not make for a high efficiency, except for very limited purposes. An orderly succession represents in most cases the optimum for intellectual efficiency. A special case is the so-called reversal of the rigid order where the W's always come last; in interpretative significance, this resembles the orderly succession.

2. *Loose and confused succession.* Loose succession is to be found where the mental capacity is not high enough to grasp a logical order fully or where the mental control for maintaining such an order is weakened either through pathological conditions or through emotional interferences. In a confused succession no trace of any logical order remains. Naturally that is only possible where the five approach-categories, W, D, d, Dd, and S, are present in sufficient numbers to permit confusion.

Rorschach claimed to have found this confusion exclusively among psychotic patients. (He mentions as one other sign of confusion the great unevenness in the production of responses to different cards.) We have occasionally found very brilliant, though erratic, normal people whose succession is also confused.

POSSIBILITIES AND LIMITS OF ESTIMATING THE INTELLIGENCE LEVEL

In attempting to appraise the different components offering material for the estimate of the intellectual level, it becomes obvious that no mechanical computation of credit points awarded to these different components will be adequate. This is a clear example of what the principle of configuration, as described in Chapter II, means. The information afforded by each one of the intelligence components must be fitted into a pattern which will give a well-integrated picture, not only of *how well* but of *how* the mind of the subject functions. This "how" is furthermore shown in an action picture of the intellectual aspects of the subject's personality. We see where and in what situations his mind works particularly well and what factors are most disturbing to its functioning.

Is there a possible rivalry between the claims of standard intelligence tests and the estimate of intelligence on the basis of a Rorschach record? It is possible to evaluate a Rorschach record and to "guess," in the majority of cases within a range of ten points, what the intelligence of the subject in terms of a Binet IQ might be; this "guessing" frequently is quite impressive to the uninitiated observer. However, most workers find discrepancies between the intellectual estimates based on Rorschach reactions and intelligence tests more interesting and important than an agreement between the two diagnostic procedures. This is true both for the clarification of research problems and for the typical guidance situation. As a practical example take the not unusual case of a youngster with an IQ of 70 to 80 (borderline intelligence). Has he reached the uppermost limit of his capacity by careful training? Has his intellectual development been arrested at a particular age level? Are his normal intellectual capacities made inefficient by some deep emotional disturbance? The answers to such questions cannot be gleaned from the ordinary intelligence test, but not uncommonly they will be found in the Rorschach record.

CHAPTER
XII

EMOTIONAL ASPECTS OF
PERSONALITY

IN THE light of the discussion at the beginning of Chapter X, it should be quite obvious that the emotional aspects of personality fall into two major areas; namely, the emotional reactions to promptings from within — what one may call the "inner reality" of human experience, or, in short, "inner life," and the emotional ties with the outer reality. The section on movement responses in Chapter IX (page 204) described how these promptings are reflected in the Rorschach material in the various types of movement responses. This chapter, like Chapter XI, serves to summarize the interpretative hypotheses suggested in Chapters IX and X.

EMOTIONAL REACTIONS TO PROMPTINGS FROM
WITHIN

1. *Significance of M.* It is impossible to discuss here the elaborate and intricate theories about M responses (*88, 141*). A few empirical facts and conclusions drawn from them must suffice. M's are rarely found among children up to eight years of age (except gifted ones), among subjects with organic brain disease, among subjects with a very rigid constriction, and among subjects of rather primitive mentality.

It would be foolish to assume that these subjects have no "inner life," especially since it is known how vivid the fantasy is in children up to eight years of age. However, although promptings from within are present in these subjects, they do not produce the personal reactions of awareness, acceptance, or rejection.

The stirrings of the imagination must be realized as a producing part of the total personality in order to become a source of self-satisfaction and a main contribution to a firm and solid balance within the whole personality. It seems, according to accumulated clinical evidence, that only if this stage of integration is reached does imaginative activity lead to the production of M. On the basis of this assumption it is not difficult to understand why M seems to be the indicator of the richness of the inner life, the creative powers, and the acceptance of one's inner promptings — i.e., how much one is at home with oneself.

2. *Relation of W and M.* Understanding the significance of M leads naturally to an understanding of the role M plays in the estimate of the higher intellectual functions. It is clear that $W : M$ is an intra-individual ratio which indicates how well the contact between a rich inner life and mental activity is established. It seems that the same degree of intellectual capacity which enables the subject to produce a certain number of M's can be turned toward the production of W's in approximately twice this number, if the subject is interested in this kind of intellectual conquest. Thus the quotient $W : M$ can be used as an indicator for what may be described as the relationship between drive for intellectual conquest and personal productive capacity to make these conquests substantial.

People with a great predominance of W, say with at

least three or four times as many W's as M's, seem always to be lacking in the best use of their creative or productive powers. They may be people with very one-sided intellectual achievements, if the W's are otherwise rich; or people with a somewhat hollow quality-ambition, if the W's are predominantly popular or noncommittal.

Where the M strongly predominates in the $W : M$ relationship, the subject seems to be inclined to lose himself in his own imagination and to be unable to utilize his imagination for creative purposes. As a working hypothesis it may be assumed that W and M show an optimum balance if the subject has at least five M's and approximately twice as many W's as M's.

3. *Relation of M and FM.* As mentioned above, Rorschach experts, almost without exception, follow Rorschach's lead in excluding animal action from the category M. It seems unreasonable that FM, after having been separated from M, should be included interpretatively in absolutely static form answers. Interest has centered, therefore, on the question of what these responses do represent, granted that their significance differs from that of M.

It now seems quite safe to assume that they represent the influence of the most instinctive layers within the personality, a hypothesis which would explain why children frequently see animals in action though they seldom see human action in their responses to the cards. Naturally it is also easier to see animals in action, since animal shapes offer themselves more readily in all blots. Thus, at a stage of mental maturation where only gifted children are able to see human figures in action, almost every normal child readily sees moving animals.

There is another more decisive and empirical confirmation of the role of *FM*. Invariably, where there is reason from other sources to assume that a subject is emotionally infantile, living on a level of instinctive prompting below his chronological and mental age, the Rorschach record of this subject shows a predominance of *FM* over *M*.

Sometimes it is hard to decide whether an action by mythological figures (like the animals in *Alice in Wonderland*) has the interpretative significance of human action or animal action. Any deviation from the natural habits of animals (boxing bears, for example) may be evaluated as a somewhat hesitant and tentative approach to the more mature level. However, if these fairy-tale *M*'s constitute all or the majority of *M*, the inner promptings seem to have found channels which do not lead straight to reality.

4. *Significance of m.* The meaning of *m*, representing mainly the effect of inanimate forces working upon objects or figures, is most easily demonstrable in its association with abstract concepts, like "forces emanating from the center," "forces whirling around," "lines of power," etc. In such responses the physical picture of these forces seems to be an almost literal reflection of tensions within the personality structure. It may be said that such *m*'s appear where the subject experiences his promptings from within as hostile and uncontrollable forces working upon him rather than as sources of energy at his disposal.

A few such *m*, in conjunction with a far greater number of *M* and *FM*, hardly seem indicative of a real disturbance within the inner life of the subject. Occasionally we are all at odds with promptings from within, without being seriously upset. However, if *m* reaches or outnumbers either *M* or *FM*, then it seems to be a danger signal indicating that these inner conflicts are too strong to permit a close coöperation between the inner and outer life. Observations in several investigations dealing with success and failure in specific occupations led to the impression that the existence of such danger signals is a favorable indicator for occupational adjustment even in otherwise not very stable or well-adjusted individuals.

5. *M, FM, and m.* Adding *FM* to the combination of *M* and *m* results in a further number of interesting variations in the picture of the inner life. In a mature, well-adjusted person it is expected that *FM* will take a medium position between the dominant *M* and the more or less insignificant *m*. Where *FM* is entirely missing, between a fairly well-developed *M* column and an equally strong *m* column, the picture of inner conflict is enhanced, since such a subject seems to be unable to accept his instinctive drives as a working part of his personality.

It is unusual to find a record in which a strong *FM* and a strong *m* appear coincidentally with a very weak *M* column. It seems that the inhibiting forces creating the *m* conflict are incompatible with an infantile domination of instinctive drives.

To give at least one numerical suggestion, a healthy balance between *M* on the one hand and *FM* and *m* on the other seems to be guaranteed where the sum of *FM* and *m* is not greater than one and a half times the number of *M*.

The additional expression *m*'s clearly indicate that some tendency to *M* has been repressed. Since the more usual way of seeing facial expressions or pointing fingers is to imagine the remaining part of the body as present, though invisible, the expression *m*'s seem to represent a superior

— i.e., more adjusted — form of inhibition to that represented by the regular *m*. This justifies their tabulation as additional *m*'s only, thus keeping them from unduly distorting the *M, FM, m* relationships just under discussion.

EMOTIONAL TIES WITH THE OUTER REALITY

The general significance of color responses has been discussed in Chapter IX. A comparatively simple explanation, or rather clarification, may be added. It must be remembered that the form responses were interpreted as an impersonal, aloof approach to the task to tell "what these blots might be." The subject is diverted from this impersonal interest in the shape, outline, or contour of the blots if he notes the manner in which the space enclosed by these outlines is filled in. The affective implications of this "fill-in," whether it is the shading or the color, penetrate into his impersonal concentration on the form as an intrusion from the outside. Many subjects experience this intrusion very vividly. Some are shocked by it, some delighted, some grow increasingly annoyed as these stimuli accumulate. Our hypothesis is that the subject's reaction to the color or shading of the blot reflects closely his general emotional reaction to outer reality.

Bright colors

Naturally the center of interest within this area lies in the reaction to the bright colors. To the majority of all subjects, the gray, black, and white portions of the cards do not represent color at all.

1. *Significance of FC.* *FC* responses (as defined in Chapter VI) imply a complete fusing of form and color.

This means that form as well as color is intended to be definite for the concept chosen, indicating that the subject is open to the emotional stimulus implied in the coloring but is not willing to react to it unless it can be done within the limits of rational considerations. It is one of the best-proved and validated assumptions that the percentage of *FC* indicates the degree of emotional adjustment to outer reality. This emotional adjustment can be accomplished in many different ways and these different ways are all clearly reflected in different constellations within the determinant graph.

Consider, for instance, the personality picture of a "pseudo-extravert" mentioned on page 222. His Rorschach record will produce a graph in which the left side is particularly well developed with an optimal relationship between *M* and *FM*, whereas on the right side of the graph in the area of bright color there will be nothing but a few carefully chosen *FC* responses, unaccompanied by any other kind of color reaction.

A similar unchallenged position of the *FC* in the bright color area may be found in the record of a subject with refined constriction, in which the constricting forces put a stop to the color influences, just after *FC* is included. Such a person feels obliged to be nice to other people in a reasonable way, but would never permit himself a more impulsive emotional reaction.

The emotional adjustment expressed in loose or forced form-color combinations $(F \leftrightarrow C)$ impresses one as being less personal, less full-bodied, than in the genuine *FC*. This form of adjustment seems to represent a merely social or superficial emotional adjustment as distinguished from a true emotional adjustment.

An *FC—* combination is a natural beginning in the course of personality development. Children as young as two years of age are able to see apples or cherries in the red spots of Card II, but beyond the preschool level such rational laxity may not be accepted as an expression of normal adjustment. From five years of age upward, any single *FC—* response must arouse strong suspicions about the efficiency of the emotional adjustment.

2. *CF and C.* There are several aspects of the emotional significance of *CF* and *C* responses which must be considered.

(1) *Significance of CF.* The *CF* combination is used by approximately as many people as is the *FC* combination. In it the consideration of rational elements is not altogether abandoned but the emotional stimulus has assumed a dominating role. Thus, all *CF* responses represent more impulsive emotional reactions than *FC*. However, it must still be investigated whether this impulsiveness is a destructive or constructive force in the individual personality.

(2) *CF and CF—.* The first way of determining the character of the impulsiveness is to investigate the form quality of *CF* responses. If the form quality is just noncommittal, as in responses like "tapestry design" or "deep-sea life" to Card X or "flames" for the red spot in Card II, an unfavorable type of impulsiveness cannot be assumed without further investigation. If, however, the impulsive color reaction has a destructive effect on the form concept — as, for instance, in a response to

Cards II or VIII like "cross sections with blood" accompanied by an unsuccessful attempt to identify the cross-sectional part of the body — this usually indicates an emotional confusion (in the example mentioned it is related to sexual conflicts and takes the form of a confused body consciousness). In such cases the color stimulus is so strong that the subject overlooks the obvious form qualities of the blots.

(3) *Significance of C/F*. *C/F* responses, like *k* responses, represent a feeble attempt to hide confusion intellectually, but in a more extraversial form than *k*. Like *k*, furthermore, *C/F* reflects an attempt to show off scientific interests.

(4) *Color description (C_{des}) and color symbolism (C_{sym})*. Color description and color symbolism responses represent a way of dealing with the color stimulus which technically belongs to the pure color responses, since the outline or shape of the blot is completely irrelevant to them. However, in their psychological significance they belong to the *CF* combination, since the impact of the pure color effect is mitigated by some rational element.

Whereas color descriptions such as the response "water colors" are mostly found among artistically inclined subjects, color symbolism is more frequent in subjects who are at odds with their own strong inclination to react to emotional stimuli from without.

(5) *FC and CF*. This relationship bears a close parallel to the relationship between *M* and *FM*. In order to represent a balanced picture, the *CF*

should not outweigh the *FC*.   However, there are more possible compensations for a lack of balance between *FC* and *CF* than there are for the imbalance between *M* and *FM*.   In cases in which the number of *M* is greater than the sum of *FC* and *CF*, there is no cause for worry lest the impulsiveness of the subject create trouble.   It may, rather, represent the free and natural responsiveness of an inwardly well-balanced person.

Prerequisite for these checks and counterbalances is, naturally, that the *CF* themselves do not belong to the negative *CF* combinations just mentioned.   It is easily understandable that a combination of unchecked predominance of *CF* over *FC*, with predominance of *FM* over *M*, gives the most unfavorable picture (except when found in children below eight years): a mixture of infantilism and lack of control.   If in addition to these symptoms there is a weakening of the form quality by color and signs of anxieties and unsuccessful inhibition (*K, m*), the worst type of hysterical behavior may be anticipated.

(6) *Color naming* (*C*n).   The pure color reaction (*C*n), excluding color description and color symbolism, can safely be called a pathological phenomenon.   It appears mainly in two forms: in the form of crude pure color associations and in color naming.

There is no difficulty in distinguishing color remarks of normal subjects from the reaction of a paranoid schizophrenic who persistently, in all five color cards, enumerates all the color nuances he can discover and refuses to do anything else with the cards. In the latter case the color enumeration seems to have an almost magic function. The emotional stimulus implied in the color represents a deadly enemy threatening to break into the carefully isolated inner world of the patient, engulfing him in the dangerous whirlpools of reality relations which he cannot master.

(7) *Crude pure C.* Reactions like "blood" or "fire" given indiscriminately to any red or pink spot in all ten cards, or like "sky" or "water" to any trace of blue, reveal that the last remainders of a rational permeation have been extinguished in the emotional reactions represented by such responses. They are very rare; most frequently they have been found in records of hebephrenic schizophrenics, and in epileptic dementia.

Achromatic colors

The significance of achromatic color responses has been discussed in Chapter X (page 243).

Texture responses

The nature of the texture response has been sufficiently clarified in Chapter X in the section on the *Fc* combination. It remains to discuss undifferentiated responses and the configuration in which texture responses appear.

As mentioned before, a plain texture reaction without a complete fusion with form — such responses as "wool," "cloth," "cotton" (mainly to Cards IV, VI, and VII) — indicates an absence of adequate control of contact impulses (see page 134). Whether the sensation represented in texture responses indicates a gross sensuality or a general sensitiveness or just a somewhat hazy desire for contact depends mainly on the configuration in which *c* responses appear.

Both texture and C' responses may be considered as an intermediate category between form and bright color which can serve two purposes: they may serve as shock absorbers for too strong emotional stimuli from without, or they may facilitate a still broader influx of impressions.

1. *Texture as shock absorber.* Three conditions can be observed which establish Fc, c, and C' as shock-absorbing qualities: ambiequality or slight extraversial predominance; signs of modified constriction; and predominance of $(Fc + c + C')$ over the sum of all bright color responses.

2. *Texture as further outlet for emotional responsiveness.* Characteristic of this role of texture responses are strong extraversial predominance, preponderance of CF over FC, and a predominance of all bright color reactions over $(Fc + c + C')$.

Whether such a configuration represents a highly differentiated artistic personality or someone entangled in his own sensuality depends on the intellectual level and the stabilizing function of the inner life.

Color dynamics

The heading "Color dynamics" has been chosen to describe the dynamic effects of color instead of the traditional term "color shock," for two reasons. First, *color shock* describes only the negative reactions to the color stimuli, whereas, interpretatively, strong positive reactions are just as revealing as strong negative reactions. Second, even within the area of negative reactions the term "color shock" is too narrow and one-sided. Reactions such as shyness, avoidance, and confusion have usually all been subsumed under the general term "color shock," which seems a rather inappropriate use of this term.

1. *Succession of color stimuli.* As mentioned in Chapter X, the succession of color stimuli within the ten cards is of prime importance. Most subjects are rather surprised by the sudden appearance of a red and black mixture in Card II. In Card III the disturbing or exciting red recedes more into the background. Then the bright color seems to disappear altogether. There are four cards in succession without a trace of it. Next Card VIII appears, colored all over. The colors themselves are not very striking, but are hard to reconcile with the forms. The situation in Card IX becomes very confusing for many subjects because the colors grow more intense; they are not as neatly separated as in Card VIII, but mix themselves freely, and one cannot find such obvious forms as the animal shapes on the side of Card VIII. The situation changes again in Card X. It depends very much on the subject whether this is a change for the better or worse. The conglomeration of color explodes like a rocket into a great many separate color details, and the colors grow even brighter. If they are used, they make it easy; if not used, they make it very difficult to form a *W* concept for this card. The objective features of this succession of color stimuli produce all the possible nuances of color reaction and color "shock."

A few examples may be cited. One subject may be surprised by the color effect in Card II, giving impulsive reactions, like "menstruation," "exploding volcano," and 'flames," and then catch himself and avoid the color persistently, till in Card X he finally finds a few chances for careful form-color combinations.

Another subject with a more elastic defense may limit the color effect in Card II to the red hats on top of the two clowns, controlling the emotional responsiveness through inner stability. Proceeding from Card III to Cards VIII, IX, and X, he becomes more and more daring and free in the use of colors.

Other subjects avoid the "hot" red spots in Cards II and III altogether, but then cannot help being affected by the avalanche of color in the last three cards. Here, again, the elasticity of defense is an important factor. Some subjects avoid the pink color just as much as the red, but are able to use green, blue, or yellow in some form combinations — e.g., "blue flags," "yellow flowers." Others cannot even afford to go that far and retreat to black, gray, and white.

2. *Differences in readiness to react to color.* Occasionally finer nuances may be observed in the general readiness to accept color stimuli. Any attempt to explain the pink color of the side *D* in Card VIII represents a more than usual striving for emotional adjustment. Solutions like "a polar bear in the sunset" or "changing chameleon" demonstrate a considerable effort to use color. To call these animals "foxes" because they are red is a simple but less-refined solution.

By far the easiest opportunity to find at least one form-color combination seems to be offered by the inner green spots in Card X. However, the caterpillar usually seen there is not always determined by color. A subject who refuses even there to acknowledge any influence of color on his responses certainly evidences an extreme reticence toward emotional entanglements. This reticence may be expressed in the inquiry by rationalized explanations denying the color, such as, "because caterpillars are brown and not green." Another rationalized denial was offered by a thirteen-year-old boy who had called the whole Card X "marine life," definitely denying that the color had any influence on his answers. When, in testing the limits, he was asked whether these green spots couldn't be caterpillars, he unhesitatingly answered, "No, caterpillars couldn't be in the water."

APPENDIX TO PART THREE

At the end of Part Three, an attempt seems in order to make the interpretation procedure more concrete by means of a sample case. In Part Two it was comparatively easy to describe the various scoring problems which the beginner is likely to encounter in a detailed and specific fashion (without, at the same time, creating the illusion that the scoring is a mechanical and foolproof procedure). In Part Three, on the other hand, it was impossible to furnish such specific and definite guides. It is not possible to say, "If you find conditions *a, b, c,* and *d* in a Rorschach record, you are dealing with personality *x*." As pointed out repeatedly in Part Three, the interpretative significance of any scorable element in a Rorschach record depends on the structure in which this element occurs. The theoretical reasons for this situation have been discussed in Chapters II and X; practically, these reasons boil down to the fact that every human personality whose structure we seek to discover through the Rorschach method is unique. All the interpretative suggestions discussed in Part Three can only point the way to the discovery of such a unique personality picture; they help to make the beginner familiar with the material from which all these structures are formed.

SAMPLE ADMINISTRATION AND INTERPRETATION

The following sample record of a young married woman 23 years of age was not selected as a routine or average case. On the contrary, so much consideration for fine points and minute elaborations is quite rare. However, these rare features afford an unusual opportunity to illustrate a great number of the scoring and interpretation problems discussed in this book.

291

ADMINISTRATION

Introduction and instructions

Examiner. You know what a "blotto" is; you put ink on a piece of paper, fold it and rub it so that the ink spreads, then you open the paper and see what picture you have.

Subject. Oh, yes.

E. The pictures on these cards which I am going to show you are such ink-blot pictures. They do not really represent anything. They are accidental blottos. All you have to do is to look at them one by one and tell me what they might be, what they could represent for you. People see all sorts of things in them; I would like to know what you will see. You understand that there is no question of right and wrong. There are also no other rules or regulations. You can take your time.

S. But what can you see in the results if there is no right and wrong and no credit for doing it quickly?

E. You see, this is a game which everyone can play in his own way because there are no rules and no conventional ways of doing it. The individual differences, the various ways in which people go about this job, is what we are interested in. We call this a projective technique, because everyone projects his own way of doing things into this task.

(The subject, the wife of a psychologist, was somewhat interested in the theoretical aspect of the procedure. However, similar questions are asked by subjects with various backgrounds and may be answered in a similar way, merely using a somewhat different terminology.)

The record of performance proper and inquiry

Actually the inquiry follows the complete performance for all ten cards, but it is reproduced here in the manner in which most Rorschach administrators record it, alongside the responses to which the inquiry information refers. The first part of the inquiry was directed to the exact location of all the responses. During the performance the subject had indicated the use of a great number of unusual and at times very small areas. Since the subject impressed the examiner as an unusually careful and explicit individual, she was asked to mark these unusual areas on the picture sheet herself, always first pointing them out on the cards. The result of this procedure is reproduced on the Location Chart which has been inserted between pages 306 and 307. The numbers of the responses were always written after the picture sheet was turned in the position in which the response was seen.

As a rule the questions and remarks by the examiner are not included in a record. They are included here in order to illustrate the technique.

RECORD
CARD I

PERFORMANCE

30 seconds

1. Looking at it this way, right side up, I see two Teutonic knights up here facing each other.

INQUIRY

Examiner. Now that you have indicated where you have seen the knights, I should like to know something about what it was in the cards that made you think of them.

Subject. I thought of knights because of the shape of these humps which are their heads. They reminded me of pictures of armor made of woven metal mesh.

E. Was it just the shape that reminded you of woven mesh?

S. And the shading here.

E. Is there anything more about these knights?

S. This looks like an upraised gauntlet.

E. Do you see their feet?

S. They stopped approximately here, the feet are not clearly outlined.

CARD I (*Cont'd*)

2. These seem to be some sort of animals, at the top corners.

2. *E.* What kind of animals could they be?
S. They are more like Scotty dogs than anything else.
E. Will you point out its main parts?
S. Here is the head and the ear. It is cocked.

3. Here I see a profile.

3. *E.* How much of the profile do you see?
S. I see a pointed nose and an eye. The mouth is not distinct. It is one of those chinless people. It could be a woman with her hat perched way forward.

4. And here might be a lion lying on its back. That's all.

4. *E.* What reminded you of a lion?
S. Here is the lion's head, the mouth is somewhere in there, this is the mane (outline features). I got a feeling of feet upright. I didn't get a definite outline for its back.

Total time for card: 3 minutes.

CARD II

PERFORMANCE

Y

10 seconds

1. Two battling bears.

1. *E.* What in the card gave the impression that they are battling?
S. They didn't seem to be passive and the front paws seem to be pushing.

CARD II (*Cont'd*)

E. Where are the faces?

S. I didn't see faces, I got a feeling of bodies rather than faces. Feet and front paws.

E. Show me the rest of the body.

S. This is the back and they are standing on hind legs, leaning back on hind legs and pushing forward with front legs.

E. Was this part of it?

S. No, none of the red was.

E. What made them look like bears rather than dogs?

S. The clumsiness. It gave me the feeling of massive animals.

E. Was it anything besides the shape?

S. A dog wouldn't be upright, a bear can walk like a man.

2. Sideways it might be a pig. A boar, a wild pig of some kind.

2. E. How much of the pig do you see?

S. (points). Face, snout, tail, leg, back, ear.

∧ 3. This, of course, is a shellfish of some kind. Lobster or something like that.

3. E. What gave you the impression of a shellfish?

S. The shell and the tentacles.

E. Can you see the shell?

S. It is the darker red portion.

E. What made the darker red portion look like a shell?

S. I dont know. Perhaps the difference in color gave me the feeling of this being more solid and this not.

∧ 4. Here within the design I see very faintly something that might be a little mouse. Just the eye and the vague outline of a body.

4. E. How much of the mouse do you see?

S. This is the eye and the front of the face. Just the general outline, not specific.

CARD II (*Cont'd*)

5. Here is a very dark cat at night, also a vague outline.

5. *E.* How much of the cat do you see?
S. Particularly the head and whiskers. Right eye, and this is the front leg, the general figure and because it is night I can't see very clearly.
E. Now a funny question: Do you see the night too, or is it only because the shape is not clear?
S. Night because it is dark. Impression of black on black.

< 6. This is some sort of long — here's an eye — some weird outlandish thing. No particular animal that I can identify but there is the eye and the back.

6. *E.* Show me the weird animal.
S. This is the eye and this is some sort of overhanging horn. Pointed chin and there is the back, and that's all I see.

Examiner. You know you needn't force yourself to see many things. The number of things you see doesn't count.

Total time for card: 3 minutes.

CARD III

PERFORMANCE

2 seconds

< 1. Two footmen bowing to each other.

INQUIRY

1. *E.* Show me the footmen.
S. They are very clear. Leg, body, head, arm, etc.
E. What made them look like footmen?
S. The stiffness. They are bowing, bent over, the shape of the black gives the feeling of a uniform.

2. Little animals falling through the air with their tails streaming behind them.

2. *E.* Would you think the animals alive or dead?
S. Alive, it seems to be resisting the fall.

CARD III (*Cont'd*)

∨ 3. These are two arms, hands reaching toward each other

3. *E.* To whom would the arms belong?
S. They are apt to be a woman's rather than a man's because they are slender and the sleeves are rather tight-fitting.
E. Could you say of what material the sleeves are made?
S. No.

4. This is an animal's head and eye.

4. *E.* Show me the animal's head.
S. Here is an eye and a nose. It gives the feeling of a bull more than anything else.
E. Could you tell what gives that feeling?
S. It has a fierce expression and the shape again.

5. This looks like a sheep.

5. *E.* First you saw this part as a sheep and then as a bear. What was the difference?
S. I saw the sheep when I held the card upside down. Here are the feet, the front and back legs. The woolly outline.
E. Only the outline?
S. Well, the whole feeling is like wool but more the outline than anything else.
E. And the bears?
S. I held the card right side up. I still see the head, the legs, and so on, but somehow this way it is more like a bear.

6. This looks like a mask down here with two eyes in it.

6. *E.* Is this any special kind of mask?
S. No, just a black kind of half-mask.

7. This could be a mouth.

7. *E.* Is the mouth human or animal?
S. Human.

CARD III (*Cont'd*)

E. Do you see only the mouth or part of the face?
S. Only the mouth.
E. The opening or the lips?
S. A closed mouth, a cupid's bow.

∧ 8. These might be a pair of very, very plump roosters, or maybe pigeons, with plump little bosoms.

8. E. What made you think of these as roosters?
S. The comb effect here.
E. The shape?
S. The shape and the jaggedness of line.
E. Nothing else?
S. No — and the fact that the color is slightly lighter than the rest.

9. What I thought was a sheep now looks like a bear.

9. (See response 5 above.)

10. Here's a man's head, a profile.

10. E. How much of the profile did you see?
S. Nose, mouth, and chin. I don't see the back of the head specifically, I just inferred it.

Total time for card: 2 minutes.

CARD IV

PERFORMANCE

INQUIRY

15 seconds

∧ 1. It looks to me like a country boy in overalls leaning back in a rocking chair, reading, with legs in larger perspective. This is his chin.

1. E. What is it in the card that makes you think of a country boy?
S. As opposed to a city boy? This wrinkled part looks like overalls. And the clumsy feet.
E. Where can you see wrinkles in the trousers?
S. In the outline and in the dark and light.
E. What in the card made you think he was reading?
S. The upper part looks as though he is holding a newspaper.

CARD IV (*Cont'd*)

E. How much of the hand do you see?

S. I don't see the hand specifically. I just get the feeling from this part.

E. Do you see the arms?

S. Again not specifically. I feel that they are through here.

E. Did you use this portion? (Upper side extensions.)

S. No. I sort of felt that was part of his chair but I didn't —

2. This could be a barking dog, a wolfhound maybe, just the middle of the body to the head.

2. *E.* What made this look like a wolfhound?

S. The length and the slenderness of the head and this is something like the fur of a wolfhound. It is fluffy.

3. A pair of ladies wearing bustles and long skirts facing each other.

3. *E.* You said these two women were facing each other. What did you mean by that?

S. They were on opposite sides of the card.

E. Do they have anything to do with each other?

S. No, they just seem to be placed there — still figures.

E. Do you see their hands?

S. Not specifically. They seem to be here because of the outline but the entire getup makes me feel that they are wearing long flowing black garments and this might be a shawl so you don't see their hands. (Tendency to live posture.)

4. Here's a leaping snake.

4. *E.* Do you see the whole snake?

S. No. I don't see it end, it might be any length.

5. And here's a profile with a pointed nose.

5. *E.* Show me the profile.

S. There is the nose, and there is the hair in the darker part.

CARD IV (*Cont'd*)

6. Another profile of an old man.

7. Here are some very shadowy — looks like a dog's face, full face, right in there. It looks very much like a dog I once had.

Examiner. You remember that you don't have to go on looking for things.

Total time for card: 2 min. 30 sec.

6. *E.* And the profile of the old man?
S. Chin, eye, eyebrow. I don't see the back of the head. Here is the mouth.

7. *E.* Do you see just the face of the dog?
S. Yes. The eyes and the mouth. It looks fluffy.

CARD V

PERFORMANCE

5 seconds

1. Here are two little gnomes facing each other wearing tall hats.

2. Here is a profile.

INQUIRY

1. *E.* Do you see the whole gnome?
S. This is the head. I get the feeling that they stop here. I don't see the lower part as distinctly as the upper.
E. What did you mean by "facing each other"?
S. The faces are here and the bodies here.
E. Do they have anything to do with each other?
S. No, no action.
E. Do you see their arms?
S. No.

2. *E.* How much of the face do you see?
S. Mouth, nose, eye, front of hair, chin. It leaves off in back again. It looks like a rather smiling face because of the shape of the mouth; the lips are parted.

CARD V (*Cont'd*)

3. And here is another profile.

    3. *E.* What about the next face?
      S. Front of head, eyes, nose, no definite chin, very snub nose. Could be tragedy and comedy masks in theater.

4. And here is one, a grotesque one.

    4. *E.* Tell me about the third profile.
      S. Here is the chin, the mouth, and the nose, quite grotesque.

5. This is the neck of a chicken or some such bird, very elongated.

    5. *E.* Is this neck part of a live chicken?
      S. Yes. If a chicken could stretch its neck so far.

6. This looks like a woman's leg kicking out.

    6. *E.* What gave you the idea that the leg was kicking?
      S. Because it seems to be jutting out from the rest of the figure and at the angle a woman's leg would be if kicking in a dance.

∨ 7. Again I see snakes: snakes' heads rising.

    7. *E.* Do you see the whole snakes?
      S. No, only their heads rising.

> 8. This looks like the nose of a wolf, pointed—just very vaguely.

    8. *E.* Did you see only the nose of the wolf?
      S. Yes.

∧ 9. Of course the total picture is a butterfly of some kind.

    9. *E.* What made you call this a butterfly?
      S. Just the outline.

Total time for card: 2 minutes.

CARD VI

PERFORMANCE

5 seconds

1. Here is a butterfly, across there.

INQUIRY

1. *E.* Is it anything besides the shape that makes it look like a butterfly?
   S. No. Oh, yes, the difference in coloring, light and dark.

CARD VI (*Cont'd*)

> 2. These look like little dogs burrowing into sand. The heads are not there but the tails and the backs of their heads are visible.

2. *E.* You explained that you saw the tail and the back of a dog. Do you see the sand?
S. Because I couldn't see the head I assumed a soft substance.
E. Is it especially like sand?
S. No, it is just that the action made me think of it.

3. Here are two very tiny human faces.

3. *E.* Do you see only the faces?
S. Yes.
E. Is there anything else about them?
S. In the one on the right I see the hair differentiated and the face lighter.

4. And here are two little mice.

4. *E.* What in the card gave you the impression of mice?
S. Their shape, like small animals. Mice have that general proportion. Also a feeling of crawling that mice have.

∧ 5. This is—the woolly texture makes it look like a sheep. The shape isn't exactly like it but here is a mouth. Maybe it is a polar bear.

5. *E.* Why did you change from sheep to polar bears?
S. I thought of sheep because of the woolliness but the shape is more that of a polar bear, and the woolliness too, I guess.

6. This looks like a doll's head, or dummy's head, something made of papier maché, very stylized, back to back.

6. *E.* Do you see only the heads of the dolls?
S. Head and bust.
E. What gave the impression of papier maché?
S. The shading and the doll-like quality.

7. Here I see little bugs.

7. *E.* What made this seem like bugs?
S. Just that it looks like a cluster of figures.

Total time for card: 3 minutes.

CARD VII

PERFORMANCE	INQUIRY
2 seconds	

1. These are cats leaping in the air, tails up.

    1. *E.* Show me the cats.
    S. Head, ears, tail, front, and back. They seem to be crouching the way cats do.

2. There is a human profile.
3. There is another.
4. And here is another.
5. And here is another. They are all different. This one looks rather stupid and this one looks like a funny-paper character. It isn't a person — just a sketch of a person.

    2, 3, 4, 5. *E.* Did you see more than the profile in any of these?
    S. No, I didn't see the backs. (These profiles are considered four separate responses because they were pointed out separately during the performance with no attempt to combine the series of profiles into one interpretation.)

6. These are two heads facing each other, talking. Might be gossiping women.

    6. *E.* What made you say the women were gossiping?
    S. The open mouths and the expression. They look as though they are talking, the fact that they are close together.

7. This looks like a pig's head. Here is the snout, eye, ear, back.

    7. *E.* You made the pig clear before.

8. This might be a bat flying with big wings.

    8. *E.* You saw a bat here; was there anything batty about it?
    S. The fact that I saw wings and I didn't feel it was a butterfly and the size of the wings. It is not a bird because of the size of the body in proportion to the wings.

Total time for card: 2 minutes.

CARD VIII

PERFORMANCE	INQUIRY
3 seconds	

Oh! this is —

1. These are climbing bears. I see a lot of animals.

    1. *E.* Did you have any special reason for calling them bears?
    S. The shape.
    E. Anything else?
    S. No.

CARD VIII (*Cont'd*)

2. This is a little fish, the little pink thing.

2. *E.* What made these look like fish?
S. Also the shape, the contrast of the pink and the blue made me think of something swimming in water.
E. What made you think of water?
S. The blue color.

3. This again looks like a shellfish with the head showing outside the shell.

3. *E.* Here you saw a shellfish.
S. The darker orange is the shell, the lighter orange is the head.

4. This is like the head of an Egyptian figure, something in stone.

4. *E.* What kind of figure is it?
S. A dog's head.
E. What gave the impression of stone?
S. I think the shading, the fact that it is very light, and the outline is not very fuzzy. (The way shading is used almost implies a rejection of the surface value.)

5. Here is a face, eyes.
6. Another face. This one has a mouth.

5, 6. *E.* Are these human faces?
S. Just sketches of faces, perhaps ghosts. Just two eyes cut into something.

7. Here is a profile facing up. Here is the hair.

7. *E.* What made it look like hair?
S. The fact that it was darker.

8. This is a small figure of a woman, the head reclining, or sitting—lounging.

8, 9. *E.* You made the woman and the dog clear before.

9. And this is like a lap dog sitting at the woman's feet, his head is on a level with her hand, she is feeding him.

10. These might be two fish swimming down to the bottom of the sea, they look as if plunging through space and the water looks as if it is in motion.

10. *E.* Show me the fish.
S. Their heads are right here. They are moving down and leaving a trail as fish would through water. The shading in the pink looks like bubbles.

CARD VIII (*Cont'd*)

11. Here again is a butterfly. I guess that's all.

11. *E.* What made you think of a butterfly?
S. The shape, the feeling of two wings, and the shading secondarily.

Total time for card: 4 minutes.

CARD IX

PERFORMANCE

INQUIRY

5 seconds
Oh, my!

1. These look like a couple of witches making incantations over a caldron.

1. *E.* Do you see the caldron?
S. Yes. This is the handle.

< 2. This looks like a cow's head. The eyes have a mild expression just like a cow I saw yesterday.

2. *E.* Besides the eye does this have any other characteristics of a cow?
S. The general shape but mostly the eye.

> 3. This is an idiot child with tongue hanging out.

3. *E.* What made this look like an idiot?
S. It's the tongue drooling.

∨ 4. This is a clumsy animal, head forward. That is its leg. It could be a lion from the shape of the head.

4. *E.* The animal is not clear; did you see the tail?
S. This would be the tail; it is crouching, I don't see the hind legs.

< 5. This looks like a very fierce head, the sort of thing you see in pictures of the devil. Open jaw looks as if it is going to devour something, to come forth with fire. Here are the eyes.

5. *E.* Is he actually devouring something now?
S. No, his mouth is open in a ferocious manner.

∧ 6. This looks like some sort of little animal, there are the eyes.

6. *E.* Do you see only the head?
S. No, the whole body. I am looking at it from the top, so I don't see the legs.
E. What kind of an animal is it?
S. I don't know.

CARD IX (*Cont'd*)

E. Is it big or small? What kind of skin has it?

S. It is not large, it wouldn't have long hair. I don't know.

< 7. This could be a squirrel.

7. E. Then you saw a squirrel?
S. Here it is, its tail up, ready to jump.

8. This could be a bone of a skeleton with little bones branching out.

8. E. Is this any specific bone?
S. No, it looks as a bone would look in a laboratory. Just a bone.
E. Is it a human or an animal bone?
S. I can't tell.

Total time for card: 3 minutes.

CARD X

PERFORMANCE

INQUIRY

5 seconds

My, oh, my!

∧ 1. I get a general impression of all kinds of squirmy animals.

1. E. You said you had a general impression of squirmy animals. What gave that general impression?

S. I think the different colors gave the impression of small areas; if it were dark I might have seen a large picture. Also the fact that they are relatively small compared with the other cards.

2. Two frogs.

2. E. Can you tell me anything about the frogs?
S. No, they're standing on their hind legs. I see an eye on this one and a front leg reaching out.

3. A couple of—what is it that has tentacles? a jellyfish—no, an octopus.

3. E. This was an octopus?
S. Just an octopus.

4. Snakes.

4. E. What kind of snakes were these?
S. I see the eye. No special kind.

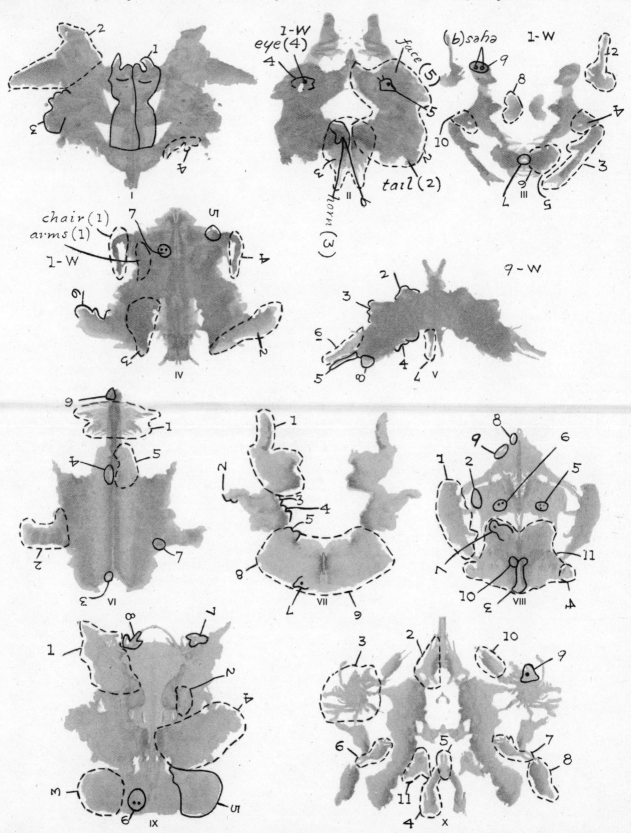

CARD X (*Cont'd*)

5. Also a rabbit's head. Ears.

5. *E.* The rabbit is clear.

6. Sort of a mouse, but the legs are in the wrong place.

6. *E.* What made you think of a mouse?
S. The general shape.
E. Just the shape?
S. And the eye.

7. This might be a horse pawing the ground, two front legs and the body out of proportion.

7. *E.* You made this clear before.

> 8. And this is a crouching— again I guess a pig. A pig is the only kind of animal that has this sort of short snout. It is lying down, crouching on front legs.

8. *E.* Did you see the whole animal?
S. Here is the head and the snout, the light part is the snout, it even has two nostrils.

∧ 9. In here the head of a unicorn. I guess that is a mythical animal but I have seen pictures of them. It resembles the horn.

9. *E.* Do you see only the head of the unicorn?
S. Yes.

10. Here are some sort of leaping little animals, this green.

10. *E.* You said green animals leaping. Why green?
S. I meant to identify the portion.

11. Here is a dog, the kind of poodle that has a big ruff around the neck and the body shaved.

11. *E.* What gave you the impression of a ruff?
S. The body is narrow and the width gave me the feeling of a ruff.

12. Wishbone of a chicken. That's all.

Total time for card: 3 minutes.

TESTING THE LIMITS

E. The only time you made use of the bright color was in the blue water. Is that correct?

S. Yes, I think so.

E. If I were to ask you to use the color, what would you do?

S. I keep seeing the things I saw before.

E. For instance, couldn't you use the color for the snakes in the last card?

S. No, I would have seen them as snakes no matter what color.

E. Can you find anything in which the specific color fits?

S. These might be lizards.

E. Now can you find some other things like that anywhere in the cards? For instance, how about the mice (in Card X)?

S. Yes, they are gray-brown, mouse color. And with the footmen (Card III) the black color, I think of uniforms in somber colors.

E. Here (Card III) you mentioned the "comb effect"; aren't combs red?

S. Yes, they are.

E. Could you accept this as a fitting color?

S. Yes.

E. But you did not think about it before?

S. No.

E. Is it the same with the shellfish?

S. Yes.

E. If you wanted to go out of your way to use color—

S. I think there are shellfish which are red—shrimp?

E. What was your feeling about color in general?

S. It helped differentiate areas.

E. Did you feel the need to use it?

S. No.

INTERPRETATION

The record represents the reactions of a "normal" subject (without a clinically manifest neurosis), of superior intelligence and with marked wariness about emotional entanglements and rather marked overemphasis on control. It is neither feasible nor important to go into the life history of the subject. On the other hand, the record lends itself in an unusual way to pointing out the interrelationships between the various layers of interpretative information. As a form of "clinical validation" the following interpretation was submitted to the subject and her husband and was accepted by both in all details.

The general personality structure

1. *Control.* One glance at the graph picturing the distribution of the determinants shows the overemphasis on control mentioned above. This overemphasis is almost evenly distributed over the various control functions. The F percentage is somewhat over 50. There is no main and only one additional response in the bright color area, and there is a considerable number of M responses.

The preoccupation with form elements pervades the record to such an extent that in many instances inquiry as to elaboration was unnecessary. Where the most detailed information about the various elements in a response was not given spontaneously in the performance, it came forth with no effort and with loving devotion after the first question in the inquiry. The use of shading as an expression of a refinement of this constrictive control is not emphasized. However, there are some main and more additional Fc. In general, her use of texture can be described as somewhat reluctant, but very careful. The subject used reasoning based on form details even in answers to "alternative questions" designed to bring out the use of other determinants (e.g., Card I, Response 2).

The reaction to bright color will receive more detailed discussion later. Here it may suffice to point out that there is no evidence of shock, but a very consistent disinclination to use color.

SCORING LIST

Card No. and Number of Response	Time and Position	Location Main	Add	Determinant Main	Add	Content Main	Add	I—U Main	Add
I (30")									
1	∧	dr		M+	Fc	H			O+
2		D		F+→	FM	A			
3	∨	d		F+		Hd			
4	(3')	dd		FM+		A		O	
II (2")									
1	∧	wx		FM+		A		P	
2	<	D		F		A		P	
3	∨	D		Fc		A			
4	∧	di		F		Ad		O	
5		di		FC'+	K	Ad		O	
6	< (3')	dr		F		A			
III (2")									
1	∧	wˣ		M	FC'	H		P	O+
2		D		FM+	Fm	A			
3	∨	D		M+		Hd			
4		d	S	F	m	Ad			
5		D		F→	Fc	A			
6		D		FC'		Obj			
7		S		F+		Hd		O+	
8	∧	D		F+	Fc	A			
9		D		F→	Fc	A			
10	(2')	de		F		Hd			
IV (15")									
1	∧	w		M+	Fc	H			O+
2	∨	dr		FM+	Fc	A			
3		D		FC+→	M	H			
4		d		FM		A			
5	<	dd		F+	Fc	Hd			
6		de		F		Hd			
7	∧ (2'30")	di		Fc		Ad		O	
V (5")									
1	∧	d		F+		(H)			
2		de		F+	M	Hd			
3		de		F+	m	Hd			
4		de		F	m	Hd			
5		dd		F		Ad		O	
6		d		M		Hd		O	O
7	∨	d		FM		Ad		O+	
8	>	dd		F+		Ad		O	
9	∧ (2')	W		F		A			O+

Card No. and Number of Response	Time and Position	Location Main	Add	Determinant Main	Add	Content Main	Add	P—O Main	Add
VI (5")									
1	∧	D		F→	Fc	A			O+
2	∨	d		F→	Fc	Hd			
3		dd		F+		A			
4		dr		Fc+		A			
5	∧	dd		Fc		(Hd)	-		
6		dd		F		A			
7	(3')								
VII (2")									
1	∧	D		FM+		A			O
2	> ∧	de		F		Hd			
3		de		F		Hd			
4		de		F		Hd			
5		de		F	m	Hd			
6	∨	dr		M+		Hd		O+	
7		dd		F+		Ad		O+	
8	(2')	D		FM		A			
VIII (2")									
1	∧	D	D	FM	CF	A		P	O
2		dd		FM	Fc	A			
3	∨	dr		F+	Fc	A			
4	<	d		F	Fc	(Ad)		O	
5		di		F	Fc	(Hd)		O	
6	.	di		F		(Hd)		O+	
7	>	dd		Fc+		H		O+	
8	∧	dd		M+		H		O+	
9		dd		FM+		A		O	
10		dd		FM	K	A	Water	O	
11	(4')	D		F	Fc	A			
IX (5")									
1	∧	D	S	M		(H)			
2	<	D		F	m	Ad			
3	>	D		F	m	Hd		O	
4	∨	D		FM		A			O+
5	<	dr		F+	m	Hd			
6	∧	di		F+		A		O	
7	<	dd		FM+		A		O+	
8	(3')	dd		F		At			
X (5")									
1	∧	W		FM		A			
2		D		FM		A			
3		D		F		A		P	P
4		D		F		A			
5		D	S	F		Ad		P	
6		D		F		A			O+
7		D		FM+	Fc	A			O
8		D		FM+		A		O+	
9		dd		F+		Ad			
10		D		FM		A			
11		D		F+		A			O+
12	(3')	D		F		Aobj			

Above is a reproduction of the Scoring List for the individual whose record appears on pages 293–308. The Tabulation Sheet and Determinant Graph for this individual are reproduced on the opposite page. The Scoring List, Tabulation Sheet, and Determinant Graph are pages 2, 3, and 4, respectively, of the Individual Record Blank; they afford a convenient means of summarizing the record preparatory to making the interpretation. See also page 183.

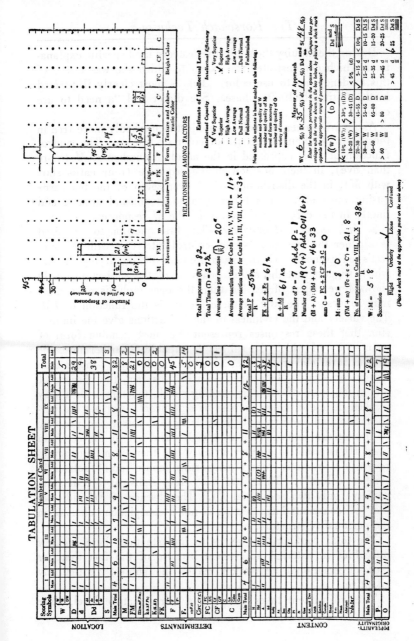

During the inquiry the subject repeatedly used specific explanations which demonstrated the extent to which she was aware of this tendency not to use color. This is most clearly illustrated in the testing-the-limits phase. She didn't feel "a need to use color."

As regards inner control, the subject is markedly more free in the use of *M* than in the use of color or texture. The control function of *M* is expressed in the absolute number of *M* (more than five), in their position in the sequence (four cards start with *M*), in the distribution of *M* over seven of the ten cards (using most of the usual but also some unusual areas), and finally in the careful elaboration of the *M* responses.

2. *Adjustment and maturity.* The first question to be raised is whether the overemphasis on control interferes with the subject's adjustment. There are a number of modifying factors which suggest that the actual behavior of the subject probably shows fewer signs of tension than the overemphasis on control may suggest. The first of these factors is the function of *FM*. The variety and the vividness of the *FM* actions give the impression that these responses represent the most genuine form of spontaneity of which the subject is capable. Furthermore, the careful form elaborations reveal a "loving devotion" rather than tension or strain. In connection with this fact, the absence of any crude form of color or shading shock, together with a very marked degree of color shyness, is significant. During the performance and inquiry only blue is used. Under the pressure of testing the limits, green is added. The red of the comb in Card III is admitted only reluctantly and there is a tendency to revert to achromatic color ("gray-brown mouse" and "footmen in somber colors"). There are very few signs of free-floating anxiety (only two additional *K*). The absence of *FK* indicates that self-conscious introspection is not a conspicuous element in the personality structure.

The total configuration seems to indicate that there are few difficulties in external adjustment because of the fact that her lack of emotional aggression makes the subject particularly adaptive.

This adjustment takes place on a fairly mature level, since

there are more than five M. However, there are certain limitations, which will be discussed in the two following sections.

3. *Erlebnistyp.* The one-sided introversial picture conveyed by the M : sum C relationship does not reveal the full story. In spite of the reluctance to use color, and in spite of the underemphasis on D, the last three cards produce at least their share of responses, indicating extraversial capacities which the subject does not use. The $(FM+m)$: $(Fc+c+C')$ proportion, which also shows an emphasis on the movement side, nevertheless holds a middle position between the M : sum C proportion and the proportion of responses to the last three cards.

This configuration indicates that the subject in all probability will always live in a more introversial way, but at present has reached a point where the extraversial development supplies a better counterbalance for the introversial inclinations than heretofore. (The subject has been married for less than a year.)

Intellectual aspects of the personality

1. *Manner of approach.* The manner of approach expressed in the distribution of W, D, d, and Dd clearly reflects a very cautious person, intent on observation of minute details.

The use of W's is most underemphasized. There is no W in the first card. Cards II, III, and IV begin and Card V ends with W. Then the W's stop, as they frequently do in records of persons who have this cautious approach. Finally, and surprisingly, one appears in Card X. Most of the five W's are well elaborated, but the W's are not the most interesting or original responses in the record.

The reluctance to use this more daring mental approach is most clearly revealed in the W : M relationship. The intellectual capacities revealed in the eight M and in the general intellectual level to be discussed below could produce between ten and twenty W's (sixteen W's represent the theoretical balance to eight M). The lack of drive in the direction of W construction represents a lack of intellectual aggression, which corresponds to the lack of emotional aggression expressed in the absence of any need to use color. The capacities indicated in the relatively high number of M seem to be used mainly in imaginative play rather than in creation, and this imaginative play is probably accompanied by some degree of self-preoccupation.

D also is underemphasized, though not so much as *W*. This may indicate that the careful attention to detail characteristic of the subject's general approach may not always be directed to the obvious but boring details of everyday living. However, this slight neglect is counterbalanced by two factors: the number of *P* indicates a readiness to think along the lines of other people; the even distribution of the *D*'s over the ten cards (about half in the first seven and about half in Cards VIII to X, corresponding to the distribution of all possible *D*'s) indicates that "common sense," the regard for the obvious, is always present, even though not particularly emphasized. It is interesting to note in this connection that the most obvious response is sometimes the last response to a card, as in the "butterfly" to Card V.

The nine *d*'s, representing the expected proportion, fit smoothly the general trend to small and unusual details. The rather even distribution of the 38 *Dd* among all kinds of *Dd*'s reaffirms the fact that her preoccupation with minor elements seems to be the outgrowth of a normal inclination rather than a neurotic limitation.

2. *Estimate of the intellectual level.* The number and quality of *W* has been discussed. So has the number of *M*. Their quality will be considered further in the next section. At this point it suffices to state that they definitely indicate superior intellectual capacities. The outstanding factor contributing to the intellectual level is the form accuracy level (33 of the total responses are designated by $+$). There is not a single response in the record with an indefinite form concept. Every main determinant is either *F* or a combination of *F* with another determinant.

The 19+11 original responses add a new aspect to the intellectual picture, especially since they form a strange contrast to the 61% animal responses, and to the fact that only three out of the 82 responses are outside the human and animal sphere: the mask in Card III, the bones in Card IX, and the wishbone in Card X.

The succession is between orderly and loose.

The combination of these various factors produces the picture of a person with superior intelligence which is being used within a very limited range of interests. However, within this range the subject shows an unusual capacity to add her personal touch to what she thinks and does.

Emotional aspects of the personality

A careful comparison of the 8+2 *M* and the 21+1 *FM* reveals an interesting picture of the subject's inner life. The action depicted in the *M* responses is characterized by restraint: bending, sitting, standing, etc., or only part of the body is seen in action, like the "kicking leg" in Card V. In some rather obvious cases such as the two gnomes in Card V the *M* is denied. On the other hand, a great many of the *FM* responses show an unusual vividness and there are no *m*'s to indicate a real conflict in the attitude to the self.

This configuration must be interpreted in the following manner: There is a definite lack of self-assertion which takes the form of timidity and shyness rather than of acute tension. The free expression of *FM* furthermore adds a great potential wealth of warm affective expression.

The fact that eight of the ten cards start with either *M* or *FM* indicates that the imaginative activity as such is not inhibited. It is only limited to rather submissive channels of expression.

The picture of the inner life serves to modify the significance of the rather extreme lack of color responses. It was emphasized earlier that there is probably no lack of adaptability and that the subject is at the point of becoming more outgoing than she has been in the past. The proportion of achromatic to bright color responses in this case in probably less an expression of specific traumatic experience than of a general timidity. This timidity is more an expression of her personal form of development than of a neurotic disturbance.

PART FOUR

CHAPTER
XIII

CLINICAL DIAGNOSIS

IN a section on the use of the Rorschach method in clinical diagnosis in a book of this type, one is faced with the difficulty of selecting sufficient material to be of value while, at the same time, excluding controversial problems. Also, since it is impossible in a work of this sort to give clinical information sufficient to enable one who is not trained in this field to do practical work, this section will be of value primarily to the medically trained professional worker or to those readers who have had extensive experience in clinical psychopathological fields.

There is no doubt, however, that an understanding of the peculiar characteristics occuring in the Rorschach reactions of various clinical groups will yield a much better understanding of the method itself. In this section, therefore, an attempt will be made to limit the clinical material in so far as is possible and to emphasize only those Rorschach factors which are based on known facts and which demonstrate the effects of various types of pathology upon the Rorschach reactions of the patient. It will also be necessary to include a somewhat more careful discussion of the literature than in the preceding parts of this book.

We shall not, however, attempt in any way to make an exhaustive survey of this material, but rather limit ourselves to those publications which represent, in our judgment, major contributions to the clinical field.

From the literature and our clinical Rorschach experience we shall attempt to indicate Rorschach patterns which are more or less characteristic for particular types of disease entities. It is obvious, of course, that one not familiar with both clinical material and current nosology should never undertake to make more than a simple personality description from a Rorschach record. It is extremely dangerous to attempt to translate such a description into diagnostic terminology with which one is unfamiliar, just as it is to make actual clinical diagnoses without any knowledge of psychiatry or neurology.

On the other hand, however, it is important for Rorschach workers coöperating with clinicians to have a general knowledge of the field so that they may better know for what to look in the Rorschach material and so that they can present to the clinician the most significant parts of the data for his use in establishing a clinical diagnosis.

In discussing the problems of clinical diagnosis with the Rorschach method, the usual problems inherent in differential diagnosis in any medical field arise. To begin with, certain types of Rorschach responses occur which, as a rule, appear only in specific disease entities. These are the so-called *pathognomonic* signs, whose appearance originally was assumed to indicate that a particular disease was undoubtedly present. Recent research has demonstrated that, while many of these responses are usually pathognomonic, none of them is limited exclusively to one single clinical entity. This is particularly true of some of the so-called schizophrenic signs, which have now been found to be present in preschool children, and of the so-called "organic" signs, which also occur in deteriorated cases of dementia praecox. There are, of course, methods of differentiating the Rorschach records of normal children from those of praecoxes and "organics," particularly by the use of combinations of responses.

These response patterns, or combinations of individual signs, have been described for many disease entities. It is obvious, of course, that the more extreme the disease under consideration, the more marked will be the pattern. In such cases the Rorschach is of little practical value because clinicians have little difficulty in diagnosing such cases by cursory studies. There is, however, marked research value in determining these patterns, since such comparatively uniform and constant Rorschach responses give us valuable clues as to the structural conditions underlying the clinical behavior. Furthermore, longitudinal case studies utilizing repeated Rorschach records, extending over a period of years, are particularly important in studies of personality disintegration or deterioration. Skalweit's studies on schizophrenic processes (*313*), or long-range studies during psychonalysis as conducted by Oberholzer, are examples of this type of research.

Therefore, as we progress beyond the single sign, supposedly pathognomonic, we find that most clinical entities produce general constellations of Rorschach responses which typically reflect the personality structure of the patient under scrutiny. We are then likely to find many signs which may indicate a general clinical condition and which may appear in most cases of a given type.

Such signs have been described for intra-cranial brain-damage cases, patients with dementia praecox, and other broad classifications of psychopathology. In any pattern of clinical signs it is obvious that certain reactions will be much more important than others, and in following discussions we shall attempt to give both the general picture and a further analysis of the signs to indicate those which are most important from a diagnostic viewpoint. A quantitative validity is not to be expected from studies of these general signs, since, clinically, all that one may hope for is that a majority of patients showing the signs will be found to possess the disease entity in question and, conversely, that the majority of patients not suffering from the disease entity will not show these Rorschach responses. It must be emphasized, therefore, that there is a grave danger of misusing such general Rorschach patterns by blindly applying them as diagnostic criteria without considering other qualitative factors and extenuating interrelationships which may be present.

From a differential diagnostic point of view the absence of such general signs is as important as their presence. In making a clinical diagnosis the clinician must weigh both the evidence at hand and also the so-called negative evidence, or findings which are not present. This negative type of diagnosis is most useful in the application of the Rorschach method. Frequently a number of signs which point in the direction of perhaps two or three clinical entities will be elicited. A careful reëvaluation of the record will then reveal that other findings, which are expected if a certain diagnosis is predicated, are lacking. Clinical experience tells whether the signs already present are sufficiently marked to lead one to expect to find these missing signs. If, according to the clinician's judgment, they should be present but are not found, the suspected pathology can be ruled out.

In other words, the signs that are not present must be evaluated in terms of those already elicited. Should those already found be sufficiently severe, the absence of other signs, usually found concomitantly, must be considered as strong evidence as the presence of the positive pathological responses.

In addition to their use in diagnosis, such sign patterns are of some value in statistical studies and are particularly useful in research projects. The distribution of such findings in specific constellations may lead us to a better understanding of many clinical entities. For example, Rorschach studies on dementia praecox to date have strongly indicated that the hebephrenic and catatonic types are much more closely related than other types — a clinical point which has been under consideration for many years.

By utilizing the methods of clinical diagnosis, realizing the limitations of general patterns, evaluating the strength of individual signs, and correlating quantitative estimates with qualitative elements, Rorschach diagnosis can be made extremely accurate and of tremendous value to the clinician.

CHAPTER
XIV

INTRACRANIAL ORGANIC
PATHOLOGY

ALTHOUGH Rorschach described a few cases of intracranial pathological conditions, most of the work in this field has been done since his time. In this chapter an attempt will be made to organize this material, which is widely scattered throughout the literature, and to correlate it with clinical and pathological findings. The term "organic personality" has been used by many workers in this field to indicate an individual suffering from actual intracranial structural brain changes. This use of the term is poor because it simply indicates a *general* disease entity and does not point to an intracranial lesion. Throughout this book whenever the term "organic" is used it is meant to indicate specific *intracranial damage*. This latter use is much better and should be employed in preference to the loose and meaningless "organic damage."

In considering the problem of the Rorschach diagnosis of intracranial brain damage we shall discuss, first, the general signs indicative of personality changes resulting from cerebral disease; second, certain Rorschach findings occuring in frontal-lobe pathology; third, those signs indicating post-traumatic brain damage; and, finally, the few known facts about other types of intracranial pathology.

Piotrowski (*257, 268*) described ten signs which, he felt, differentiated patients with cortical and sub-cortical pathology from other groups of patients. He suggested that the presence of any single sign meant little but felt that if five or more of the signs were present the patient being studied was undoubtedly suffering from brain damage. These findings, however, are not completely confirmed in Nadel's study (*239*) in which are reported subjects with tumors in other areas than the frontal lobe who showed fewer than five of the Piotrowski signs — two showing only three such signs, two only one sign, and one no sign at all.

Piotrowski felt that his ten signs occurred with any type of intracranial disease but in his early work did not attempt to localize the lesion. It is important, however, in the practical use of these signs to remember that the Rorschach method is a method for studying the personality of an individual and is not a technique designed to localize pathology of the central nervous system. One may reasonably expect that there might occur in the brain discrete focal lesions which would not produce any personality change and consequently would not be disclosed by the Rorschach method. On the other hand, discrete lesions, if accompanied by changes in intracranial pressure or cortical function, may produce personality deviants which can be interpreted by a study of the Rorschach responses. Ross (*287*) suggested that Piotrowski's signs, as first delineated, are not entirely reliable, as they may occur in varying degrees with temporary disturbances of the nervous system, and that their significance is psychological rather than clinical. This is an obvious conclusion flowing from the fundamental concepts of the Rorschach method; clinical interpretation is necessarily based on the personality configuration portrayed by the responses. These signs do, however, if present, point to a severe disturbance of the personality. It can also be accepted that, if certain of these signs do occur, there is a strong probability of the individual's personality having been upset by structural changes.

Harrower-Erickson (*108*), in a study of cerebral lesions, concluded that the location of the lesion is not an important factor in Rorschach responses and that the outstanding characteristics of records of patients with tumors are uniformity and constriction. She made graphs showing the distribution of the determinants which she felt were of value and verified Piotrowski's findings in most of her cases, although she also found some intracranial tumor cases in which only two or three signs occurred.

In considering the localization of intracranial lesions one would be most amazed to find any Rorschach personality pattern pointing to a lesion in any specific area of the brain, with the possible exception of the frontal lobes. A study of patients with intracranial tumors preoperatively, even with coöperation of the patient, may be of little value in determining the personality effect of the destruction of any specific area in the brain unless an unusually discrete tumor is found.

It seems safe to conclude that most intracranial endogenous lesions will disturb the normal physiology of the brain to a degree great enough to result in personality changes which will be evident in the Rorschach responses, even though the responses will not indicate the localization of the lesion. This would also be true of post-traumatic states where the pathology is usually widespread, and of

certain postoperative conditions, particularly those involving surgical procedures in the frontal lobe. Finally, as
Rorschach himself pointed out, the generalized damage
resulting from arteriosclerotic changes, paresis and other
infectious processes, senile states, atrophies, etc., would
be clearly reflected in the Rorschach record.

Conversely, we would not expect to find such personality changes occurring in discrete cerebral lesions. We
would expect to find in such cases few or, perhaps, no
indications in the Rorschach of the presence of small localized tumors, tiny scars, or localized centers of atrophy or
infection. This assumption is borne out by the work of
Harrower-Erickson (*109*), who, in studying focal epilepsy, found that no one typical personality was present
and that psychoneurotic manifestations and all varieties
of mental approach might occur.

As Putnam (*273*) has pointed out, the concomitant
changes in most types of intracranial lesions are apt to be
widespread. If the Rorschach is skillfully administered
and interpreted, the tiny personality shifts resulting from
the organic changes will be elicited and demonstrated in
the great majority of cases. Frequently, in fact, these
minute personality deviations are easily seen in the
Rorschach findings, in many instances even before they can
be determined by clinical study, as shown by Piotrowski
and Kelley (*271*), and others. For this reason the
Rorschach is an important adjunct in the diagnosis of
intracranial organic lesions and, as such, may offer important corroborative support to clinical findings or may,
by itself, offer leads for other diagnostic procedures. It
should be utilized by the neurologist and neurosurgeon in
exactly the same way that X-rays, spinal fluid findings,

and other techniques are employed—to complement clinical findings and not as a specific diagnostic agent by itself. Finally, the Rorschach record may also be of value in estimating the amount as well as the direction of the personality deviation and may give useful data for prognosis, as shown by Harrower-Erickson (*108*) and Piotrowski (*266, 269*).

Let us now turn to the actual Rorschach findings and attempt to correlate them — with some suggested refinements — with what is known of the neurophysiological and psychological changes occurring as a result of intracranial lesions. We may begin with a study of Rorschach findings resulting from known intracranial pathology and take up a discussion of the general signs occurring in all intracranial lesions, particularly in intracranial neoplasms. These general Rorschach indications of cerebral lesions are applicable not only to brain tumors but also to diffuse arteriosclerotic diseases, demyelinating pathology, and other generalized organic structural changes. As a rule, the more extensive the pathology the more obvious the Rorschach signs. We would expect, therefore, to find brain tumors, when unaccompanied by increased pressure, giving us the fewest symptoms, while advanced stages of senile dementia and arteriosclerosis yield more abundant signs.

Looking at the general configuration of cerebral lesions, we may note first the findings of Harrower-Erickson(*108*). She described the general picture as being restricted and constricted and usually showing (1) a poor output; (2) a W to D to d to S proportion too heavily weighted with W, and without an adequate number of clear precise forms; (3) a percentage of F responses higher than normal; (4) a poor range of psychic reactivity — i.e., a more constricted and uniform personality structure (M : sum C barely 1 : 1); and (5) absence of K and FK throughout. This general picture was obtained in 28 cases of patients with tumors of the brain and, in general, seems to hold for most tumor cases. It is, however, not at all specific for intracranial lesions in its general picture of constriction, since constriction may occur in normals, depressives, the feeble-minded, and certain neurotics. The poor output, poor W and $F-$ responses, of course, do not occur in normals, neurotics, or depressives. Mentally deficient cases can easily be distinguished by the presence of large numbers of $F-$ responses and oligophrenic details.[1] Although the shading responses, K and FK, did not occur in any of Harrower-Erickson's records, certain shading responses are present in intracranial lesions, particularly in the post-traumatic type. Earl,[2] who has studied many cases with intracranial lesions, considers the absence of FK the most unvarying and valuable sign in differentiating doubtful cases. These responses will be discussed later. In general, the configuration described by Harrower-Erickson is merely a summation of effects and indicates the probable nature of a record of a patient with an intracranial neoplasm. In work with individual patients it is not to be taken too specifically, but, rather, as a general configuration acting as a guide.

The most important method for general diagnosis of in-

[1] This response, described by Rorschach and scored *Do* (Oligophrenic detail), is indicated when the subject sees only a part of a figure usually seen as a whole. The heads of the men in Card III, or the feet in the same card, seen as independent details without seeing the men, are examples of such responses.

[2] Personal communication to the writer.

tracranial lesions was offered by Piotrowski in a series of studies (*257, 259, 268*) describing his ten signs.

His sign "*R,*" meaning that the number of responses is not more than 15, indicates the inability of the patient with structural brain pathology to synthesize details and wholes into a large number of responses. It is not an important finding, as it occurs with depressives, neurotics, mentally deficients, and normals and is merely one of the lesser indicators. The same may be said of the sign "*T,*" indicating an average time per response of more than one minute. This is more valuable than the "*R*" but less valuable than other signs. The sign "*M,*" indicating that the number of movement responses is no more than one, is an important sign, although it too may be found in neurotics, schizophrenics, depressives, feeble-minded, and normals. Human movement responses may also occur in large numbers (three or more) in post-traumatic cases, general paresis, encephalitis, and cases with post-traumatic damage to the frontal lobes, in which the personality changes are slight.

The "*F+%*" sign,[3] which indicates that the percentage of good form responses is below 70, is important only as an accessory sign, for it may also occur among mentally deficient, schizophrenics, and excited patients. Combinations of good form and poor form responses may represent deterioration but are also common in dementia praecox. The "*P%*" sign, which indicates that the percentage of popular responses is below 25 per cent, has been modified by Piotrowski, who feels that the percentage of popular responses need not be computed if the total number of re-

---

[3] See footnote on page 234. It was necessary to use the *F +* symbol in its traditional sense in Part Four, since this Part summarizes literature in which the *F +* symbol is so used.

sponses exceeds 25. In long records $P\%$ ceases to be useful because of the limited number of popular responses.

The color-naming (C_n) sign, indicating that the record contains at least one color denomination, is, if properly elicited, one of the most important findings in the entire series. This C_n designation, as described in an earlier chapter, is assigned to a response if the response is considered satisfactory by the patient although it contains only the name and description of a blot — e.g., "Red, this is a red spot and here is a black one," or "This card has lots of colors — here it is green and here orange and here pink." In all these responses the blot is not used except for its color value, to which the proper name is given, and in every case the subject is satisfied that this is a response and that he has given a sufficient amount of effort toward its determination. It is particularly important to differentiate this response from the responses of neurotic and superior normals with artistic trends who frequently give responses mentioning the colors but without actually considering them adequate responses. They may describe a card as "like a daub of paint" (C_{des}), or may simply enumerate the colors, but only as an enumeration, not considering it a response; for example, they may offer such statements as "These colors are orange, green, and pink, and this mixture is not artistic," or "This red color is impossible; it has no meaning to me," or, "I don't like this red color; it is a horrible shade." In these cases the patients are either describing the card in a casual sort of way or are showing their inability to utilize the color and eliminating it by the process of mentioning it. However, the color naming in these instances is not given as a simple declarative statement in which naming is the only element involved, as it is in the responses of "organics."

From empirical findings it appears that this color-naming sign is very important. Experimental studies (*167*) revealed that during acute alcoholic intoxication, where there was reason to suspect the existence of some temporary organic disorganization, 50 per cent of the cases showed color naming, whereas no cases at all showed it previous to the intoxication. Recent work by Lowenbach and Stainbrook (*214*) in post-electric-shock states has confirmed this impression. These authors, working with confused patients immediately after shock treatments, discovered a high proportion of color-naming responses which tended to disappear as the confusion cleared. From this study, together with the alcoholic study mentioned above, it seems fairly definite that the color-naming sign indicates mental confusion and represents a reversible temporary process. This sign, then, if it occurs in the true organic fashion, may be considered one of the most important indicators.

The remaining four signs are all equally important and are qualitative signs which in many cases must be elicited during the inquiry or in testing the limits. The first of these is repetition (*Rpt*), standing for the repetition or perseveration of the same response to several ink blots. If three similar responses are given in a record without regard to form, repetition may be scored. It is important to note, however, that should some sudden change in the structure of the cards occur — as, e.g., the appearance of color in Card VIII — a repetitive process begun in Card VI may be stopped. Perseveration may also occur in some cases of dementia praecox, but in this type of perseveration the praecox patient, having a fixed idea, utilizes the actual form of the card more frequently and attempts to mold the perseveration to the card. In the organic perseveration, the differences among the individual cards seem to matter little to the patient. The patient seems to feel compelled to respond to each card rather than keep silent, and repeats an earlier response which may have no correspondence to the card in question.

The next sign, impotence (*Imp*), indicates the giving of a response in spite of the recognition of its inadequacy. Here the patient understands the inadequacy of the response but is unable to withdraw it or to improve it. Examples of this impotence are, "Here, I think, may be a reindeer (for the orange area in Card IX), but a kind of sick-looking reindeer." These responses are given by normal patients and neurotics. Piotrowski (*268*) felt that impotence should be scored only in the presence of repetition or perseveration. Impotence may occur, however, even without perseveration, and in the organic patient it represents the futile clinging of the patient to any response, even when he knows the response is inadequate. In neurotic responses simulating impotence, the responses are usually accurate, but are simply not good enough for the neurotic's overemphasized desire for accurate form. Here we have the rejection or qualification of an acceptable form simply because it does not come up to the patient's impression. Impotence in the organic patient indicates his realization that the response is essentially poor and yet that he is unable to do anything to improve it.

Perplexity (*Plx*) is associated with the distrust of one's own ability and a request for reassurance. Here the patient recognizes his own incompetence but seeks reas-

surance from the examiner. The patient shows four
specific symptoms: (1) marked interest in the result obtained; (2) a complete lack of ability to decide for himself whether or not this result is adequate; (3) a need for
reassurance from the examiner to indicate that he has
performed his task well; and (4) satisfaction or frustra-
tion according to whatever he is told about his performance. Perplexity is essentially a modification of impotence on a deeper level, in that the perplexed patient by
himself is unable even to offer an opinion regarding his
response, whereas in impotence he is at least able to realize
that the response is poor. Schenck (*300*) felt that these
two signs, *Imp* and *Plx,* are most important and point to
cerebral organic lesions even in the absence of all other
Rorschach organic signs. These two signs do not occur in
healthy adults, but they do occur in a certain percentage
of neurotics with very profound personality disturbances
— *Imp* in about 8 per cent and *Plx* in about 2 per cent.
In addition, an even greater percentage of neurotics will
offer responses which simulate impotency and perplexity,
but which, in reality, are only comments regarding the
responses or a general request for reassurance.

The last sign, automatic phrases (*Ap*), has been described by Oberholzer (*241*), and is scored when the patient uses a phrase in an indiscriminate fashion. The
phrase may be complimentary, as "That is good," or the
patient may state with each card, as he receives it and before he looks at it, "I cannot say anything about it," or "I
do not know what it is," or he may routinely, as he gives
the card back, state, "That's all I can say. These are very
hard. I do not understand them." Every individual studying the cards may give an occasional phrase such as these,

but they do not persist in giving them for card after card. If the same automatic phrase is given for over half of the cards, it may be scored. If it occurs without the patient's troubling to note whether such a phrase is reasonable or not, it is almost pathognomonic of an intracranial lesion.

In concluding a discussion of these specific signs, it must be pointed out that they may not necessarily be expected to appear in patients under the age of eighteen, because, as suggested by Piotrowski, age has a specific effect upon the incidence of these signs. Many of the signs, as M and $F\%$, may occur normally in children, but signs such as perplexity and impotency are based upon a mature viewpoint which is not developed in children.

Piotrowski also emphasized the fact that it is advisable to adhere to the specific definitions of the signs and, when in doubt, to leave out a sign and not score it. If there are less than five signs found, no specific diagnosis can be made. However, if the signs present include among them color naming, perplexity, impotence, or automatic phrases, a suspicion of organic cerebral disease is certainly justified, regardless of the number of other signs present.

Occasionally a few cases which are not organic will show more than five signs. In some of these cases the signs are falsely produced by the occurrence of anatomical perseveration as described by Ross (*285*). In this type of perseveration the patient in practically all the responses gives only a description of parts of the body. If this performance takes place, Ross's suggestion that the test be readministered, with a request that the patient see things other than parts of the body, should be followed. If this is done, it is quite probable that the true picture will be discovered. The only other usual type of case in which

five or more possible signs may be found is the deteriorated dementia praecox patient. In these records — and
they are rare — the qualitative aspects, which must always
complement the computation of the signs, will determine
the diagnostic decision. It is tempting to speculate upon
the similarity of organic brain disease and schizophrenic
records, but discussion along this line is beyond the scope
of this book.

The qualitative aspect of these findings may be somewhat more clearly indicated by a discussion of lesions of
the frontal lobes. Here no evidence of absurd ideas is
found and only a few of the signs described above may
occur. Certain other fine discriminatory differences may
be elicited, one of the most important of which is the inability of the patient to compare reliably parts of the ink
blots with parts of animals or objects or whatever may
have been projected into these ink blots. This inability
was described by Piotrowski (263); it can be elicited only
by a careful inquiry. The patient is unable to show the
correspondence between blot and concept — i.e., he may
give a general response, but when a careful inquiry is
made, will demonstrate an ability to respond only to the
outstanding details of the situation and will not be able to
justify the response by describing the smaller, less important details. Such patients are, however, capable of
visually separating details from wholes; i.e., they can see
details or parts of blots where more advanced cases can
see only crude whole responses. Another important
characteristic of these patients is the utilization of their
total ability in the original administration. These patients are always coöperative and attentive, try to do their
best, and seem to realize that they are unable after effort

to improve their responses. This is most easily observed in the testing-the-limits period, and it is particularly valuable to utilize a specific routine for this phase of the administration. First, after the inquiry is finished, the patient is told that there are certain other responses which will occasionally be suitable and that the examiner is interested in knowing what he thinks about them. The cards are then shown and the popular or commonly seen forms, or other forms of a level equivalent to the patient's, are mentioned. These are not outlined to the patient, but he is asked to find them. For example, if he has not seen the usual figures in motion in Card III, the card is shown to him with the remark, "Some people see two figures, perhaps human-like figures possibly dressed in evening clothes, bowing to each other. Can you show them to me?" Occasionally these patients will be able to see some of the more obvious whole responses but will be unable to pick out any of the more complicated responses, as the bears in Card II or the worms or rabbit in Card X. After this procedure has been carried out, the patient is shown the cards again and the responses not yet found are outlined in the cards. He is then asked whether he can now see them and if so, what he thinks of them. In almost every example these organic patients are unable to show how a suggested interpretation fits the ink blot or to locate a suggested form if it is not pointed out. When the form is finally outlined, they are unable to utilize it and cannot accept intelligently the suggestions offered by the examiner in regard to responses which they themselves have not originally given.

All other types of patients, except certain cases of dementia praecox, are able in some way to describe in detail what is seen and, if suggestions are given, are generally able to utilize them very well. Cases of dementia praecox may not agree to suggestions made but will generally be able to employ them. However, some cases of schizophrenia, as described by Kelley (*166*), may also show this sign. Organic cases will merely agree in a vague sort of way and will usually state that it is a poor idea and that it is not well seen. These findings suggest the general conclusion that the patient is probably incapable of analytical reasoning and cannot think on an abstract level. This impression is suggested by Piotrowski (*263*) and is in accordance with the belief of Weigl (*369*), who felt that in cases of cortical damage the essential difference between the normal adult and the patient in sorting cardboard figures of different colors and forms was revealed when they were asked to arrange the material a second time or, in other words, to shift them around. The normal subject could classify on the basis of color or form with little difference in difficulty. The patient, having adopted one way of classifying, could not voluntarily shift to another. This ability to shift an attitude is associated with abstract behavior.

These signs both for general intracranial pathology and pathology of the frontal lobes are of course not specific for any one etiological agent. The brain-tumor group, on the whole, will more often show the constricted configuration described by Harrower-Erickson, but in general, until further refinements of the method are delineated, it is better merely to recognize the fact that there is intracranial pathology and leave it to the clinician to determine whether this pathology represents an intracranial tumor, a hemorrhage, or a deteriorating process.

There is, however, one group of cases of intracranial pathology which shows very definite trends in the Rorschach; these are the cases of post-traumatic brain damage. Here it is necessary to differentiate, as did Schilder (*367*), neuroses occurring after head injuries, other traumatic neuroses resulting from injuries elsewhere in the body, and post-concussion syndromes. True post-traumatic neuroses may develop after head injuries as a result of the production of certain changes in the cerebral mechanism facilitating the neuroses, and because of the specific psychological value placed upon the head. They may occur in cases without obvious organic impairment or in cases with marked organic defects in which persistent dizziness, headache, and vasomotor instabilities encourage the neuroses, In the purely psychogenic types, organic Rorschach findings do not occur and the neurotic findings are pronounced. In most cases, however, there are some findings which point to organic damage with concomitant neurotic findings, and these clinically represent neurotic manifestations superimposed upon actual cortical damage. Finally, signs of deterioration resulting from diffuse organic brain damage without prominent neurotic components may occur. All these conditions can be differentiated by the Rorschach technique.

Post-traumatic cases in general show a great number of unusual details, or they show a number of confabulatory whole responses. Oberholzer (*242*) felt that these wholes, which are poor responses, have the same symptomatic value as rare details and are really not interpretations. Oberholzer stated that, if the percentage of unusual details is not greater than 25, only slight effects will be found clinically. Cases with clinical evidence of moderate damage show up to 32 per cent unusual details, and 50 per cent or more of rare details are found only in traumatic or Korsakoff psychoses. Among the normal population these rare details comprise only approximately 6 per cent of the total responses. In cases in which there is a large number of poor whole responses this percentage will not hold.

The second important finding is the large number of pure form responses, many of which are poor. In addition there will appear considerable disturbance in the succession, some pure color responses, and a very definite increase in the shading responses. The shading responses are believed to indicate depressed, irritated, anxious moods, and may contain elements which are gruesome and threatening. These responses, somewhat similar to the so-called *Hd* responses of Binder, are usually of a diffuse type utilizing the shading in a vague sort of way (K) in combination with some perspective, or they may include some surface shading (c) with again a sense of distant perspective. Such responses appear, for example, in Card IV, which "looks like a body — a furry body, and you could see around the back of it," or in Card I, which "is something like grass tangled here, you know the way it is when you look down through the water at the bottom of a river where the fish are." Clouds, X-rays, smoke, and other responses bordering on K are very common. This particular type of shading response is practically pathognomonic of post-traumatic cases if it occurs more than two or three times, and its elicitation is most important. From the psychological point of view, taking it to represent feelings of inadequacy or free-floating anxiety, its appearance would be expected in such cases of post-traumatic head injury.

Finally, in post-traumatic cases color shock is common. While it may always be taken to represent neurotic elements, it may occur in cases of post-traumatic brain injury, frontal-lobe damage, encephalitis, or dementia praecox. It has never been known to occur in manic-depressive psychoses. The color shock occurring in cases of organic brain damage and post-traumatic injury represents neurotic components of the personality, but in these cases it is a vague, indefinite, and indistinct type of color shock as compared to the precise disabling shock of neurotics. The differentiation of the color shock is important, for in a post-traumatic hysteria without observable evidence of brain damage the color shock will be of the neurotic variety, and in the same sort of patient with organic damage it will be of the organic type. Color shock has been well described by Brosin and Fromm (49); its presence in organic cases is comparable to the catastrophic reaction described by Goldstein (364). Clear-cut neurotic color shock is demonstrated by an increased reaction time for the color cards, exclamation of newly aroused emotions with comments by the subject indicating anxiety, tension, and stress at the color cards, decline in number and quality of responses and irregular succession on the color cards, an impoverished content of responses or rejection of the color cards, a decreased ability to see popular configurations on these cards, and absence of color-determined responses in individuals otherwise able to use color.

Brain-damage cases demonstrating color shock may show time prolongation and decrease in the F accuracy.

They may also show some crude color responses or color naming. They would not show, however, the intense psychological upset indicated by anxiety, tension, exclamations, rejections, and dislike of these cards. These are neurotic findings and the organic shows his color shock only by a decrease in form, a prolongation of time, irregular succession, and crude color responses. These organic patients may also show shading shock, but only as a rule when the neurotic element is more pronounced than the organic one. In some cases, of course, the neurotic symptoms may be so conspicuous as to overshadow the evidences of active organic brain disorders. This condition, however, is important to diagnose, and hence the method is of great value in these cases. The Rorschach is also particularly valuable in differentiating between conversion hysteria and compensation neurosis, in that the latter usually shows little color shock and the former will show a decrease in form. Compensation hysterias will show a greater number of anatomy interpretations. Both syndromes can be differentiated from mixed organic neurotic cases by a lack of the organic signs.

Malingering in these cases can also be determined by the Rorschach method by reëxamination. In cases of malingering the Rorschach psychograms of retests of a subject will generally disagree. Psychograms of coöperative subjects are practically identical unless the personality undergoes a definite change between testings. In this consideration it must be borne in mind that the organic type of color shock is characterized by its inconsistency and may vary markedly on retesting. Malingerers, however, show no true organic signs. Also they can be discovered during the inquiry and testing the limits by their

capacity to improve and by the suggestion of certain answers with the indication that these are expected responses.
In retesting, the malingerer, unless he is actually an expert
in the method himself, will invariably include these responses regardless of their applicability, whereas a patient
with true organic damage cannot utilize them at any time.

Rorschach findings in the other organic fields are not
so well worked out. Cases of encephalitis are characterized by the presence of movement responses, uncertain
and inadequate form structure, perseveration, confabulation, a predominance of color responses, oligophrenic
details, and an $F + \%$ [4] between 50 and 70, together with
disturbed succession and marked variation between successive tests. This variation from test to test occurs primarily in these cases and is a particularly good method
for their diagnosis in obscure cases. Variation within a
single test — i.e., the giving of very good answers together
with a number of very poor answers — may occur particularly in cases of general paresis, certain types of epilepsy, and some brain tumors. Rorschach pointed out
certain signs for late organic, psychotic pathology, including senile states, arteriosclerosis, and Korsakoff psychosis; cases of Pick's disease have been described by Piotrowski (*258*) and Sanders, Schenk, and Van Veen (*292*).
In cases of gross organic damage the "organic signs" will
occur with constant regularity and in sufficient number to
make the diagnosis an easy one.

These late cases are of value, however, in that they
furnish leads pointing to the correlation of the Rorschach
findings with the actual psychological changes occurring
in the patient. Studies by Klopfer and Tallman (*198*)

[4] See footnotes on pages 329 and 330.

of Brickner's case and Piotrowski's case of Pick's disease are especially valuable here. In cases with lobectomies or gross organic structural damage to the frontal lobes, the crude color responses, color enumerations, and color naming may indicate the confusion of these patients in relation to the environment and represent the emotional lability and instability which occurs so frequently. The deterioration of intellectual functions with memory loss, lack of concentration, and inability to think clearly are represented by the low F accuracy, low $P\%$, increased reaction time, and few responses. As the patients deteriorate, automatic phrases become more frequent, just as do repetition and perseveration. The small number of M responses can be correlated with this intellectual deterioration, and the general constriction in the personality can be related, to a certain extent, to personality changes described in the patients. As Freeman and Watts (86) have pointed out, these patients have an impairment of imagination as related to themselves, and this observation was definitely substantiated by the few human-movement responses. The most important correlations, however, lie in the association of certain findings with loss of abstract thinking in organics. Goldstein (364) has shown that patients with a loss of "categorical behavior" have "lost the capacity to deal with that which is not real." They are unable to "transcend concrete experience in order to act" and show impairment of the capacity to "comprehend the essential features of an event." Correspondingly, in their Rorschach responses is to be found a lack of M, inability to utilize suggested interpretations, and a failure to relate their general reactions to the actual details on the card. The relationship of the shading responses to anxiety and to Goldstein's "catastrophic reactions" has been indicated previously. Goldstein has also described the attempt by the patient to escape or to avoid dangerous situations as resulting in a personality characterized by "orderliness" of the simple, concrete, "primitive" type. This is shown in the markedly constricted Rorschach patterns described by Harrower-Erickson. Also this underlying anxiety and constant dread of catastrophic shocks would account for the presence of the color and shading shock reactions in these patients and would explain the need for reassurance indicated by their perplexity.

Such patients are also dominated by the principle of optimal performance, and as Hanfmann and Kasanin (*365*) state, "coöperate too well at times; they are too eager and frequently perseverate with the test." This mechanism is a point of differentiation from schizophrenics who frequently fail to coöperate. (When they do, little difficulty in differential diagnosis is found.) It also explains certain other organic Rorschach findings. Perseveration or repetition occurs as a result of the patient's intense drive to succeed. Since they usually believe that the blots actually represent specific objects to be identified, in itself an example of concrete thinking, they produce an idea and then, being unable to vary it, they apply the concept to succeeding cards, because of their inability to perceive defects. This tendency to exclusion of defects, described by Goldstein, also accounts for the impotency of these patients and, coupled with anxiety, would explain their inability to decide on the merits of a response and their dependency upon the examiner.

This primary drive to maximum performance together with the inability of the patient to shift his attitudes accounts for his inability to improve during the inquiry or to utilize new suggestions offered during the testing of the limits. Such impairment of abstract behavior, demonstrated with other methods by Goldstein, Weigl, Bolles (363), and others, is an important sign which has not yet been sufficiently emphasized. It is a demonstrable finding in these patients; and, since many cases of organic brain damage that show few other signs do show this finding, the value of a careful inquiry and exhaustive testing of the limits cannot be overemphasized.

The loss of "categorical behavior," as indicated by the Rorschach method, has been described by Kelley (166) and found to occur only in cases of intracranial lesions or dementia praecox. While not a pathognomonic sign, it is of major value, and its presence or absence should always be checked. If impairment of abstract behavior is present, it represents a positive sign to be added to Piotrowski's ten. It may be indicated by the symbol (*Abs*), indicating that the power of abstraction is impaired or lost.

In employing all the above material, the methods of clinical differential diagnosis must be used. This means that, after the record has been taken and the limits have been carefully checked, all the possibilities which may be present must be considered. Differential diagnosis in organic patients is, if the qualitative aspect is taken into consideration, usually limited to certain profound neurotics, deteriorated schizophrenics, and the feeble-minded. The deteriorated schizophrenics can usually be ruled out by the presence of certain bizarre types of response, qualitative findings, and the occurrence of certain pathognomonic responses, such as contamination, marked variability in form accuracy, etc., together with the other signs described by Kelley and Klopfer (*170*). If the record shows neurotic shock, psychoneurosis can be ruled out by a careful study of the shock and, if necessary, one or more repetitions of the test. If the patient is a neurotic, the shock will strongly persist, whereas in organics there will be considerable variability as regards this point. In addition, careful qualitative studies of the responses will reveal significant differences in questionable responses of the perplexed and impotent type. Mentally deficient patients usually present little difficulty, as the answers are generally stereotyped and on a lower form level and there is little realization by the patients of the poor results. *Po* responses [5] *F* — responses, and poor originals also will be present. It must be borne in mind that many cases of mental deficiency have an organic basis, and these cases will show organic signs. In this connection the appearance of deterioration — i.e., the presence of some responses which are very good together with responses which are poor, indicating a previously higher level of ability — is an important finding.

If fewer than five organic signs are found, the record must be carefully scrutinized in an effort to pick up the most important findings, such as color naming, perplexity, impotence, and impairment of abstract thinking. If these occur, other findings must be considered merely as supporting elements. If they do not occur, the other signs must be in considerable number (at least five or six) before diagnosis of organic intracranial pathology is seriously considered.

[5] These are responses determined only by the position or numerical aspect of a stimulus. Typical examples are "Heart, because it is in the middle," or "Father and mother, because there are two of them." (Cf. page 163.)

CHAPTER
XV

DEMENTIA PRAECOX

FOLLOWING the appearance of *Psychodiagnostik*, little work was done with the Rorschach test in the field of schizophrenia until the important monograph of Skalweit in 1934(*313*). Skalweit was chiefly interested in the problem of whether or not schizophrenia is merely an accentuation of the normal schizothymic type of personality or whether it is an actual disease process which will provoke measurable changes in personality. His case records followed some twenty-three acute cases with repeated Rorschach administrations over a period of years, and tend to substantiate his claim that the profound changes accompanying the progressing personality deterioration are manifestations of a disease process that attacks and changes the basic personality and are not just exaggerations of traits already present in the individual. The most striking example is a change in the personality from an introversive to a extratensive type, as shown by decrease of the *M* and an increase of the *C* reactions approaching pure color. His records over a period of years show this change clearly.

In addition, Skalweit has pointed out many schizophrenic signs in the Rorschach test. It is not possible to present all his conclusions, but his most conspicuous findings can be briefly summarized. In chronic cases of dementia praecox he found 50 per cent showing confused succession and only 14 per cent showing normal emphasis on D. The other cases stressed W or Dd or both. Over half the patients showed more than 50 per cent original responses, but the greater the number of originals given, the poorer the quality. Only 21 per cent of the cases showed any M at all, and these in most instances gave only one. Skalweit found three predominant reactions to color. First, the small group which exhibited the best rapport and were in closest contact with reality, showed more FC than CF, and no C responses. Second, the abulic or simple type of schizophrenic, who shows a lack of energy, usually gave only CF responses and no C or FC answers. Third, the group possessing the severest psychiatric defects reacted with C and some CF responses but never gave those of an FC type. He stressed the fact that the presence of crude color responses does not indicate excitement. Eight cases with only pure C responses were patients who, clinically, were depressed, blocked, and stuporous, but who demonstrated a latent irritability which was occasionally manifested by a severe impulsive outburst.

Since Skalweit's article most research on Rorschach reactions in schizophrenia has been done in America. Hackfield (*98*) published his work in 1935 and Dimmick (*62*) in 1936; both papers have been reviewed by Beck (*13*). The year 1938 seems to have been most productive, for papers by Benjamin (*28*) and Rickers-Ovsiankina (*277*) appeared then, as did Beck's book, *Personality Structure in Schizophrenia.* It is chiefly with these three sources that this chapter deals. All of them reveal a careful approach to this problem; and, while a critical reader may find numerous controversial points, he will find much of genuine significance.

Benjamin's article is primarily a check on the diagnostic validity of the Rorschach test, but is of particular interest in that it shows how accurately Rorschach personality descriptions may be made. His study concerns forty-six cases of which eleven were schizophrenic or had questionable schizophrenic traits. Some of the analyses were so-called "blind" interpretations, and in others the test was personally administered by the interpreter. Benjamin points out, however, that this actually makes little difference in the accuracy of the results. His report is, unfortunately, merely confined to a table comparing the Rorschach and clinical diagnosis, and it is felt that a more detailed treatment of the material would be of great value to all Rorschach workers. Some of his Rorschach diagnoses show very fine shades of interpretation, as "very mild early (latent) schizophrenia with marked hysterical superstructure and depression," or "early schizophrenia, primarily hebephrenic, with catatonic features." A knowledge of the Rorschach signs used in making these refined diagnoses would prove of real value to every Rorschach student. In all the schizophrenic cases listed the Rorschach and clinical diagnoses compare very well, and this preliminary report indicates clearly the value of the test as a diagnostic tool.

The Rickers-Ovsiankina paper and Beck's book are the most comprehensive surveys of the Rorschach test in schizophrenia as yet available. Naturally there are numerous disputable points in them, but both cover this field well, and from them certain tentative criteria may be derived which will enable us to secure a more comprehensive and easily recognizable picture of the schizophrenic process as reflected in the Rorschach test.

It must first be strongly emphasized that there is no single definite Rorschach or personality picture typical of schizophrenia as a whole. Also it should be realized that diagnoses are not made directly but by inference from the personality picture constructed out of the Rorschach material. Furthermore, it must be borne in mind that the psychiatric classification of the various schizophrenic processes in use today leaves much to be desired. Pure and unmixed clinical schizophrenic entities are rare. Usually each case shows some admixture of the hebephrenic, catatonic, and paranoid syndromes and, further, may have some affective or psychoneurotic coloring. All these clinical behavior patterns are reflected in the test, and as a result the Rorschach patterns of a group of patients all labeled "schizophrenic" may be tremendously varied. Research of any type in dementia praecox should first include a segregation of the various types. Inasmuch as schizophrenia is but a syndrome — a name given to certain groups of patients who may show widely varying behavior complexes — it is too much to expect that any known method of investigation, if applied indiscriminately to all the members of this group, will ever show any definite results. Rickers-Ovsiankina has taken a step in this direction in pointing out the higher $F+\%$ and $O+\%$ in paranoids as compared to hebephrenics ($F+$ between 70 and 80 per cent, and $O+$ more than 50 per cent in paranoids; and $F+$ less than 60 per cent, and $O+$ less than 30 per cent in hebephrenics).

There are, however, a few signs which seem to be, when present, almost certain indicators of the schizophrenic process, and there are certain others which, if found together, tend to point to such diagnosis. These signs, of course, are still in the "raw" state in that we are not sure, in the case of many of them, to what types of schizophrenic reaction they point. Empirically, however, it would seem that if enough of them are present a diagnosis of schizophrenia is justified; and, until further research work is done, we must content ourselves with assembling them into their most usable combinations. It must be further remembered, too, that no one case will present all the signs and many will present only a few. Each case must be evaluated separately and the number and value of the so-called schizophrenic signs must be weighed. We are unable to specify numerically the total quantity of signs necessary to indicate a schizophrenic process. Rather, the entire pattern must be studied and each sign evaluated by itself and in relationship to the other signs which may happen to be present in the record.

Ewald Bohm added to the third edition of Rorschach's *Psychodiagnostik* (*282*) a set of tables summarizing the Rorschach findings in various diseases. In the table referring to schizophrenia, he made a number of points which should be listed both as a matter of historical interest and because all of them have been verified by recent research. He listed three signs which he considered pathognomonic of the schizophrenic process. Unfortunately these three signs do not appear in the records too commonly, and their absence does not necessarily mean that the case is not schizophrenic. However, when the signs are found, the diagnosis is usually very easily made.

The first sign is the presence of *Po* (see page 347). Although Guirdham (*96*) has noted this phenomenon in epileptic patients and it has been found to occur occasionally in organic cases, it is probably most common among the schizophrenics.

The second sign is the presence of extreme variation in the form quality of the responses. This is true both of the *F* and of the *O*. Rickers-Ovsiankina (*277*) stated: "Probably more significant than the total score of a schizophrenic subject is the variation within a single record. In the same person may be found very poor and frequently absurd responses as well as ordinary good ones, or even responses which are considerably above the average with respect to fine and differentiated form perception." Thus in a single card will be found an *F* or *O* response of high quality immediately followed or preceded by a far-fetched or even absurd response.

The third point listed by Bohm is the presence of contaminated answers. These are answers in which the subject gives to one blot or part of a blot two entirely incompatible interpretations or responses. For example, for the green details in Card IX, an *F* response — e.g., "bear" — may be used, or a *C* response, "grass." Should the normal individual desire to use both *F* and *C* simultaneously, he would perhaps say, "an old bronze figure of a bear covered with verdigris." The schizophrenic subject "contaminates" these two responses by putting them together in a rather abnormal manner to create a new concept — as, for example, "grass-bear." Or, to use Rorschach's own example for the definition of contaminatory *W*, Card IV is seen as a degenerated liver, and then as a happy man sitting on a stool; the two responses are contaminated into the response, "liver of a solidly living politician." Contamination is found, in adults, only among schizophrenics.

While these signs have been described as pathognomonic, it must again be emphasized that there are no true pathognomonic signs in the Rorschach method. The appearance of pseudopsychotic signs in preschool children, where contaminated and position responses and extreme variation may occur, has been discussed earlier in this book. In addition, deteriorating processes of any type may cause marked variation in quality of the responses; position answers, as has been previously indicated, obviously occur in other conditions. These signs are, however, most commonly found in cases of schizophrenia. If the Rorschach method is used in diagnostic conjunction with clinical findings, such differential problems will seldom present themselves.

In addition to these three most typical signs of schizophrenia, there are a number of others that have been emphasized by Rorschach and more recent research workers. The more of these signs that are present in any given record, the more reliable is the assumption that a schizophrenic personality is reflected. As a convenient summary, we have assembled, following Piotrowski's method, a table of twenty Rorschach signs, showing the different qualities of each as it appears in the schizophrenic. It will be necessary to describe briefly each of these twenty signs and to summarize the various research findings relative to each. In this discussion the symbols used for scoring will correspond as closely as possible to those used by the various research workers, preference being given always to the English symbol.

1. *The manner of approach* (*Ap*). In this category the only agreement among the various workers is that the mode of apperception (*Erfassungstypus*) in the schizophrenic group is loose or confused. Rorschach points out that in paranoids it may be normal. Beck, in an excellent table (*13*), found that *DW* (confabulatory response) is a common schizophrenic approach and emphasized that the expected *W–Dd* approach is not borne out. This is exactly contrary to the opinion of Rickers-Ovsiankina (*277*), who found that the most common approach is *W–Dd–D*. This apparently great difference in results can probably be explained by the fact that in many schizophrenic cases the *D* responses consist to a large extent of borderline reactions, which are either close to *Dd* or are practically *W* responses. In Beck's scoring he did not make use of the finer differences between *D* and *Dd* nor did he use the "cut-off" *W* response, which would easily account for his emphasis on the *D* responses. Other research workers have found the most common approach always to be the *W–Dd* type.

2. *Whole responses* (*W*). As indicated in the preceding paragraph, Rickers-Ovsiankina and most of the other research workers found an increase in the number of *W*'s together with a decrease in their quality. Beck actually found fewer *W*'s in his schizophrenic records than in normals, a condition which would make one strongly suspect some variation in his scoring. Rickers-Ovsiankina in addition used a *Wv* scoring for configurations of a simple and rather vague nature, based upon the crudest outlines. These are not generally *F–* but are definitely platitudinous interpretations, and in the schizophrenic

many of the *W* responses are of this crude and undifferentiated type.

3. *Confabulatory W's.* Beck, Rickers-Ovsiankina, and Rorschach all agreed that this is a common sign. The confabulatory *W* answer, *DW*, is one in which the subject really identifies only one more or less significant detail in a whole card, and is carried away by his "whole intention" to such a degree that he attaches an interpretation to the entire card which derives only from the tiny detail. For example, from the detail of the "cat's whiskers" in Card VI he may interpret the whole card as a cat. A more sophisticated subject would interpret it as a badly skinned cat, which is not a confabulatory but a fabulatory response, as described by Schneider (*304*). Another example is the response to Card VI inverted, if the topmost tiny protrusion is seen as an eagle's beak, and, immediately, the card as a whole is reported as an eagle.

4. *Contamination.* This has previously been described and is mentioned by both Beck and Rorschach.

5. *Unusual detail (Dd).* Both Beck and Rickers-Ovsiankina pointed out that there is a tremendous amount of scatter in the number of details, some patients having few and some having a great number. The schizophrenic patient will usually pick out bizarre or unclear details.

6. *Movement (M).* All the research work tends to point to the fact that the number of *M* in schizophrenic patients is below normal. Rorschach found one exception, in that *M* responses are fairly high in the paranoid type.

7. *Color.* Both Beck and Rickers-Ovsiankina put considerable emphasis on the color responses of the schizo-

phrenic. Both felt that sum *C* is not particularly significant but that the ratio of the various components to one another is extremely important. Both found that the schizophrenic records were high in *CF* and *C* responses but low in *FC* responses. Rickers-Ovsiankina further pointed out that subjects not showing *FC* responses but showing several *CF* and *C* responses generally evidence considerable deterioration. Thus the ratio of the various factors is more important than their total.

8. *Erlebnistypus* (*M* : sum *C*). In the schizophrenic picture the *M* to *C* ratio is of considerable importance and, according to all workers, shows a domination of the color over the movement. Occasionally in certain types of schizophrenia — as, for example, the paranoid — one will find a record with a large number of *M* and a small number of other *C*, although there may be considerable color naming. The usual case is the one with a small number of *M* and a considerable number of real *C*. In many cases the schizophrenic record will show only one or the other and there never will be a real balance between them. A record showing many *M* together with many real *C* would not be a schizophrenic at all. The paranoid types tend to show the greatest number of *M* responses and the hebephrenic and the catatonic types the greatest number of color responses.

9. *Color naming* (*C$_n$*). Rickers-Ovsiankina, following Skalweit, found *C$_n$* fairly common in schizophrenic patients. In addition, Piotrowski (*257*), Skalweit (*314*) and others found it as an organic manifestation. *C$_n$* is the mere naming of a color and is scored separately from the color responses. If found with other more typical schizophrenic signs, it may be construed as an added point. Care

must be taken, however, that it is not indicative of some organic disorder. Skalweit looked upon C_n as the sign of an organic schizophrenic defect. In the discussion of organic findings color naming has been more completely described, and while it occurs frequently in schizophrenics, it should more properly be considered an organic indication. It may well be that the color naming can be differentiated into an organic and schizophrenic variety or, more probably, C_n may be found to represent inability on the part of the patient to orient himself clearly in his relationships to the environment — a condition common both to schizophrenics and organics.

10. *Good form* ($F+$). Here again there is universal agreement that the percentage of $F+$ is definitely decreased in the schizophrenic. Beck felt that the low number of accurately perceived forms is the factor with the highest discriminative value.

11. *Popular responses* (P). Next to $F+$, Beck found this the second most discriminative factor; and inasmuch as it is scored objectively, there being only few possible responses that may be scored P, he felt that the fact that the percentages are always lower than normal is a reliable indication. This has been borne out by Rickers-Ovsiankina.

12. *Variability*. A marked variation in form accuracy within a single record is a significant finding. This variability may also be noted in the number of responses and choice of location for the various cards. In some cases a patient will give a great number of responses to some of the cards, and few or none to the others. Again, they will carry on through four or five cards with a single W answer and then begin the sixth with a Dd response.

13. *Blocking.* In line with this variability is the more frequent rejection of certain cards and not of the same cards as normal subjects refuse. Rorschach and Beck both pointed this out. The normal subject who rejects any cards will usually refuse Card IX and possibly one or two others. The schizophrenic may refuse any one or all of them. Piotrowski has also found this to be an organic sign.

14. *Original responses* (O). All the authors are in agreement that the O responses are usually minus responses; Rickers-Ovsiankina and Rorschach pointed out that these O — responses tend to occur rather frequently. Rickers-Ovsiankina indicated that perseveration in the carrying of one answer through several cards will frequently result in unconventional interpretations, therefore scored O —. Moreover, good O answers and bizarre ones are apt to be found side by side.

15. *Animal responses* (A). Animal responses, *per se*, are not of great significance, but Rickers-Ovsiankina emphasized the very pertinent relation between the A and O responses. Only in exceptional cases in normal subjects does an $A\%$ of more than 50 coincide with an $O\%$ that exceeds 25. In schizophrenics, on the other hand, 77 per cent of the subjects showing an A percentage greater than 50 have at the same time a percentage of O responses which ranges between 25 and 75.

16. *Shading.* Beck found no particular shading variations, but Rickers-Ovsiankina found that undifferentiated shading responses occurred in few normal subjects but in 13 per cent of the schizophrenics, and considered it an important finding.

17. *Position.* This type of response has been dis-

cussed before, and its significance is agreed upon by all workers.

18. Abstract and personal reference responses seem to occur more frequently in schizophrenics and are mentioned by all workers.

19. Perseveration is another feature of schizophrenic records, as was mentioned by both Beck and Rickers-Ovsiankina. This perseveration differs somewhat from the organic type of perseverative response. Such perseveration may also occur in preschool children, particularly superior ones. Here perseveration is most common in the last three cards. In organic cases little difference is found in the perseveration in reactions to the colored as compared with the achromatic cards. The organic perseveration is a sort of "stickiness" in which the subject is unable to shift from an already established chain of thought to another one, regardless of the structure of the card. In dementia praecox a patient, while perseverating the response, fits it in more accurately to the structure of the card and does not seem so completely unable to change his trend of thought.

20. Description of a card as an ink blot, a design, or a line is a schizophrenic type of response suggesting dearth of ideas and inflexibility in thinking. Such descriptions also are found in organic cases and appear in the records of some neurotic individuals. Patients of the semi-hysterical type, who are not particularly interested in the test but who coöperate sufficiently well to take it, frequently will merely describe the cards, thereby feeling that they have given some response with a minimum of effort. The organic and schizophrenic patients, on the other hand, will apply tremendous effort to the attempt

to find something in the cards, but their achievement level is so reduced that the best they can do is simple card description. The attitude of the subject is of considerable importance in differentiating these two types of card description. The cards may also be described by malingerers, who feel that here is a simple way of following an obvious process which to them appears so innocuous that it could not possibly give them away. Differentiation of this group depends on the absence of other findings typical of schizophrenic or organic deterioration.

In addition to these findings, Beck also mentioned that occasionally a schizophrenic will reverse the figure and background, but this is not rare in normals. He also points out that some schizophrenics produce neologisms and new words in response to the test stimuli. These cases can usually be identified after a few minutes' discussion, and the Rorschach hardly need be used for diagnosis.

From the above data the table on pages 362 and 363 has been prepared for ready reference, showing the findings of various research workers for each of these twenty categories among schizophrenic subjects.

Thus we find, after carefully surveying the various "schizophrenic findings," that there is no single symptom typical of the process. This is to be expected in view of the multifarious manifestations which the disease may present and in view of the fact that the clinical symptomatology is markedly variable. Almost no work has been done to differentiate the simple, paranoid, catatonic, and hebephrenic types, although these types may be recognized in the individual case. Generally we have found that paranoid cases of dementia praecox show many human movement responses and, on the whole, a better-integrated

TABLE 2

OCCURRENCE OF CERTAIN RORSCHACH SIGNS AMONG SCHIZOPHRENIC SUBJECTS, ACCORDING TO VARIOUS INVESTIGATORS.

	BECK	RICKERS-OVSIANKINA	RORSCHACH	KELLEY AND KLOPFER
1. Manner of approach	Confused; DW most typical	Confused; W-Dd-D	Confused; W-Dd	Confused; W-Dd-D-DW
2. W	Fewer than normal	Higher than normal. W of poor quality		Crude W or DW
3. Confabulatory DW	Present	Present	Present	Present
4. Contamination	Present		Pathognomonic	Usually pathognomonic
5. Rare detail (Dd)	Scattered. Schizophrenics sensitive to them	Qualitatively but not quantitatively important		Frequent; qualitatively and quantitatively important
6. M	Low	Low	High in paranoids, low in others	High in paranoids, low in others
7. Color	High C and CF, low FC	Ratio of CF and C to FC important		C and CF high in hebephrenics, low in paranoids and simple schizophrenics
8. Erlb.	Dominance of C	Dominance of C		Dominance of C

		Present		Occasionally present
9. C_n		Present		
10. $F+$	Low	Low	Low	Low
11. $P\%$	Low	Low	Low	Low
12. Variability in quality ($F-$ to F)	Very important	Very important	Pathognomonic	Very important but not pathognomonic
13. Blocking (rejections)	Present	Present	Present	Present
14. Original responses	Poor quality	Increased number; poor quality; vary in quality	Increased number; presence of $O+$ and bizarre $O-$ together	Increased $O+$ and $O-$
15. $A\%$		Relation of $A\%$ to $O\%$ important		$A\%$ to $O\%$ important
16. Shading		Present		K and c common; FK, Fc and C rare
17. Po	Present	Present	Pathognomonic	Present and usually pathognomonic
18. Abstract and personal references	Present	Present	Present	Present
19. Perseveration	Present	Present	Present	Present
20. Description of card	Present	Present	Present	Present

363

general picture. They also show considerable ability in the handling of the color cards, although they may show some color shock. As has been previously indicated, color shock can occur in schizophrenia as well as in the organic states. Catatonics usually give markedly constricted records which are frequently bizarre. In many instances it is impossible to secure a record from a mute catatonic, but we have found that in these cases intravenous sodium amytal in prenarcotic doses will produce transient ameliorating effects which will permit the securing of an adequate record. Studies with this drug reveal that it produces no other changes in the patient's Rorschach responses than to permit a free flow of replies and an extension of the record. It is, therefore, of great value for any individuals who refuse to respond to the cards, or in those cases where rejections are numerous. Catatonics notoriously reject many cards; but this in itself is not diagnostic, since occasionally hebephrenics, profound depressives, and neurotics will also refuse to respond to more than two or three cards.

The hebephrenic records are very similar to the catatonic in their bizarre content but different in that the strangeness of their responses is less well-organized and is more absurd in character. They show a jumble of fixed ideas and frequent marked perseveration, and may or may not show large amounts of *CF* or *C* responses. Cases of dementia simplex show a much more normal type of record but may produce some color naming or present some of the other signs typically found in dementia praecox. Latent schizophrenia is also manifested by discrepancies in a record which otherwise appears fairly normal.

In general, in the average record of the patient with schizophrenia we would expect to find emotional extremes with an absence of the normal relationship between the M and O responses and the $W : M$ ratio. In this last ratio, W and M may be equal, or in paranoid types there may actually be more human movement responses. The important finding is the abnormal relationship among the various factors. This is borne out by clinical data which show a lack of real balance between the inner life of the schizophrenic and his relationship to his environment.

The relationship of the factors in the Rorschach to the known clinical findings in dementia praecox is also of considerable importance. The failure of the patient's control is demonstrated in the lower percentage of $F+$ or in a high $F\%$ with a large number of $F-$ responses. This same lack of control is seen in the absence of the differentiated shading responses (FK or Fc). The inability of the schizophrenic to handle everyday situations, as a result of his lack of contact with everyday life, coupled with his futile though ambitious attempts to achieve recognition, are shown in his approach, which is characterized by crude or confabulated wholes and a lack of D. Further, his attention to tiny details represents the preoccupation with inconsequential and unimportant details which is typical of his everyday life. His difference from normally expected activity is shown by the small percentage of D responses, the disproportion between $O\%$ and $P\%$, and also between the $A\%$ and the $O\%$. It has also been noted that in the ratio $H + A : Hd + Ad$, schizophrenics depart from the usual ratio of two to one and generally stress the details. This, again, is a departure from nor-

mal expectations and shows the inherent personality differences of the schizophrenic. The lack of human-movement responses in the schizophrenic corresponds to their
lack of differentiated and constructive inner life, while
the increase in M in the paranoid corresponds to his over-
developed intellectualized fantastic delusions. The
blocking of the dementia praecox is shown in the rejection of the cards and in the frequent application of abstract and personal references to the cards themselves.
Perseveration is reflected in the responses and indicates
the patient's inability to shift a concept once he has accepted it. This lack of categorical behavior is somewhat
similar to that found in the organics; and, as has been
previously pointed out, the failure of the capacity for
abstract thought can be found in some cases of dementia
praecox. This finding is much more common in organics,
but if found in conjunction with other signs may point
to a schizophrenic process. The regression of the schizophrenic, as defined by White (*370*), represents a dropping
back to the use of simpler mechanisms for handling reality. This regression to a childish level is a regression to
a different kind of order or, as expressed by Korzybski
(*366*), to a lower order of abstraction. In the Rorschach responses the regression is manifested by the appearance of responses which are commonly found in preschool children, such as position responses, contamination,
perseveration, poor form, crude color, increased $A\%$, and
curious originals. In addition, the deterioration is further evidenced by the presence of remarkably good and
remarkably poor form responses, which indicates a previously higher intelligence functioning on a lower level.
  Certain basic mechanisms common to children and

praecoxes have been described by Storch (*368*), White, and others. They are seen in conjunction with the language of schizophrenia, as emphasized by the so-called "law of Storch" which points out that "language develops from feeling, concreteness, and perception in the direction of reasoning, differentiation, and abstraction." These mechanisms are also evident in the Rorschach responses. The condensation of words, sentences, and phrases, described by these authors, is obvious in the contamination responses. The lack of differentiation and abstraction and the presence of concrete perception is shown in the description of the cards, the patient's belief that the cards represent real objects, personal references, and the lack of demonstrable ability in the field of abstract behavior. The dementia praecox patient feels that the cards arc real entities and takes them as a part of his environment, to be included directly into his personality reactions and utilized as an active part of his surroundings.

Finally, the impulsive reactions of catatonics and hebephrenics are shown in their crude color responses, and the illogic of these types is manifested by bizarre answers, confused color reactions, and deteriorated patterns.

There is one more important area to be considered in relation to Rorschach work in schizophrenia; namely, the future possibilities for research in this field. It has been pointed out that obvious signs of schizophrenia in the Rorschach, such as the formation of neologisms, are hardly of value as diagnostic criteria, since these signs are apparent as soon as the patient begins to speak. This does not mean that tests should not be made in these cases. The Rorschach test is a research tool as well as a diagnostic one, and in this field the possibilities are unknown and therefore, as yet, unlimited. It is a recognized fact that there is a clear cleavage between the Rorschach records of paranoid types of schizophrenics on the one hand and of hebephrenics and catatonics on the other. Therefore there is a real need for research to study the justification of the currently accepted diagnostic symptoms from the point of view of basic personality factors and to reëvaluate them if necessary. Certainly our present clinical classifications are in many instances far from satisfactory, and a true knowledge of the actual differences in underlying personality structure occurring in cases presenting superficially similar syndromes would be of value in reorganizing our trends of thought.

Secondly, research work has been started by Piotrowski (*266, 269*) in an effort to discover prognostic possibilities of the Rorschach method in the insulin treatment of schizophrenia. His papers published to date suggest certain criteria which, if present, tend to point toward a better prognosis under treatment. In general, of course, the more the pretreatment record approaches "normal," the better the prognosis. Patients giving human-movement responses, color responses, and good form responses can be said to present the best prognostic criteria.

One other important use of the Rorschach in this field is in the determination of cases of early or incipient schizophrenia, even before they are clinically apparent. Such processes are manifested by the presence of abnormal basic ratios coupled with patterns comprising some of the schizophrenic findings. It is, of course, true that many such cases are functioning moderately well and are getting along outside of hospitals. Their Rorschach records will be more nearly normal than hospital cases, but, if careful search is made, disturbances in the underlying personality structure will be revealed. Occasional early cases will be missed, for the Rorschach is a test which reveals the underlying personality structure; and, obviously, if no definite personality changes have been produced, no change in the Rorschach test can appear. If, however, the developing process has produced some change in the personality, the Rorschach test will frequently uncover the beginnings of the disintegrating process before the definite clinical diagnosis is possible.

Thus it can be clearly seen that the Rorschach test will be of great usefulness when applied in the field of mental hygiene as an aid to early diagnosis or the discovery of incipient personality defects.

From these and many other points of view, the Rorschach test can be applied to the solution of the problems of the disease syndrome known as schizophrenia. Indeed, the methods of approach are limited only by the resourcefulness and ingenuity of the worker, and virtually any approach should prove of value both to the worker and to psychiatry in general.

CHAPTER
XVI

MENTAL DEFICIENCY

A NOTHER field which has been intensively studied by the Rorschach method is that of mental deficiency. Rorschach himself in *Psychodiagnostik* concluded that the method is of value, not only in evaluating the intelligence level but also in the estimation of grades of mental deficiency. Furthermore, the method, since it results essentially in an evaluation of the total personality of the individual rather than in a quantitative determination of one particular aspect, is of value in depicting the influence of the patient's emotional life in inhibiting or expediting intellectual functions, and in demonstrating inherent but perhaps unrealized capacities in the personality of the subject.

In addition Rorschach also pointed out that the mentally deficient patients as a group show a response pattern characterized by poor form perception, with the use of definitions of the test cards rather than interpretations, many C responses, no M responses, frequent poor DW responses, few W responses, loose succession, little content variety with a high animal per cent, and frequent oligophrenic details.

Beck, quoting Rorschach, has tabulated norms for the incidence of the various scoring categories at different levels of intelligence, as follows:

INTELLIGENCE LEVEL	W	M	C	F+%	A%	O%
Very superior	10 or more	5 or more	4–7	90–100	10–20	30–50
Superior	7–10	5 or more	1.5–3.5	80–100	20–35	20–30
Average	4–7	2–4	.5–2.5	70–80	30–55	0–20
Low average	3–4	0–2	1.5–6	60–70	50–70	0–20
Morons [1]	1–3	0	4–7	45–60	60–80	30–40
Imbeciles [1]	0–2	0	5.5–8.5	0–45	80–100	40–70

[1] Rorschach uses the terms "Debile" and "Imbezile." The classifications are not stated to have been made on the basis of any instrument of intelligence measurement.

Pfister (*251*) and Beck (*23*) agreed with Rorschach, except in the matter of oligophrenic details, which they were unable to verify. Beck, on the basis of the most extensive study in this particular phase of the Rorschach method, confirmed Rorschach's findings as regards the *C*, *F+%*, and animal responses, but found a slightly higher *W* range. This finding would be expected since Rorschach did not score most of the incomplete whole responses as *W* and labeled almost all parts of responses as main details. We found the proportion of *W* responses slightly higher than that found by Rorschach and noted that the wholes include chiefly combinatory, confabulatory, or low-quality "cheap" whole responses.

As regards the movement (*M*) responses, Rorschach scored *M* very strictly and did not use the *FM* and *m* scores as advocated by many present workers. For this reason many of his cases must have appeared deficient in inner life; we have found this to be present but represented chiefly by infantile *FM* responses together with an occasional *M* response.

Rorschach, although not including the total response number, *R*, among his diagnostic criteria, mentioned that the feeble-minded tended to exceed the median of normals (15–30), a finding not confirmed by Pfister or Beck, who report a mean of about 21. Both these authors verified the value of *P* (popular) responses as an accurate measure of the patients' adaptability, as judged by their usefulness in the wards or participation in social activities.

Other early studies of Juarros and Soriano (*157, 158*) and Kerr (*178*), confirm the findings of Rorschach, Beck, and Pfister, although some of their norms are slightly higher. Ganz, quoted by Vernon (*339*), found little difference in the *R*, *M*, or sum *C* of normals and of mental deficients; these factors, however, would not be expected to show much change except in extreme cases. Müller (*235*) found the method of great value and claimed that the Rorschach diagnosis of intelligence is usually found to be more revealing than the Binet test results.

Case studies by Behn-Eschenburg (*26*), Schneider (*304*), Löpfe (*213*), Beck (*23*), and Sill (*310*) tend to verify this statement. Recent work by Davidson and Klopfer (*59*) confirms Rorschach's primary findings and further indicates the value of the method in determination of the intellectual level.

In discussing the problem of intelligence determination, Vernon points out that "the Rorschach test is stated to possess peculiar advantages in the diagnosis of intelligence:

"(1) Because it does not employ verbal material and is therefore relatively uninfluenced in its results by schooling.

"(2) Because it can be applied at every mental age level from the lowest to the highest, children and adults alike.

"(3) Because the experimental situation is less constrained, less liable to arouse emotional tensions and inhibitions than Binet testing.

"(4) Because the test does not merely supply a single numerical score for intelligence but indicates also the abstract intellectual type, the practical and material, the analytic or meticulous, the broad organizing or synthetic, and the original creative types of intelligence."

Rorschach based his estimate of intelligence upon the following factors:

(1) Percentage of $F+$
(2) Number of M
(3) Number of W
(4) Apperception type
(5) Succession type
(6) Percentage of animal responses
(7) Percentage of original responses

It seems essential at this point to mention that some authors have attempted to validate the Rorschach method by comparing these individual factors with the stated IQ's of their subjects. In these attempts only the $F+\%$ holds up as a single factor with adequate statistical validity. This does not mean in any sense, however, that the other individual factors, when taken not as separate entities but as parts of a whole response pattern, are not valid. (See Chapter XI.)

Probably the only pattern of response similar to the one commonly seen in mentally deficient subjects is found in certain schizophrenics, and Piotrowski (253) has been able to differentiate these groups. He states, "(1) perseveration of one idea which seems to be closely connected with a personal experience of the child, (2) uneven performance level characterized by the presence of few good responses and autocritical remarks together with many vague and not infrequently absurd responses, (3) large percentage of poor original responses, and (4) absence of inductive reasoning, distinguish the schizophrenic from the mentally defective individual."

In considering the application of the Rorschach method of personality analysis to problems of the mentally deficient, it seems that, as contrasted with other methods having determination of the intelligence level as the primary and perhaps sole aim, the Rorschach method may evaluate the intelligence level only as one aspect of the total personality of the individual. The essential function of the Rorschach method is to evaluate the total assets and liabilities of the personality, actual and potential. It is, therefore, of particular value in its application to problems of the mentally deficient because, as seems obvious, such patients are not of importance merely because they have IQ's of a certain value; they are definite clinical problems. The detection of the nature and magnitude of their personality trends is perhaps the most valuable function of the Rorschach method. The discovery of such elements in the total personality of the mentally deficient patient may be of great assistance in dealing with problems of guidance, reëducation, social adaptability, etc. Orientation as to the clinical handling and prognosis of such patients is indeed of great practical value and the Rorschach method, indicating as it does the existence of certain potentialities or trends in addition to a certain intelligence level, may justly be applied to problems of investigation of the mentally deficient. Intelligence, after all, is for the psychiatrist only one aspect of the personality and not always the most important aspect. Many problems in psychiatry are concerned more with the affective integrations of the personality. These problems are not less important in the mentally deficient individual, especially the borderline case, than in the usual psychiatric case.

In summary, the Rorschach method may be considered an instrument for the estimation of intellectual ability whose primary value is in the determination of the influence of the emotional life on the inhibition or the stimulation of the intellectual functions; it is also of value in indicating clinically important assets and liabilities which may orient the physician as regards care and prognosis of the mentally deficient patient.

CHAPTER

XVII

CONVULSIVE STATES

THE problem of the manifestation of convulsive states in Rorschach protocols has been considered by numerous authors and the Rorschach findings have been fairly well established. The Rorschach worker is here confronted with the same basic problems which the clinician must face when considering convulsive states. The recent trend in neuropsychiatry to consider a convulsion as a symptom rather than as a disease entity has clarified the picture and at the same time sharply indicated the impossibility of delineating any specific pattern typical of patients manifesting this symptom. Indeed, if it is recalled that a low blood sugar, the injection of metrazol, a focal brain tumor, or any one of a number of other conditions, many of which are only remotely related to the brain, can cause the same sort of convulsive attack, we can easily understand why no specific, clear-cut Rorschach pattern, applicable to epilepsy *per se*, can be expected. Most of the work which has been done on epileptics by Guirdham (*96*) and Stauder (*318*) has dealt with cases of idiopathic epilepsy, generally of long duration and evidencing considerable deterioration.

It is obvious that, in investigations of patients who show no specific type of pathological lesion, but in whom for one reason or another fits occur and in whom mental deterioration is present, signs common to those found in cases of actual organic brain damage will occur. On the other hand, epileptic spells resulting from lesions or physiological disturbances elsewhere in the body would not necessarily be expected to show any organic signs and might show only the presence of some anxiety as a result of the concern of the patient with his disease. Indeed, epilepsy resulting from focal lesions in the brain itself may be accompanied by very few signs of intracranial damage as previously described.

Harrower-Erickson (*109*) has shown in focal epileptics that no typical personality is found but that all cases seem to show evidences of personality difficulties. These studies further indicated that approximation of the tumor psychogram was correlated only with extensive or diffuse cerebral damage. She was, however, unable to compare her results to any great degree with those of other workers, since her patients were a specially selected group in whom the exact extent of the lesion had been carefully determined.

For practical purposes we shall limit our discussion to known facts and consider the work dealing with idiopathic epilepsy of long duration. Rorschach felt that epileptics in general tend to define pictures rather than interpret them and that their average number of responses tends to exceed the average for normal subjects. Their reaction time tends to be greater than average and they have a considerable number of poor form responses. As regards human-movement responses, he found that the most demented give the most M and that those in whom the dementia appears slowly over a period of years may have the least amount of human movement. Epileptics in general show an inverse relationship between M and $F+$; that is, the better the form, the fewer M, or the less sharp the form, the more M. Many of these M are really minus responses. Rorschach also described certain peculiar responses which he classed as a kind of primary C response but which are really color-naming responses of the organic type.

Rorschach felt that black and white responses are as significant as the rest of the color responses in this group. Epileptics in general show many color responses, particularly pure C, and though FC responses occur frequently, they are accompanied by large numbers of CF and C answers. DW are also common among this group and the succession is generally loose or confused. Rorschach stressed the perseveration of epileptics, which generally is concerned with an adherence to one word or concept; but he also emphasized the fact that, for the most part, a large variability of responses is evidenced and no animal or anatomy stereotypy appears. He pointed out that in the matter of content, more whole human figures than body parts are seen and that, frequently, large numbers of inanimate objects are named by epileptics. Epileptics in general appeared to have more ability for extratensive than introversive rapport and always show a predominance of the color side of the psychogram. Rorschach felt that the number of movement and color responses increases as the epileptic dementia progresses; and that the color responses, in particular, are not unlike a scale expressing the degree of dementia. He did indicate, however, that an epileptoid or a person with epileptic-like characteristics may have a majority of responses on the movement side of the psychogram.

Guirdham (*96*) felt that there is no uniform type of epileptic reaction, but noted several characteristics which set the epileptic apart from the normal. One of these is perseveration of a kind found in subjects of a more concrete intelligence, who stress an approach of the $D-Dd$ type, or those of a higher potential intelligence where, frequently, exceptionally well-preserved form is sought. This perseveration is, as a rule, very different from the schizophrenic type and is very much like the organic variety, although the form structure tends to be much better. As regards the M to sum C balance, it is extratensive or ambiequal, and in general sum C is considerably greater than M. This led Guirdham to believe that epileptics have a much less well-developed introversive life than normals.

Guirdham's findings suggested that the color responses of epileptics are characterized by the presence of many CF and C responses, which indicate different degrees of unadapted affectivity. As regards areas of response, he found many W's which are repetitious (perseveration), and many poor W's, some of the confabulatory type. As regards succession, he found that the loose, reversed, and irregular types are overwhelmingly more common. He found that ordered succession, when it occurs, is vitiated by the poor types of apperception. From this he concluded that there is in epilepsy a deficiency in the process of abstract synthesis, as shown by the concrete and overmeticulous types of approach revealed by the overaccentuation of D, Dd, and its allied comprehension types.

Guirdham also called attention to the large number of poor forms which are found and emphasized that $P\%$ is usually lower than average.

He agreed with Rorschach that epileptics show fewer indications of stereotypy in content than normals, and that, though their original responses are numerically greater, the quality of these originals on the whole is rather poor. He also verified Rorschach's findings that the animal responses are fewer in epileptics than in normals and concluded that epileptics show more preoccupation with parts of the human body than with animal forms. In considering shading responses, Guirdham found that they frequently occur in epileptics, particularly those with an extratensive preponderance. In cases showing marked intellectual impairment, shading responses seem to diminish, which is precisely according to expectation from our understanding of these responses. He also mentioned the tendency in epileptics to non-interpretative responses, such as description of the cards, and emphasized the appearance of what he calls "geometric answers," which are the responses we have referred to as position (Po) responses. These descriptive or position responses occur generally with marked deterioration and, when coupled with a low $F+\%$ and a high percentage of poor original forms, point to an impoverishment of genuine associational processes. Guirdham stressed the fact that abstract responses are common among epileptics. This point was briefly mentioned by Rorschach, who indicated that epileptics frequently will call a blue area "heaven." They also quite often give large numbers of sexual responses and responses referring to themselves, which are known as "ego" responses.

Guirdham, finally, introduced one other phenomenon, which he termed "staccato." This involves a waxing and waning of the flow of interpretation independent of the effects of inattention or fatigue. It seems to concide with the uneven and staccato nature of the mental process, which is regarded by Bleuler as one of the salient features of the epileptic type and occurs in the Rorschach almost as though good interpretations were followed by a negative phase during which the faculty of association becomes inaccessible to further stimuli.

Guirdham's work on Rorschach signs in epilepsy represents one of the most comprehensive studies in the field and has contributed as much to our understanding of the problem as Rorschach's original work.

Stauder's study (*318*) suggested that genuine epileptics of long duration, and cases recently showing convulsions but without any clinical signs of personality change, both show a specific Rorschach pattern which is indicative of an "epileptic personality." This Rorschach syndrome occurs in full form in about two thirds of the patients, and to a modified degree in the rest. However, it is found in all patients in the confused state immediately following a convulsion. Stauder worked with "genuine epileptics" which are comparable to our idiopathic cases. He believed that perseveration in the Rorschach responses is the most direct yardstick of the epileptic personality change and occurs independently of dementing factors. This diagnosis was based on a specific type of perseveration which is determined by a fairly normal response to the first card, this response then being carried through the remaining plates. He differentiated this perseveration from the bizarre schizophrenic type.

Stauder reported that of 358 cases of idiopathic epilepsy studied, 222 had from 90 to 100 per cent perseveration, while of 74 "traumatic epileptics" only 18 showed a like percentage. Clinical study of these cases, however, convinced Stauder that all 18 of these patients showed symptoms similar to the idiopathic type. This finding of such extreme perseveration is interesting but has never been verified by any other worker. Perseveration is an important and frequent finding in these patients, but 90 to 100 per cent perseveration is decidedly not common.

Stauder also described certain other findings which he included in an "abortive syndrome," applied to those patients failing to show extreme perseveration. These signs, suggesting intracranial damage, include the sign R (average number of responses is less than 15); the sign M (92 per cent show no M); and the sign T (average response time is 1.5 minutes). Stauder emphasized that the response time does not parallel the degree of perseveration, but is positively correlated with the increase in $A\%$, suggesting that stereotypy and perseverative factors are not identical.

Stauder believed that the Rorschach findings do not confirm the frequent clinical assumption that irritability, explosiveness, abruptness, or morose moods are components of the personality, except in a small per cent of the patients. He suggested that the affective elements are overstressed clinically and that the Rorschach gives a truer picture than the ordinary clinical assumptions.

The records of epileptic patients may be expected to show, in cases of idiopathic epilepsy, a sufficient number of definite signs to permit diagnosis to be made directly from the Rorschach records.

As can be seen from the above discussion, many of the signs enumerated for organic intracranial disease will appear, particularly the following:

(1) Prolonged response time
(2) Lack of popular responses
(3) Poor form responses
(4) Few human-movement responses
(5) Color naming
(6) Perseveration

In addition, epileptics may show some impotence and perplexity and will show a concrete approach to the task, coupled in some instances with a loss of categorical behavior. The value of these signs in epilepsy has been indicated by Piotrowski and Kelley (*271*). Oberholzer (*241*) has also mentioned the appearance of such responses in post-traumatic epileptic states. Differential diagnosis of these records must be made in the customary medical fashion. The usual problems are the differentiation of these pictures from cases of schizophrenia and actual intracranial structural diseases. Schizophrenia can usually be distinguished by means of the specific signs which have been previously described. The *DW* approach may occur among epileptics, and confused succession, position responses, poor original responses, perseveration, and poor form may simulate a schizophrenic picture. However, the variation in perseveration, the low *A*%, the preoccupation with human detail, the presence of typical organic signs, particularly color naming and organic perseveration, and the extratensive general pattern should enable one to make a diagnosis. In addition, a lack of bizarre responses, curious personal references, contamination, and other typical schizophrenic findings are of considerable value. It is impossible in many cases to differentiate the pattern of these epileptics from definite known cases of intracranial damage. In general it may be said that an epileptic record showing enough signs so that it is confused with an organic one will be, on the whole, a much better record than that of the organic patient. By this we mean that, if the epileptic record is sufficiently advanced to present such diagnostic difficulty, the epileptic record will still contain a number of good forms, human-movement responses, and original responses, and will not show so many of the typical organic signs, such as automatic phrases, marked impotence, and complete lack of abstractive power. In general an epileptic record will not present a great number of organic signs, but if it should, differential diagnosis can be worked out without too great difficulty from the other aspects of the record, which is typically superior from both a qualitative and quantitative point of view. Such types of differential diagnosis have been demonstrated by Kelley and Margulies (*173*).

It must be borne in mind that no one has to date been able to elicit signs for convulsions *per se*. We are at present justified only in making a diagnosis of a Rorschach pattern which is compatible with convulsive states; we are not able to say specifically from the record alone whether the individual under scrutiny clinically manifests convulsions. It must further be borne in mind that actual cases of intracranial pathology — as, for example, tumors — may show marked organic records while accompanied clinically by convulsive symptoms. In these cases a Rorschach diagnosis of organic brain disease is indicated and it is possible that the convulsive aspects may be missed.

XVIII

PSYCHONEUROSES

R ORSCHACH findings in psychoneurosis are quite variable, and indications of neuroses are found not only in psychoneuroses themselves but in almost every other type of psychopathology. This situation is reasonable in view of the fact that some degree of anxiety may appear in any individual and that compulsive obsessive traits are common in the general population. Probably the most important single sign of a neurotic reaction is color shock; all students of the method have found that neurotics invariably show such shock, and only a small percentage of normals and other types of psychopathology display it. It is true, however, that color shock does occur and has been reported in all types of psychopathy except manic-depressive psychoses and that it also appears in approximately one fifth of the records of normal subjects.

By color shock is meant here any indication of disturbance in responses to the color cards. In the neurotic the color seems to constitute a new and catastrophic situation which requires a shift in the behavior pattern. The criteria for such color shock have been best described by Brosin and Fromm (49) and are as follows:

(1) Time. There will be a significant delay prior to the first scorable response. Occasionally on a card with an easily seen form — for example, Card VIII — this delay will not occur until after the simple form is given; or, occasionally, preoccupation with the shock of the color cards may be carried over and result in a prolongation of reaction time to the succeeding cards.

(2) Exclamations indicative of newly aroused emotions different from those produced by uncolored cards.

(3) Comment by the subject indicative of anxiety, tension, stress, newly mobilized defense mechanisms such as undue irritation, aggressiveness, passivity, and so forth. These comments may be given during the succeeding cards and refer to the cards which provoke them.

(4) Decline in the total number of responses to the color cards, particularly the last three, as compared with the uncolored ones.

(5) Decline in the quality of the responses. The $F + \%$ will decline and the quality of the responses as to originality and complexity will be poor.

(6) Impoverished content of responses. The meaning of the response rather than its structure is here considered for a decline in richness, originality, expansiveness, and ingenuity. There is usually evidence of satisfaction with commonplace, banal, or indifferent responses. This characteristic is often striking in intelligent neurotics.

(7) Rejection of the card, refusal to touch it, or the quick return of the card to the examiner.

(8) Irregular succession appearing on colored cards when the succession on uncolored cards is orderly.

(9) Decreased ability to see popular configurations when these are quickly or easily seen on the uncolored cards.

(10) Color shyness and absence of color-determined responses in an individual who shows the ability to give them by verbal references to the color but who is unable to use them to advantage in combination with form.

When such color shock occurs, it undoubtedly indicates some neurotic element in the patient's make-up. However, this sign alone is not sufficient to warrant a diagnosis of a psychoneurotic process.

A second important type of shock which has been considered in the literature since Rorchach's time is shading shock. Shading shock implies a reaction to the shaded cards similar to color shock. Cards IV and VI are the most conspicuous in this connection, although Card VII also frequently produces this effect. If the shock is extremely marked, even Cards I and V may provoke some reaction of this type.

Shading shock is manifested by the same reactions as is color shock and indeed frequently occurs in conjunction with color shock. Particularly important in the diagnosis of shading shock are increased reaction time, exclamations, and comments indicative of anxiety, tension, horror, etc., a decrease in the number and quality of the responses, and rejection of the cards in question.

Color shock is so widespread in its occurrence that it seems to indicate a rather common, superficial emotional disturbance. Shading shock, on the other hand, is most frequently found in those individuals who have feelings of inadequacy and are afraid of external contacts. It seems to indicate, more than does color shock, that the individual is aware of his personality instability and that the disturbance is deeply rooted.

In considering the neuroses in general, Miale and Harrower-Erickson (*230*) have described the following nine signs which occur in neurotic records and which serve to differentiate them to some extent from normals.

(1) The number of responses is not more than 25.
(2) The number of *M* is not more than one.
(3) *FM* or animal movement responses outnumber the human movement responses.
(4) Color shock occurs.
(5) Shading shock occurs.
(6) There is refusal or rejection of one or more cards.
(7) More than 50 per cent pure form responses occur.
(8) *A%* is greater than 50.
(9) The number of *FC* responses is not more than one.

These original nine signs have been somewhat modified by Harrower-Erickson as a result of a more exhaustive study, including one hundred persons tested while manifesting neurotic behavior and some five hundred normal controls. This study is to be published shortly. Studies carried on since these signs were suggested have shown that while in general they are of value in differential diagnosis, cases of organic brain disease or dementia praecox, and occasionally normal subjects, may show almost all these signs. A recent study reveals that many of these signs occur in the records of chronic alcoholics, although clinically these individuals were not demonstrably psychoneurotic. The problem here is the same as that occurring in the use of signs in any category. Differential diagnosis is not made by the signs in and of themselves. The signs merely indicate a general trend which further study of the record will either establish or disprove.

Other signs which occur frequently in neurotics but which are not mentioned by these authors are perplexity and impotence. These signs have been taken up in the discussion of organics and will not be further discussed here. They are indications of a profound neurotic disturbance and must be differentiated from actual organic processes.

Certain of the signs, particularly the number of responses, lack of M, color shock, shading shock, refusals, $A\%$, and number of FC responses will be found in schizophrenics, organics, and, except for color and shading shock, in affective depressions. Consequently, while these signs do tend to differentiate the neurotic from the normal, which was the original plan of those who proposed them, they do not differentiate to any great degree the neurotic from other types of psychopathy. Differential diagnosis here depends generally more upon the presence of additional findings which enable us to diagnose other conditions when present. In other words, the neurotic pattern, if it occurs by itself without other demonstrable evidence of more serious disorder, is sufficient indication of a psychoneurotic disorder. If other evidences are present, these signs only indicate concomitant neurotic reaction occurring either as a part of, or as a reaction to, a more profound disease process.

Very little work has been published dealing with the differentiation of the various types of neuroses. In general, pure anxiety states will show, in addition to the above-enumerated signs, a considerable preoccupation with the shading, including K, k, FK, Fc, and C' responses. Also, individuals of this type may show an increase in the m responses, which seems to indicate an actual physiological translation of their anxiety as expressed by their tense and contracted body musculature. Hysterias and obsessive-compulsive neurotics, on the other hand, frequently show very little anxiety and little reaction to the shading elements in the cards. Hysterias frequently fail to respond to the cards, generally because they feel that the procedure is silly and they are too sensitive to expose themselves. Rorschach emphasized this point and indicated further that these individuals, if carefully encouraged, will respond to the cards. This is in distinction to organics and schizophrenics, who cannot, as a rule, be induced to respond adequately to a card, once they have refused it. Hysterias also show profound color shock and frequently show a large amount of reaction to the color cards in the form of pure color and CF responses, indicating their egocentricity, uncontrolled affectivity, and dependence upon and marked influence by the external environment. Their form responses may or may not be good but usually are much poorer than in the anxiety states or in the obsessive-compulsive types. Anxiety states frequently are more introversive, whereas hysterias are usually more on the extratensive side.

Obsessive-compulsive neurotics generally show a particularly profound color shock, which frequently is emphasized by remarks that the colored cards are difficult and that the subjects are unable to use them. They usually show a rigid succession, a high $A\%$, a large number of details, particularly *dd*, and frequent *Do* responses, where only part of a customarily seen response is given. Obsessive-compulsives are more ambiequal concerning the ratio of *M* to sum *C*, approaching ambiequality on the introversive side when obsessive phenomena are prominent and on the extratensive side when compulsive habits predominate.

Rorschach felt that a central position or exact ambiequality occurs in the compulsive doubter. These individuals also may show a number of rejections to the cards together with marked perplexity. This is not because they are unable to see good form but because their neurotic requirement for form is set at so high a standard that they will not give responses which are ordinarily considered good. Finally, in these individuals there is a marked degree of stereotypy and an increase in the $F+\%$ and $A\%$.

Hysterias do not tend to show so much preoccupation with the quality of the response and show much more anxiety, particularly *Fc*, than do the obsessive-compulsive neurotics. In general, differential diagnosis of this group consists in first establishing the presence of a neurotic process by the appearance of color shock, anxiety, and the other signs mentioned above, and then eliminating any more profound disorder by careful scrutiny of the record for responses indicating a more disintegrating type of personality disorder. If nothing more than a neurotic structure can be elicited and if the neurotic elements are sufficiently definite to preclude the possibility of the subject being merely a deviant normal, exact diagnosis is made either by a consideration of the amount of free anxiety, which is paramount in the anxiety states, or of the *erleb-*

nistyp or the general reaction as evidenced by the hysteria cases, or of the whole configuration which characterizes the obsessive-compulsive group. It must be borne in mind that pure examples of the psychoneuroses are clinically rare and, consequently, pure Rorschach patterns will be equally infrequent. We must expect to find admixtures of anxiety, hysterias, and compulsions throughout most records. Neurasthenia is generally evidenced in the Rorschach record by the passivity of the movement responses, as indicated by human-movement responses employing bending, and an introversive psychogram, together with a complete lack of ambition, which is shown in poor responses, description, card rejection, and overemphasis on popular or "cheap" whole answers. In addition, there will usually be marked color shock, shading shock, and considerable preoccupation with the shading elements.

CHAPTER

XIX

DEPRESSIVE STATES

CONSIDERABLE work has been done with the Rorschach method in the study of depressions; but, as in almost all the other branches of psychopathology, the subject has been studied as a whole and finer differentiations of the subgroups included under major headings are yet to be made.

Rorschach believed that the depressive mood improves the form perception, makes the succession more rigid, decreases the number of whole responses, decreases the variability, raises the $A\%$, decreases the number of original responses, and decreases markedly the number of M and color responses. Depressive individuals find their associative processes cut down to such a degree that they frequently are blocked and everything they perceive appears changed or strange. Their records are filled with side remarks, such as "I do not know what I am interpreting; it must be something else," or "I have never seen these cards and I can't tell what they are; they must be something else than what I see." Rorschach felt that, in general, depressives give an average or somewhat less than the usual number of responses and their reactions have less the character of interpretations than of perceptions. They frequently show a prolonged reaction time and tend to subordinate all other considerations to form. This leads to stereotypy and impoverishes the content of interpretation, high $A\%$ being frequent.

These individuals experience the interpretations of the cards as painful uncertainties, and their criticisms of the perceptive process and of their own functions is frequently most caustic. They frequently see many body parts (Ad) and Hd rather than A and H, and Do responses occur occasionally. Their *erlebnistyp* is markedly coarcted, and human movement and color responses are either completely absent or reduced to a minimum. Depressives give a smaller number of responses in these two categories, but the relationship between the two changes very little or not at all.

Guirdham (*94, 95*) in studying such patients also noted a profound decrease in the color and movement responses, but disagreed with Rorschach in that he found a decrease in the percentage of $F+$ and an increase in W responses. Guirdham contended that there was also an increase in the popular responses and in the human details. He felt that the approach is of the W–Dd–D variety, which is at variance with Rorschach's findings, where the importance of Do responses is emphasized. Guirdham also emphasized the shading responses as an index of anxious affectivity occurring in depressions, particularly psychogenic depressions. Beck (*11*) summarizes the records of typical manic-depressive depressives as being over-particular in regard to form, showing low organizing energy and having few or no human movement or color responses. He states, "Low productivity, painful uncertainty, rejection, pedantic self-correction, qualification of responses, self-depreciation, are all characteristic of this group."

Varvel (*331*) corroborated the findings of Beck and Rorschach with regard to the decreased number of movement and color responses in this group. He found the score for organizing energy reduced, as did Beck, but in contradistinction to Guirdham found that the $F + \%$ is increased. He also found that whole responses are few in relation to normal detail and rare detail responses, again in contradistinction to Guirdham, and that such whole responses as do appear are generally banal or vague, requiring little intellectual energy. He also emphasized the appearance of shading responses, chiefly in neurotic depressives.

Comparing this summary of the literature with our experience, we would agree with these authors that the picture described by Rorschach is generally adequate. The depressive group, thus, may be said to be characterized by a constricted psychogram, high $F + \%$, high $A\%$, stereotypy, an approach employing D and Dd at the expense of W, poor perceptual organization, and marked reduction in movement and color responses. Differential diagnosis of this group is not difficult, although cases of neurasthenia, occasional organics, malingerers, and pedantic normals will have to be considered.

Differential diagnosis within the group itself is somewhat more difficult, although certain aids may be given. Patients showing agitated types of depression, psychogenic depressions, and involutional melancholia tend to show a larger number of human-movement responses, and the presence of any movement response should point rather definitely away from a true affective psychotic process.

Color responses may appear in impulsive types, or in atypical depression, or occasionally in psychoneurotics. This finding is at variance with Rorschach's statement that psychoneurotics give few if any color responses. Such color responses are invariably CF or of the C type. Psychoneurotic depressions and atypical depressions frequently show color or shading shock, which is never found in true manic-depressive depressions. Also, neurotic depressions will show shading shock and frequent FK, K, and Fc responses. Another factor which occurs in reactive or neurotic depressions and is fairly common in our experience is the use of black as a color (C'). The use of black as color also occurs in early manic-depressive depressions and seems to indicate a depressive trend resulting from reactions to the environment. This response disappears in true affective depressions, however, when they become profound.

The depressive picture is probably the most difficult for fine diagnostic procedure because the very mechanisms of depression give us a markedly constricted, scanty record which makes the diagnosis of the depression itself easy but obscures the finer nuances necessary for accurate differentiation of the individual type of reaction present.

CHAPTER

XX

MISCELLANEOUS CLINICAL PROBLEMS

IN THIS concluding discussion we shall present known Rorschach findings on a number of unrelated clinical entities, on which little work has as yet been done. These findings suggest areas where important extensive work can be undertaken in the future.

Excitements

Under the heading of excitements, mention should be made of psychotic excitements, confusions, and mania. Levy and Beck (*205*), as well as Rorschach, studied manic-depressive manic phases with the Rorschach method and concluded that these records vary considerably with the degree of excitement. The manic phases, however, were very definite, particularly in contrast to melancholic phases.

In mania, confabulatory, careless, poor whole responses are common and the forms seen are usually at a low level of quality. There is much combining of details, and fabulation and confabulation predominate. The number of original answers generally is high, although poor orig-

397

inal answers, carelessly seen, are the general expectancy. Both human-movement and color responses increase and, as excitement progresses, the color responses tend to become more frequent, with emphasis on the crude type. The animal responses remain high, and may actually increase with a concomitant increase in animal-movement responses. Shading responses are generally not so prominent, but white space answers, particularly in combination with loosely constructed whole responses, are common. Control is definitely decreased, and as the mania becomes more intense the $F + \%$ drops and poor human-movement together with crude color responses become most prominent.

In other states of confusion these general trends are also seen. Organically confused cases, such as toxic exhaustive states, post-electric-shock cases, etc., show an increase in whole responses which are definitely poor and vague. In addition these cases show much less human-movement than acute affective excitements, and their color responses show a much greater trend to color naming. Perseveration predominates, and original answers are much less common.

From these Rorschach findings diagnosis of an acute excitement can be made, and intrinsic differential diagnosis is usually obvious from closer studies. Epileptic and organic excitements will show definite organic patterns, whereas excitements occurring in cases of dementia praecox yield bizarre and obviously schizophrenic responses. Purely manic-depressive manic excitements show neither schizophrenic nor organic coloring, never show any signs of color shock, and generally present simply a picture of pure excitement with increased but crude M and C, as indicated above.

Effects of alcohol

Acute alcoholic intoxication, both at mild levels and at severe ones, does not give any pathognomonic findings, and no typical Rorschach pattern can be described. This is because personality reactions to alcoholic intoxications are apparently dependent upon the personality of the individual intoxicated, and consequently the clinical picture varies markedly from subject to subject. In general, acute alcoholic intoxication, particularly if it is severe, results in an increase in both color and movement responses. The records are very similar to those records found in affective excitements, although original answers are not so prominent and there may be some emphasis on shading responses, particularly *Fc*. White space answers also are increased and in acute intoxication actual color naming may occur. Usually the *M* to sum *C* ratio is shifted to the color side, but in certain cases the reverse trend is found. Odd, bizarre, schizophrenic-like responses never occur in intoxicated normals but if the degree of stupor is profound, confusion, perseveration, color naming, and extremely poor form simulating an organic type of record may be elicited.

To date, studies which have been carried out on chronic alcoholics yield little or no specific information. In general, chronic alcoholics show no typical Rorschach pattern, except that most chronic alcoholics yield Rorschach records which deviate considerably from the so-called normal. This is exactly what we would expect from clinical experience in view of the fact that people take to alcohol for many different reasons and that the underlying psychopathology may differ markedly in different cases. If chronic alcoholic deterioration has not become apparent, records of confirmed drinkers generally show neurotic, schizophrenic, depressive, or psychopathic personality trends. These individuals usually show an increase in *FM* over *M* and an increase in *CF* and *C* over *FC*. In addition they may show an increase in poor form responses and generally present evidence of anxiety in a preoccupation with the shading responses. As deterioration develops, organic signs make their appearance.

Miscellaneous pathological conditions

A number of other studies have been undertaken to correlate Rorschach findings with various types of medical pathology. Booth (*42, 43*), studying personality in chronic arthritics, found in general that such patients showed about the same number of *W* as of *D*, a considerable excess of *W* in the *W : M* ratio, a tendency to give a maximum of whole responses even in records otherwise inhibited, a very low number of color responses and a frequency of shading and color shock, and descriptive responses indicating anxiety, inhibition, and fears of giving in to their feelings.

Hackfield's study (98) on cases of hypertension, Grave's disease, and gastrointestinal disfunction indicated that many of these patients yield similar Rorschach psychograms, characterized by increased details, constriction, sensitivity, and anxiety.

Recent studies by Mulholm and Kelley [1] of cases of spastic colitis have borne out these findings and revealed the rigid coarcted personality structure of these patients, who give records with a preponderance of details, emphasis on excellent form, almost no *M* or *C* responses, a

[1] Unpublished data.

considerable number of *FM* responses, extreme color shock, few shading responses, and markedly aggressive content.

In addition, studies carried out on patients with facial pain and known trigeminal neuralgia or carcinoma of the face or neck have yielded results which are surprisingly normal. The records of these patients show some constriction together with a slight increase in the shading responses, as might be expected, but otherwise their records are entirely normal. However, patients who have the same symptoms but without evidences of organic structural disease yield records which show *FM* greater than *M*, *CF* and *C* greater than *FC*, a decrease in *M*, and definite neurotic color and shading shock.

The presence of long-continued chronic disease, as shown in Booth's study (*42*), may superimpose a more or less definite reaction pattern upon individuals who otherwise may have profound and marked variations in their personality types. Finally, the method may be of considerable value in differentiating between psychological and organic etiologies in cases which present identical clinical syndromes.

Numerous other isolated research projects on various medical problems have been carried out, but the ones cited above are sufficient to indicate that Rorschach studies can be of great value not only in neuropsychiatry but also in the general medical field.

In studies such as those cited, great care must be utilized in limiting the clinical disorder under investigation. In general, such studies should be undertaken only by an individual who is an expert both in the Rorschach method and as a clinician, or by specialists in both fields working in close association. The Rorschach expert will need but little advice, as his methods have been fairly definitely developed for the administration, scoring, and evaluation of results. In dealing with clinical groups, however, he must be mindful to set down, with the utmost care, the criteria by which he selects his various clinical groups. It is not at all sufficient in a research study to report that it is based on records of 100 schizophrenics or 100 manic-depressives. Care must be taken in each case to specify the exact diagnosis, and the criteria upon which it was made should be carefully set forth in writing in the records. There are many clinical classifications in use today in the psychiatric and neurological field, and it is utterly impossible from a mere classification scheme to know what type of patient actually is indicated unless careful descriptive terminology is employed.

This point has often been emphasized by Nolan Lewis in his discussions on the study of constitutions; as, e.g., the vascular constitution in relation to certain groups in mental disorder. If a study is to be undertaken on a group of patients who are diagnosed as catatonic praecox cases, it will be especially necessary that all the criteria upon which the diagnosis of catatonic praecox was made be explicitly stated. For practical use this means that descriptive terminology should be used in preference to mere classification.

Unfortunately, when a new and somewhat sensational technique is developed, there is frequently a tendency for many workers to substitute this single technique for general clinical procedure. This is a great error because, after all, medicine deals with essentially total reactions of an individual, and while various methods may reveal certain pictures or appearances in selected aspects of the individual, physicians and scientists must interpret such results in relation to the total clinical situation.

Juvenile delinquency

In conclusion, a word may be said concerning problems of juvenile delinquency. Beck (*11*), studying problem children covering the entire range of a behavior clinic, found that in general they tend to show a decrease in the color and movement responses suggesting constriction, although an almost equal number with extratensive trends and a smaller number of introversive ones are found. Individual studies of these records, however, show that the introversive tendencies result from a suppression of extratensive traits and that the reverse is true of the extratensive group. He concluded, therefore, that these children show constricted psychic potentialities, a tendency to rigid adherence to form, increase in *Hd, Ad,* and *Do* responses, and increase in the shading responses. Beck felt that these children are suffering from anxiety attitudes and inadequate personality development.

These findings are somewhat opposed to the findings of Zulliger (*361*), who described a delinquency pattern which included three primary signs, as follows: (1) a presence of confabulatory responses (*DW*); (2) a predominance of crude color responses (*CF* + *C*) over *M* + *FC* + shading responses; and (3) an ever-present extratensive *erlebnistyp.*

He also indicated four secondary syndrome symptoms which are usually present: (1) confused or loose succession; (2) a strong component of white space responses; (3) a high *A%*; and (4) a low *H%*.

This syndrome, according to Zulliger, is fairly representative of juvenile thieves. Obviously, however, it cannot be considered as such, since at best this syndrome can only be concluded to represent a personality pattern of an individual who has been a thief. If the same results were found in the study of another subject, one could not, from the Rorschach record alone, conclude that the individual being studied actually was a thief. Furthermore, studies by Kelley and Flicker [2] on juvenile thieves contradict these findings. These workers, like Beck, found that juvenile thieves and other juvenile delinquents show a variety of Rorschach patterns which are similar only in that they are not as a rule normal. Juvenile thieves, and probably juvenile delinquents in general, may show either introversive or extraversive emphasis but, as Beck has indicated, tend to show a repression of some part of their personality in addition to signs of marked anxiety and shading responses, coupled in some cases with abnormal proportions of W or D. FM predominates over M, and marked aggression is usually shown in the content. The only cases in their study which showed similarity to Zulliger's syndromes were those with unusually low intelligence, and it is possible that Zulliger's group was composed exclusively of these individuals.

Compulsive thieves tend to show an ambiequal M : sum C ratio and present a generally marked obsessional picture which is also indicated by the presence of a large number of DW's or poorly combined whole responses. This entire field still requires much investigation; the studies cited suggest the direction future research may take.

[2] Unpublished data.

Effects of drugs

In addition to the studies in the field of medical problems, further research in the reactions of individuals to drugs should be conducted. Studies on the effect of histamine have been reported by Robb, Kovitz, and Rapaport (*279*), and studies of amytal by Kelley and co-workers (*172*) and by Orbison, Eisner and Rapaport (*245*). Work with mescaline was reported by Wertham and Bleuler (*346*), but these studies have barely scratched the surface. Studies on chronic morphine addiction are being undertaken at present by the United States Public Health Service, but the results as yet have not been released.

Military medicine

Recently the Rorschach method has been suggested by Harrower-Erickson (*112, 114*) and by Bigelow (*29*) as an adjunct in military medicine. We touched upon this topic briefly at the end of Chapter I, but a complete discussion is beyond the scope of the present work. The hypothesis in general is that it may be possible to utilize the method in the determination of the personality of officers, aviators, and other personnel of the military service; if certain character weaknesses could be detected, individuals with psychological defects could be removed from, or prevented from attaining, important positions.

From this discussion it will be evident that the Rorschach method can be of the utmost value in medical fields both as an instrument for diagnosis and prognosis and, in some cases, as an indication of possible therapeutic attack.

BIBLIOGRAPHY [1]

(Through January, 1942)

1. AGUIAR, W. E. DE. ("Application of the Rorschach Psychological Test in Forensic Psychopathology.") *Med. Leg. e Criminol, Sao Paulo,* 1935, Vol. 6, pages 62–63.

2. —— ("Possibilities of the Clinical Application of the Psychological Rorschach Method.") *Rev. Neurol. Psiquiat, Sao Paulo,* 1935, Vol. 1, pages 447–454.

3. (Anon.) "A Review of Rorschach Scoring Samples." *Rorschach Res. Exch.,* 1936–1937, Vol. 1, pages 94–102.

4. APOLCZYN, L. "Metoda Rorschacha: Technika Eksperymentów." (Rorschach's Method: Experimental Technique.) *Psychol. Wychow,* 1938–1939, Vol. 11, pages 27–37, 53–66.

5. ARLUCK, E. "A Study of Some Personality Characteristics of Epileptics." *Arch. Psychol.,* 1941, Vol. 263, Pp. 77.

6. —— "A Study of Some Personality Differences between Epileptics and Normals." *Rorschach Res. Exch.,* 1940, Vol. 4, pages 154–156.

7. BARRY, H., and SENDER, S. "The Significance of the Rorschach Method for Consulting Psychology." *Rorschach Res. Exch.,* 1936–1937, Vol. 1, pages 157–167.

8. BECK, S. J. "Autism in Rorschach Scoring: A Feeling Comment." *Character and Pers.,* 1936, Vol. 5, pages 83–85.

9. —— "Configurational Tendencies in Rorschach Responses." *.Amer. J. Psychol.,* 1933, Vol. 45, pages 433–443.

10. —— "Error, Symbol, and Method in the Rorschach Test." *J. Abnorm. Soc. Psychol.* 1942, Vol. 37, pages 83–103.

11. —— "Introduction to the Rorschach Method: A Manual of Personality Study." *Amer. Orthopsychiat. Ass. Monog.,* 1937, Vol. 1, Pp. xv+278.

12. —— "Personality Diagnosis by Means of the Rorschach Test." *Amer. J. Orthopsy.,* 1930, Vol. 1, pages 81–88.

13. —— "Personality Structure in Schizophrenia: A Rorschach Investigation in 81 Patients and 64 Controls." *Nerv. Ment. Dis. Monog.,* 1938, Vol. 63, Pp. ix+88.

14. —— "Problems of Further Research in the Rorschach Test." *Amer. J. Orthopsy.,* 1935, Vol. 5, pages 100–115.

15. —— "Psychological Processes and Traits in Rorschach's Findings." *Psychol. Bull.,* 1935, Vol. 32, pages 683–684.

[1] See 1946 Supplement, pages 453–468, for Supplementary Bibliography.

16. BECK, S. J. "Psychological Processes in Rorschach Findings." *J. Abnorm. Soc. Psychol.*, 1937, Vol. 31, pages 482–488.

17. —— "Some Present Research Problems." *Rorschach Res. Exch.*, 1937, Vol. 2, pages 15–22.

18. —— "Sources of Error in Rorschach Test Procedures." *Psychol. Bull.*, 1940, Vol. 37, pages 516–517.

19. —— "The Rorschach Method and Personality Organization: Balance in Personality." *Amer. J. Psychiat.*, 1933, Vol. 13, pages 519–532.

20. —— "The Rorschach Method and Personality Organization: The Psychological and the Social Personality." *Amer. J. Orthopsy.*, 1934, Vol. 4, pages 290–297.

21. —— "The Rorschach Method and the Organization of Personality: Basic Processes." *Amer. J. Orthopsy.*, 1933, Vol. 3, pages 361–375.

22. —— "The Rorschach Test and Personality Diagnosis: The Feeble-Minded." *Amer. J. Psychiat.*, 1930, Vol. 10, pages 19–52.

23. —— "The Rorschach Test as Applied to a Feeble-Minded Group." *Arch. Psychol.*, 1932, Vol. 136, Pp. 84.

24. —— "The Rorschach Test in Problem Children." *Amer. J. Orthopsy.*, 1931, Vol. 1, pages 501–509.

25. —— "Thoughts on an Impending Anniversary." *Amer. J. Orthopsy.*, 1939, Vol. 9, pages 806–808.

26. BEHN-ESCHENBERG, H. *Psychische Schüleruntersuchungen mit dem Formdeuteversuch.* (Use of Rorschach in School Testing.) Ernst Bircher Verlag, Bern u. Leipzig, 1921, Pp. 67.

27. BENJAMIN, J. D. "Discussion on 'Some Recent Rorschach Problems.'" *Rorschach Res. Exch.*, 1937, Vol. 2, pages 46–48.

28. —— and EBAUGH, F. G. "The Diagnostic Validity of the Rorschach Test." *Amer. J. Psychiat.*, 1938, Vol. 94, pages 1163–1178.

29. BIGELOW, R. B. "The Evaluation of Aptitude for Flight Training: The Rorschach Method as a Possible Aid." *J. Aviat. Med.*, 1940, Vol. 11, pages 202–209.

30. BINDER, H. "Comments concerning the Beck-Klopfer Discussion." *Rorschach Res. Exch.*, 1937, Vol. 2, pages 43–44.

31. —— "Die Helldunkeldeutungen im Psychodiagnostischen Experiment von Rorschach." (Shading Responses in Rorschach Reactions.) *Schweiz. Arch. Neurol. Psychiat.*, 1932–1933, Vol. 30, pages 1–67, 233–286. Reprinted by Orell Fussli, Zurich, 1932, Pp. 123.

32. —— "The 'Light-Dark' Interpretations in Rorschach's Experiment." *Rorschach Res. Exch.*, 1937, Vol. 2, pages 37–42.

33. —— BLEULER, M.; BENJAMIN, J. D.; BOOTH, GOTTHARD, C.; HERTZ, M. R.; KLOPFER, B.; PIOTROWSKI, Z. A.; and SCHACHTEL, E. "Discussion on 'Some Recent Rorschach Problems.'" *Rorschach Res. Exch.*, 1937, Vol. 2, pages 43–72.

34. BINSWANGER, L. "Bemerkungen zu Hermann Rorschach's Psychodiagnostik." (Comments on Rorschach's Psychodiagnostic.) *Z. f. Psychoanal.*, 1923, Vol. 9, pages 512–523.

35. BLEULER, M. "Der Rorschachsche Formdeuteversuch bei Geschwistern." (The Rorschach Method Applied to Siblings.) *Zbl. f. d. Ges. Neuro. u. Psychiat.,* 1929, Vol. 118, pages 366–398.

36. —— "Der Rorschach-versuch als Unterscheidungsmittel von Konstitution und Prozess." (The Rorschach Method as a Means of Distinguishing Biological Constitution and Disease Process.) *Z. Ges. Neurol. Psychiat.,* 1934, Vol. 151, pages 571–578.

37. —— "Discussion on 'Some Recent Rorschach Problems.' " *Rorschach Res. Exch.,* 1937, Vol. 2, pages 45–46.

38. —— "The Shaping of Personality by Environment and Heredity." *Character and Pers.,* 1933, Vol. 1, pages 286–300.

39. —— and R. "Rorschach's Ink-Blot Test and Racial Psychology." *Character and Pers.,* 1935, Vol. 4, pages 97–114.

40. BOOTH, GOTTHARD C. "Comments concerning the Beck-Klopfer Discussion." *Rorschach Res. Exch.,* 1937, Vol. 2, pages 48–53.

41. —— "Objective Techniques in Personality Testing." *Arch. Neurol. Psychiat.,* 1939, Vol. 42, pages 514–530.

42. —— "Personality and Chronic Arthritis." *J. Nerv. Ment. Dis.,* 1937, Vol. 85, pages 637–652.

43. —— and KLOPFER, B. "Personality Studies in Chronic Arthritis." *Rorschach Res. Exch.,* 1936–1937, Vol. 1, pages 40–49.

44. —— KLOPFER, B., and STEIN-LEWINSON, THEA. "Material for a Comparative Case Study of a Chronic Arthritis Personality." *Rorschach Res. Exch.,* 1936, Vol. 1, pages 49–54.

45. BORGES, J. C. C. "The Rorschach Test in Epilepsy." *Neurobiologia, Pernambuco,* 1938, Vol. 1, pages 29–35.

46. BOSS, M. "Psychologisch-charakterlogische Untersuchungen bei antisozialen Psychopothen mit Hilfe des Rorschachschen Formdeuteversuches." (The Rorschach Test Applied to Anti-Social Psychopaths.) *Zbl. f. d. Ges. Neuro. u. Psychiat.,* 1931, Vol. 133, pages 544–575.

47. BÖSZÖRMENZI, G., and MÉREI, F. "Zum Problem vom Konstitution und Prozess in der Schizophrenie auf Grund des Rorschach-Versuches." (Contributions of the Rorschach Test to the Problem of Biological Constitution and Disease Process in Schizophrenia.) *Schweiz. Arch. Neurol. Psychiat.,* 1940, Vol. 45, pages 276–295.

48. BRATT, N. "Noget om det Rorschachske Formtydningsforsög og dets Praktiske Anvendelse." (About the Rorschach Configuration Experiment and Its Practical Application.) *Ugeskr. Laeg.,* 1938, Vol. 100, pages 534–537.

49. BROSIN, H. W., and FROMM, E. O. "Rorschach and Color Blindness." *Rorschach Res. Exch.,* 1940, Vol. 4, pages 39–70.

50. —— and FROMM, E. O. "Some Principles of Gestalt Psychology in the Rorschach Experiment." *Rorschach Res. Exch.,* 1942, Vol. 6, pages 1–15.

51. BROWN, J. F., and ORBISON, W. D. "A Program for the Experimental

Psychological Investigation of Convulsion Therapy." *Bull. Menninger Clin.,* 1938, Vol. 2, pages 151–154.

52. BRUSSEL, J. A., and HITCH, K. S. "The Rorschach Method and Its Uses in Military Psychiatry." *Psychiat. Quart.,* 1942, Vol. 16, pages 3–29.

53. CARDONA, F. "Il Test di Rorschach Nella Diagnostica Psychiatrica." (The Rorschach Test in Psychiatric Diagnosis.) *.Riv. Patol. Nerv. Ment.,* 1937, Vol. 49, pages 252–267.

54. CHENEY, C. O., and CLOW, H. E. "Prognostic Factors in Insulin Shock Therapy." *Amer. J. Psychiat.,* 1941, Vol. 97, pages 1029–1039.

55. COPELMAN, L. S. *Psihodiagnosticul Rorschach in Lumina Activitatii Dinamice a Scoartei Cerebrale.* (Rorschach Psychodiagnosis Considered in the Light of the Dynamic Activity of the Brain.) Bucuresti: Societatea Romana de Cercetari Psihologice, 1935, Pp. 48.

56. COSTA, A. "Le Tavole del Rorschach Quale Mezzo di Ricerca per la Psicologia Normale e Patologica." (The Rorschach Test as a Tool of Research in Normal and Abnormal Psychology.) *Arch. Ital. Psicol.,* 1939, Vol. 17, pages 17–28.

57. COWIN, MARION. "Reporting Group Discussion: What Constitutes a Single Response?" *.Rorschach Res. Exch.,* 1936, Vol. 1, page 4.

58. DAVIDSON, H. H., and KLOPFER, B. "Rorschach Statistics: Part I — Mentally Retarded, Normal, and Superior Adults." *Rorschach Res. Exch.,* 1937–1938, Vol. 2, pages 164–169.

59. —— and KLOPFER, B. "Rorschach Statistics: Part II — Normal Children." *Rorschach Res. Exch.,* 1938, Vol. 3, pages 37–43.

60. DAY, F., HARTOCH, A., and SCHACHTEL, E. "A Rorschach Study of a Defective Delinquent." *J. Crim. Psychopath.,* 1940, Vol. 2, pages 62–79.

61. DIETHELM, O. "The Personality Concept in Relation to Graphology and the Rorschach Test." *Proc. Ass. Res. Nerv. Ment. Dis.,* 1934, Vol. 14, pages 278–286.

62. DIMMICK, G. B. "An Application of the Rorschach Ink-Blot Test to Three Clinical Types of Dementia Praecox." *J. Psychol.,* 1935–1936, Vol. 1, pages 61–74.

63. DROHOCKI, Z. "Psychologiczne Badania nad Epilepsja przy Pomocy Metody Rorschacha." (Psychological Investigations of Epilepsy with the Aid of the Rorschach Method.) *Nowiny Psychjatryczne,* 1928, Vol. 1, pages 32–33.

64. —— "Znaczenie Typologiczne Orjentacji przy Pomocy Barwy lub Ksztaltu. Studium nad Znaczeniem Diagnostycznem Testow Rorschacha." (The Typological Significance of Orientation with the Use of Color or of Form. A Study of the Diagnostic Significance of the Rorschach Test.) *Pol. Arch. Psychol.,* 1932, Vol. 5, pages 406–426.

65. DROPE, D. ("Critical Reflections on the Rorschach and Graphology.") *Arch. Ges. Psychol.,* 1939, Vol. 104, pages 353–379.

66. DUBITSCHER, F. "Der Rorschachsche Formendeuteversuch als Diagnostisches Hilfsmittel." (Rorschach Method as an Aid in Diagnosis.) *Zbl. f. d. Ges. Neuro. u. Psychiat.*, 1932, Vol. 138, pages 515–535.

67. —— "Der Rorschachsche Formendeuteversuch bei Erwachsenen Psychopathen sowie Psychopathischen und Schwachsinnigen Kindern." (Rorschach Method Applied to Adult Psychopaths and Pychopathic and Dull Children.) *Zbl. f. d. Ges. Neuro. u. Psychiat.*, 1932, Vol. 142, pages 129–158.

68. —— "Die Persönlichkeitsentwicklung des Schulkindes im Rorschachischen Formendeuteversuch." (Personality Development of School Children Reflected in their Rorschach Reactions.) *Z. Kinderforsch.*, 1933, Vol. 41, pages 485–494.

69. DUNMIRE, H. "An Evaluation of Beck's Norms as Applied to Young Children." (Paper read before Midwestern Psychological Association, 1939). *Psychol. Bull.*, 1939, Vol. 36, page 629.

70. DWORETZKI, G. "Le Test de Rorschach et l'évolution de la Perception." (The Rorschach Test and the Evolution of Perception.) *Arch. Psychol., Genève*, 1939, Vol. 27, pages 233–396.

71. EARL, C. J. "A Note on the Validity of Certain Rorschach Symbols." *Rorschach Res. Exch.*, 1941, Vol. 5, pages 51–61.

72. ENDARA, J. "A Proposito de Los Examines Biopsicologicos en Delincuentes." (Biopsychological Examinations of Delinquents.) *Arch. Criminol. Neuropsiquiat.*, 1938, Vol. 2, pages 229–234.

73. —— "Psicodiagnóstico de Rorschach y Delincuencia: Clasificación de las Respuestas." (Rorschach's Test and Delinquency: Classification of Answers.) *An. Inst. Psicol. Univ. B. Aires*, 1938, Vol. 2, pages 207–252.

74. —— "Psicodiagnóstico de Rorschach y Delincuencia: Psigramas de dos Homicidas Reincidentes." (The Rorschach Test and Delinquency: Psychograms of Two Habitual Homicidal Criminals.) *Psiquiat. y Criminol*, 1937, Vol. 2, pages 45–50.

75. ENKE, W. "Die Bedeutung des Rorschachschen Formdeuteversuches für die Psychotherapie." (The Significance of the Rorschach Test for Psychotherapy.) *Sitzungsber d. Ges. z. Forderg d. Ges. Naturw. Marburg*, 1927, Vol. 62, pages 621–633.

76. —— "Die Konstitutionstypen in Rorschachschen Experiment." (The Constitutional Types in the Rorschach Test.) *Zbl. f. d. Ges. Neuro. u. Psychiat.*, 1927, Vol. 108, pages 645–674.

77. —— "Experimentalpsychologische Studien zur Konstitutionsforschung." (Studies in Experimental Psychology as a Contribution to Research on Biological Constitutions.) *Zbl. f. d. Ges. Neuro. u. Psychiat.*, 1928, Vol. 114, pages 770–794.

78. FLEISCHER, R. O., and HUNT, J. McV. "A Communicable Method of Recording Areas in the Rorschach Test." *Amer. J. Psychol.*, 1941, Vol. 54, pages 580–582.

79. FOSBERG, IRVING A. "An Experimental Study of the Reliability of the

Rorschach Psychodiagnostic Technique." *Rorschach Res. Exch.*, 1941, Vol. 5, pages 72–84.

80. FOSBERG, IRVING A. "Rorschach Reactions under Varied Instructions." *Rorschach Res. Exch.*, 1938, Vol. 3, pages 12–31.

81. FRANK, L. K. "Comments on the Proposed Standardization of the Rorschach Method." *Rorschach Res. Exch.*, 1939, Vol. 3, pages 101–105.

82. —— "Projective Methods for the Study of Personality." *J. Psychol.*, 1939, Vol. 8, pages 389–413.

83. —— "Projective Methods for the Study of Personality." *.Trans. N. Y. Acad. Sci.*, 1939, Vol. 1, pages 129–132.

84. FRANKEL, F., and BENJAMIN, D. "Der Rorschachsche Formdeuteversuch als Differentialdiagnostisches Mittel für Gutachter." (The Rorschach Test as an Aid for Differential Diagnoses in Legal Opinion.) *Ärztl. Sachverst. Ztg.*, 1932, Vol. 38, pages 20–23.

85. —— and BENJAMIN, D. "Die Kritik der Versuchsperson beim Rorschachschen Formdeuteversuch." (Criticisms by the Subject in the Rorschach Test.) *Schweiz. Arch. Neurol. Psychiat.*, 1934, Vol. 33, pages 9–14.

86. FREEMAN, W., and WATTS, J. W. "An Interpretation of the Functions of the Frontal Lobe Based upon Observations in 48 Cases of Prefrontal Lobectomy." *Yale J. Biol. Med.*, 1939, Vol. 11, pages 527–539.

87. FURRER, A. *Der Auffassungsvorgang beim Rorschachschen Psychodiagnostischen Versuch.* (The Apperceptive Process in Rorschach Reactions.) Zurich: Buchdruckerei zur Alten Universität; 1930.

88. —— "Uber die Bedeutung der 'B' im Rorschachschen Formdeuteversuch." (The Significance of Movement Responses in Rorschach Reactions.) *Imago* (Wien), 1925, Vol. 11, pages 362–365.

89. GANZ, E., and LOOSLI-USTERI, M. "Le Test de Rorschach Appliqué à 43 Garçons Anormaux." (The Rorschach Test Applied to 43 Abnormal Boys.) *Arch. Psychol., Genève*, 1934, Vol. 24, pages 245–255.

90. GARDNER, G. E. "Rorschach Test Replies and Results in 100 Normal Adults of Average IQ." *Amer. J. Orthopsy.*, 1936, Vol. 6, pages 32–60.

91. GOLDFARB, W. "Personality Trends in a Group of Enuretic Children Below the Age of Ten." *Rorschach Res. Exch.*, 1942, Vol. 6, pages 28–38.

92. GOLDSTEIN, KURT. "Personality Studies of Cases with Lesions of the Frontal Lobes: The Psychopathology of Pick's Disease." *Rorschach Res. Exch.*, 1937, Vol. 1, pages 57–64.

93. GUIRDHAM, A. "On the Value of the Rorschach Test." *J. Ment. Sci.*, 1935, Vol. 81, pages 848–869.

94. —— "Simple Psychological Data in Melancholia." *J. Ment. Sci.*, 1936, Vol. 82, pages 649–653.

95. —— "The Diagnosis of Depression by the Rorschach Test." *Brit. J. Med. Psychol.*, 1936, Vol. 16, pages 130–145.

96. GUIRDHAM, A. "The Rorschach Test in Epileptics." *J. Ment. Sci.*, 1935, Vol. 81, pages 870–893.

97. —— "Weitere Beobachtungen nach Rorschach's Testmethode." (Further Observations on the Rorschach Test.) Schweiz. Arch. Neurol. *Psychiat.*, 1938, Vol. 41, pages 8–16.

98. HACKFIELD, A. W. "An Objective Interpretation by Means of the Rorschach Test of the Psychobiological Structure Underlying Schizophrenia, Essential Hypertension, Graves' Syndrome, Etc." *Amer. J. Psychiat.*, 1935, Vol. 92, pages 575–588.

99. HALLOWELL, A. I. "The Rorschach Method as an Aid in the Study of Personalities in Primitive Societies." *Character and Pers.*, 1941, Vol. 9, pages 235–245.

100. —— "The Rorschach Test as a Tool for Investigating Cultural Variables and Individual Differences in the Study of Personality in Primitive Societies." *Rorschach Res. Exch.*, 1941, Vol. 5, pages 31–34.

101. HALPERN, F. "Rorschach Interpretation of the Personality Structure of Schizophrenics Who Benefit from Insulin Therapy." *Psychiat. Quart.*, 1940, Vol. 14, pages 826–833.

102. HALVORSEN, H. "Eine Korrelation zwischen Rorschach Test und Graphologie." (A Correlation between the Rorschach Test and Graphology.) *Z. Agnew. Psychol.*, 1931, Vol. 40, pages 34–39.

103. HANFMANN, E. "Personal Patterns in the Process of Concept Formation." *Psychol. Bull.*, 1940, Vol. 37, page 515 (Abstract).

104. HARRIMAN, P. L. "The Rorschach Test Applied to a Group of College Students." *Amer. J. Orthopsy.*, 1935, Vol. 5, pages 116–120.

105. HARROWER-ERICKSON, M. R. "Diagnosis and Prognostic Value of the Rorschach Test in Neurological Cases." (Paper read before Eastern Psychological Association, 1939.) *Psychol. Bull.*, 1939, Vol. 36, page 662.

106. —— "Directions for Administration of the Rorschach Group Test." *Rorschach Res. Exch.*, 1941, Vol. 5, pages 145–153.

107. —— "Modification of the Rorschach Method for Use as a Group Test." *Rorschach Res. Exch.*, 1941, Vol. 5, pages 130–144.

108. —— "Personality Changes Accompanying Cerebral Lesions: I. Rorschach Studies of Patients with Cerebral Tumors." *Arch. Neurol. Psychiat.*, 1940, Vol. 43, pages 859–890.

109. —— "Personality Changes Accompanying Cerebral Lesions: II. Rorschach Studies of Patients with Focal Epilepsy." *Arch. Neurol. Psychiat.*, 1940, Vol. 43, pages 1081–1107.

110. —— "Personality Studies in Cases of Focal Epilepsy." *Bull. Canad. Psychol. Assn.*, 1941 (February), pages 19–21 (Abstract).

111. —— "Personality Studies in Patients with Cerebral Lesions." *Bull. Canad. Psychol. Assn.*, 1940 (December), pages 9–10 (Abstract).

112. —— "Psychological Factors in Aviation." *J. Canadian Med. Assn.*, 1941, Vol. 44, pages 348–352.

113. —— "Psychological Studies in Patients with Epileptic Seizures," Chapter 20 in *Epilepsy and Cerebral Localization*, by W. Penfield and

T. C. Erickson, C. Thomas, Publisher, Springfield, Illinois, 1941, Pp. xii+623.

114. HARROWER-ERICKSON, M. R. "The Contribution of the Rorschach Method to Wartime Psychological Problems." *J. Ment. Sci.*, 1940, Vol. 86, pages 366–377.

115. —— and MIALE, F. R. "Personality Changes Accompanying Organic Brain Lesions: Pre- and Post- Operative Study of Two Pre-Adolescent Children." *.Rorschach Res. Exch.*, 1940, Vol. 4, pages 8–25.

116. HARTOCH, A., and SCHACHTEL, E. "Über Einige Beziehungen zwischen Graphologie und Rorschachs Psychodiagnostik." (Some Comparative Aspects of Graphology and the Rorschach Test.) *Psyche; Schweiz. Monats.*, 1936, Vol. 3, No. 4, 5.

117. HENRY, J. "Rorschach Technique in Primitive Cultures." *Amer. J. Orthopsy.*, 1941, Vol. 11, pages 230–235.

118. HERTZ, H. "Binder's Shading Responses." *.Rorschach Res. Exch.*, 1937–1938, Vol. 2, pages 79–89.

119. HERTZ, H. and WOLFSON, R. "A Rorschach Comparison between Best and Least Adjusted Girls in a Training School." *Rorschach Res. Exch.*, 1939, Vol. 3, pages 134–150.

120. HERTZ, M. R. "Discussion on 'Some Recent Rorschach Problems.'" *Rorschach Res. Exch.*, 1937–1938, Vol. 2, pages 53–65.

121. —— *Frequency Tables to Be Used in Scoring the Rorschach Ink-Blot Test.* Brush Foundation, Western Reserve, Cleveland, Ohio; 1936.

122. —— "On the Standardization of the Rorschach Method." *.Rorschach Res. Exch.*, 1939, Vol. 3, pages 120–133.

123. —— *Percentage Charts for Use in Computing Rorschach Scores.* Brush Foundation and the Department of Psychology, Western Reserve University, Cleveland, Ohio; 1940.

124. —— "Personality Changes in 35 Girls in Various Stages of Pubescent Development Based on the Rorschach Method." Paper read before the Midwestern Psychological Association, Ohio University, Athens, Ohio; April, 1941.

125. —— "Pubescence and Personality." *.Psychol. Bull.*, 1941, Vol. 38, page 598 (Abstract).

126. —— "Recording the Responses to the Rorschach Ink-Blot Test." *Rorschach Res. Exch.*, 1942, Vol. 6, pages 16–27.

127. —— "Rorschach Norms for an Adolescent Age Group." *.Child Developm.*, 1935, Vol. 6, pages 69–76.

128. —— "Rorschach: Twenty Years After." *Rorschach Res. Exch.*, 1941, Vol. 5, pages 90–129.

129. —— "Scoring the Rorschach Ink-Blot Test." *J. Genet. Psychol.*, 1938, Vol. 52, pages 15–64.

130. —— "Scoring the Rorschach Test with Specific Reference to 'Normal Detail' Category." *Amer. J. Orthopsy.*, 1938, Vol. 8, pages 100–121.

131. —— "Some Personality Changes in Adolescence as Revealed by the Rorschach Method." *Psychol. Bull.*, 1940, Vol. 37, pages 515–516.

132. —— "The Method of Administration of the Rorschach Ink-Blot Test." *Child Developm.*, 1936, Vol. 7, pages 237–254.

133. HERTZ, M. R. "The Normal Details in the Rorschach Ink-Blot Test." *Rorschach Res. Exch.*, 1936–1937, Vol. 1, pages 104–121.

134. —— "The 'Popular' Response Factor in the Rorschach Scoring." *J. Psychol.*, 1938, Vol. 6, pages 3–31.

135. —— "The Reliability of the Rorschach Ink-Blot Test." *J. Appl. Psychol.*, 1934, Vol. 18, pages 461–477.

136. —— "The Rorschach Ink-Blot Test: Historical Summary." *Psychol. Bull.*, 1935, Vol. 32, pages 33–60.

137. —— "The Shading Response in the Rorschach Ink-Blot Test; a Review of Its Scoring and Interpretation." *J. Gen. Psychol.*, 1940, Vol. 23, pages 123–167.

138. —— "Validity of the Rorschach Method." *Amer. J. Orthopsy.*, 1941, Vol. 11, pages 512–520.

139. —— and BAKER, E. "Personality Changes in Adolescence as Revealed by the Rorschach Method: 'Control' Patterns." Paper read before the Midwestern Psychological Association, Ohio University, Athens, Ohio; April, 1941.

140. —— and BAKER, E. "Personality Changes in Adolescence: Color Patterns." *Rorschach Res. Exch.*, 1941, Vol. 5, page 30 (Abstract).

141. —— and KENNEDY, S. "The *M* Factor in Estimating Intelligence." *Rorschach Res. Exch.*, 1940, Vol. 4, pages 105–106 (Abstract).

142. —— and RUBENSTEIN, B. "A Comparison of Three 'Blind' Rorschach Analyses." *Amer. J. Orthopsy.*, 1939, Vol. 9, pages 295–315.

143. —— "Evaluation of the Rorschach Method in Its Application to Normal Childhood and Adolescence." *Character and Pers.*, 1941, Vol. 10, pages 151–162.

144. HIRNING, L. C. "Case Studies in Schizophrenia." *Rorschach Res. Exch.*, 1939, Vol. 3, pages 66–90.

145. HOEL, H. "Pseudodebilitet." (Pseudodebility.) *Svenska Läkartidn*, 1938, Vol. 35, pages 1521–1533.

146. HOLZMAN, G. G., and E. E. "An Evaluation of Personality Analysis in the General Practice of Medicine." *Rorschach Res. Exch.*, 1941, Vol. 5, pages 67–71.

147. HUNT, T. "The Application of the Rorschach Test and a Word-Association Test to Patients Undergoing Prefrontal Lobotomy." *Psychol. Bull.*, 1940, Vol. 37, page 546 (Abstract).

148. HUNTER, M. "Responses of Comparable White and Negro Adults to the Rorschach Test." *J. Psychol.*, 1937, Vol. 3, pages 173–182.

149. —— "The Practical Value of the Rorschach Test in a Psychological Clinic." *Amer. J. Orthopsy.*, 1939, Vol. 9, pages 287–295.

150. HYLKEMA, G. W. "De Rorschach-Test bij Schizophrenen." (The Application of the Rorschach Test to Schizophrenics.) *Ned Tijdschr. Psychol.*, 1938, Vol. 6, pages 1–15.

151. INGEBRECTSEN, E. "Some Experimental Contributions to the Psychology and Psychopathology of Stutterers." *Amer. J. Orthopsy.*, 1936, Vol. 6, pages 630–649.

152. IONESCU-SISESTI, N., and COPELMAN, L. "Le Profil Mental des Parkin-

soniens." (Mental Profiles of Parkinsonians.) *Anal. Psihol.*, 1938, Vol. 5, pages 156–165.

153. IONESCU-SISESTI, N.; COPELMAN, L.; and TUMIN, L. "Profilul Mintal al Parkinsonienilor Post-Encefalitici." (Mental Profile of Cases of Post-Encephalitic Parkinsonism.) *Anal. Psihol.*, 1939, Vol. 6, pages 180–186.

154. JACOBSON, W. T. "A Study of Personality Development in a High School Girl." *Rorschach Res. Exch.*, 1937, Vol. 2, pages 23–35.

155. JASTAK, J. "Rorschach Performances of Alcoholic Patients." *Delaware St. Med. J.*, 1940, Vol. 12, pages 120–123.

156. JUARROS, C. "El Método de Rorschach y Sus Nuevas Aplicaciones." (The Rorschach Method and Its New Applications.) *Rev. Criminol., B. Aires*, 1935, Vol. 22, pages 507–530.

157. —— and SORIANO, M. ("Comparative Results of Normal and Abnormal Children on the Rorschach Test.") *Arch. Españ. Pediatr.*, 1929, Vol. 13, pages 609–613.

158. —— and SORIANO, M. "Le Psychodiagnostic de Rorschach Chez les Enfants Anormaux." (The Rorschach Test Applied to Abnormal Children.) *Conf. Internat. de Psycho. de Paris*, 1927, pages 595–605.

159. KALLMANN, F. J.; BARRERA, S. E.; HOCH, P. H.; and KELLEY, D. M. "The Rôle of Mental Deficiency in the Incidence of Schizophrenia." *Amer. J. Ment. Def.*, 1941, Vol. 45, pages 514–539.

160. KAPLAN, A. H.; MIALE, F. R.; and CLAPP, H. "Clinical Validation of a Rorschach Interpretation." *Rorschach Res. Exch.*, 1937–1938, Vol. 2, pages 153–163.

161. KATZ, H. "Rorschach Investigations on Schizophrenics Treated with Insulin." *Monats. f. Psychiat.*, 1941, Vol. 104, pages 15–33.

162. KELLER, A. *Normale und Unternormale Intelligenz im Rorschachtest.* (Normal and Below Normal Intelligence in the Rorschach Test.) Cologne: Orthen; 1939, Pp. 54.

163. KELLEY, D. M. "A Questionnaire for the Study and Possible Standardization of the Technique of the Rorschach Method." *Rorschach Res. Exch.*, 1941, Vol. 5, pages 62–66.

164. —— "Report of the First Annual Meeting of the Rorschach Institute, Inc." *Rorschach Res. Exch.*, 1940, Vol. 4, pages 102–103.

165. —— "Survey of the Training Facilities for the Rorschach Method." *Rorschach Res. Exch.*, 1940, Vol. 4, pages 84–87.

166. —— "The Rorschach Method as a Means for the Determination of the Impairment of Abstract Behavior." *Rorschach Res. Exch.*, 1941, Vol. 5, pages 85–88.

167. —— and BARRERA, S. E. "Rorschach Studies in Acute Experimental Alcoholic Intoxication." *Amer. J. Psychiat.*, 1941, Vol. 97, pages 1341–1364.

—— and BARRERA, S. E. "The Present State of the Rorschach Method as a Psychiatric Adjunct." *Rorschach Res. Exch.*, 1940, Vol. 4, pages 30–36.

169. —— and BARRERA, S. E. "The Rorschach Method in the Study of

Mental Deficiency: A Résumé." *Amer. J. Ment. Def.*, 1941, Vol. 45, pages 401–407.

170. KELLEY, D. M., and KLOPFER, B. "Application of the Rorschach Method to Research in Schizophrenia." *Rorschach Res. Exch.*, 1939, Vol. 3, pages 55–66.

171. —— and LEVINE, K. "Rorschach Studies during Sodium Amytal Narcoses." *Rorschach Res. Exch.*, 1940, Vol. 4, page 146 (Abstract).

172. —— LEVINE, K.; PEMBERTON, W.; and LILLIAN, K. K. "Intravenous Sodium Amytal Medication as an Aid to the Rorschach Method." *Psychiat. Quart.*, 1941, Vol. 15, pages 68–73.

173. —— and MARGULIES, H. "Rorschach Case Studies in the Convulsive States." *Rorschach Res. Exch.*, 1940, Vol. 4, pages 157–190.

174. —— MARGULIES, H.; and BARRERA, S. E. "The Stability of the Rorschach Method as Demonstrated in Electric Convulsive Therapy Cases." .*Rorschach Res. Exch.*, 1941, Vol. 5, pages 35–43.

175. —— and RIETI, E. "The Geneva Approach to the Rorschach Method." *Rorschach Res. Exch.*, 1939, Vol. 3, pages 195-201.

176. KENYON, V. B.; RAPAPORT, D.; and LOZOFF, M. "Note on Metrazol in General Paresis." *Psychiatry*, 1941, Vol. 4, pages 165–176.

177. KERR, M. "Temperamental Differences in Twins." *Brit. J. Psychol.*, 1936, Vol. 27, pages 51–59.

178. —— "The Rorschach Test Applied to Children." *Brit. J. Psychol.*, 1934, Vol. 25, pages 170–185.

179. KISKER, M. A., and MICHAEL, N. "A Rorschach Study of Psychotic Personality in Uniovular Twins." *J. Nerv. Ment. Dis.*, 1941, Vol. 94, pages 461–465.

180. KLOPFER, B. "Discussion on 'Some Recent Rorschach Problems.'" *Rorschach Res. Exch.*, 1937, Vol. 2, pages 66–68.

181. —— "Personality Aspects Revealed by the Rorschach Method." .*Rorschach Res. Exch.*, 1940, Vol. 4, pages 26–29.

182. —— "Personality Diagnosis in Early Childhood: The Application of the Rorschach Method at the Preschool Level." *Psychol. Bull.*, 1939, Vol. 36, page 662 (Abstract).

183. —— "Personality Differences between Boys and Girls in Early Childhood." *Psychol. Bull.*, 1939, Vol. 36, page 538 (Abstract).

184. —— "Personality Studies of Cases with Lesions of the Frontal Lobes; Rorschach Study of a Bilateral Lobectomy Case — Interpretation." *Rorschach Res. Exch.*, 1936–1937, Vol. 1, pages 83–88.

185. —— "Pseudopsychotic Reactions in Rorschach Records of Preschool Children." *Psychol. Bull.*, 1941, Vol. 38, page 597 (Abstract).

186. —— "Should the Rorschach Method Be Standardized?" *Rorschach Res. Exch.*, 1939, Vol. 3, pages 45–54.

187. —— "The Interplay between Intellectual and Emotional Factors in Personality Diagnosis." *Proc. 6th Inst. Except. Child., Child. Res. Clin.*, 1939, pages 41–47.

188. —— "The Present Status of the Theoretical Development of the

Rorschach Method." *Rorschach Res. Exch.*, 1936–1937, Vol. 1, pages 142–148.

189. KLOPFER, B. "The Shading Responses." *Rorschach Res. Exch.*, 1937–1938, Vol. 2, pages 76–79.

190. —— "The Technique of the Rorschach Performance." *Rorschach Res. Exch.*, 1937, Vol. 2, pages 1–14.

191. —— BURCHARD, M. L.; KELLEY, D. M.; and MIALE, F. R. "Theory and Technique of Rorschach Interpretation." *Rorschach Res. Exch.*, 1939, Vol. 3, pages 152–194.

192. —— DAVIDSON, H. H. *Record Blank for the Rorschach Method of Personality Diagnosis.* Rorschach Institute, Inc., New York; 1941.

193. —— DAVIDSON, H.; HOLZMAN, E.; KELLEY, D. M.; MARGULIES, H.; MIALE, F. R.; and WOLFSON, R. "The Technique of Rorschach Scoring and Tabulation." *Rorschach Res. Exch.*, 1940, Vol. 4, pages 75–83.

194. —— KRUGMAN, M.; KELLEY, D. M.; MURPHY, L.; and SHAKOW, D. "Shall the Rorschach Method Be Standardized?" *Amer. J. Orthopsy.*, 1939, Vol. 9, pages 514–529.

195. —— and MARGULIES, M. A. "Rorschach Reactions in Early Childhood." *Rorschach Res. Exch.*, 1941, Vol. 5, pages 1–23.

196. —— and MIALE, F. R. "An Illustration of the Technique of the Rorschach Interpretation: The Case of Anne T." *Rorschach Res. Exch.*, 1937–1938, Vol. 2, pages 126–153.

197. —— and SENDER, S. "A System of Refined Scoring Symbols." *Rorschach Res. Exch.*, 1936–1937, Vol. 1, pages 19–22.

198. —— and TALLMAN, G. "A Further Rorschach Study of Mr. A." *Rorschach Res. Exch.*, 1938, Vol. 3, pages 31–36.

199. KOGAN, W. "Shifts in Rorschach Patterns during a Critical Period in the Institutional Experience of a Group of Delinquent Boys." *Rorschach Res. Exch.*, 1940, Vol. 4, pages 131–133.

200. KRAFFT, M. R. "Value of the Rorschach Test to Case Work." *Smith Coll. Stud. Soc. Work*, 1940, Vol. 11, pages 153–154 (Abstract).

201. KRUGMAN, M. "Out of the Inkwell: The Rorschach Method." *Rorschach Res. Exch.*, 1940, Vol. 4, pages 91–101. Also in *Character and Pers.*, 1940, Vol. 9, pages 91–110.

202. —— "Rorschach Examination in a Child Guidance Clinic." *Amer. J. Orthopsy.*, 1941, Vol. 11, pages 503–512.

203. KUHN, R. "Der Rorschachsche Formdeuteversuch in der Psychiatrie." (The Rorschach Test in Psychiatry.) *Mschr. Psychiat. Neurol.*, 1940, Vol. 103, pages 59–128.

204. LAYMAN, J. W. "A Quantitative Study of Certain Changes in Schizophrenic Patients under the Influence of Sodium Amytal." *J. Gen. Psychol.*, 1940, Vol. 22, pages 67–86.

205. LEVY, D. M., and BECK, S. J. "The Rorschach Test in Manic-Depressive Psychosis," In *Manic-Depressive Psychosis.* The Williams & Wilkins Company, Baltimore; 1931, pages 167–181. Also in *Amer. J. Orthopsy.*, 1934, Vol. 4, pages 31–42.

206. LINARES, A. ("Experiments on Normal Spanish Children with the Rorschach Test.") *Arch. Neurobiol.*, 1932, Vol. 12, pages 693–738.

207. LINE, W., and GRIFFIN, J. D. M. "Some Results Obtained with the Rorschach Test, Objectively Scored." *Amer. J. Psychiat.*, 1935, Vol. 92, pages 109–114.

208. —— "The Objective Determination of Factors Underlying Mental Health." *Amer. J. Psychiat.*, 1935, Vol. 91, pages 833–842.

209. LOOSLI-USTERI, M. *Le Diagnostic Individual Chez L'enfant au Moyen du Test de Rorschach.* (Individual Diagnosis of the Child by Means of the Rorschach Test.) Paris: Hermann; 1937. Pp. 92.

210. —— "Le Test de Rorschach Appliqué à Différents Groupes l'enfants de 10–13 Ans." (The Rorschach Test Applied to Groups of 10–13 Year Old Children.) *Arch. Psychol.*, 1929, Vol. 22, pages 51–106.

211. —— "Les Interpretations dans le Test de Rorschach. Interprétations, Kinesthésiques et Interprétations-Couleur." (Interpretations of the Rorschach Test. Kinesthetic and Color Interpretations.) *Arch. Psychol.*, *Genève* 1932, Vol. 23, pages 349–365.

212. —— "Von Der Geistes — und Seelenverfassung der Anstaltskinder." (The Mental and Emotional Conditions of Children in Institutions.) *Psychol. Rundschau*, 1930, Vol. 2, pages 45–49.

213. LÖPFE, A. "Uber Rorschachische Formdeuteversuche mit 10–13 Jahrigen Knaben." (The Rorschach Test Applied to Boys 10–13 Years.) *Z. Angew. Psychol.*, 1925, Vol. 26, pages 202–253.

214. LOWENBACH, HANS, and STAINBROOK, C. J. "Observations on Mental Patients after Electro-Shock." Read before the American Psychiatric Association, Richmond, Virginia, May 9, 1941.

215. MACCALMAN, D. R. "The Rorschach Test and Its Clinical Application." *J. Ment. Sci.*, 1933, Vol. 79, pages 419–423.

216. MADOW, L. "Can the Rorschach Ink-Blot Test Be Used to Predict Hypnotizability?" Master's Thesis, The Ohio State University, Columbus, Ohio, 1938.

217. MAHLER-SCHÖENBERGER, M. "Rorschach Findings in a Patient with Generalized Tic and other Tic Patients." (To be published.)

218. —— and SILBERPFENNIG, I. "Der Rorschach'sche Formdeuteversuch als Hilfsmittel zum Verständnis der Psychologie Hirnkranker: I. Zur Psychologie Der Amputierten." (The Rorschach Test as an Aid to Psychological Understanding of Cerebral Disorders: I. Contribution to the Psychology of the Amputee.) *Schweiz. Arch. Neurol. Psychiat.*, 1938, Vol. 40, pages 302–327.

219. MANDOWSKY, C. "Uber die Bedeutung des Rorschach'schen Formdeuteversuchs." (The Significance of the Rorschach Test.) *Die Biologie der Person* (ed. T. Brugsch and F. H. Lewey), 1931, pages 1044–1059.

220. MARINESCU, G.; KREINDLER, A.; and COPELMAN, L. "Essai d'une Interprétation Physiologique du Test Psychologique de Rorschach. Son Application à L'étude de la Dynamique Cérébrale des Jumeaux." (An Attempt at a Physiological Interpretation of the Rorschach Psy-

chological Test. Its Application to the Study of the Cerebral Activity of Twins.) *Anal. Psihol.*, 1934, Vol. 1, pages 14–26.

221. MARINESCU, KREINDLER, A.; and COPELMAN, L. "Le Test de Rorschach et la Dynamique de l'Écorce Cérébrale d'après les Lois des Réflexes Conditionnels de Pavlov." (The Rorschach Test and the Dynamics of the Cerebral Cortex According to Pavlov's Laws of the Conditioned Reflex.) *Ann. Med. Psychol.*, 1935, Part 1, Vol. 93, pages 614–623.

222. MATSKEVITCH, A. N. K. "Metodike Otiskani ja Skritogo Pathologicheskogo Koniplexa po Metodai Rorschacha." (The Method of Detecting Hidden Psychological Complexes According to the Rorschach Method.) *Trudi Ukr. Psikhonevr. Instit.*, 1931, Vol. 15, pages 44–51.

223. MAZA, A. LINARES. "Diagnóstico de Niños Anormales y Superdotados." (Diagnosis of Abnormal and Superior Children.) *Rev. de Ped.*, 1931, Vol. 10, pages 412–417, 456–464.

224. —— "Investigaciones con el Psicodiagnóstico de Rorschach en Niños Normales Españoles." (Experiments on Normal Spanish Children with the Rorschach Test.) *Arch. Neurobiol.*, 1932, Vol. 12, pages 693–738.

225. MELTZER, H. "Personality Differences among Stutterers as Indicated by the Rorschach Test." *Amer. J. Orthopsy.*, 1934, Vol. 4, pages 262–282.

226. —— "Personality Differences between Stuttering and Non-Stuttering Children as Indicated by the Rorschach Test." *Psychol. Bull.*, 1933, Vol. 30, pages 726–727.

227. —— "Talkativeness in Stuttering and Non-Stuttering Children." *J. Genet. Psychol.*, 1935, Vol. 46, pages 371–390.

228. MIALE, F. R. "The Rorschach Forum at the Sixteenth Annual Meeting of the American Orthopsychiatric Association, February 23, 1939." *Rorschach Res. Exch.*, 1939, Vol. 3, pages 106–119.

229. —— CLAPP, H., and KAPLAN, A. H. "Clinical Validation of a Rorschach Interpretation." *Rorschach Res. Exch.*, 1938, Vol. 2, pages 153–162.

230. —— and HARROWER-ERICKSON, M. R. "Personality Structure in the Psychoneuroses." *Rorschach Res. Exch.*, 1940, Vol. 4, pages 71–74.

231. MIRA, L. E. "Exploración de la Afectividad." (Explorations into Affectivity.) *Rev. Médica de Barcelona*, 1930, Vol. 14, pages 222–259.

232. —— "Sobre el Valor del Psicodiagnostico de Rorschach." (Validity of the Rorschach Test.) *Progressos de la Clinica*, 1935, Vol. 30, pages 808–845.

233. MONNIER, M. "La Technique Actuelle du Test Psychodiagnostique de Rorschach (Revision et Criticism)." (The Present Technique of the Rorschach Psychodiagnostic Test. Revision and Criticism.) *Ann. Med. Psychol.*, 1938, Vol. 96, pages 15–22.

234. —— "Le Test Psychologique de Rorschach." (The Rorschach Test.) *Encéphale*, 1934, Vol. 29, pages 189–201, 247–270.

235. MULLER, MAX. "Der Rorschachsche Formdeuteversuch seine Schwie-

regheiten und Ergebrisse." (The Rorschach Test, Difficulties and Results.) *Z. Ges. Neurol, Psychiat.*, 1929, Vol. 118, pages 598–620.

236. MUNROE, RUTH. "Inspection Technique." *Rorschach Res. Exch.*, 1941, Vol. 5, pages 166–191.

237. —— "The Use of the Rorschach in College Guidance." *Rorschach Res. Exch.*, 1940, Vol. 4, pages 107–130.

238. MUNZ, E. "Die Reaktion des Pykniches im Rorschachschen Psychodiagnostischen Versuch." (Rorschach Reactions of the Pyknic Type.) *Z. Ges. Neurol, Psychiat.*, 1924, Vol. 91, pages 26–92.

239. NADEL, A. B. "A Qualitative Analysis of Behavior Following Cerebral Lesions." *Arch. Psychol., New York*, 1938, Vol. 224, Pp. 60.

240. OBERHOLZER, E. "Rorschach's Experiment in Traumatic Mental Disorders." Paper read before the annual meeting of the American Psychiatric Association, Chicago, 1939.

241. —— "Zur Differenzialdiagnose Organischpsychischer und Psychogen Bedingter Störungen nach Schädel-und Hirnstraumen Vermittels des Rorschachschen Formdeuteversuchs." (Contributions of the Rorschach Test to Differential Diagnoses in Psycho-Organic and Psychogenetic Disturbances after Skull Fractures and Cerebral Lesions.) *Bericht Am. I. Internat. Neurologischen Kongress in Bern*, 1931.

242. —— "Zur Differentialdiagnose Psychischer Folgezustände nach Schädeltraumen Mittels des Rorschachschen Formdeuteversuchs." (Contributions of the Rorschach Test to Differential Diagnoses of the Psychological After-Effects of Skull Fractures.) *Z. Ges. Neurol. Psychiat.*, 1931, Vol. 136, pages 596–629.

243. OESER, O. A. "Some Experiments on the Abstraction of Form and Color: Part II. Rorschach Tests." *Brit. J. Psychol.*, 1932, Vol. 22, pages 287–323.

244. OPPENHEIMER, E., and SPEYER, N. "Uitkomsten van de Rorschachproef bij een Geval van Dementia Paralytica Voor en na de Malariakuur." (Results of the Rorschach Test in a Case of Dementia Paralytica before and after Malaria Treatment.) *Psychiat. Neurol. Bl., Amst.*, 1937, Vol. 3, pages 3–8.

245. ORBISON, W. D.; EISNER, E.; and RAPAPORT, D. "Psychiatric Implications of Rorschach Studies with Sodium Amytal." Read before the American Psychiatric Association, Cincinnati, Ohio, 1940.

246. PATTERSON, M., and MAGAW, D. C. "An Investigation of the Validity of the Rorschach Technique as Applied to Mentally Defective Problem Children." *Proc. Amer. Ass. Ment. Def.*, 1938, Vol. 43, No. 2, pages 179–185.

247. PAULSEN, A. "Rorschachs of School Beginners." *Rorschach Res. Exch.*, 1941, Vol. 5, pages 24–29.

248. PESCOR, M. J. "A Further Study of the Rorschach Test Applied to Delinquents." *Publ. Hlth. Rep.*, 1941, Vol. 56, pages 381–395.

249. —— "Age of Delinquents in Relationship to Rorschach Test Scores." *Publ. Hlth. Rep., Wash.*, 1938, Vol. 53, pages 852–864.

250. PESCOR, M. J. "Marital Status of Delinquents in Relationship to Rorschach Test Scores." *Publ. Hlth. Rep., Wash.*, 1939, Supp. No. 153, page 6.

251. PFISTER, O. "Ergebnisse des Rorschachschen Versuches bei Oligophrenen." (Results of the Rorschach Test with Oligophrenics.) *Allg. Z. Psychiat.*, 1925, Vol. 82, pages 198–223.

252. PIOTROWSKI, Z. A. "A Comparative Table of Main Rorschach Symbols." *Psychiat. Quart.*, 1942, Vol. 16, pages 30–37.

253. —— "A Comparison of Congenitally Defective Children with Schizophrenic Children in Regard to Personality Structure and Intelligence Type." *Proc. Amer. Ass. Ment. Def.*, 1937, Vol. 42, pages 78–90.

254. —— "A Simple Experimental Device for the Prediction of Outcome of Insulin Treatment in Schizophrenia." *Psychiat. Quart.*, 1940, Vol. 14, pages 267–273.

255. —— "Blind Analysis of a Case of Compulsion Neurosis." *Rorschach Res. Exch.*, 1937–1938, Vol. 2, pages 89–111. Also in *Kwart. Psychol.*, 1939, Vol. 11, pages 231–264.

256. —— "Comments Concerning the Beck-Klopfer Discussion." *Rorschach Res. Exch.*, 1939, Vol. 2, pages 68–69.

257. —— "On the Rorschach Method and Its Application in Organic Disturbances of the Central Nervous System." *Rorschach Res. Exch.*, 1936–1937, Vol. 1, pages 23–40. Also in *Kwart. Psychol.*, 1937, Vol. 9, pages 29–41.

258. —— "Personality Studies of Cases with Lesions of the Frontal Lobes: II. Rorschach Study of a Pick's Disease Case." *Rorschach Res. Exch.*, 1936–1937, Vol. 1, pages 65–77.

259. —— "Positive and Negative Rorschach Organic Reactions." *Rorschach Res. Exch.*, 1940, Vol. 4, pages 147–151.

260. —— "Psychological Difference between the Schizophrenic and Organic Patient as Revealed in the Rorschach Technique." Paper read before the annual meeting of the Rorschach Institute, New York, 1940.

261. —— "Recent Rorschach Literature." *Rorschach Res. Exch.*, 1937–1938, Vol. 2, pages 172–175.

262. —— "Rorschach Manifestations of Improvement in Insulin Treated Schizophrenics." *Psychosom. Med.*, 1939, Vol. 1, pages 508–526.

263. —— "Rorschach Studies of Cases with Lesions of the Frontal Lobes." *Brit. J. Med. Psychol.*, 1937, Vol. 17, pages 105–118.

264. —— "The Fallacy of Measuring Personality by the Same Methods as Intelligence." *Psychol. Bull.*, 1937, Vol. 34, pages 546–547 (Abstract).

265. —— "The M, FM, and m Responses as Indicators of Changes in Personality." *Rorschach Res. Exch.*, 1936–1937, Vol. 1, pages 148–157.

266. —— "The Prognostic Possibilities of the Rorschach Method in Insulin Treatment." *Psychiat. Quart.*, 1938, Vol. 12, pages 679–689.

267. —— "The Reliability of Rorschach's Erlebnistypus." *J. Abnorm. Soc. Psychol.*, 1937, Vol. 32, pages 439-445.

268. —— "The Rorschach Ink-Blot Method in Organic Disturbances of the

Central Nervous System." *J. Nerv. Ment. Dis.*, 1937, Vol. 86, pages 525–537.

269. PIOTROWSKI, Z. A. "The Rorschach Method as a Prognostic Aid in the Insulin Shock Treatment of Schizophrenics." *Psychiat. Quart.*, 1941, Vol. 15, pages 807–822.

270. —— "The Rorschach Method of Personality Analysis in Organic Psychoses." *Psychol. Bull.*, 1936, Vol. 33, page 795 (Abstract).

271. —— and KELLEY, D. M. "Application of the Rorschach Method in an Epileptic Case with Psychoneurotic Manifestations." *J. Nerv. Ment. Dis.*, 1940, Vol. 92, pages 743–751.

272. POWELL, M. "Relation of Scholastic Discrepancy to Free Associations on the Rorschach Test." *Kentucky Person. Bull.*, 1935, No. 14.

273. PUTNAM, TRACY J. "The Significance of the Alterations of Mental and Emotional Processes Produced by Diseases of the Brain." *Res. Publ. Ass. Nerv. Ment. Dis.*, 1939, Vol. 19, pages 81–107.

274. RICCI, A. "Studi di Diagnosi Differenziale col Reattivo del Rorschach." (Studies of the Differential Diagnosis Attained with the Rorschach Test.) *Cervello*, 1939, Vol. 1, pages 11–20.

275. RICKERS-OVSIANKINA, M. "Description of the First-Grade Normal Details for the Ten Test-Plates." Appendix to Klopfer's article in *Rorschach Res. Exch.*, 1936, Vol. 1, pages 16–17.

276. —— *Rorschach Scoring Samples.* Worcester State Hospital, Worcester, Massachusetts; 1938.

277. —— "The Rorschach Test as Applied to Normal and Schizophrenic Subjects." *Brit. J. Med. Psychol.*, 1938, Vol. 17, pages 227–257.

278. RIZZO, C. ("Preliminary Researches on Normal Italian Adults by Rorschach's Method.") *Riv. Sper. Freniat.*, 1937, Vol. 61, pages 1124–1150.

279. ROBB, R. W.; KOVITZ, B.; and RAPAPORT, D. "Histamine in the Treatment of Psychosis." *Amer. J. Psychiat.*, 1940, Vol. 97, pages 601–610.

280. ROEMER, G. A. "Über die Anwendung des Psychodiagnostischen Verfahrens nach Rorschach auf Fragen der Berufsberatung." (The Use of the Rorschach Test for Problems of Vocational Guidance.) *Kong. f. Exper. Psychol.*, Marburg, 1921, Vol. 7, pages 165–167.

281. —— "Vom Rorschach zum Symboltest." (From the Rorschach to the Symbol Test.) *Zbl. Psychother Sonderh.*, 1938, Vol. 10, pages 310–370.

282. RORSCHACH, H. *Psychodiagnostik: Methodik und Ergebnisse eines Wahrnemungsdiagnostischen Experiments. Deutenlassen von Zufallsformen.* (Psychodiagnostic: Method and Results of an Experiment in Apperceptual Diagnosis by Means of Interpretation of Random Forms.) 1st ed., Ernst Bircher, Bern; 1921, Pp. 174. 2nd ed., Huber, Bern; 1932, Pp. 227. 3d ed., Huber, Bern; 1937, Pp. 255. 4th ed., Huber, Bern; 1941, Pp. 277.

283. —— and OBERHOLZER, E. "Zur Auswertung des Formdeuteversuchs für die Psychoanalyse." *Z. Ges. Neurol. Psychiat.*, 1923, Vol. 82,

pages 240–274. Also translated as "The Application of the Interpretation of Form to Psychoanalysis." *J. Nerv. Ment. Dis.*, 1924, Vol. 60, pages 225–248, 359–379.

284. ROSENZWEIG, S. "Outline of a Cooperative Project for Validating the Rorschach Test." *Amer. J. Orthopsy.*, 1935, Vol. 5, pages 121–123.

285. ROSS, W. D. "Anatomical Perseveration in Rorschach Records." *Rorschach Res. Exch.*, 1940, Vol. 4, pages 138–145.

286. —— "The 'Anxiety Neurosis' Rorschach Record Compared with the Typical Basically Neurotic Record." *Rorschach Res. Exch.*, 1940, Vol. 4, pages 134–137.

287. —— "The Contribution of the Rorschach Method to Clinical Diagnosis." *J. Ment. Sci.*, 1941, Vol. 87, pages 331–348.

288. —— "The Incidence of Some Signs Elicited by the Rorschach Method." *Bull. Canad. Psychol. Assn.*, 1941, February, pages 21–22.

289. RYMER, C. A.; BENJAMIN, J. D.; and EBAUGH, F. G. "The Hypoglycemia Treatment of Schizophrenia." *J. Amer. Med. Assn.*, 1937, Vol. 109, pages 1249–1251.

290. SALAS, J. "El Psicodiagnóstico de Rorschach." (The Psychodiagnostic of Rorschach.) *Arch. Neurobiol.*, 1932, Vol. 12, pages 316–339.

291. —— "La Clasificación de las Respuestas en el Psicodiagnostico de Rorschach." (The Classification of Responses in the Rorschach Test.) *Arch. Neurobiol.*, 1933, Vol. 13, pages 45–80.

292. SANDERS, J.; SCHENK, V. W. D.; and VAN VEEN, P. "A Family with Pick's Disease." *Verh. Akad. Wet. Amst.*, 1939, Sec. 2, Part 38, No. 3, pages 1–124.

293. SANFORD, R.; ADKINS, M. M.; and COBB, E. A. "An Experiment to Test the Validity of the Rorschach Test." *Psychol. Bull.*, 1939, Vol. 36, page 662 (Abstract).

294. SARBIN, T. R. "Rorschach Patterns under Hypnosis." *Amer. J. Orthopsy.*, 1939, Vol. 9, pages 315–319.

295. SAUDEK, R. "A British Pair of Identical Twins Reared Apart." *Character and Pers.*, 1934, Vol. 3, pages 17–39.

296. SCHACHTEL, E. "The Dynamic Perception and the Symbolism of Form." *Psychiatry*, 1941, Vol. 4, pages 79–96.

297. —— and HARTOCH, A. "Discussion on 'Some Recent Rorschach Problems.'" *Rorschach Res. Exch.*, 1937, Vol. 2, pages 70–72.

298. —— and HARTOCH, A. "The Curve of Reactions in the Rorschach Test: A Contribution to the Theory and Practice of Rorschach's Psychodiagnostic Ink-Blot Test." *Amer. J. Orthopsy.*, 1937, Vol. 7, pages 320–348.

299. SCHATIA, VIVA. "The Incidence of Neurosis in Cases of Bronchial Asthma as Determined by the Rorschach Test with Psychiatric Examination." *Psychosom. Med.*, 1941, Vol. 3, pages 157–169.

300. SCHENK, V. W. D. "Der Formdeuteversuch Rorschach bei Organischen Hirnerkrankungen." (The Rorschach Test in Organic Brain Disease.) *Psychiat. Neurol. Bl.*, 1938, No. 3, page 23.

301. SCHNEIDER, E. "Der Rorschachsche Formdeuteversuch." (The Rorschach Test.) *Industr. Psychotech.*, 1935, Vol. 12, pages 223–230.

302. —— "Die Bedeutung des Rorschachschen Formdeuteversuches zur Ermittlung Intellektuel Gehemmter." (The Significance of the Rorschach Test for Diagnosis of Intellectual Retardation.) *Z. Angew. Psychol.*, 1929, Vol. 32, pages 102–163.

303. —— "Eine Diagnostische Untersuchung Rorschachs auf Grund der Helldunkeldeutungen Ergänzt." (A Diagnostic Investigation in the Field of Shading Interpretations.) *Z. Ges. Neurol. Psychiat.*, 1937, Vol. 159, pages 1–10.

304. —— *Psychodiagnostisches Praktikum. Eine Einführung in Hermann Rorschachs Formdeuteversuch.* (Psychodiagnostic Technique. An Introduction to the Rorschach Test.) Barth, Leipzig; 1936. Pp. viii+132.

305. SENDER, S. and KLOPFER, B. "Application of the Rorschach Test to Child Behavior Problems as Facilitated by a Refinement of the Scoring Method." *Rorschach Res. Exch.*, 1936, Vol. 1, pages 5–17.

306. SHAPIRO-POLLACK, ——. *Contribution à L'étude Psychologique de la Puberté à l'aide du Test de Rorschach.* (Contribution to the Psychological Study of Puberty by Means of the Rorschach Test.) Soc. Nouv. d'Imprim., Paris; 1935. Pp. 115.

307. SHUEY, H. "A New Interpretation of the Rorschach Test." *Psychol. Rev.*, 1933, Vol. 40, pages 213–215.

308. —— "Further Discussion on 'Some Recent Rorschach Problems.'" *Rorschach Res. Exch.*, 1937–1938, Vol. 2, pages 170–171.

309. SICHA, K. and M. "A Step toward the Standardization of the Scoring of the Rorschach Test." *Rorschach Res. Exch.*, 1936–1937, Vol. 1, pages 95–101.

310. SILL, J. B. "A Case Study Comparing the Performance on the Binet and on the Rorschach." *Rorschach Res. Exch.*, 1937–1938, Vol. 2, pages 112–124.

311. SINGEISEN, F. "Rorschachbefunde bei Chronisch Lungentuberkulösen und Herzkranken." (Rorschach Findings of Chronic Tubercular and Heart Diseased Persons.) *Schweiz. Arch. Neurol. Psychiat.*, 1940, Vol. 45, pages 230–247.

312. SKALWEIT, W. "Der Rorschach-Versuch als Unterscheidungsmittel von Konstitution und Prozess." (The Rorschach Test as a Means of Differentiation between Biological Constitution and Disease Processes.) *Z. Ges. Neurol. Psychiat.*, 1935, Vol. 152, pages 605–610.

313. —— *Konstitution und Prozess in der Schizophrenie.* (Biological Constitution and Disease Process in Schizophrenia.) Georg Thieme, Verlag, Leipzig; 1934. Pp. 88.

314. —— "Praktisch-diagnostische Verwertung des Rorschachschen Formdeuteversuches." (Application of the Rorschach Test in Clinical Diagnoses.) *Vers. Norddtsch. Psychiate. u. Neurol.*, 1931, Vol. 10, pages 24–25. Also in *Zbl. f. d. Ges. Neuro. u. Psychiat.*, 1932, Vol. 63, page 21 (Abstract).

315. SKALWEIT, W. "Schizophrenie." (Schizophrenia.) *Fortsch. Neurol. Psychiat.*, 1939, Vol. 11, pages 331–349.

316. SOUKUP, F. ("The Study of Personality by the Rorschach Test.") *Čas. Lék. Česk.*, 1931, Vol. 1, pages 881–887. Also in *Zbl. f. d. Ges. Neuro. u. Psychiat.*, 1932, Vol. 61, page 564 (Abstract).

317. STAINBROOK, EDWARD J. "A Modified Rorschach Technique for the Description of Transitory Post-Convulsive Personality States." *Rorschach Res. Exch.*, 1941, Vol. 5, pages 192–203.

318. STAUDER, K. H. *Konstitution und Wesensänderung der Epileptiker.* (Constitution and Character Changes in Epileptics.) Georg Thieme, Leipzig; 1938. Pp. 196.

319. STERREN, H. A. v. D. " 'Moelijke' Kinderen En Rorschachs Psycho-diagnosiek." ("Difficult" Children and Rorschach's Psychodiagnostic.) *Psychiat. Neurol. Bl., Amst.*, 1938, Vol. 42, pages 416 ff.

320. SUARÈS, N. D. "Personality Development in Adolescence." *Rorschach Res. Exch.*, 1938, Vol. 3, pages 2–12.

321. SUNNE, D. "Rorschach Test Norms of Young Children." *Child Developm.*, 1936, Vol. 7, pages 304–313.

322. SZÉKELY, B. "Teoría y Práctica del 'Psicodiagnóstico de Rorschach.' " (Theory and Application of "Rorschach's Psychodiagnostic.") *An. Inst. Psicol. Univ. B. Aires*, 1941, Vol. 3, pages 429–481.

323. TALLMAN, GLADYS. "Further Results of Retesting Mr. A." *Rorschach Res. Exch.*, 1938, Vol. 3, pages 35–36.

324. —— and KLOPFER, B. "Personality Studies of Cases with Lesions of the Frontal Lobes: III. Rorschach Study of Bilateral Lobectomy Case." *Rorschach Res. Exch.*, 1936–1937, Vol. 1, pages 77–89.

325. THORNTON, G. R. "A Note on the Scoring of Movement in the Rorschach Test." *Amer. J. Psychol.*, 1936, Vol. 48, pages 524–525.

326. —— and GUILFORD, J. P. "The Reliability and Meaning of *Erlebnistypus* Scores in the Rorschach Test." *J. Abnorm. Soc. Psychol.*, 1936, Vol. 31, pages 324–330.

327. TROUP, E. "A Comparative Study by Means of the Rorschach Method of Personality Development in Twenty Pairs of Identical Twins." *Genet. Psychol. Monogr.*, 1938, Vol. 20, pages 461–556.

328. —— and KLOPFER, B. "Sample Case Studies" (from No. 327, study of identical twins). *Rorschach Res. Exch.*, 1936–1937, Vol. 1, pages 121–140.

329. TULCHIN, S. H. "The Pre-Rorschach Use of Ink-Blot Tests." *Rorschach Res. Exch.*, 1940, Vol. 4, pages 1–7.

330. VARVEL, W. A. "Suggestions toward the Experimental Validation of the Rorschach Test." *Bull. Menninger Clin.*, 1937, Vol. 1, pages 220–226.

331. —— "The Rorschach Test in Psychotic and Neurotic Depressions." *Bull. Menninger Clin.*, 1941, Vol. 5, pages 5–12.

332. —— "The Rorschach Test in Relation to Perceptual Organization and to Intelligence." Paper read before the Midwestern Psychological Association, Ohio University, Athens, Ohio, April, 1941.

333. VAUGHN, J., and KRUG, O. "The Analytic Character of the Rorschach Ink-Blot Test." *Amer. J. Orthopsy.*, 1938, Vol. 8, pages 220–229.

334. VEIT, H. "Der Parkinsonismus nach Encephalitis Epidemica im Rorschach'schen Fundamentalversuche." (Rorschach Reactions of Post-Encephalitic Parkinsonians.) *Z. Ges. Neurol. Psychiat.*, 1927, Vol. 110, pages 301–324.

335. —— "Der Rorschachsche Versuch als Klinisches Hilfsmittel." (The Rorschach Test as a Clinical Aid.) XLIV. Jahresversammlung der Sudwesldtsch. Psychiater, Freiburg; 1926. Also in *Zbl. f. d. Ges. Neuro. u. Psychiat.*, 1927, Vol. 45, page 840 (Abstract).

336. VERNON, P. E. "Recent Work on the Rorschach Test." (Bibliography, No. II.) *J. Ment. Sci.*, 1935, Vol. 81, pages 894–920.

337. —— "Rorschach Bibliography No. III." *Rorschach Res. Exch.*, 1936–1937, Vol. 1, pages 89–93.

338. —— "The Matching Method Applied to Investigations of Personality." *Psychol. Bull.*, 1936, Vol. 33, pages 149–177.

339. —— "The Rorschach Ink-Blot Test." (Bibliography No. I.) *Brit. J. Med. Psychol.*, 1933, Vol. 13, pages 89–118, 179–200, 271–291.

340. —— "The Significance of the Rorschach Test." *Brit. J. Med. Psychol.*, 1935, Vol. 15, pages 199–217.

341. WALLS, H. G. v. D. "Uber die Beziehungen Zwischen dem Associations-Experiment nach Jung und der Psychodiagnostik nach Rorschach." (The Relationship between the Jung Association and the Rorschach Test.) *Schweiz. Arch. Neurol. Psychiat.*, 1938, Vol. 42, pages 377–403.

342. WEBER, A. "Delirium Tremens und Alkoholhalluzinose im Rorschachschen Formdeutenversuch." (Delirium Tremens and Alcoholic Hallucinosis in the Rorschach Test.) *Z. Ges. Neurol. Psychiat.*, 1937, Vol. 159, pages 446–500.

343. WECHSLER, D.; HALPERN, F.; and JAROS, E. "Psychometric Study of Insulin-Treated Schizophrenics." *Psychiat. Quart.*, 1940, Vol. 14, pages 466–476.

344. WEIL, ANDRÉ A. "The Rorschach Test in Diagnosis of Psychoses and Psychoneuroses." *J. Maine Med. Assn.*, 1941, Vol. 32, pages 35–39.

345. WELLS, F. L. "Rorschach and the Free Association Test." *J. Gen. Psychol.*, 1935, Vol. 13, pages 413–433.

346. WERTHAM, F., and BLEULER, M. "Inconstancy of the Formal Structure of the Personality. Experimental Study of the Influence of Mescaline on the Rorschach Test." *Arch. Neurol. Psychiat.*, 1932, Vol. 28, pages 52–70.

347. WOLFSON, R. "Scoring, Tabulation, and Interpretation of Two Sample Cases." *Rorschach Res. Exch.*, 1939, Vol. 3, pages 140-150.

348. WOOD, AUSTIN; ARLUCK, EDWARD; and MARGULIES, HELEN (Compilers). "Report of a Group Discussion of the Rorschach Method." *Rorschach Res. Exch.*, 1941, Vol. 5, pages 154–165.

349. YOUNG, R. A., and HIGGINBOTHAM, S. A. "Behavior Checks on the Rorschach Method." *Amer. J. Orthopsy.*, 1942, Vol. 12, pages 87–94.

350. ZUBIN, J. "A Psychometric Approach to the Evaluation of the Rorschach Test." *Psychiatry*, 1941, Vol. 4, pages 547–566.

351. —— "A Quantitative Approach to Measuring Regularity of Succession in the Rorschach Experiment." *Character and Pers.*, 1941, Vol. 10, pages 67–68.

352. ZULLIGER, H. "De Rorschachtest ten Dienste van den Opvoedkundige en de Beroepskeuze." (The Use of the Rorschach Test in Education and Vocational Guidance.) *Ned. Tijdschr. Psychol.*, 1937, Vol. 5, pages 50–88.

353. —— "Der Rorschachsche Testversuch im Dienst der Erziehungsberatung." (The Rorschach Test as an Aid in Guidance.) *Z. f. Psychoanal. Päd.*, 1932, Vol. 6, pages 489–495.

354. —— "Der Rorschachtest im Dienste der Erziehungs-und Berufsberatung." (The Rorschach Test as an Aid in Child Guidance and Vocational Guidance.) *Gesundh. u. Wohlf.*, 1934, Vol. 14, pages 273–286.

355. —— "Diagnostische Schwierigkeiten bei einem 'Merkwürdigen Bub' und der Rorschach'sche Test." (Diagnostic Difficulties in the Case of a "Peculiar Boy" and the Rorschach Test.) *Z. Kinderpsychiat.*, 1935, Vol. 2, pages 149–156.

356. —— "Die Angst im Formdeutversuch nach Dr. Rorschach." (Anxiety in the Rorschach Test.) *Z. f. Psychoanal. Päd.*, 1933, Vol. 7, pages 418–420.

357. —— *Einführung in Den Behn-Rorschach Test.* (Introduction to the Behn-Rorschach Test.) Hans Huber, Bern; 1941.

358. —— "Erscheinungsformen und Bedeutung des Farbschocks beim Rorschachschen Formdeutversuch." (Varieties and Meaning of Color Shock in the Rorschach Test.) *Z. Kinderpsychiat.*, 1938, Vol. 4, pages 145–153.

359. —— "Hat der Rorschachsche Formdeutversuch dem Volks-Schullehrer etwas zu Bieten?" (Does the Rorschach Test Offer Anything to the Elementary School Teacher?) *Schweiz. Erzieh. Rdsch.*, 1935.

360. —— "het Optreden en de Beteekenis van den Kleurschok bij den Test van Rorschach." (The Occurrence and Significance of Color Shock in the Rorschach Test.) *Ned. Tijdschr. Psychol.*, 1938, Vol. 6, pages 162–175.

361. —— *Jugendliche Diebs im Rorschach-Formdeutversuch. eine Seelenkundliche und Erzieherische Studie.* (Young Thieves and the Rorschach Test. A Psychological and Pedagogical Study.) Haupt, Bern; 1938. Pp. 166.

362. —— ("The Rorschach Test in Child Guidance.") *Psychother. Praxis*, 1938, Vol. 3, pages 102–107.

The following are non-Rorschach sources referred to in Part Four.

363. BOLLES, M. M. "The Basis of Pertinence." *Arch. Psychol.*, 1937, Vol. 212, Pp. 51.

364. GOLDSTEIN, K. "The Organism." American Book Company, 1939.

365. HANFMANN, E., and KASANIN, J. "A Method for the Study of Concept Formation." *J. Psychol.*, 1937, Vol. 3, pages 521–540.
366. KORZYBSKI, A. "Science and Sanity." Science Press, N. Y., 1941.
367. SCHILDER, P. "Neuroses Following Head and Brain Injuries." The Williams and Wilkins Company, 1940.
368. STORCH, A. "The Primitive Archaic Forms of Inner Experiences and Thought in Schizophrenia." *Nerv. Ment. Dis. Monog.*, 1924, No. 36.
369. WEIGL, E. "On the Psychology of So-called Processes of Abstraction." *J. Abnorm. Soc. Psychol.*, 1941, Vol. 36, pages 3–33.
370. WHITE, W. A. "The Language of Schizophrenia." *Arch. Neurol. Psychiat.*, 1926, Vol. 16, pages 395–413.

Key to Foreign Language Periodicals in the Bibliography

Allg. Z. Psychiat. Allgemeine Zeitschrift für Psychiatrie und Psychiatrisch-Gerichtliche Medizin.
An. Inst. Psicol. Univ. B. Aires. Anales del Instituto de Psicologia, Universidad de Buenos Aires.
Anal. Psihol. Anallee de Psihologie.
Ann. Med. Psychol. Annales médico-psychologiques.
Arch. Criminol. Neuropsiquiat. Archivos de criminología y neuropsiquíatria.
Arch. Españ. Pediatr. Archivos Españoles de Pediatrici.
Arch. Ges. Psychol. Archiv für die Gesamte Psychologie.
Arch. Ital. Psicol. Archivio Italiano di Psicologia.
Arch. Neurobiol. Archivos de Neurobiologia.
Arch. Psychol., Genève. Archives de Psychologie, Genève.
Ärztl. Sachverst Ztg. Ärztliche Sachverständigenzeitung.
Čas. Lék. Česk. Casopis lékafá českých.
Cervello. Il Cervello; Giornale di Neurologia.
Conf. Internat. de Psycho. de Paris. Conférence Internationale de Psychotechnique de Paris.
Encéphale. L'Encéphale.
Fortschr. Neurol. Psychiat. Fortschritte der Neurologie und Psychiatrie.
Gesundh. u. Wohlf. Gesundheit und Wohlfahrt.
Industr. Psychotech. Industrielle Psychotechnik.
Kong. f. Exper. Psychol. Kongress für Experimental Psychologie.
Kwart. Psychol. Kwartalnik Psychologiczny.
Med. Leg. e. Criminol., Sao Paulo. Medicina Legal e Criminología, Sao Paulo.
Monats. f. Psychiat. Monatschrift für Psychiatrie.
Mschr. Psychiat. Neurol. Monatschrift für Psychiatrie und Neurologie.
Ned. Tijdschr. Psychol. Nederlandsch Tijdschrift voor Psychologie.
Neurobiologia, Pernambuco. Neurobiologia. Recife-Pernambuco.
Nowiny Psychjatryczne. Nowiny Psychjatryczne.
Pol. Arch. Psychol. Polskie Archiwum Psychologji.
Progressos de la Clinica. Progressos de la Clinica (Madrid).

Psiquiat. y. Criminol. Revista de Psiquiatría y Criminología.

Psyche; Schweiz. Monats. Psyche; Schweizerische Monatschrift.

Psychiat. Neurol. Bl., Amst. Psychiatrische en Neurologische Bladen. Amsterdam.

Psychol. Rundschau. Psychologische Rundschau.

Psychol. Wychow. Psychologia Wychowawcza.

Psychother. Praxis. Psychotherapeutische Praxis.

Rev. Criminol., B. Aires. Revista de Criminología, Buenos Aires.

Rev. de Ped. Revista de Pediología.

Rev. Neurol. Psiquiat., Sao Paulo. Revista de Neurologia e Psiquiatria de Sao Paulo.

Rev. Medica de Barcelona. Revista Médica de Barcelona.

Riv. Patol. Nerv. Ment. Rivista di Patologia Nervosa e Mentale.

Riv. Sper. Freniat. Revista Sperimentale di Freniatria e Medicina Legale Delle Alienazioni Mentali.

Schweiz. Arch. Neurol. Psychiat. Schweizer Archiv für Neurologie und Psychiatrie.

Schweiz. Erzieh. Rdsch. Schweizer Erziehungsrundschau.

Sitzungsber. d. Ges. z. Förderg. d. Ges. Naturw. Sitzungsbericht der Gesellschaft zur Förderung der Gesamten Naturwissenschaft, Marburg.

Svenska Läkartidn. Svenka Läkartidningen.

Trudi Ukr. Psikhonevr. Instit. Trudy Ukrainskogo Psikhonevrologicheskogo Instituta.

Ugeskr. Laeg. Ugeskrift for Laeger.

Verh. Akad. Wet. Amst. Verhandelinger der Akademie van Wetenschappen te Amsterdam.

Vers. Norddtsch. Psychiater. u. Neurol. Versommlung Norddeutscher Psychiater und Neurologen.

Z. Angew. Psychol. Zeitschrift für Angewandte Psychologie und Charakterkunde.

Z. f. Psychoanal. Zeitschrift für Psychoanalyse.

Z. Ges. Neurol. Psychiat. Zeitschrift für die Gesamte Neurologie und Psychiatrie.

Z. Kinderforsch. Zeitschrift für Kinderforschung.

Z. Kinderpsychiat. Zeitschrift für Kinderpsychiatrie.

Z. f. Psychoanal. Päd. Zeitschrift für Psychoanalysische Pädogogik.

Z. Psychol. Zeitschrift für Psychologie.

Zbl. f. d. Ges. Neuro. u. Psychiat. Zentralblatt für die Gesamte Neurologie und Psychiatrie.

Zbl. Psychother Sonderh. Zentralblatt für Psychotherapie, Sonderhefte.

1946 SUPPLEMENT

NEW TRENDS
IN RORSCHACH DEVELOPMENT

Introduction

The manuscript for the first printing of *The Rorschach Technique* was virtually completed before Pearl Harbor. From that time until the third printing, which is to be accompanied by this Supplement, the United States was actively at war and methods for quick and adequate selection of personnel for the armed forces were wanted. The last war witnessed the development of techniques for testing the *intelligence* of large groups of individuals. In this war the demand was not only for the development of techniques for testing intelligence of individuals, but also for the purpose of detecting deviates in *personality structure*. Experience of the last war with psychoneurotic and psychotic casualties intensified this demand. For the discovery of these personality difficulties which might lead to eventual breakdown, the Rorschach method seemed to supply the necessary vehicle. It is one of the two most widely used projective techniques [1] to attract the interest of psychologists and psychiatrists, both inside and outside the armed forces.

Research in rapid methods of administration and evaluation of the Rorschach method during this period, therefore, overshadows to some degree other developments.

Large-scale administration

That the Rorschach could be used as a group test was first indicated by Vernon, who said that "it should be theoretically possible to give the test in group form" but felt that it would not yield valuable results (*339*).[2] It was not until 1941, when Harrower-Erickson and Steiner proposed a scheme for using the

---

[1] The other being the Thematic Apperception Test.
[2] Italic numbers in parentheses refer to the Bibliography.

Rorschach as a group test (*106, 107*), that this idea received a great deal of attention. Since the publication of their first two articles on the subject, the method of group administration has been discussed and used in research by many workers, notably Hertz (*472*), Hertzman (*484*), Lindner (*524, 527*), Munroe (*542, 546*), and Sender (*603*).

Large-scale interpretation

The need for reducing the amount of time in administering the Rorschach method was temporarily met by these proposals. However, the time and training necessary to interpret the results of a Rorschach protocol still remained a problem. To reduce both the time needed for an interpretation and to serve as an aid to the Rorschach worker, three procedures for more rapid interpretation were used. The first, one that was developed before 1941, may be designated as the "sign" approach. "Signs" have been used in studies of differential diagnosis (*581, 586*), in studies of vocational aptitude (*563, 564*), and in studies of general adjustment (*419, 434, 532*). The possible uses and essential improvements of the sign approach are fully discussed by Ross in several papers (*579, 581, 586*). The second procedure, the "inspection technique," developed by Munroe (*542, 547*), permits rapid scanning of a Rorschach protocol for an ultimate evaluation as to quality of adjustment. The third short-cut method is the multiple-choice technique developed by Harrower and Steiner (*466*). The first two methods attempt to use as far as possible a limited number of objective aspects of the Rorschach in order to arrive at a diagnosis. The interpreter has to discover these aspects — "signs" or "patterns" as used in the inspection technique — in the record of the subject's spontaneous Rorschach responses. The Rorschach worker obviously needs some training to be able to do this. The multiple-choice technique represents an attempt to eliminate this need through the use of selected responses with an *a priori* adjustment value; these are offered to the subject with the task of checking the ones he thinks best fit the blot instead of recording his spontaneous responses. The hopes of the authors of the multiple-choice technique that such a method could be used effectively without any Rorschach training were not fulfilled. Some experimenters who tried to use the multiple-choice technique in such a completely mechanical way found that it did not yield useful results (*412, 497, 635*). On the other hand, experimenters who applied Rorschach interpretation principles to the material yielded by the multiple-choice technique achieved promising results (see *466*, papers by Wright, Due, and Wright). It is apparent that further research with all these methods is needed.

Parallel series

The increased and extended demand for Rorschach material resulted in the offering of at least two parallel series of blots — one new (*460*), the other older but only recently made available in the United States (*357*). Whether or not these are really parallel series in the psychometric sense remains to be investigated.

Textbooks and general surveys

After many years of waiting, there appeared in 1942 an authorized English translation of Rorschach's *Psychodiagnostik* (*574*). It was received with enthusiasm by non-German-reading Rorschach workers. In 1943, the *Journal of Consulting Psychology* devoted an entire issue to a discussion of the Rorschach method in its many aspects (*388, 429, 457, 478, 508, 514, 550, 563*). A number of books on the Rorschach method in general have appeared (*411, 517, 604*). The most important new general contribution in English is the two volumes by Beck (*382, 383*). While the first volume presents merely a description of the various scoring categories, with numerous examples, the second presents a valuable survey of Rorschach records covering a number of clinical entities.

Another important general contribution is one by Rapaport which includes the Rorschach along with other diagnostic devices in the study of the total personality (*568*). The fact that the Rorschach method is most useful when applied in conjunction with other psychometric and projective measures is being more and more widely recognized (*439, 448, 491, 504, 506, 551, 568, 569, 591, 618*).

Methodological problems

Matters of technique of administration and scoring have definitely receded into the background, except possibly the scoring of F+ and of organizational activity (437, 479, 510). Interest is now centered rather in the establishment of norms for various age groups, particularly among children (see especially 413, 433, 473, 474, 475, 481, 482, 500, 552, 592, 617, 630), and on the validation of the method (470, 476, 513, 542, 614, 615).

Clinical application

The original purpose of the Rorschach method — that is, to provide an objective means for differential diagnosis in a clinical situation — is still of primary concern. It should be mentioned at this point that the *Graphic Rorschach* (444), used as a supplement to the usual procedure, may aid in establishing a definitive diagnosis. Not only as a diagnostic aid, but also for the purpose of planning treatment (477, 599, 608) and predicting its outcome (540), the Rorschach method is proving to be of value. In research employing the Rorschach method the following clinical entities have received special attention: schizophrenia, depression, disturbances of the central nervous system, psychopathic personality, epilepsy, homosexuality, malingering, and psychosomatic medicine.

Other fields of application

The Rorschach method has become a valuable adjunct in many fields of work: in anthropological and sociological studies, both of primitive societies (415, 416, 421, 422, 445, 446, 554, 593) and of modern societies (373, 419, 610, 624); in vocational guidance and selection of personnel (376, 377, 450, 561, 563); in mental hospitals (534, 625); in penal institutions (459, 621); in school and college guidance (417, 434, 546); in social case work (436, 439, 440, 512, 600, 601); and in child-guidance clinics (513, 514, 533).

The application of the Rorschach method from Rorschach's first publication up to the present time has not been predicated upon any particular theory of personality. Nevertheless, a number of the newer publications indicate that use of the method is having a stimulating effect on the development of such a theory.

FORM-LEVEL RATING

A Preliminary Proposal for Appraising Mode and Level of Thinking as Expressed in Rorschach Records

I. INTRODUCTION

In an opinion survey among teachers of psychology at American universities and colleges recently conducted by the Rorschach Institute (426), one of the most frequently expressed criticisms of the Rorschach method was that many of its adherents appear to use a magic procedure rather than a method which can be scientifically described and verified. The best way to dispel such a misconception seems to be to develop methods which will enable any professionally trained psychologist or psychiatrist to understand the various criteria used in arriving at a Rorschach interpretation.

The aim of the present report is to propose a method for the purpose of objectifying one area of Rorschach interpretation — namely, the area of intellectual functioning as expressed in the form level. The writers experimented with teaching this procedure in a number of different Rorschach classes during the last three years and found it not only teachable but especially helpful for beginners in the use of the Rorschach method. Nevertheless, the method proposed is in an experimental stage and is offered at this time in order that research workers may experiment with it.

The form-level rating as proposed here is intended to supplement the usual psychometric procedures which, by themselves, give a more precise estimate of the intellectual efficiency level. However, a combination of the routine psychometric picture with a projective picture of intellectual functioning as revealed by the Rorschach method seems to yield a more adequate description of the mental abilities of an individual. Such a twofold approach is quite indispensable in treatment planning for educational and therapeutic work. Other important areas of application of form-level rating are discussed at the end of this section.

II. Definition of Form Level

The term "form level" as used in these considerations refers to certain form qualities of the subject's Rorschach responses — namely, accuracy, specification, and organization.

A. Accuracy

The term "accuracy" as traditionally used in the Rorschach literature refers to the degree of fit between the total outline characteristics of the blot area used for a response and the generally accepted form qualities of the concept given in response to this blot area. One prerequisite for evaluating the accuracy of a response is that the concept chosen for a response have a sufficiently *definite* form to make a comparison between it and the form of the blot areas meaningful. Evasive concepts like map, X ray, anatomical chart, and clouds, which are chosen by subjects for the very purpose of avoiding the test of accuracy, are essentially *indefinite* in character and are as a rule (unless chosen for a conspicuously inappropriate blot area or card) outside the range of the concept of accuracy or inaccuracy as here used. The fact that the distinction between definite and indefinite concepts has not been sufficiently considered in previous attempts at evaluation of accuracy is the cause of most of the confusions which arise in scoring accuracy. This actually is at the basis of most inconsistencies in the plus and minus scores published in Rorschach's *Psychodiagnostics* (575).

B. Specification

"Specification" refers to the use of specific elements within a chosen blot area either for justifying or for refining and elaborating the concept chosen in response to this area.[3] *Positive,* constructive forms of *specification* are described later in the sections on form-level credits and sample responses. However, not all specifications mentioned by subjects spontaneously during the performance proper or in the inquiry are constructive in that they serve the purpose of justification or refinement. Non-constructive or *negative specification* may be distinguished as follows:

[3] The term "specification" replaces the term "elaboration" as used throughout *The Rorschach Technique*.

1. *Specifications irrelevant to the form level.* Some specifications are merely embellishments and actually do not contribute in any way to the form level of the responses. For instance, the usual animals in Card VIII are described as walking from rock to rock, but then the subject points out that one foot is on the blue rock and the other on the gray rock. The specification of the position of the feet is irrelevant, since it does not raise the form level of the response beyond the specification of walking.

2. *Specifications which lower the form level.* Less frequently, but still within the range of normal (non-psychotic and not mentally deficient) subjects, one finds specifications which are unjustifiable within the context of the response. Instead of refining the concept, they make it appear in some particular more crude or sloppy or infantile. A not too infrequent example is offered by the light-gray outer-side protrusions in Card V. Subjects who do not feel free to omit any part of the blot material in the card but do not have the ingenuity to find a proper explanation for these protrusions often attach them as extra legs or as hands of some winged creature which they see in this card. To give another example, in the inquiry to "a long-eared rabbit" seen in the usual inner green portion in Card X, a subject first pointed out very carefully "two eyes, nose, smiling mouth, and two straight ears above." Then she decided to add the darker-green areas and used for this purpose a favorite device of calling the rabbit an "Alice in Wonderland character." However, instead of interpreting these dark-green portions as the folds of a scarf or the back of a throne or using any other appropriate explanation, she attached to the rabbit two more "long green curly ears," a forced and far-fetched idea which not only does not contribute to the total form level of the concept but actually detracts from it. In another response, given to Card II, the inappropriateness of the specification is based on an intrinsic contradiction of details given: the subject saw two cows' heads and described the eyes as closed, but at the same time mentioned the pupils of the eyes.

3. *Specifications which destroy the total form level.* This kind of specification is exemplified by what Rorschach described as "confabulatory combination." For example, some subjects see

the face of an animal in Card I, using the white spaces as eyes and mouth, and attach to this face some of the smaller protrusions as legs and tails. This kind of response occurs frequently among preschool children, but among adults of at least average intelligence such destructive specifications are quite rare.

The destructive effect of this third type of specification lies in the fact that the inconsistencies within the concept leave no essential part of the concept unaffected, in contradistinction to the second type described above, which affected merely peripheral parts of the concept, leaving an acceptable core undistorted.

C. Organization

The term "organization" refers to the procedure used by a subject in order to combine the various blot areas into a meaningful concept — whether he uses all the blot material on a card or only parts of it.

These three qualities of accuracy, specification, and organization should form an adequate basis for a quantifiable evaluation of the form level of each Rorschach response.

III. History of the Form-Level Rating

Previous efforts to use quantitative rating scales for evaluating form level were limited to rating either accuracy or organization. Rorschach suggested a very rough distinction between accurate and inaccurate responses which he described as F+ and F—. He was merely interested in discovering to what extent the concept formation of a subject fell below the minimum requirements for accuracy expected from a non-psychotic subject of at least average intelligence. He therefore used the form characteristics of the most popular responses as a yardstick for establishing his minimum requirements, suggesting that any response at least as accurate as a popular response be rated F+ and that any response not measuring up to these minimum requirements be rated as F—. He paid no attention to the problems of specification as described previously, nor did he distinguish between definite and indefinite responses. Nevertheless, his statistical principle of using the most popular responses as a basis for establishing the minimum requirements for accuracy seems entirely sound and has been used in the rating scale proposed in the present treatise.

Rorschach also distinguished between various forms of organization relating primarily to the W response, such as simple and combinatorial W's and simultaneous and successive combinations. Rorschach seemed to feel that the number of W's used by a subject was more an indication of the ability to organize or synthesize, in contrast to the F+ per cent, which was more an indication of the capacity for analysis and logical thinking.

Beck, too, realized that the principle of organization played at least as important a role in establishing the level of thinking as did accuracy. He went farther than Rorschach and recognized that "organizing energy" may be extended to the partial use of blot material (detail responses). He developed a quantitative scale for evaluating "organizing energy" and distinguished the following forms of organization: (1) responses using adjacent details; (2) responses using distant details which are separated either by white space or by solid portions; (3) responses which combine white spaces with adjacent solid portions; (4) responses where the portions of the figures are broken up and the elements recombined into meaningful percepts; (5) the use of the whole blot material on one card for one concept (9). However, he still thought that it might be possible to evaluate organizing ability independently of accuracy. It is this separate evaluation of organization and of form accuracy in part which accounts for the interpretative limitations of Beck's Z score.

Beck's Z score is further limited by the fact that he simply states that all whole responses are scored for Z. But it is everyone's experience that different subjects may use the whole blot material in any one of the ten cards in very different fashion. A three-year-old child who calls each one of the ten cards "doggie," paying little or no attention to the differences in the blot material of each card, certainly does not use much "organizing energy" by using W ten times. Likewise, a brain-tumor patient, completely preoccupied with his sickness, may describe each one of the ten cards as "insides of the human body," making feeble efforts to identify roughly the side contours of the blot material with the outlines of the chest, hips, or any other part of the human anatomy. In either case, the lack of interest in or ability for organizing the blot material is evident. The inadequacy of the undifferentiated organization score is not limited to such extreme cases. It is certainly equally true for all indefinite and evasive responses (clouds, islands, bones, etc.) frequently used by more or less emotionally disturbed subjects. In other words, the scoring of the organizational elements aimed at in Beck's Z score gives an adequate picture of the subject's thinking only in so far as it takes into account accuracy and specification of the total concept. This fact is succinctly demonstrated in a recent study of organization activity in the Rorschach (437).

There is one procedure published in the literature which attempts to overcome the shortcomings of Beck's Z score. This is Hertz's "g" score (479), which is a refinement of Vernon's "g" score (336). Hertz, as did Vernon and others, recognized that the rating of accuracy and organization cannot be separated. Her procedure selects responses involving organization which are weighted according to their accuracy level. She distinguishes three accuracy levels: first, the inaccurate and P responses; second, the accurately perceived but not original responses; and third, the accurately perceived but original responses. In two separate studies, Hertz found correlations of .954 and .958 between her "g" score and Beck's Z score.[4] These high correlations of Beck's Z score, which assumes accuracy and weights organization, with a score which assumes organization and weights accuracy, demonstrates conclusively that any form-level evaluation separating accuracy and organization must be inadequate and artificial. Accuracy and organization are mutually interdependent.

For this reason the rating scale now proposed attempts to combine all three aspects of form level — namely, accuracy, specification, and organization — in one numerical rating. It is hoped that this combined rating will give a more accurate picture of the level of a subject's thinking.

---

[4] According to personal communication, Beck's Z score was applied in such a manner that only responses with definite form were rated, thus omitting the indefinite whole responses which would necessarily interfere with a high correlation.

IV. The Rating Scale

A. General description

The scale as now proposed evolved from preliminary experimentation with various numerical schemes. It seemed to cover most adequately the form-level differences found in Rorschach responses. The scale is arranged around a *zero value* representing Rorschach responses with indefinite form and extends from there two main steps in the minus direction and two main steps in the plus direction. Minus two (—2.0) responses are the irrational concepts found chiefly in psychotic records; minus one (—1.0) responses are the inaccurate concepts given by subjects with a mental capacity below that of the average adult or by those functioning below their normal capacity. Plus two (+2.0) responses are the logical, original responses found chiefly in records of high average or superior people. Plus one (+1.0) responses are the usual responses found in records of intellectually average adult subjects or of subjects functioning not above this level due to emotional reasons.

In order to differentiate further superior form level in Rorschach responses, the basic ratings of +1.0 and +2.0 can be increased by credits for additional spontaneous and accurate specifications and for organization. A plus five (+5.0) form-level rating has been found to be the practical upper limits for this rating scheme.[5]

The extremes of the scale (—2.0 and +5.0), therefore, describe form-level values most rarely found in Rorschach responses; the middle values (0.0 and +1.0) describe the run-of-the-mill responses found most frequently in any random selection of records. This is to be expected, due to the fact that the form-level value of +1.0 is based on the form level of "popular responses" — that is, those occurring most frequently. The manner in which the ratings are assigned is explained below. It might be noted

---

[5] To simplify the scale, Dr. William Goldfarb suggested that the possibility of increasing the basal ratings of plus one (+1.0) and plus two (+2.0) by giving credit for specifications be eliminated and rather use these ratings as such, to which a weighted organization score be added instead. This idea deserves further experimentation.

that beginners unused to the intricacy of a method feel more at ease, the more quantitative choices they have for intermediate decision. For this reason half-point values have been inserted in the rating scale.

For further clarification, the following descriptive definitions of the main points in the rating scale are given.

Zero rating. Zero rating is given to those responses where the form element is indefinite or is completely disregarded in favor of shading color, or abstract movement. This zero rating, however, is not assigned to such responses when they are given to a blot or blot area with a very definite form configuration which is grossly disregarded. In such cases, rather, a minus rating is assigned.

Minus ratings. There are two main levels which need to be distinguished on the minus side of the rating scale:

—*1 rating* is assigned to the inaccurate responses where some effort on the part of the subject to reconcile the shape of the blot area chosen and the form elements of the concept is recognizable, but where this effort is ineffectual.

—*2 rating* is used for irrational responses where for one reason or another the subject does not bother at all to try to reconcile the shape of the blot area chosen with the form elements of the concept.

An intermediate rating between these two main minus levels (the rating —1.5) may be given to the classical confabulatory response which starts with some effort on the part of the subject to reconcile the shape of the blot with the concept chosen, but where this effort is subsequently completely abandoned.

Plus ratings. As discussed in the section on the history of form-level rating, Rorschach's principle of using the most frequent responses or the so-called popular responses as an assessing point in gauging the accuracy of other responses was also used in the present rating scale for determining the *basal rating* to be assigned a response. Therefore, the most frequent responses — that is, the popular responses — are given a basal rating of

+1.0. The most unusual but obviously keen responses (the so-called good original responses) are given a basal rating of +2.0.

Intermediate ratings of +0.5 and +1.5 may be used: the +0.5 rating may be given to responses which are fairly usual and not inaccurate but *semi-definite* in shape, like "peninsula" to the outer d in Card I or "autumn leaf" to the lower D in Card VIII; the +1.5 rating may be given to responses which are almost as frequent as the popular responses, like the "two people dancing" in Card II or "totem pole" to the upper D in Card VI.

B. Form-level credits

1. *Adding credits.* Each constructive specification or organizational elaboration adds one-half point credit to the basal rating under the following conditions.

   a. The specification must be spontaneous. Each addition which is to be credited must be offered spontaneously by the subject either in the performance proper or in the inquiry. Information secured once the examiner begins to prod cannot be credited. General inquiry questions or following clues offered by the subject are not considered prodding.[6]

   b. The specification must exceed the essential elements of the concept. This may take the form of: (1) mentioning a part of a concept not usually included (like seeing the claws of the bat or the protruding round eyes of the moth in Card I, along with the body and wings) or (2) pointing out a specific position (like bending over of the men in Card III or the stretching neck of a snake seen in the small upper side detail of Card IV).

   c. The specification must be independent. For example, the pointing out of several interdependent details like the snout and ears of the usual animal heads in Card II or the eyes and eyebrows of the face in the top detail of Card IV are counted as only *one* specific elaboration and therefore given

---

[6] The kind of information necessary for rating form level may not be available in records obtained by the group method, not supplemented by an individual inquiry, or where the coöperation of the subject is not secured. In such cases, the form-level rating can only be estimated.

just one-half credit. Also, the use of other determinants (color, shading, or abstract movement) besides form counts as a specific elaboration only when the use of such a determinant makes the concept more precise. The red tall hats of the clowns in Card II, for example, count as just one specific elaboration because the use of the color does not make the concept "tall hats" more precise. However, "pieces of red clothing visible through the black over-garments" would be credited as an additional specific elaboration.

d. *Organization.* When successful effort to organize the blot material is demonstrated, one-half point of credit is added. This organizational activity is evident when two or more areas of the ink blots are perceived as separate concepts but in relationship to each other. This is the case whether or not separate details or a detail combined with white space or the entire ink blot is used in such a manner. Credit for organization would be given, for example, if the animals in Card VIII are seen climbing a mountain, or if the white space in Card II is used as a lake in front of a castle, the castle being the usual top center detail, or if the entire area of Card I is perceived as two gentlemen carrying a lady or the entire area of Card X as an aquarium of tropical fish. Credit for organization is given only when the form level of a response is +1.0 or better.

2. *Subtracting credits.* Specifications which lower the form level as described on page 437 apply only to plus ratings. (No decrement can occur in a minus form-level rating, since by definition minus ratings are assigned to totally inaccurate responses which cannot become more inaccurate.)

Each inaccurate specification may decrease a plus form-level rating by one-half point of credit except in the case of +1.0 ratings. A plus one (+1.0) rating can only be lowered for inaccurate specification to a —0.5 rating, since the ratings 0.0 and +0.5 are reserved for concepts which lack *definiteness* and not for those which lack accuracy. Thus the rating —0.5 represents responses which do not fulfill the accuracy requirements of a $+1.0$ response but which are not completely inaccurate.

3. *Unchanged credit.* The form-level rating of a concept remains unchanged when irrelevant specifications are mentioned by the subject. The nature of these irrelevant specifications is described on page 437.

Specific samples for various form-level ratings will be given in the next section. To illustrate the whole process of raising the form level of a popular concept by specification and organization, let us consider the popular response to Card III, "two people." Heads, bodies, and legs are the essential prerequisites of this very popular response. Pointing out their peculiar bent-over position is one way of going beyond these minimum requirements. Organizing the blot material in such a way that the bottom center detail is used for something definite they are lifting or holding in their hands is another way to earn additional form-level credit. Using the red spots as decorative backdrop may add more credit along organizational lines. Furthermore, there are endless opportunities for using some of the details in the blot area for further specification; for instance, the white space between "body and legs" as the vest coming out between coat and pants; another little white spot in the "body" area as a handkerchief in the vest pocket; the lowermost part of the "leg" area as high-heeled shoes, the light gray part in this area as spats; the inner protrusion on the "leg" part as coattails blown by the wind; the protrusion of the upper inner edge of the "body" part as flowers on their lapels; the light-gray color of the "neck" area as high stiff collars; the lower edge of the "head" area as goatee; some of the lighter shadings in the "head" area as sideburns; some others as the bald part of the head.

V. Sample Responses for Various Form-Level Ratings [7]

Examples of responses for the several rating levels are listed below. The list is to be read as follows: the *final form-level rating* assigned the response along with the scoring of the re-

[7] The majority of these samples were supplied by Mrs. Comfort Gilder, New York, N.Y.

sponse is shown in parentheses. The way in which the final rating was arrived at also is indicated — the *base rating* from which all additions or subtractions are counted is in italics; the additions or subtractions, as the case may be, are shown in parentheses next to the item which justifies them. The inquiry is separated from the performance by starting a new line.

CARD I   (W cF N 0.0)
Gives me a feeling of being of stone or rock. *0.0*

CARD VII   (W K Clouds 0.0)
Just clouds — it looks like it. *0.0*

CARD III   (W Fm,KF Smoke +0.5)
Very stylized kind of smoke coming up from fire down here (all black). *0.0*
Springing quality of it, and swirling of it as it spreads out and gets wider and wider. (0.5)

CARD IX   (W mF,CF Abst. +0.5)
Sea and earth and sky, symbolic, earth and powers under earth, and sky connect. Of first importance is movement upward. *0.0*
Middle green part is earth. Sunlight in sky. Pink is under the earth, fire. Green thing suggests grass. (0.5)

CARD X   (D F Ad P +1.0)
Here is a rabbit's head — here are the long ears, eyes, and mouth. *1.0*

CARD X   (D F A P +1.0)
Octopus because of the many legs. *1.0*

CARD II   (D FC Pl +1.5)
Complicated flower (inner red) *1.0* with stamen shooting up (1.5) and a great many petals, not a real flower, long spikes, red color.

CARD V   (W FM A P +1.5)
Also idea of winged thing *1.0* moving fast (1.5) like a bat. (Raised ½ point because of specification of movement.)

CARD V   (W Fc obj additional 0 +2.0)
Fan with queer double handles. *1.5*
Double handle elaboration on top. Feathery fan (2.0), it's a black fan with a black handle. (Since the black color and double handle do not make the total concept more precise, they are not credited.)

CARD V   (d F → FM Ad +2.0)
Pair of serpents' heads (lower extension) stylized *1.5* like bronze statues facing each other — confronting each other (2.0). (Raised ½ point because of organization of separate details.)

CARD X   (D FM A P +2.0)
On either side delicately shaded blue crabs *1.0* as if holding something green (1.5). (Raised ½ point because of organization.)
Wiggling legs, probably swimming (2.0); color only to identify.

CARD IX   (D Fc,M Hd +2.5)
> Two faces looking down (green area), plump-looking faces looking downward away from each other. *1.5*
Button of nose (2.0) and eyes deep set, plump, fleshy cheeks. (2.5)

CARD III   (D Fe,FM A +2.5)
∨ Another pair of birds here (part of middle black). *1.5*
Heads of birds facing away from each other. Suggestion of feathers, cross between feathers and fur (2.0); has a white eye; the birds are in flight. (2.5)

CARD II   (dr M Hd o +2.5)
Feet of bowlegged person (top red and adjacent black *2.0* trying to toe dance (2.5).

CARD I   (W̶ M,m (H) +3.0)
Figure on either side *1.5* hooded like witches (2.0) riding on a broomstick (2.5); tall caps, breeze blowing clothes back (3.0), capes hiding contour of broomstick.

CARD VII   (W M H +3.0)
∨ Dancing girls *1.5*, very kittenish, coquettish poses (2.0). See legs, body, dress (2.5), bodies twisting, wriggling, fur hats (3.0).

CARD X   (D FM A O +3.0)
∨ Suggests two turtles (usual side gray). *2.0*
Head raised on slant (2.5); legs here and tail. (3.0)

CARD V   (W M,Fc,FC′ H +3.5)
Figure of a dancer *1.5* who is weighted down (2.0) by one of those feather costumes, black feathers. She is pointing toes in wrong way (2.5). Two-peaked headdress with hollow in middle (3.0); might be bright jeweled thing. Has texture of heavy feathers (3.5). Looks tired and knock-kneed.

CARD III   (W̶ M,FC′,Fc H +4.0)
∨ Dance movement *1.5*, Negro dance, violent effect (2.0), club foot in whirl (2.5), one leg up (3.0).
Blackness makes me see it (3.5); back of heads is clearly marked, hair in denser black (4.0). Black men, hair gives it, shape of heads.

CARD VII   (W M H +4.0)
Two ladies gossiping *1.5*; lively conversation over cups of tea; have hats on (2.0); arms extended (2.5) and knees together (3.0).

CARD II Shape and coloration of face gives it; face is dark (3.5) gives accent of force, makes it more animated; hair curled up (4.0), gay.
(W M,FC,Fc H +4.5)

CARD II Two clowns *1.5* dancing (2.0) with hands held up in dance number, red hats (2.5), almost can see faces.
Feet in red below (3.0), red boots, knees up (3.5); costume has red touches on shoulder (4.0); looks like paintbrush strokes (4.5) across it in black ink.
(W M,FC,Fc H +5.0)

CARD II Two people *1.5* with red nightcaps (2.0) putting hands against each other (2.5); on one knee (3.0); look Chinese because one eye is drooping (3.5).
Blurred red feet; knee bent up here, other leg out of sight (4.0), each has hand up, head bent (4.5) with slanting eyes; effect of plump face (5.0).
(D → W CF,m Fire —0.5)

CARD II There is a fire blazing in a stove (lower red area). *0.0*
The fire is red and the stove I saw in other card (—0.5).
(Decreased ½ point because of inaccurate specification — the stove.)
(W F Geo —0.5)
Map (all black area, white space filled in) *0.0* Australia and here is Melbourne, Sydney, and Perth (—0.5). (Decreased ½ point because of inaccurate specification.)

CARD VIII (W F A —1.0)
A butterfly *—1.0*
Points out wings (usual animals), body (orange and blue) veins (usual skeleton), little ears (top gray).

CARDS II–X (W F— obj —2.0)
Airplane. *—2.0*
The response "airplane" given first to Card I on a rational basis is perseverated then for the remaining nine cards in an entirely irrational manner.

VI. USES FOR FORM-LEVEL RATING

The quantification of form level with the help of this rating scale has the effect of bringing into clearer relief qualitative aspects of intellectual functioning. This has practical value in every area of living. The planning of a school program, the giving of vocational guidance and training, the diagnosing of mental deterioration, the prognosing of treatment, are just a few of the areas where it is essential to know how much mental ability a person has at his disposal, in what way it functions optimally, or where its weaknesses lie.

A Rorschach analysis which highlights these qualitative aspects of intellectual functioning can serve as a basis for such decisions.

A. The rating of form qualities of a Rorschach response will serve to point up the qualitative aspects of intelligence

Comparison of the form-level ratings of the scoring categories for location is the main procedure for evaluating such qualitative aspects. This analysis must take into consideration three variables: (1) the general form level of the record; (2) the relative form level of the various location categories; and (3) the quantitative emphasis on each location category.

For instance, in a record with a generally mediocre form level (average around +1.0), with a comparatively low form-level rating of the whole responses as compared to the various types of detailed responses and an underemphasis on whole responses, we may be dealing with a subject who is limited in abstract forms of thinking and, realizing his limitation, tries to concentrate on those procedures where he feels more able to cope with the task. In another situation, where the only difference is that the general form level of the record is high (above +2.0), we deal with a subject who is very intelligent but is too cautious and perhaps too constricted to make use of the capacities that he has to draw general conclusions or to synthesize his experience.

The combination of relatively low W form level (as we had before) but with an overemphasis on whole responses gives the picture of some kind of mental inflation. If this occurs in a record where the general form level is average, it indicates that the subject does not know his own limitations and tries to bite off more than he can chew; in a record where the general form level is superior, it represents a tendency to get lost in abstractions.

The number of such combinations obviously are many. These may suffice as examples at this time.

B. Form-level rating serves to refine the picture of the interplay between the intellectual and the emotional factors in personality

Qualitative comparisons of scoring categories are obviously not limited to location scores. Form-level comparisons between the main determinant categories yield equally interesting results relating primarily to the interplay of emotional and intellectual factors. Conspicuous lowering of the form level in response to the strongly shaded or colored cards is a much finer indicator of color and shading disturbances than any of the other expressions of such disturbances. On the other hand, the use of any particular determinant (movement, color, and shading) combined with a raising in the form level of the responses above the general level is an indication of the stimulating function of the emotional sphere. It may be the imaginative life of the subject (M), his response to outside stimulation (color), or his general longing for affection and contact (differentiated shading), which produces this effect.

C. Form-level rating gives a more precise and objective basis for comparing Rorschach results with psychometric results

In quantifying the form quality of Rorschach responses and thus making it possible to obtain a numerical rating,[8] statistical comparison with psychometric test results becomes feasible.

The following suggestion is offered at this time with reference to obtaining the average form-level rating of a record. We have found it advisable to give double weight to every form-level score of $+2.5$ or over. Naturally, the total sum obtained in this way is still divided by the actual number of responses. Since superior scores are, by definition, rare, such a procedure leads to better differentiation of final ratings on the higher levels. If the total rating is used rather than an average, the general productivity of the subject is taken into consideration in addition.

Not only the final rating but also the amount and kind of scatter of the form-level ratings may be of interest to the ex-

[8] In computing the average form-level rating of a record, additional responses given spontaneously during the inquiry may be included.

perimenter. A large scatter (where even only one response is two points or more above the average of the record) may have important diagnostic value, especially in the recognition of unused intellectual potentialities.

VII. Pictorial Presentation

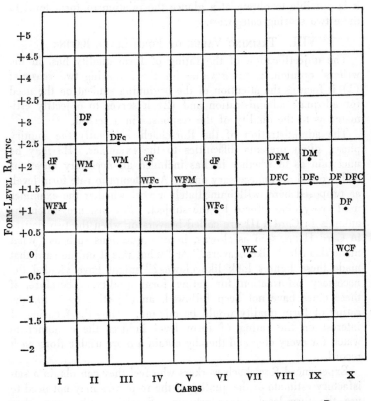

R = 20
Total = 31.5
Raw Average = 1.6
Weighted Average = 1.9
(Scores of 2.5 or over
are doubled)

Averages for Location
Categories
W = 1.1
D = 1.8
d = 2.0

Averages for Determi-
nant—Categories
M = 2.0   Fc = 1.3
FM = 1.5   FC = 1.8
F = 1.9

For ease in obtaining a quick picture of the results, the graphic scheme shown on page 451 is suggested. There are ten spaces along the horizontal axis — one for each card; the form-level ratings are represented along the vertical axis. It is then possible to plot each response to each card according to its form-level rating. If the location score and the main determinant score are indicated, it is possible to obtain at a glance the relation of form level to these two scoring categories.

VIII. Training Value of Form-Level Rating

The objectification of the rating of form quality has, in the writers' opinion, training value for the following two reasons: (1) it focuses the attention of the beginning student on the need for adequate administration and (2) it serves to objectify estimates as to the quality of the responses in a record.

The administration of the Rorschach, especially the inquiry phase, often presents difficulties to the examiner. He may be uncertain as to whether he has included all necessary questions and avoided all unnecessary ones. An attempt to rate form level, as proposed here, will immediately reveal whether the examiner used every clue offered by the subject. For instance, when the animals in Card VIII are called beavers or when the two figures in Card II are seen as clowns, inquiry questions such as "What made them look like beavers?" or "What was it on the card that made these figures look like clowns?" might have yielded the necessary information for rating form quality. Therefore, if these clues have not been followed, an objective basis for the rating of form quality would be missing. Thus the focusing of interest on the rating of form level induces the examiner to watch for every clue and thereby obtain a more usable Rorschach record.

Experienced Rorschach workers who feel they can obtain a satisfactory estimate of the quality of the responses may not need to use the form-level rating scheme. Sometimes, however, they may want to use it either as an objective check on their estimates or for purposes of research. For inexperienced workers, this check is indispensable if they are to arrive at an adequate personality picture.

SUPPLEMENTARY BIBLIOGRAPHY[1]

(Through September, 1945)

371. ABBOTT, W. D.; DUE, F. O.; and NOSIK, W. A. "Subdural Hematoma and Effusion as a Result of Blast Injuries." *J. Amer. Med. Assn.*, 1943, 121, 739–741.

372. ABEL, T. M. "The Rorschach Test and School Success among Mental Defectives." *Rorschach Res. Exch.*, 1945, 9, 105–110.

373. —— PIOTROWSKI, Z. A.; and STONE, G. "Responses of Negro and White Morons to the Rorschach Test." *Amer. J. Ment. Def.*, 1944, 48, 253-257.

374. ANDRESEN, H. "Ueber die Auffassung diffus optischer Eindrücke; ein Beitrag zur Bedingungserforschung der Leistungsvollzüge heim Rorschach test." (The Perception of Diffuse Optical Impressions; a Contribution to the Rorschach Test.) *Z. Psychol.*, 1941, 150, 6–91.

375. BAKER, E. "Personality Changes in Adolescence as Revealed by the Rorschach Method." *Psychol. Bull.*, 1941, 38, 705 (Abstract).

376. BALINSKY, B. "A Note on the Use of the Rorschach in the Selection of Supervisory Personnel." *Rorschach Res. Exch.*, 1944, 8, 184–188.

377. —— "The Multiple Choice Group Rorschach Test as a Means of Screening Applicants for Jobs." *J. Psychol.*, 1945, 19, 203–208.

378. BARISON, F. "Il fattore tempo nel reattivo di Rorschach." (The Time Factor in the Rorschach Method.) *Riv. Psicol. Norm. Pat.*, 1940, January-June.

379. —— "Il reattivo di Rorschach in 74 fanciulli ferraresi di 9–12 anni." (The Rorschach Test on 74 Children of Ferrara, 9–12 Years Old.) *Arch Psicol. Neurol. Psychiat.*, 1940, 2, 1–77.

380. BAUMGARTEN-TRAMER, F. "Zur Geschichte des Rorschachtests." (History of the Rorschach Method.) *Schweiz. Arch. Neurol. Psychiat.*, 1942, 50, 1–13.

381. BECK, S. J. "Effects of Shock Therapy on Personality, as Shown by the Rorschach Test." *Arch. Neurol. Psychiat.*, 1943, 50, 483–484 (Abstract).

382. —— *Rorschach's Test. Vol. I: Basic Processes.* New York: Grune & Stratton, Inc.; 1944. Pages 223.

383. —— *Rorschach's Test. Vol. II: A Variety of Personality Pictures.* New York: Grune & Stratton, Inc.; 1945. Pages 402.

384. —— "Stability of the Personality Structure." *Psychol. Bull.*, 1942, 39, 512 (abstract).

[1] The numbering of this Bibliography continues the numbering of the Bibliography in *The Rorschach Technique*, pages 407–429.

385. BECK, S. J. "The Rorschach Experiment: Progress and Problems." *Amer. J. Orthopsy.*, 1945, 15, 520–524.

386. —— "The Rorschach Test in a Case of Character Neurosis." *Amer. J. Orthopsy.*, 1944, 14, 230–236.

387. —— "The Rorschach Test in Men Discharged from the Armed Forces." *War Psychiatry*. Proceedings of the Second Brief Psychotherapy Council. Chicago: Institute for Psychoanalysis; 1944. Pages 55.

388. —— "The Rorschach Test in Psychopathology." *J. Consult. Psychol.*, 1943, 7, 103–111.

389. BENTON, A. L. "Rorschach Performances of Suspected Malingerers." *J. Abnorm. Soc. Psychol.*, 1945, 40, 94–96.

390. BERGMANN, M. S. "Homosexuality on the Rorschach Test." *Bull. Menninger Clin.*, 1945, 9, 78–83.

391. BILLIG, O. "The Rorschach Test; an Important Aid in the Personality Diagnosis." *N. C. Med. J.*, 1943, 4, 46–50.

392. —— and SULLIVAN, D. J. "Personality Structure and Prognosis of Alcohol Addiction: a Rorschach Study." *Quart. J. Stud. Alcohol*, 1943, 3, 554–573.

393. —— "Prognostic Data in Chronic Alcoholism." *Rorschach Res. Exch.*, 1942, 6, 117–125.

394. BINDER, H. "Die Klinische Bedeutung des Rorschach'schen Versuches." (Clinical Value of the Rorschach Method.) *Schweiz. Arch. Neurol. Psychiat.*, 1944, 53, 12–29.

395. BINSWANGER, W. "Über den Rorschach'schen Formdeuteversuch bei akuten Schizophrenien." (The Rorschach Method in Acute Schizophrenia.) *Schweiz. Arch. Neurol. Psychiat.*, 1944, 53, 101–121.

396. BOCHNER, R., and HALPERN, F. *The Clinical Application of the Rorschach Test*. New York: Grune & Stratton, Inc.; 1945. Pages 330. Second Edition.

397. BOVET, T. "Der Rorschachversuch bei verschiedenen Formen von Epilepsie." (The Rorschach Method in Various Forms of Epilepsy.) *Schweiz. Arch. Neurol. Psychiat.*, 1936, 37, 156–157.

398. BOYNTON, P. L., and WALSWORTH, B. M. "Emotionality Test Scores of Delinquent and Non-Delinquent Girls." *J. Abnorm. Soc. Psychol.*, 1943, 38, 87–92.

399. BRENMAN, M., and REICHARD, S. "Use of the Rorschach Test in the Prediction of Hypnotizability." *Bull. Menninger Clin.*, 1943, 7, 183–187.

400. BROWN, R. R. "The Effect of Morphine upon the Rorschach Pattern in Post-Addicts." *Amer. J. Orthopsy.*, 1943, 13, 339–343; also in *Psychol. Bull.*, 1942, 39, 512–513.

401. BRUNO, A. M. L. "Movimiento Rorschach no Brasil." (The Rorschach Movement in Brazil.) *An. Paulist de Med. Cir.*, 1944, 47, 377–401.

402. —— "Psicograma de Rorschach: Ficha para seu registo." (Rorschach's Psychogram.) *Arq. Policia Civil, S. Paulo*, 1942, 4, 185–198.

403. BRUSSEL, J. A.; GRASSI, J. K.; and MELNICKER, A. "The Rorschach Method and Postconcussion Syndrome." *Psychiat. Quart.*, 1942, 16, 707–743.

404. BUCKLE, D. F., and COOK, P. H. "Group Rorschach Method: Technique." *Rorschach Res. Exch.*, 1943, 7, 159–165.

405. BUHLER, C. "Father and Son." *Rorschach Res. Exch.*, 1943, 7, 145–158.

406. BURGEMEISTER, B. B., and TALLMAN, G. "Rorschach Patterns in Multiple Sclerosis." *Rorschach Res. Exch.*, 1945, 9, 111–122.

407. CAMERON, D. C. "The Rorschach Experiment — X ray of Personality." *Dis. Nerv. Syst.*, 1942, 3, 374–376.

408. CARVALHAL RIBAS, J. "Psico-diagnostico de Rorschach." (The Rorschach Method.) *Rev. Clin. S. Paulo*, 1942, 11, 31–34.

409. CAVALCANTI BORGES, J. C. "Da psicologia de epilepticos genuinos. Respostas de côr primaria no psicodiagnostico de Rorschach." (The Psychology of Idiopathic Epilepsy. Pure Color Responses in Rorschach Records.) *Rev. Med. de Pernambuco*, 1936, 6, 185–187.

410. ——"O teste de Rorschach em epilepticos." (The Rorschach Method in Epilepsy.) *Neurobiologia*, 1938, 1, 29–35.

411. CERQUEIRA, LUIZ. *Psicodiagnóstico de Rorschach.* (The Rorschach Method.) Bahia-Tip. Moderna, 1945. Pages 106. (Contains a bibliography of 21 titles of Rorschach papers published from 1934–1943 in Brazil.)

412. CHALLMAN, R. C. "The Validity of the Harrower-Erickson Multiple-Choice Test as a Screening Device." *J. Psychol.*, 1945, 20, 41–48.

413. CLARDY, E. R.; GOLDENSOHN, L. N.; and LEVINE, K. "Schizophrenic-like Reactions in Children: Preliminary Report: Studies by Electroencephalography, Pneumoencephalography, and Psychological Tests." *Psychiat. Quart.*, 1941, 15, 100–116.

414. COLLIN, A. G. "Review — European Rorschach Findings." *Rorschach Res. Exch.*, 1943, 8, 169–181.

415. COOK, P. H. "Mental Structure and Psychological Field: Some Samoan Observations." *Character and Pers.*, 1942, 10, 296–308.

416. ——"The application of the Rorschach Test to a Samoan Group." *Rorschach Res. Exch.*, 1942, 6, 51–60.

417. COWIN, M. "The Use of the Rorschach in Schools." *Rorschach Res. Exch.*, 1945, 9, 130–133.

418. CRANFORD, V., and SELIGER, R. V. "Understanding the Alcohol Patient, Part I." *J. Clin. Psychopath. and Psychother.*, 1944, 6, 323–334.

419. DAVIDSON, H. H. *Personality and Economic Background: A Study of Highly Intelligent Children.* New York: King's Crown Press; 1943. Pages 189.

420. DE OLIVEIRA, W. I. *O Psicodiagnóstico de Rorschach em epilepticos.* (The Rorschach Method in Epileptics.) Rio de Janeiro: Companhia Editora Americana; 1945. Pages 93.

421. DU BOIS, C. *The People of Alor; a Social Psychological Study of an East Indian Island.* Minneapolis: University of Minnesota Press; 1944. Pages 654.

422. —— and OBERHOLZER, E. "Rorschach Tests and Native Personality in Alor, Dutch East Indies." *Trans. N. Y. Acad. Sci.*, 1942, 4, 168–170.

423. DUNBAR, F. *Psychosomatic Diagnosis.* New York: Paul B. Hoeber, Inc.; 1943. Pages 741.

424. ENDACOTT, J. L. "The Results of 100 Male Juvenile Delinquents on the Rorschach Ink Blot Test." *J. Crim. Psychopath.*, 1941, 3, 41–50.

425. ENDARA, J. "Psicodiagnóstico de Rorschach y sus aplicaciones clinicas." (Rorschach's Psychodiagnostics and Its Clinical Applications.) *Arch. Criminol. Neuropsiquiat., Quito*, 1940–1941, 4–5, 90–111.

426. FATERSON, H. F., and KLOPFER, B. "A Survey of Psychologists' Opinions Concerning the Rorschach Method." *Rorschach Res. Exch.*, 1945, 9, 23–29.

427. FOSBERG, I. A. "How Do Subjects Attempt Fake Results on the Rorschach Test?" *Rorschach Res. Exch.*, 1943, 7, 119-121.

428. FRAENKEL, D. "Explication de l'ivresse de haschisch par le test de Rorschach." (Explanation of the Hashish Elation with the Help of the Rorschach Method.) *Hyg. Ment.*, 1935, 30, 66–68.

429. FRANK, L. K. "The Rorschach Method." *J. Consult. Psychol.*, 1943, 7, 63–66.

430. —— and Others. "Psychosomatic Disturbances in Relation to Personnel Selection." *Ann. N. Y. Acad. Sci.*, 1943, 44, 541–624.

431. FREEMAN, H.; RODNICK, E. H.; SHAKOW, D.; and LEBEAUX, T. "The Carbohydrate Tolerance of Mentally Disturbed Soldiers." *Psychosom. Med.*, 1944, 6, 311–317.

432. FUNKHOUSER, J. B., and KELLEY, D. M. "The Rorschach Ink-Blot Method." *Virginia Med. Mon.*, 1942, 69, 139–144.

433. GAIR, M. "Rorschach Characteristics of a Group of Very Superior Seven-Year-Old Children." *Rorschach Res. Exch.*, 1944, 8, 31–37.

434. GANN, E. *Reading Difficulty and Personality Organization.* New York: King's Crown Press; 1945. Pages 149.

435. GOLDFARB, W. "A Definition and Validation of Obsessional Trends in the Rorschach Examination of Adolescents." *Rorschach Res. Exch.*, 1943, 7, 81–108.

436. —— "Effects of Early Institutional Care on Adolescent Personality: Rorschach Data." *Amer. J. Orthopsy.*, 1944, 14, 441–447.

437. —— "Organization Activity in the Rorschach Examination." *Amer. J. Orthopsy.*, 1945, 15, 525–528.

438. —— "The Animal Symbol in the Rorschach Test and an Animal Association Test." *Rorschach Res. Exch.*, 1945, 9, 8–22.

439. —— "The Effects of Early Institutional Care on Adolescent Personality (Graphic Rorschach Data)." *Child Developm.*, 1943, 14, 213–223.

440. —— and KLOPFER, B. "Rorschach Characteristics of 'Institution Children.'" *Rorschach Res. Exch.*, 1944, 8, 92–100.

441. GOLDMAN, G. S., and BERGMAN, M. S. "A Psychiatric and Rorschach Study of Adult Male Enuresis." *Amer. J. Orthopsy.*, 1945, 15, 160–166.

442. GOLDSTEIN, K., and ROTHMANN, E. "Physiognomic Phenomena in Rorschach Responses." *Rorschach Res. Exch.*, 1945, 9, 1–7.

443. GRASSI, J. R. "Contrasting Schizophrenic Patterns in the Graphic Rorschach." *Psychiat. Quart.*, 1942, 16, 646–659.

444. —— and LEVINE, K. N. "The Graphic Rorschach Manual." *Psychiat. Quart.*, 1943, 17, 258–281.

445. HALLOWELL, A. I. "Acculturation Processes and Personality Changes as Indicated by the Rorschach Technique." *Rorschach Res. Exch.*, 1942, 6, 42–50.

446. —— "The Rorschach Technique in the Study of Personality and Culture." *Amer. Anthrop.*, 1945, 47, 195–210.

447. HANFMANN, E. "A Study of Personal Patterns in an Intellectual Performance." *Character and Pers.*, 1941, 9, 315–325.

448. HARRISON, R. "The Thematic Apperception and Rorschach Methods of Personality Investigation in Clinical Practice." *J. Psychol.*, 1943, 15, 49–74.

449. HARROWER, G. J. "Medical Technologists' Group Personality Estimate." *Canad. J. Med. Technol.*, 1942, 4, 177–178.

450. —— and COX, K. J. "The Results Obtained from a Number of Occupational Groupings on the Professional Level with the Rorschach Group Method." *Bull. Canad. Psychol. Assn.*, 1942, 2, 31–33.

451. HARROWER, M. R. (HARROWER-ERICKSON). "A Multiple-Choice Test for Screening Purposes (for Use with the Rorschach Cards or Slides)." *Psychosom. Med.*, 1943, 5, 331–341; also in *American Society for Research in Psychosomatic Problems,* Proceedings of the Military Session, May 9, 1943, pages 9–19.

452. —— "Clinical Use of Psychological Tests." *McGill Med. J.*, 1941, 11, 105–109.

453. —— "Developments of the Rorschach Test for Large Scale Application." *Rorschach Res. Exch.*, 1944, 8, 125–140.

454. —— "Diagnosis of Psychogenic Factors in Disease by Means of the Rorschach Method." *Phychiat. Quart.*, 1943, 17, 57–66.

455. —— "Directions for Administration of the Rorschach Group-Test." *J. Genet. Psychol.*, 1943, 62, 105–117.

456. —— "Group Test Techniques: A Discussion of an Eclectic Group Method." *Rorschach Res. Exch.*, 1942, 6, 147–152.

457. —— "Large Scale Investigation with the Rorschach Method." *J. Consult. Psychol.*, 1943, 7, 120–126.

458. —— "Personality Changes Accompanying Organic Brain Lesions: III. A Study of Preadolescent Children. *J. Genet. Psychol.*, 1941, 58, 391–45.

459. HARROWER, M. R. (HARROWER-ERICKSON). "Personality Testing in Penal Institutions." *Probation,* 1943, 22, 1–6.

460. ——*Psychodiagnostic Inkblots.* New York: Grune & Stratton, Inc.; 1945. Manual and ten plates.

461. ——"The Patient and His Personality." *McGill Med. J.,* 1941, 11, 25–40.

462. ——"The Rorschach Method in the Study of Personality." *Ann. N. Y. Acad. Sci.,* 1943, 44, 569–583.

463. ——"The Rorschach Test." *J. Assn. Amer. Med. Coll.,* 1944, 19, 193–200.

464. ——"The Use of the Multiple Choice Test (Rorschach) in the Military Services." *War Psychiatry.* Proceedings of the Second Brief Psychotherapy Council. Chicago: Institute for Psychoanalysis; 1944. Pages 55.

465. ——"The Value and Limitations of the So-Called 'Neurotic Signs.'" *Rorschach Res. Exch.,* 1942, 6, 109–114.

466. —— and STEINER, M. E. *Large Scale Rorschach Techniques; a Manual for the Group Rorschach and Multiple-Choice Test.* Springfield, Illinois: Charles C. Thomas; 1945. Pages 149.

467. —— and STEINER, M. E. "Modification of the Rorschach Method for Use as a Group Test." *J. Genet. Psychol.,* 1943, 62, 119–133.

468. —— WASHBURNE, A. C.; and JACOB, J. S. L. "A Preliminary Screening Test for Disturbances in Personality." *Bull. Canad. Psychol. Assn.,* 1944, 4, 4–6.

469. HERTZ, M. R."Comments on the Standardization of the Rorschach Group Method." *Rorschach Res. Exch.,* 1942, 6, 153–159.

470. ——"Evaluation of the Rorschach Method and Its Application to Normal Childhood and Adolescence." *Character and Pers.,* 1941, 10, 151–162.

471. ——*Frequency Tables to Be Used in Scoring the Rorschach Ink-Blot Test* (Rev. Ed.). Cleveland: Western Reserve University Press, Department of Psychology; 1942. Pages 275.

472. ——"Modification of the Rorschach Ink-Blot Test for Large Scale Application." *Amer. J. Orthopsy.,* 1943, 13, 191–212.

473. ——"Personality Patterns in Adolescence as Portrayed by the Rorschach Ink-Blot Method: 1. The Movement Factors." *J. Gen. Psychol.,* 1942, 27, 119–188.

474. ——"Personality Patterns in Adolescence as Portrayed by the Rorschach Ink-Blot Method: III. The 'Erlebnistypus' (a Normative Study)." *J. Gen. Psychol.,* 1943, 28, 225–276.

475. ——"Personality Patterns in Adolescence as Portrayed by the Rorschach Method: IV. The 'Erlebnistypus' (a Typological Study)." *J. Gen. Psychol.,* 1943, 29, 3–45.

476. ——"Rorschach: Twenty Years After." *Psychol. Bull.,* 1942, 39, 529–572.

477. —— "The Role of the Rorschach Method in Planning for Treatment." *Rorschach Res. Exch.*, 1945, 9, 134–146.

478. —— "The Rorschach Method: Science or Mystery." *J. Consult. Psychol.*, 1943, 7, 67–79.

479. —— "The Scoring of the Rorschach Ink-Blot Method as Developed by the Brush Foundation." *Rorschach Res. Exch.*, 1942, 6, 16–27.

480. —— "The Validity of the Rorschach Group Method." *Psychol. Bull.*, 1942, 39, 514 (abstract).

481. —— and BAKER, E. "Personality Patterns in Adolescence as Portrayed by the Rorschach Ink-Blot Method: II. The Color Factors." *J. Gen. Psychol.*, 1943, 28, 3–61.

482. —— and EBERT, E. H. "The Mental Procedure of 6- and 8-Year-Old Children as Revealed by the Rorschach Ink-Blot Method." *Rorschach Res. Exch.*, 1944, 8, 10–30.

483. HERTZMAN, M. "A Comparison of the Individual and Group Rorschach Tests." *Rorschach Res. Exch.*, 1942, 6, 89–108.

484. —— "Recent Research on the Group Rorschach Test." *Rorschach Res. Exch.*, 1943, 7, 1–6.

485. —— and MARGULIES, H. "Developmental Changes as Reflected in Rorschach Test Responses." *J. Genet. Psychol.*, 1943, 62, 189–215.

486. —— ORLANSKY, J.; and SEITZ, C. P. "Personality Organization and Anoxia Tolerance." *Psychosom. Med.*, 1944, 6, 317–331.

487. —— and SEITZ, C. P. "Rorschach Reactions at High Altitudes." *J. Psychol.*, 1942, 14, 245–257.

488. HIRNING, L. C. "Report of the Research Committee." *Rorschach Res. Exch.*, 1942, 6, 177.

489. HITCH, K. S. "A Rorschach Diagnosis of Cerebral Arteriosclerosis." *Psychiat. Quart.*, 1943, 17, 81–86.

490. —— "Rorschach Examinations in Acute Psychiatric Admissions." *J. Nerv. Ment. Dis.*, 1943, 97, 27–39.

491. HUTT, MAX L. "The Use of Projective Methods of Personality Measurement in Army Medical Installations." *J. Clin. Psychol.*, 1945, 1, 123–140.

492. HYLKEMA, G. W. "De Veranderingen in het Rorschach Protocol in het Verloop van de moderne Schizophreniebehandeling Een Casuistisch Onderzoek." (Changes in the Rorschach Records in the Course of Modern Treatment of Schizophrenics.) *Diss. Amsterdam;* 1938.

493. INTI LUNA, R. "Ensayo de la prueba de Rorschach en 104 niños." (Study of the Rorschach Method with 104 Children.) *Rev. Neuro-Psiquiat, Lima*, 1941, 4, 249–262.

494. JACOB, Z. "Some Suggestions on the Use of Content Symbolism." *Rorschach Res. Exch.*, 1944, 8, 40–41.

495. JACOBSEN, W. "Charaktertypische Arten des Deutens von Helldunkelbildern." (Personality Types in Interpreting Light-Dark Pictures.) *Z. Psychol.*, 1937, 140, 86–108.

496. JACOBSON, L. "Evaluation of Beck's Rorschach Norm as Applied to Children." *Tr. Kansas Acad. Sc.*, 1938, 41, 257–258.

497. JENSEN, M. B., and ROTTER, J. B. "The Validity of the Multiple-Choice Rorschach Test in Officer Candidate Selection." *Psychol. Bull.*, 1945, 42, 182–185.

498. KAMMAN, G. R. "The Rorschach Method as a Therapeutic Agent." *Amer. J. Orthopsy.*, 1944, 14, 21–28.

499. KATZ, H. "Untersuchungen an insulinbehandelten Schizophrenen mit dem Rorschach'schen Formdeutversuch." (Rorschach Investigations of Schizophrenics Treated with Insulin Shock.) *Mschr. Psychiat. Neurol.*, 1941, 104, 15–33.

500. KAY, L. W., and VORHAUS, P. G. "Rorschach Reactions in Early Childhood. Part II. Intellectual Aspects of Personality Development." *Rorschach Res. Exch.*, 1943, 7, 71–77.

501. KELLEY, D. M. "Requirements for Rorschach Training." *Rorschach Res. Exch.*, 1942, 6, 74–77.

502. KEMPLE, C. "Contributions of the Rorschach Test to Psychosomatic Diagnosis." Chapter XI, Section IV, in *Psychosomatic Diagnosis*, by Dunbar, F. New York: Paul B. Hoeber, Inc.

503. —— "Rorschach Method and Psychosomatic Diagnosis: Personality Traits of Patients with Rheumatic Disease, Hypertensive Cardiovascular Disease, Coronary Occlusion, and Fracture." *Psychosom. Med.*, 1945, 7, 85–89.

504. KENDIG, I. V. "Projective Techniques as a Psychological Tool in Diagnosis." *J. Clin. Psychopath. and Psychother.*, 1944, 6, 101–110.

505. KIMBLE, G. A. "Social Influence on Rorschach Records." *J. Abnorm. Soc. Psychol.*, 1945, 40, 89–93.

506. KISKER, G. W. "A Projective Approach to Personality Patterns during Insulin Shock and Metrazol-Convulsive Therapy." *J. Abnorm. Soc. Psychol.*, 1942, 37, 120–124.

507. —— "The Rorschach Analysis of Psychotics Subjected to Neurosurgical Interruption of the Thalamo-Cortical Projections." *Psychiat. Quart.*, 1944, 18, 43–52.

508. KLOPFER, B. "Instruction in the Rorschach Method." *J. Consult. Psychol.*, 1943, 7, 112–119.

509. —— "Personality Diagnosis in Children." Chapter V in *Modern Trends in Child Psychiatry*. Edited by Lewis, N. D. C., and Pacella, B. L. New York: International Universities Press, Inc.; 1945.

510. —— and DAVIDSON, H. H. "Form-Level Rating; a Preliminary Proposal for Appraising Mode and Level of Thinking as Expressed in Rorschach Records." *Rorschach Res. Exch.*, 1944, 8, 164–177.

511. —— and HIRNING, L. C. "'Signs,' 'Syndromes,' and Individuality Patterns in Rorschach Reactions of Schizophrenics." *Psychol. Bull.*, 1942, 39, 513 (Abstract).

512. KRAFFT, M. R., and VORHAUS, R. C. "The Application of the Rorschach Method in a Family Case Work Agency." *Rorschach Res. Exch.*, 1943, 7, 28–35.

513. KRUGMAN, J. I. "A Clinical Validation of the Rorschach with Problem Children." *Rorschach Res. Exch.*, 1942, 6, 61–70.

514. KRUGMAN, M. "The Rorschach in Child Guidance." *J. Consult. Psychol.*, 1943, 7, 80–88.

515. KUHN, R. "Über Rorschach's Psychologie und die psychologischen Grundlagen des Formdeutversuches." (Rorschach's Psychology and the Psychological Basis of His Method.) *Schweiz. Arch. Neurol. Psychiat.*, 1944, 53, 29–47.

516. LANDIS, C., and BOLLES, M. M. *Personality and Sexuality of the Physically Handicapped Woman.* New York: Paul B. Hoeber, Inc.; 1942. Pages 171.

517. LEME LOPES, J. *Das Interpretações Claro-escuro no Psicodiagnóstico de Rorschach e os Estados de Ansiedade.* (The Shading Responses in Rorschach Records in Anxiety States.) Rio de Janeiro: Imprensa Nacional; 1943. Pages 191.

518. —— "O psico-diagnóstico de Rorschach na consulta medico-psicologica." (The Rorschach Method in Medico-Psychological Consultation.) *Bol. Inst. de Puericult.*, 1938, 1, 63–94.

519. LEVINE, K. N. *A Comparison of Graphic Rorschach Productions with Scoring Categories of the Verbal Rorschach Record in Normal States, Organic Brain Disease, Neurotic and Psychotic Disorders.* *Arch. Psychol.* (New York), 1943, No. 282, Pages 63.

520. —— and GRASSI, J. R. "The Relation between Blot and Concept in Graphic Rorschach Responses." *Rorschach Res. Exch.*, 1942, 6, 71–73.

521. —— GRASSI, J. R.; and GERSON, M. J. "Hypnotically Induced Mood Changes in the Verbal and Graphic Rorschach; a Case Study." *Rorschach Res. Exch.*, 1943, 7, 130–144.

522. —— GRASSI, J. R.; and GERSON, M. J. "Hypnotically Induced Mood Changes in the Verbal and Graphic Rorschach: a Case Study. Part II: The Response Records." *Rorschach Res. Exch.*, 1944, 8, 104–124.

523. LEVIT, L. "Consideraciones sobre el 'Psicodiagnostics' de Rorschach." (Considerations Regarding Rorschach's Psychodiagnostics.) *Rev. Med. de Rosario*, 1939, 29, 772–785.

524. LINDNER, R. M. "A Further Contribution to the Group Rorschach." *Rorschach Res. Exch.*, 1943, 7, 7–15.

525. —— "Some Significant Rorschach Responses." *J. Crim. Psychopath.*, 1944, 5, 775–778.

526. —— "The Rorschach Test and the Diagnosis of Psychopathic Personality." *J. Crim. Psychopath.*, 1943, 5, 69–93.

527. —— and CHAPMAN, K. W. "An Eclectic Group Method." *Rorschach Res. Exch.*, 1942, 6, 139–146.

528. —— CHAPMAN, K. W.; and RINCK, E. C. "The Development of a Group Rorschach Technique in a Federal Penal Institution with Special Reference to the Problem of Psychopathic Personality." *Psychol. Bull.*, 1942, 39, 513–514.

529. LUKE, BROTHER. "The Rorschach Method Applied to Delinquent and Non-Delinquent Boys; Summary of Research." *Bull. Canad. Psychol. Assn.,* 1943, 3, 52–53, also in French in Bull. 5, *L'institut Pedagogique Saint-Georges,* 1942, University of Montreal.

530. LYNN, J. G.; LEVINE, K. N.; and HEWSON, L. W. "Psychologic Tests for the Clinical Evaluation of Late 'Diffuse Organic,' 'Neurotic,' and 'Normal' Reactions after Closed Head Injury." *Assn. for Research in Nerv. and Mental Dis.,* 1945, 24, 296–378.

531. MANN, I., and ARCHIBALD, D. "A Study of a Selected Group of Women Employed on Extremely Fine Work." *Brit. Med. J.,* 1944, 1, 387–390.

532. MARGULIES, H. *Rorschach Responses of Successful and Unsuccessful Students. Arch. Psychol.* (New York), 1942, No. 271. Pages 61.

533. MELTZER, H. "Personality Differences Between Stuttering and Non-Stuttering Children as Indicated by the Rorschach Test." *J. Psychol.,* 1944, 17, 39–59.

534. MICHAEL, J. C., and BUHLER, C. "Experiences with Personality Testing in a Neuropsychiatric Department of a Public General Hospital." *Dis. Nerv. Syst.,* 1945, 6, 205–211.

535. MILLER, J. S., and GAIR, M. "A Traumatic Neurosis of World War I 23 Years After: Psychiatric and Rorschach Investigations." *J. Nerv. Ment. Dis.,* 1943, 97, 436–446.

536. MOHR, P. "Die Inhalte der Deutungen beim Rorschach'schen Formdeuteversuch und ihre Beziehungen zur Versuchsperson." (The Contents of the Interpretations in the Rorschach Method and Their Relationships to the Subject.) *Schweiz. Arch. Neurol. Psychiat.,* 1941, 47, 237–270.

537. —— "Die schwarze und sehr dunkle Tönung der Rorschach'schen Tafeln und ihre Bedeutung für den Versuch." (The Black and Very Dark Shading in the Rorschach Pictures and Their Meaning for the Method.) *Schweiz. Arch. Neurol. Psychiat.,* 1944, 53, 122–123.

538. MONS, W. E. R. "Air Raids and the Child." *Brit. Med. J.,* 1941, 2, 625–626.

539. MORHARDT, P. E. "Nouvelle Methode d'Examen mental: le Psychodiagnostic de Rorschach." (The Psychodiagnosis of Rorschach: A New Method of Mental Examination.) *Pr. Méd.,* 1941, 49, 30–32.

540. MORRIS, W. W. "Prognostic Possibilities of the Rorschach Method in Metrazol Therapy." *Amer. J. Psychiat.,* 1943, 100, 222–230.

541. —— "Prognostic Possibilities of the Rorschach Method in Metrazol Therapy." *Arch. Neurol. Psychiat.,* 1943, 49, 927–928.

542. MUNROE, R. "An Experiment in Large Scale Testing by a Modification of the Rorschach Method." *J. Psychol.,* 1942, 13, 229–263.

543. —— "Considerations on the Place of the Rorschach in the Field of General Psychology." *Rorschach Res. Exch.,* 1945, 9, 30–40.

544. —— "Discussion of the Paper, 'The Rorschach Method in the Study of Personality.'" *Ann. N. Y. Acad. Sci.*, 1943, 44, 583–588.

545. —— "Objective Methods and the Rorschach Blots." *Rorschach Res. Exch.*, 1945, 9, 59–73.

546. —— *Prediction of the Adjustment and Academic Performance of College Students by a Modification of the Rorschach Method.* Appl. Psychol. Monog., Stanford University Press, 1945, No. 7. Pages 104.

547. —— "The Inspection Technique: A Method of Rapid Evaluation of the Rorschach Protocol." *Rorschach Res. Exch.*, 1944, 8, 46–70.

548. —— "The Rorschach Test: A Report of Its Use at Sarah Lawrence College." *J. Higher Educ.*, 1945, 16, 17–23.

549. —— "Three Diagnostic Methods Applied to Sally." *J. Abnorm. Soc. Psychol.*, 1945, 40, 215–227.

550. —— "Use of the Rorschach Method in College Guidance." *J. Consult. Psychol.*, 1943, 7, 89–96.

551. —— LEWINSON, T. S.; and WAEHNER, T. S. "A Comparison of Three Projective Methods." *Character and Pers.*, 1944, 13, 1–21.

552. MURPHY, L. B. "Personality Development of a Boy from Age Two to Seven." *Amer. J. Orthopsy.*, 1944, 14, 10–21.

553. MYERS, M. C. "The Rorschach Method." *Psychol. Bull.*, 1941, 38, 748 (abstract).

554. OBERHOLZER, E. "Rorschach's Experiment and the Alorese." Chapter 22 in *The People of Alor*, by Du Bois, C. Minneapolis: University of Minnesota Press; 1944.

555. —— "Zur Auswertung des Rorschachschen Versuchs bezüglich Diagnose und Krankheits — resp. Heilungsablauf." (The Use of the Rorschach Method for Diagnosis, Disease, and Healing Processes.) *Schweiz. Arch. Neurol.*, 1929, 24, 141.

556. PARSONS, F. H. "Eight Cases of Section of Corpus Callosum in Individuals with a History of Epileptic Seizures: Psychological Tests." *J. Gen. Psychol.*, 1943, 29, 227–241.

557. PASTER, S., and GRASSI, J. R. "Clarification of Rorschach Responses of the Graphic Rorschach Method." *J. Clin. Psychol.*, 1945, 1, 28–36.

558. PEMBERTON, W. H. "General Semantics and the Rorschach Test." *Papers Amer. Congr. Gen. Semant.*, 1943, 2, 251–260.

559. PIOTROWSKI, Z. A. "A Note on the 'Graphic Rorschach' and the 'Scoring Samples.'" *Rorschach Res. Exch.*, 1943, 7, 182–184.

560. —— "On the Rorschach Method of Personality Analysis." *Psychiat. Quart.*, 1942, 16, 480–490.

561. —— "Tentative Rorschach Formulae for Educational and Vocational Guidance in Adolescence." *Rorschach Res. Exch.*, 1943, 7, 16–27.

562. —— "The Modifiability of Personality as Revealed by the Rorschach Method: Methodological Considerations." *Rorschach Res. Exch.*, 1942, 6, 160–167.

563. —— "Use of the Rorschach in Vocational Selection." *J. Consult. Psychol.*, 1943, 7, 97–102.

564. PIOTROWSKI, Z. A.; CANDEE, B.; BALINSKY, B.; HOLTZBERG, S.; and VON ARNOLD, B. "Rorschach Signs in the Selection of Outstanding Young Male Mechanical Workers." *J. Psychol.*, 1944, 18, 131–150.

565. PRADOS, M. "Rorschach Studies on Artists — Painters. I. Quantitative Analysis." *Rorschach Res. Exch.*, 1944, 8, 178–183.

566. RABIN, A. I. "Rorschach Test Findings in a Group of Conscientious Objectors." *Amer. J. Orthopsy.*, 1945, 15, 514–519.

567. RAINES, G. N., and BROOMHEAD, E. "Rorschach Studies on Combat Fatigue." *Dis. Nerv. Syst.*, 1945, 6, 250–256.

568. RAPAPORT, D. "Principles Underlying Projective Techniques." *Character and Pers.*, 1942, 10, 213–219.

569. —— GILL, M.; and SCHAFER, R. *Diagnostic Psychological Testing* (Two volumes). Chicago: Year Book Publishers; 1945.

570. —— and SCHAFER, R. "The Rorschach Test: A Clinical Evaluation." *Bull. Menninger Clin.*, 1945, 9, 73–77.

571. RICHARDS, T. W. "The Appraisal of Naval Psychiatric Casualties by the Rorschach Method." *Naval Med. Bull.*, 1943, 41, 788–799.

572. RICHARDSON, L. H. "A Personality Study of Stutterers and Non-Stutterers." *J. Speech Disorders*, 1944, 9, 152–160.

573. RICKERS-OVSIANKINA, M. "Some Theoretical Considerations Regarding the Rorschach Method." *Rorschach Res. Exch.*, 1943, 7, 41–53.

574. ROCHLIN, G. N., and LEVINE, K. N. "The Graphic Rorschach Test I." *Arch. Neurol. Psychiat.*, 1942, 47, 438–448.

575. RORSCHACH, H. *Psychodiagnostics, a Diagnostic Test Based on Perception.* (Translated by Lemkau, P., and Kronenberg, B.) New York: Grune & Stratton, Inc.; 1942. Pages 226.

576. RORSCHACH, O. Über das Leben und die Wesensart von Hermann Rorschach." (The Life and Personality of Herman Rorschach.) *Schweiz. Arch. Neurol. Psychiat.*, 1944, 53, 1–11.

577. ROSENBERG, S. J., and FELDBERG, T. M. "Rorschach Characteristics of a Group of Malingerers." *Rorschach Res. Exch.*, 1944, 8, 141–158.

578. ROSENZWEIG, S. "A Note on Rorschach Pre-History." *Rorschach Res. Exch.*, 1944, 8, 41–42.

579. ROSS, W. D. "A Contribution to the Objectification of Group Rorschach Scoring." *Rorschach Res. Exch.*, 1943, 7, 70–71.

580. —— "A Quantitative Use of the Rorschach Method." *Amer. J. Psychiat.*, 1944, 101, 100–104.

581. —— "Notes on Rorschach 'Signs' in Diagnosis and Research." *Rorschach Res. Exch.*, 1942, 6, 115–116.

582. —— "The Contribution of the Rorschach Method to Clinical Diagnosis." *J. Ment. Sci.*, 1941, 87, 331–348.

583. —— "The Rorschach Performance with Neurocirculatory Asthenia." *Psychosom. Med.*, 1945, 7, 80–84.

584. —— "The Uses of the Rorschach Method in the Canadian Army." *Rorschach Res. Exch.*, 1944, 8, 159–161.

585. —— DANCEY, T. E.; and BROWN, F. T. "Rorschach Scores of Parachute Troopers in Training." *Bull. Canad. Psychol. Assn.*, 1943, 3, 26–27.

586. —— and McNAUGHTON, F. L. "Objective Personality Studies in Migraine by Means of the Rorschach Method." *Psychosom. Med.*, 1945, 7, 73–79.

587. —— and Ross, S. "Some Rorschach Ratings of Clinical Value." *Rorschach Res. Exch.*, 1944, 8, 1–9.

588. ROTTERSMAN, W. "Green Ink: Preliminary Report." *J. Nerv. Ment. Dis.*, 1944, 100, 507–510.

589. —— and GOLDSTEIN, H. H. "Group Analysis Utilizing the Harrower-Erickson (Rorschach) Test." *Amer. J. Psychiat.*, 1945, 101, 501–503.

590. RUESCH, J., and FINESINGER, J. E. "The Relation of the Rorschach Color Response to the Use of Color in Drawings." *Psychosom. Med.*, 1941, 3, 370–388.

591. ST. CLAIR, W. F. "The Self-Recording Technique in Rorschach Administration." *Rorschach Res. Exch.*, 1943, 7, 109–118.

592. SARBIN, T. R., and MADOW, L. W. "Predicting the Depth of Hypnosis by Means of the Rorschach Test." *Amer. J. Orthopsy.*, 1942, 12, 268–271.

593. SARGENT, H. "Projective Methods: Their Origins, Theory, and Application in Personality Research." *Psychol. Bull.*, 1945, 42, 257–293.

594. SCHACHTEL, A. H. "The Rorschach Test with Young Children." *Amer. J. Orthopsy.*, 1944, 14, 1–10.

595. —— HENRY, J.; and HENRY, Z. "Rorschach Analysis of Pilagá Indian Children." *Amer. J. Orthopsy.*, 1942, 12, 679–713.

596. —— and LEVI, M. B. "Character Structure of Day Nursery Children in Wartime as Seen through the Rorschach." *Amer. J. Orthopsy.*, 1945, 15, 213–222.

597. SCHACHTEL, E. G. "On Color and Affect; Contributions to an Understanding of Rorschach's Test II." *Psychiatry*, 1943, 6, 393–409.

598. —— "Some Notes on Firesetters and Their Rorschach Tests." *J. Crim. Psychopath.*, 1943, 5, 341–350.

599. SCHENK, V. W. D., and COLTOF, F. ("Changes in the Rorschach Test after Insulin Treatment.") *Psychiat. Neurol. Bl., Amst.*, 1940, 44, 435–445.

600. SCHMIDL, F. "The Rorschach Personality Test in Family Case Work." *The Family*, 1943, 24, 83–90.

601. —— "The Use of the Rorschach Method in Social Work Treatment of Adults." *Rorschach Res. Exch.*, 1945, 9, 123–125.

602. SCHMIDT, H. O. "Test Profiles as a Diagnostic Aid: The Rorschach." *J. Clin. Psychol.*, 1945, 1, 222–227.

603. SELIGER, R. V., and CRANFORD, V. "The Rorschach Analysis in the Treatment of Alcoholism." *Med. Rec., N. Y.*, 1945, 158, 32–38.

604. SELINSKY, H.; KLOPFER, B.; and EMERY, M. "Inferences Drawn from Rorschach Tests in Convulsive States." *J. Nerv. Ment. Dis.*, 1936, 84, 322–323.

605. SENDER, S. "The Influence of Variations in Rorschach Group Method Administration upon the Scorability of the Records." *Rorschach Res. Exch.*, 1943, 7, 54–69.

606. SEREBRINSKY, B. *El Psicodiagnóstico de Rorschach en los Homicidas.* (The Rorschach Method in Homicides.) Argentina: Cordoba; 1941. Pages 198.

607. —— "Psicodiagnóstico de Rorschach e Inventario Personal de Bernreuter en los Homicidas." (The Rorschach Method and the Bernreuter Personality Inventory in Homicides.) *Rev. Psiquiat. Crim., B. Aires*, 1941, 6, 602–610.

608. SHASKAN, D.; YARNELL, H.; and ALPER, K. "Physical, Psychiatric, and Psychometric Studies of Post-Encephalitic Parkinsonism." *J. Nerv. Ment. Dis.*, 1942, 96, 653–662; also in *Arch. Neurol. Psychiat.*, 1942, 48, 666–688.

609. SIEGEL, M. G. "The Rorschach Test as an Aid in Selecting Clients for Group Therapy and Evaluating Progress." *Ment. Hyg.*, 1944, 28, 444–449.

610. —— "The Use of the Rorschach Test in a Treatment Program." *Rorschach Res. Exch.*, 1945, 9, 126–129.

611. STAINBROOK, E. "The Rorschach Description of Immediate Post-Convulsive Mental Function." *Character and Pers.*, 1944, 12, 302–322.

612. —— and SIEGEL, P. S. "A Comparative Rorschach Study of Southern Negro and White High School and College Students." *J. Psychol.*, 1944, 17, 107–115.

613. STAVRIANOS, B. "An Investigation of Sex Differences in Children as Revealed by the Rorschach Method." *Rorschach Res. Exch.*, 1942, 6, 168–175.

614. —— "Location of Responses." *Rorschach Res. Exch.*, 1943, 7, 78.

615. STEINZOR, B. "Rorschach Responses of Achieving and Non-Achieving College Students of High Ability." *Amer. J. Orthopsy.*, 1944, 14, 494–504.

616. —— STERN, K., and MACNAUGHTON, D. "Capras' Syndrome, a Peculiar Illusionary Phenomenon Considered with Special Reference to the Rorschach Findings." *Psychiat. Quart.*, 1945, 19, 139–163.

617. SWIFT, J. W. "Matchings of Teachers' Descriptions and Rorschach Analyses of Preschool Children." *Child Developm.*, 1944, 15, 217–224.

618. —— "Relation of Behavioral and Rorschach Measures of Insecurity in Preschool Children." *J. Clin. Psychol.*, 1945, 1, 196–205.

619. —— "Reliability of Rorschach Scoring Categories with Preschool Children." *Child Developm.*, 1944, 15, 207–216.

620. —— "Rorschach Responses of Eighty-Two Preschool Children." *Rorschach Res. Exch.*, 1945, 9, 74–84.

621. SYMONDS, P. M., and KRUGMAN, M. "Projective Methods in the Study of Personality." *Rev. Educ. Res.*, 1944, 14, 81–98.

622. TAVARES BASTOS, A. "A Constatacao de Fatores Psicogenicos em Pacientes Epilepticas, ao Test de Rorschach." (Observation of Psychogenic Factors in Epileptics, with the Rorschach Method.) *An Colôn Gustavo Riedel*, 1943, 6, 115–145.

623. —— "Sôbre a Identidade de Certas Expressôes nas Repostas de Casais e Pessôas afins ao Test de Rorschach." (Identity of Certain Expressions in the Rorschach Responses of Married and Closely Attached Persons.) *An Côlon Gustavo Riedel*, 1943, 6, 57–82.

624. TORRANCE, K. "The Rorschach Method in a Correctional Institution." *Ment. Hlth. Bull. Ill. Soc. Ment. Hyg.*, 1943, 21, 14–16.

625. TRANQUE GARCIA, F. "Color y Claroscuro en el 'Test' de Rorschach." (Color and Shading in the Rorschach Method.) *Psicotecnia*, 1942, 3, 428–433.

626. TSCHUDIN, A. "Chronische Schizophrenien beim Rorschach'schen Versuch." (Chronic Schizophrenia and the Rorschach Method.) *Schweiz. Arch. Neurol. Psychiat.*, 1944, 53, 79–100.

627. TULCHIN, S. H., and LEVY, D. M. "Rorschach Test Differences in a Group of Spanish and English Refugee Children." *Amer. J. Orthopsy.*, 1945, 15, 361–368.

628. URBAITIS, J. C., and WATERMAN, J. "Application of the Rorschach Test to Practice in Mental Disease Hospitals." *Arch. Neurol. Psychiat.*, 1941, 45, 383–384.

629. VAN BARK, B., and BARON, S. "Neurotic Elements in the Rorschach Records of Psychotics." *Rorschach Res. Exch.*, 1943, 7, 166–168.

630. VARVEL, W. A. "The Rorschach Test in Relation to Perceptual Organization and to Intelligence." *Psychol. Bull.*, 1941, 38, 705 (abstract).

631. VEIT, R. "Do Valor Diagnostico do 'Test' de Rorschach." (The Diagnostic Value of the Rorschach Method.) *Rev. Neurol. Psiquiat, São Paulo*, 1942, 8, 24.

632. VICTORIA, M. "Presentacion del Test de Rorschach." (Description of the Rorschach Method.) *Rev. Otol. Neuro. Oftal. y Cir. Neur. Sud. Amer.*, 1937, 12, 29–35.

633. VORHAUS, P. G. "Rorschach Reactions in Early Childhood. Part III. Content and Details in Pre-School Records." *Rorschach Res. Exch.*, 1944, 8, 71–91.

634. WEBER, A. "Der Rorschach'sche Formdeutversuch bei Kindern." (The Rorschach Test as Applied to Children.) *Schweiz. Arch. Neurol. Psychiat.*, 1944, 53, 47–61.

635. WEISSENFELD, F. "Der Rorschach'sche Formdeutversuch als Hilfsmittel zur Differentialdiagnose zwischen genuiner Epilepsie und Übererregbarkeitsepilepsie." (The Rorschach Test as an Aid in the Differential Diagnosis of Idiopathic Epilepsy and Epilepsy Caused by Overexcitability.) *Z. Ges. Neurol. Psychiat.*, 1941, 171, No. 1–3.

636. WEISSKOPF, E. A. "The Influence of the Time Factor on Rorschach Performances." *Rorschach Res. Exch.*, 1942, 6, 128–136; also in *Psychol. Bull.*, 1942, 39, 51 (Abstract).

637. WERNER, H. "Perceptual Behavior of Brain Injured, Mentally Defective Children: An Experimental Study by Means of the Rorschach Technique." *Genet. Psychol. Monogr.*, 1945, 31, 51–110.

638. —— "Rorschach Method Applied to Two Clinical Groups of Mental Defectives." *Amer. J. Ment. Def.*, 1945, 49, 304–306.

639. WITTSON, C. L.; HUNT, W. A.; and OLDER, H. J. "The Uses of the Multiple-Choice Group Rorschach Test in Military Screening." *J. Psychol.*, 1944, 17, 91–94.

640. YAWGER, N. S. "The Rorschach Ink Blot Tests." *Philadelphia Med.*, 1943–1944, 39, 548–551.

641. ZOLLIKER, A. "Schwangerschaft-Depression und Rorschach'scher Formdeuteversuch." (Pregnancy Depression and the Rorschach Method.) *Schweiz. Arch. Neurol. Psychiat.*, 1944, 53, 62–78.

642. ZUBIN, J.; CHUTE, E.; and VENIAR, S. "Psychometric Scales for Scoring Rorschach Test Responses." *Character and Pers.*, 1943, 11, 277–301.

Supplementary Key to Foreign Language Periodicals in the Bibliography [1]

An. Colôn Gustavo Riedel. Anais da Colônia Gustavo Riedel.

An. Paulist de Med. e Cir. Anais paulistas de medicina e cirurgia, S. Paulo.

Arch. Psicol. Neurol. Psychiat. Archivio di psicologia e neurologia e psichiatria.

Arq. Policia Civil, S. Paulo. Arquivos da policia civil de São Paulo.

Bol. Inst. de Puericult. Boletim do Instituto de Puericultura.

Hyg. Ment. L'Hygiène Mentale.

Pr. Méd. Presse Médicale.

Psicotecnia. Psicotecnia, órgano del Instituto nacional de Psicotecnia, Madrid.

Rev. Clin., S. Paulo. Revista clinica de São Paulo.

Rev. Med. de Pernambuco. Revista medica de Pernambuco.

Rev. Med. de Rosario. Revista médica del Rosario.

Rev. Neuro-Psiquiat., Lima. Revista de neuro-psiquiatría, Lima.

Rev. Otol. Neuro. Oftal. y Cir. Neur. Sud. Amer. Revista otologia-neurologia-oftalmológica y de cirugía neurológica Sud-Americana.

Rev. Psiquiat. Crim., B. Aires. Revista de psiquiatría y criminología, Buenos Aires.

Riv. Psicol. Norm. Pat. Rivista di psicologia normale e patelogica.

[1] Supplementary to the Key to Foreign Language Periodicals in *The Rorschach Technique*, pages 429–430.

INDEX

Numbers included in brackets refer to entries in the Bibliography.

469